ADVANCE PRAISE FOR *POGIEBAIT'S WAR*

"More than a family memoir or nostalgic wartime reminiscence, *Pogiebait's War* is a colorful, poignant and personal tribute to a tough, patriotic Leatherneck. From Parris Island to the Pacific and back home to Tennessee, we follow the author's meticulous exploration of his father's wartime experiences. Whether you are an avid World War Two enthusiast, historian, veteran, or general reader, McCall will have you on the edge of your seat."

—LISA M. BUDREAU—
PhD, military, cultural historian, and author

"More than a tale of heroism in wartime, McCall gives us a thoughtful and eloquent tribute from a son to his father. This book shows the impact of war across the generations down to our own time."

—MICHAEL NEIBERG—
Professor of History, Chair of War Studies, US Army War College

"A riveting, moving account of the Pacific theater. *Pogiebait's War* is in equal parts a biography, a history and, ultimately, a sheer labor of love by a son for his father. Highly recommended."

—JOHN C. MCMANUS—
PhD, Curators' Distinguished Professor, Missouri University of Science and Technology, author of *Island Infernos: The U.S. Army's Pacific War Odyssey, 1944*

"Nick McCall provides an intimate, eminently readable, and now timely personal perspective on a defining period in the history of the U.S. military—and of the United States and Asia."

—EDWARD G. LENGEL—
PhD, Chief Historian, National Medal of Honor Museum

"Begun as a labor of love to better understand the World War II experiences of his father who served with the US Marines in the Pacific, Jack H. (Nick) McCall, Jr. has crafted an impeccably researched and engaging work that deserves a wide audience. Part biography, part operational history of the Ninth Marine Defense Battalion at Guadalcanal, Rendova, New Georgia, and Guam, McCall tells, a story of valor and courage. But McCall, an attorney by profession, avoids hagiography and is unflinchingly honest about the racism endemic among the Marines who fought with his father and the other brutalities of the Pacific War. We will always be indebted to McCall for interviewing Jack "Pogiebait" McCall and his comrades to make sure their stories got into history books before it was too late."

—G. KURT PIEHLER—
teacher at Florida State University,
author of *A Religious History of the American GI in World War II*

"The death of his father in 1997 launched Jack McCall Jr. on a journey to discover his father's wartime legacy, which he beautifully chronicles in *Pogiebait's War*. Armed with family stories, archival records, and interviews with veterans, McCall follows his father's path from a small town in Tennessee to the far Pacific, from Guadalcanal and the Solomon Islands to Guam and the Marianas. The end result is not only a wonderful testimony of a son's amazing love for his father, but a reminder of what we as a nation owe to the incredible veterans of the Greatest Generation."

—JAMES M. SCOTT—
Pulitzer Prize finalist and author of *Target Tokyo* and *Rampage*

POGIEBAIT'S WAR

POGIEBAIT'S WAR

A Son's Quest for His Father's Wartime Life

SECOND EDITION

Jack H. McCall Jr.

THE UNIVERSITY OF TENNESSEE PRESS
Knoxville

Frontispiece:
Portrait of Jack McCall, taken in spring 1945 while serving as a corporal
in the III Amphibious Corps. Author's collection.

All the maps were prepared by Erin Greb, Erin Greb Cartography.

LIBRARY OF CONGRESS CATALOGING-IN-PUBLICATION DATA
Names: McCall, Jack H., Jr., 1961- author.
Title: Pogiebait's war : a son's quest for his father's wartime life / Jack H. McCall Jr.
Description: Second edition. | Knoxville : The University of Tennessee Press, [2022] |
Series: Legacies of war | Includes bibliographical references and index. |
Summary: "This revised version of a work self-published in 2000 by Jack H.
McCall Jr. provides biographical details of the author's father, an ordinary
Tennessean who, like so many able-bodied young men, signed up with the military
services (in this case, the Marines) in the wake of the attack on Pearl Harbor.
The younger McCall's approach goes beyond family memoir or nostalgic wartime
reminiscence to provide a painstakingly researched biography set within a rich,
engaging study of the US Marine Corps, particularly the elder McCall's
understudied unit, the Ninth Defense Battalion—the "Fighting Ninth." The author
provides a window into the day-to-day service of a Marine during World War II,
with important coverage of fighting in the Pacific Theater. Especially noteworthy
in this regard is the chapter on Guam, a very unpleasant late-war "mopping-up"
action that has received little scholarly attention. McCall also depicts life in wartime
Franklin, Tennessee, and offers a poignant, personal tribute to his father"
—Provided by publisher.
Identifiers: LCCN 2022039150 (print) | LCCN 2022039151 (ebook) |
ISBN 9781621907565 (paperback) | ISBN 9781621907572 (kindle edition) |
ISBN 9781621907589 (pdf)
Subjects: LCSH: McCall, Jack H., Sr., 1922-1997. | United States. Marine Corps.
Defense Battalion, 9th—Biography. | World War, 1939-1945—Campaigns—Pacific Area. |
United States. Marine Corps—Biography. | Franklin (Tenn.)—Biography.
Classification: LCC D767.9 .M39 2022 (print) | LCC D767.9 (ebook) |
DDC 940.54/26 [B]—dc23/eng/20220823
LC record available at https://lccn.loc.gov/2022039150
LC ebook record available at https://lccn.loc.gov/2022039151

For Margaret

They will live a long time, these men of the South Pacific.
They had an American quality. They, like their victories,
will be remembered as long as our generation lives. After that,
like the men of the Confederacy, they will become strangers.
Longer and longer shadows will obscure them, until the name
Guadalcanal sounds distant on the ear like Shiloh and Valley Forge.

—JAMES MICHENER—
Tales of the South Pacific

[In] the end, of course, a true war story is never about war....
It's about love and memory. It's about sorrow.

—TIM O'BRIEN—
The Things They Carried

CONTENTS

ILLUSTRATIONS

Maps

PREFACE

Since its original publication in 2000,[1] I have long wanted to do a revised version of this book. While I had no regrets in publishing when I did—especially as it enabled me to get copies of this book into the hands of an all-too-rapidly dwindling number of aged Marine Corps veterans and, as importantly, the hands of their families while fathers and grandfathers were still alive—some practical limitations were imposed in the original publication's format. Those limited me in realizing the full intent and scope originally planned for *Pogiebait's War*, including the inclusion of appropriate footnotes and sources and a better selection of maps to aid the reader in following the movement of "Pogiebait" Jack McCall and the Marines' Ninth Defense Battalion across the expanses of the South and Central Pacific. This edition remedies those limitations; accordingly, it includes footnotes as to my sources (many of them original interviews and documents); better maps and better-quality photographs and illustrations; the opportunity to condense and refine several sections that could benefit from slightly more adept editing; and substantively, several updates and amendments based on additional research available since the original publication date.

For starters, the declassification and release by the National Archives and Records Administration (NARA) in 2012 of a wealth of previously classified after-action and operations reports from the Ninth Defense's files provided enormous clarity and helped immeasurably in cross-checking and critically evaluating a host of dates, claims, and testimonies my father and other members of his unit provided to me. In addition, recent research on Japanese aviation units and their combat losses in the Pacific has helped clarify some issues that members of the Ninth have heatedly debated since July 1943. All of those revisions and changes are now reflected where appropriate in this narrative. In general, though, unless edits or updates were needed, I strived to retain as much as possible of the original 2000 edition.

This book has three essential themes and purposes. First—and as noted more extensively in my original introduction and prologue—it was principally intended to serve as a son's recounting of the wartime biography and experiences of his father and his Marine comrades-in-arms. During this process, however, I realized that I was opening a window to a second theme and purpose: an exploration of the history, role, and functions of the Marines' Ninth Defense Battalion during its campaigns across the Pacific. Akin to that is a closely related third theme, which was to provide unique insights into the daily life and experiences of average Marines, touching on several subjects that have often been explored only briefly—if at all—in other accounts. In doing so, the book may help shed light on certain broader aspects of what one might term the "social history" of the Marine Corps of the Second World War—or at least, of one of its units.

One particular aspect may be noteworthy at this juncture.

Several readers of the original edition have noted that the attitude expressed by Jack McCall and many (but not all) of his fellow Ninth Defense Battalion "leathernecks" toward the Japanese came as a bit of a surprise. Despite the frequent use of a certain common American epithet toward the foes of 1941-45 and obvious references toward war crimes and abuses between the sides, one can discern, at least in Pogiebait McCall's case, something like grudging respect mixed with pity, in some later instances, toward his Japanese opponents. I believe that to be true, and perhaps this attitude should not be so surprising to modern readers. Of course, one can have a measure of professional respect for an adversary, even as one fears or hates that adversary, I suppose.[2] Nevertheless, the measure of continuing hatred or, at the least, distrust engendered between American and Japanese combatants in that war varied significantly as I talked with Jack and interviewed and corresponded with other veterans of his battalion. By the later portion of his life, Jack (and several other Ninth veterans) demonstrated more of a "live and let live" outlook toward the enemy of forty or fifty years earlier. As my father often said to me, "They [the Japanese] were just doing their job, like we were, and most of them were drafted; they didn't have any choice." On the other hand, as will be seen, this outlook was shared neither by all members of the Ninth nor, of course, by all Marine or other American veterans of the savage fighting across the Pacific—some of whom, as I came to learn in the course of my research, correspondence, and interviews, still harbored resentments and anger toward the Japanese, even across the years.

What was a labor of love for me to capture my father's reminiscences and memories had become, by the time *Pogiebait's War* was first published in 2000, much the same effort for the host of his fellow Marines and veterans who contributed so greatly to this account. As one would expect in the intervening sixteen years, so many of these contributors and friends have themselves died. I could never have undertaken this effort without them. A postscript has been added to reflect the invaluable contribution of all of those men and women who truly helped this work become a practical reality and who have died in the intervening years since the original publication.

I must also take this opportunity to thank a range of friends and other recent contributors for their invaluable assistance. The family members of several other Ninth Defense Battalion veterans—most notably, Dr. Christopher S. Donner III; Mrs. Marilyn Galloway; Dr. Jonathan Slater; Dr. Davis Tracy; and Mr. Joe Pratl Jr. and his wife Denise—have lent me invaluable support and have provided a measure of continuity across the generations, as each of us have lost our fathers (in Maril's case, her spouse) and watched the Ninth fade away.

The maps for this new edition have been prepared by Erin Greb of Erin Greb Cartography, and photographic assistance was provided by researcher Gina McNeely and by Thompson Photo Products of Knoxville, Tennessee. Japanese aircraft researcher and model hobbyist (and my friend and fellow church parishioner) Mike Driskill deserves a special note of thanks for having brought to my attention Japanese sources that helped crack the mystery (briefly referred to above) that has vexed both researchers and the Fightin' Ninth's veterans since two epic days of air raids and bombing occurred in early July 1943.

A sadly belated note of thanks is owed to the late Colonel Dye Ogata, wartime *Nisei* intelligence officer and translator, who helped verify the provenance of a unique Japanese diary that is cited in the chapter on Rendova and New Georgia. Along with Joe Pratl of the Ninth, Dye was one of the greatest cheerleaders for the earlier edition of *Pogiebait's War*. I will never forget Joe or Dye, or their incredible kindness to me and my family over the last years of their lives.

For the preparation and support of this edition, I owe considerable thanks and the highest appreciation to several more persons: first, the director of the University of Tennessee Press, Scot Danforth, and his staff, especially Jonathan Boggs. Scot's keen editor's eye helped craft and refine this edition, and his excitement about UT Press's republication of this updated version of *Pogiebait's War* helped keep my own enthusiasm kindled through the process. In very close tandem with my thanks to Scot and Jonathan are my thanks to Professor G. Kurt Piehler, director of the Florida State University Institute of World War II and the Human Experience, associate professor of history at FSU, and book series editor for Fordham University Press's World War II: The Global, Human, and Ethical Dimension series and UT Press's Legacies of War series. Since serving earlier as director for the University of Tennessee's Center for the Study of War and Society around the time this book was originally published, Kurt has been highly supportive of my efforts. As we discussed a potential republication of *Pogiebait's War*, Kurt was instrumental in helping me keep UT Press squarely in mind, with the revised version as a candidate for UT's Legacies of War book series. Likewise, I am enormously grateful to UT Press's independent readers, Lisa M. Budreau, senior military curator of the Tennessee State Museum, and Professor B. Franklin Cooling III of the National Defense University's Dwight D. Eisenhower School for National Security and Resource Strategy, for their incisive and extremely helpful comments and suggestions. I am also highly grateful to Katie Little for her keen editorial support and editing of the manuscript. Any errors and omissions contained herein are, of course, entirely my own and attributable to no one but myself.

Last but by all means not least: my deepest thanks to my family: my wife, Jennifer Ashley-McCall; my daughter, Margaret McCall; and my sister, Holly McCall. "Big Jack" McCall would be mighty proud of you all, as would his spouse and Holly's and my late mother, Patricia H. McCall.

POGIEBAIT'S WAR

INTRODUCTION

Definition of "Pogey Bait": Candy. Old naval term.

—HENRY BERRY—
*SEMPER FI, MAC: LIVING MEMORIES OF
THE U.S. MARINES IN WORLD WAR II*

My father, Jack McCall, Sr., was a lifelong resident of Franklin, Tennessee, a small town nestled in the rolling hills just south of Nashville. Apart from spending part of his early years in various cities around the Southeast, Jack called Franklin home during almost all of his seventy-five years. After moving back to Franklin with his family around 1928, he seldom spent more than a few weeks or months away from Franklin for the rest of his life—with one notable exception. That exception was four years of service in the United States Marine Corps during World War II.

As his son, I thought I knew how much the time he spent in service during the war years affected my father. A favorite Friday-night childhood pastime of ours was for my sister Holly and me to ask him to tell us a story. He was a natural-born storyteller and raconteur, but of all the stories he told, we would most frequently prompt him with the inevitable request: "Tell us what you did in World War II, please, Dad?" This prompted him to regale us with his favorite "war stories."

The litany of geographical names routinely cropping up in these tales were mysterious, yet alliterative and lyrical things, like some destinations out of a boy's adventure book: *Guantanamo; Noumea; Guadalcanal; Nalimbiu; Tenaru; Gavutu; Rendova; Munda; Vella Lavella; Roviana; Banika; Eniwetok; Bangi Point; Agana; Pago Bay; the Golden Gate.* Sometimes after his storytelling, the family would troop upstairs to a big cedar chest to unload his war souvenirs: his dress green uniform, a tattered Japanese flag, an Imperial Navy sailor's cap, a tin case full of crumbling Japanese cigarettes, and other artifacts he'd salvaged from some Pacific battlefield twenty or twenty-five years before.

Some of my earliest memories of my sister often feature Holly wearing her favorite headgear: my dad's battered campaign hat (which she and I called the "Sergeant Carter hat" after Gomer Pyle's much-harassed drill sergeant, who wore a similar hat in the TV series), perched precariously on her head as she toddled around the yard or snacked in the kitchen. Occasionally one of my Cub Scout buddies would gape at a finger-sized hole in the crown of the hat and, awestruck, ask as he fingered it: "Wow! I'll bet you were shot at by a sniper, weren't you, Mr. McCall?" "Aw, no, that's not how I got that hole!" my father would respond. Inevitably to my friends' disappointment that something bloodier had not occurred, he would explain that a large rat had once nibbled on the hat while he was stationed at Guantanamo Bay, Cuba—that is, until my dad caught the rat in the act. The hat was damaged, but the rat had met its end.

On every Fourth of July, there would be two or three phone calls along these lines: "Hey, little Jack. Where's *Pogiebait*?[1] You know, kid; your old man?" Within a few minutes, I would hear my father chortling into the phone: "That was the best Fourth of July I ever had! I love you like a brother!" It was a mystery to me what he was talking about so jovially and to whom, except that when I asked him, he'd simply reply with a name seldom heard during the rest of the year and say: "He's an old Leatherneck buddy of mine." As much as my father laughed with these strangers—and as much as I heard him occasionally argue and bicker heatedly with my uncles over every topic imaginable—I began to suspect that, just maybe, he loved these mysterious callers *more* than his real brothers.

As for his wartime pals' favorite nickname, frequently used to his family's wonderment whenever these buddies called or wrote him, he confessed to having earned the moniker "Pogiebait" while a young recruit at Boot Camp in an escapade involving his lifelong and incorrigible sweet tooth. When I was a teenager, he would tell me that his unit never got any real leave once it was sent overseas and that, for its one "R&R" break, his battalion was stationed in a swamp. When I challenged him on that, cynical and dubious teen that I was—*Come on, Dad, don't pull my leg; they wouldn't put you in a swamp while you were on R&R!*—he testily responded as he peered irritably at me over his glasses: "Son, don't you think I know what a *swamp* is?"

My father's war stories themselves were exciting and usually humorous, but on the whole, they suggested that he'd never really been in *that* much danger—except maybe from an attack or two of food poisoning or tropical disease and, most definitely, in self-inflicted danger from the Japanese hand grenades he tried to deactivate during his months on New Georgia by soaking them in a helmet full of kerosene under his cot. ("Don't let me ever catch *you* trying to do something that dumb, son!" he'd sternly lecture me.) From hearing these stories, no one would ever have mistaken my father for Audie Murphy, Chesty Puller, or George S. Patton. Still, they were enough to set me on a lifelong interest in history, and they partly contributed to my own decision late in high school to try the military as a career.

Yet, for many years, there was also a certain distance to my father. He always seemed to be at work on something very important: his slide rule in hand, calculating weekly or monthly sales figures; checking through his ledgers to see what was left in his inventory and what needed to be reordered; either going to or returning from the Chicago or Dallas clothing marts, sample cases of his wares in hand. He was at times oddly overprotective of my sister and me, too, in ways that were strikingly different from so many of our peers' parents, who were five to twenty years younger than him. *No BB guns for the boy . . . no bunk beds for the kids, they might roll out and break their necks in the middle of the night . . . no football or baseball, he might break a bone . . . did we really give our son a chemistry set for Christmas? My God, Pat, what were we thinking? Your son might blow himself up. . . .* And on, and on. What was he protecting us from? And why was he going to such extremes?

By the time I entered high school, this overprotectiveness no longer seemed to be a mere personal quirk; to me, it seemed positively neurotic. Despite my best efforts to be a good son, my father and I fought pitched battles over almost everything: over the times I stayed out late (even if it was only for a track or cross-country meet out of town), over driving lessons, over the first time I dented the car, over my first date. Yet, despite his lectures and our verbal grappling and arguments, I did not feel any closer to understanding what made him tick. It was not until after I entered the military myself that I began to get a better inkling, and it was not until very close to the end of his life, after I had completed my military service and become a father myself, that I truly began to "get" the insights I lacked for so long. Sadly, the greatest insights would only come after his death, when it was too late for me to say: *Now, at last, I see. I think I finally understand, Dad, what you were about.*

Some thirty years passed from the times I first recall hearing my dad's war stories to the day in late May 1997 when he lay in a hospital room in Franklin. My father lay propped up in his bed at a forty-five-degree angle to ease his breathing, which was coming shallow and fast. He was covered only by a thin hospital smock and sheet. He was dying, and we—and he—knew it. In fact, he had been dying in front of our eyes for eight years. Years of massive cigarette smoking had taken its toll, and in spring 1990, he was diagnosed with emphysema. On the day my father learned it in March 1990, before he underwent what should have been minor nasal surgery, his physician had pushed open the door and tossed a batch of x-rays on his chest. "Mr. McCall, do you have any idea what these are?" the physician curtly asked. As I could feel my anger rising at the doctor's harshness—*the jerk, just who the hell does he think he is to do that to my dad!*—but before anyone could utter a word, the doctor continued in a deliberate and icy cold tone: "Mr. McCall, these are the worst lungs of any *living* man I've ever seen. *You have emphysema.* Do you understand me?" This blunt but effective pronouncement finally succeeded in doing what Jack's family had strived for years to do—he immediately stopped smoking, cold turkey—but the worst damage had already been done, and it was far too late to reverse its course. A living death sentence had effectively been pronounced on my father, albeit one with a seven-year stay of execution. In spring 1990, his doctor had expected him to last less than five.

By Memorial Day 1997, however, my father's stay of execution was lifted, and his life was ebbing quickly as pneumonia set in. Watching someone die of any disease can be, in its own way, as emotionally and spiritually debilitating to the family and loved ones as it is physically to the sufferer. Emphysema has its own hideous etiology. The convulsive and shuddering coughs would often be followed by his hacking, as he expectorated fluid from the weakened lungs, and by a gentle, sad wheezing as he gulped in air. The onset of sudden losses of breath made him claustrophobic and panicky, and every breath was painful. His debilitated condition sometimes left him embarrassed and, most unlike the energetic man of my youth, tired to the core of his soul. He lacked the energy to walk farther than a few paces before becoming desperately short of breath. It was somewhat like watching someone drown in slow motion on dry land. I could not help but sometimes think of the doughboy gas victims of World War I that Jack had seen as a young boy not long after that war ended as I watched my own father suffer what must have been a similar fate, at least physiologically speaking.

By six months before he died, Jack's world, his very field of vision, had narrowed to only three rooms in his home. He would pace from the bedroom, to the easy chair in the den, then to the bathroom—all the time tethered to life, like a deep-sea diver, by a plastic tube and an oxygen-generating machine. His body had become its own prison, but the tortures it imposed extended far beyond what he felt. Jack's family watched this once robust man dwindle to a specter of his former self, yet his humor remained largely intact to the end. This fight was for his life: it took all of his available energy to wage it, and he did not dare let down his guard until the very end.

As he lay in his bed in the intensive care unit of the Williamson Medical Center late that May, my father gripped my hand with both of his, with an amazing strength for one so weakened. He had a lifelong love of history and genealogy, but the passion of his request still surprised me. "Son, when the county historical association . . . wanted to interview me . . . oh, I wished I had done it . . . but I just never felt up to it." "Don't worry, Dad," I responded, partly out of despair and partly hoping against hope to give him something that would perk him up. "Between what you've told me and Holly and what I can find out from your friends, Uncle Al and Mom, I'll do a biographical sketch for you. Okay?" "I'd appreciate that, son," he gently replied, and he closed his eyes and laid his head down on his pillow for a fitful nap.

Then, a few hours later, the bitter realization dawned: "Son, tell me the truth. *I'm not coming out of here, am I?*" It was there, it was out in the open, and nothing would work but the truth, although I failed immediately to grasp his full meaning. "Yeah, sure, Dad. You'll probably be here for a few weeks or so, but you'll be out of the hospital soon enough if you keep trying." He saw through my temporizing immediately. "You're one hell of an actor, kid; you ought to be on the stage," he muttered bitterly, looking me straight in the eyes, when I vainly tried to reassure him that he'd be all right. Then, bluntly, a few minutes later: "You're a lawyer. Can't you tell me what a person has to do to get out of *here*?" The truth hit me: the "here" to which he was referring wasn't the hospital, it was *life*, and he both was resigned to death and maybe welcomed it as a release. My father had long said that he would not want to face an existence in a nursing home or as a burden on his family, and he saw that these were about the only certainties for him if he survived this round of pneumonia.

He began to shrug off my mother's and Holly's and the nurses' efforts to cheer him up as well. Five days earlier, Jack had already told his wife that he felt the closeness of death; he could *sense* it, and it was closer now than at any time since the war. He had told his family in the past that death could be felt, could be perceived, like a tangible sensation—but, cynics and disbelievers that we were, we did not wholly believe him. We could not grasp it, we could not let ourselves believe it, and so we refused to believe.

Within two more days, my father was dead, and his request became more than a mere wish—it became a son's last duty to his father and his father's memory. It also became a tribute to other men like my father, who themselves are quickly shrinking in number as the bloody twentieth century nears its end, and it is my attempt to preserve a portion of their memories as well.

I realized even better what my father had really gone through with these wartime buddies when I picked up his address book the day after his death and began making calls to tell his friends, business associates, and other family members the news. Jack McCall's relatives and business cronies were saddened, sure, but their responses were often more in the way of persons used to accepting bad news, especially since he had been ill for so long. Yet, as I called his Marine Corps friends, not just their words, but the tenor of their responses, were utterly different from what I had expected: to my amazement, many of them *cried*, more so than his other family and friends. One of them, Al Downs, a pal since Boot Camp, told me how much my father had meant to him in these words: "You don't go through what we all went through without becoming close. He and I shared our last cola together just before I left the Ninth Defense and came back stateside in '44. I knew he'd be left out there, and I worried for a long time that he'd be killed." Another, Frank Chadwick, also cried as he took the news, but then he said: "Your father was such a good man, Nick. You know, I think we talked every July 4th for the last twenty years. I guess he must have told you about the time he was nearly blown up on Guam. We all thought we'd lost him that time, for sure."

I was flabbergasted. Of all the stories my father had shared, this one was news to me. "No, Frank. He never told me about that."

Likewise, Bill Galloway, another Marine buddy, told me on that same day: "Well, I'm sure your dad must have told you about how he was almost killed when my crew's Long Tom"—a heavy artillery piece, of which my father had often spoken—"exploded." Again, I was stupefied. *My father, nearly blown up by an exploding cannon?* "No, sir. That's all news to me." "Well, Nick," Bill continued, "I still carry around a hunk of metal inside me today from that gun. Your dad was damn lucky that day. He was a good man."

And the trickle of information I received on June 1, 1997 as to what my father had *really* experienced in World War II—far beyond the usually humorous tales of my childhood—became a torrent over the next few months as more of his friends and wartime buddies contacted me and as I reached out to them to learn more of my father's life in those grim years.

This work is my obligation to the man who, more than anyone I have ever encountered, has taught me what life—and death—ultimately means. He died well and bravely. I have come to suspect that what my father had faced fifty years before, as a mere teenaged boy in the jungles of the Pacific, somehow helped give him the courage and dignity he needed to face death one last time; to grasp that death, too, is a part of life; and to die with enormous dignity and grace—to "die well." It was a hard death, but he did die well, and he tried to make as much of his life as he could while there was yet time. His buddies would have been proud of the man they once called "Pogiebait."

It has only been after his death that I now truly appreciate how much his wartime experience irrevocably altered Jack McCall's life and my family's lives as well. I have better learned how truly hazardous service in the Pacific was, even to those not always in direct combat, and how indebted today's Americans are to the sacrifices of those like him—both those who came home and those who did not. One thing that becomes readily apparent from Jack's account—something forgotten or, at best, half understood by modern Americans, while remembered by almost all the surviving veterans of the Pacific War—is the fact that the Pacific fighting was very much, in the Duke of Wellington's trenchant summary of the Battle of Waterloo, a "damned close-run thing." The final American victory was by no means inevitable for much of the war. In 1941-42, the Allies' situation looked grim. This was certainly true for much of the Guadalcanal campaign, and in many respects, the prospect of final victory was still debatable as late as 1944, at least to those at the front. Several circumstances, both fortunate and unfortunate, marked the conduct of the Central Solomons campaign in mid-1943 in which my father participated. Instances of "friendly fire" casualties abounded, including the sinking of the command ship for the New Georgia campaign. Likewise, the presence of a large undetected reef off the invasion beaches jeopardized the American initial landings on Guam and, more personally, nearly led to Jack's death.

Jack's physical condition in his last few months of life severely limited his ability to follow through on his wish to provide a personal history of his war years. This narrative is partly a payment of my debt to my father, and it is also my way to help him honor his desire to preserve a small, highly individual part of the history of World War II. Obviously, while this narrative may not necessarily reflect what he would have said were he still alive today, I hope that this account will accurately record many of his recollections. These reminiscences were provided to me by him (some of which, in the form of his war stories, form some of my earliest childhood memories) and also by his relatives, friends, and Marine buddies. It is also my hope that this will help give the reader an idea of "what it was all about" and "what it was like," at least as viewed through the eyes of one young and low-ranking participant, some eighty years later.

My father did take some steps to record at least a fraction of his wartime history in his own words. He began a short, typewritten manuscript, which he never finished but which gives some of this history as he saw it. I will, therefore, begin each chapter of this narrative with his words, as an introduction.

I have strived to use Jack's own words to the greatest degree possible, although many of these words, I admit, I have reconstructed from memory. I have, however, sought to corroborate every significant event or incident he recounted to me, either by the historical record or by the testimony of other veterans of his battalion. In many respects, then, this story is not just a retelling of Jack McCall's wartime life but also of the lives of his buddies, the men of the Marines' Ninth Defense Battalion with whom he served.

Some Ninth Defense veterans may feel slighted in that this account centers around one part of this unique and heterogeneous battalion, the 155mm Group, being the portion of the battalion to which Jack belonged. While there are more tales yet to be told about the Ninth's antiaircraft gunners and tank and radar crews, each of whom pioneered new methods of warfare in the South Pacific's jungles, those must be told in detail elsewhere. Still, as will be seen, the stories of these other key elements of the Ninth will overlap with Jack's experiences.

Another word is necessary and appropriate here: this being as to the racial composition of American forces in the Pacific. To a significant degree—but by no means entirely—the saga of the average Marine in the South and Central Pacific involved ground combat actions fought largely by white men. One must remember that the Second World War was fought by America's last segregated military: racial desegregation did not follow until the Truman Administration issued Executive Order 9981 as to desegregation of the armed forces in 1948. Nevertheless, the World War II Marine Corps ultimately formed two African American defense battalions as sister units to the Ninth at Montford Point, North Carolina. By 1944, Black Marines served at Peleliu, on Guam, and in other late-war campaigns. Of course, African American sailors, stevedores, and laborers played an invaluable and greatly underappreciated role in serving as the muscles and sinews for much of America's logistical efforts across the Pacific.[2] Both combat and non-combat Navy vessels often had Black and Filipino stewards and crewmen aboard. The Ninth Defense would also encounter Fijian native commandos in combat during the fighting on New Georgia.[3] However, in the highly segregated Marine Corps and US military of the day, interactions with Black military personnel tended to be limited, especially in the Pacific combat zone of 1942–44. The same was largely true for women, both service personnel and Red Cross and USO workers. In the Solomon and Russell Islands and later on Guam, the Ninth Defense's men would have interactions with local villagers, although the combat environment tended to make these more limited. In my research, the Ninth's veterans, in short, seemed to write and talk little about both the Black servicemen they met and the largely Melanesian inhabitants of the South Pacific islands where they served from autumn 1942 until summer 1944. To borrow Ralph Ellison's eloquent term, the Black soldiers, Marines, sailors and Merchant Mariners were the "Invisible Men" of the Pacific campaign.

Regrettably, however, some instances of what can only be recognized as flat-out racism toward non-white allies and peers arose in some conversations with a very limited number of the battalion's veterans. I wish I could say that this were not true, but—whether from racism, or a form of snobbery from having enlisted before the acceptance and formation of Black and female Marine Corps units and also K9 scout-dog squads—the highly charged and offensive put-down, "I was in the Marine Corps before women, dogs, and [a racial insult toward Blacks]," was encountered on several occasions. No excuses or justifications can be offered for such a comment, and no attempt to legitimate the attitudes demonstrated therein will be made.

While comic moments are described throughout this account, this is certainly not always a happy or uplifting story. The memories of sacrifices made by a generation are being lost to time. There are some frank admissions of feelings shared by my father and his fellow veterans of the Pacific theater toward their old adversary, Japan and her people. Consequently, certain wartime events are recounted which, to the present-day reader, may be despicable or horrifying. For the sake of presenting as complete a picture as possible of the life and times of a fairly average Marine-enlisted man in the Pacific War from his worm's-eye point of view—why and how he fought; why he fought in the manner he did; what his fears and hopes were; how he survived and kept his sanity intact—I find it necessary to be as candid as possible and include unpleasant reminders of the ancient hatreds of some eighty years ago. Those sentiments were often an integral factor in the reasons he and others enlisted in the Marine Corps. They were very much a factor in the ways that the fighting developed and were an adjunct to the greater geopolitical events that shaped the larger war.

For those readers who may find this too brutal or insensitive, I ask your indulgence. I also ask you to remember: for better or worse, those times *were* different, and such things did occur, much as they still occur today. We can look back and marvel or be disturbed (sometimes simultaneously) at what transpired on the islands and waters of the Pacific more than fifty years ago. The average Marine, sailor, Seabee, or Army dogface—or, for that matter, their respective Japanese counterparts—seldom had the luxury of time to contemplate an often-brutish existence that encompassed both the heights and depths of the human experience. Again, my goal has been to capture the events and attitudes of those times—most importantly, Jack McCall's and his friends' recollections—as authentically as possible. To be true to this goal, this narrative will occasionally adhere to General Sherman's admonition: "War is cruelty, and you cannot refine it."

There were, however, good times, too, mainly arising from the camaraderie of men thrown together for three years in a sometimes ridiculous, *Catch-22*-like situation. As several of Jack's Marine buddies have noted, the Pacific War's veterans have to talk among themselves and at their reunions about their good times in the last "good war," to use Studs Terkel's expression. "Otherwise, it just wouldn't be worth talking about," as more than one of them commented to me.

While a son can never truly know and understand all aspects of his father's life, it is clear to me that my father's service in World War II was a defining period in his. This book is, above all, one son's recollections and attempts to reconstruct this defining season.

PROLOGUE

To one young Marine, all hell broke loose on Friday, July 2, 1943, at about 1:35 p.m.—1335 hours, in military time—on Rendova, a stiflingly muggy island two hundred miles north of Guadalcanal in the South Pacific.

Rendova is a semi-volcanic outcropping barely ten miles long and at its narrowest point, less than one mile away from the much larger island of New Georgia. Hundreds of land crabs and ravenous ants scuttered through its untended coconut groves, abandoned by its British and Australian plantation masters over a year earlier when the islands were seized by the Japanese. Those Japanese forces were now in the second day of opposing a new invasion, this time by hosts of US Marines and Army troops massing on Rendova to bombard and seize New Georgia's prize: a large Japanese airfield on that island's rocky southwestern tip, Munda Point.

That Friday morning it rained heavily, much as it had periodically for the last two days, and the area around Rendova Harbor emitted an ether of steam and other more pungent miasmas: of jungle decay and rot, of sweat, of death. The reek of putrefaction was noticeable, as several of the dead Japanese defenders, killed the previous day, lay unburied and hidden in the dense foliage. Piles of boxes, supplies, and equipment were stacked up around a group of open-sided, corrugated-metal sheds, formerly the property of Lever Brothers. Large landing craft disgorged heavy artillery pieces, towed by Caterpillar tractors and accompanied by the cursing and shouting of sergeants and troops. During the unloading process, others aboard the landing craft or awaiting orders noted a large group of planes passing over the dormant peak of Mount Rendova, debating their make, model, and mission. "Must be our guys," several of the onlookers speculated, "heading back to the Canal"—Guadalcanal. Others were not so sure.

Nearby, a lanky, young Marine, just under six feet tall and looking vaguely like a clean-shaven and younger version of Clark Gable, looked up, too, as he widened his small foxhole. His faded green shirt opened wide to fight the heat, the "Pfc."—private, first class—leaned on his shovel, took a brief puff, and went back to work. He glanced over at a mass of hoses and boxes, collapsible canvas tubs, and a pump, and sighed. The young Marine was a "gizmo"—a technical specialist, the bane of all Marine sergeants, and in this case, a water purification man—and he cursed to himself as he imagined having to set up his equipment after having finished his small foxhole. He was sopping wet with perspiration; his platoon sergeant was nowhere to be found—no surprise there, he was probably nursing that ever-present sick headache of his—so the odds of getting a couple of helping hands were fading fast.

As the young Marine glumly pondered how to set up all this gear by himself before nightfall, he heard the roar of multiple aircraft engines, straining in a dive, and a belated chorus of screams: "Take cover, now! *They're Japs!*" Having already had his "bells rung" by a marauding squadron of Japanese planes earlier that day while offloading a landing craft, he had quickly learned to recognize the sound of Zero fighters' engines, and he leapt into his shallow hole.

As the Japanese planes soared overhead, their Rising Sun "meatball" insignia now easily visible, many of the men cluttering the narrow beachhead were caught in the open without warning. The more experienced Marines and sailors yelled "*Condition Red! Take cover!* Hit the deck!" long before the keening sirens, ships' bells, and blasts of air horns erupted from the landing craft and ships bobbing in Blanche Channel. Clusters of Marines and Seabees near the beach ran for either the nearest cover or gun position, but there were also lines of heavily laden troops from the Army's Forty-Third Infantry Division struggling off a line of beached LCI infantry landing craft. While wading through the surf to the beach, these troops were caught squarely in the open and suffered terribly. "Now the earth began to vibrate with blasts," Lieutenant Christopher Donner, a young Marine officer, recalled of his huddling in a foxhole with eleven others. "Above the sound of the firing came the high scream of planes diving, and bullets smacked into the palms over our heads."[1] Drums of gasoline and diesel, boxes of ammunition, and the Forty-Third Division's casualty clearing station were all hit, and five tons of Navy construction engineer ("Seabee") demolition materials exploded in brilliant flames. Jack McCall, the young Marine gizmo, later recalled that it was "absolute pandemonium."

Caught in the open without foxholes, on the hard coral of the small peninsula, the Navy's Twenty-Fourth Seabee Battalion took the brunt of the attack, surrounded by drums and crates of fuel and ammo. The colossal explosion of the Seabees' demolition dump on a peninsula jutting into Rendova Harbor arguably "[caused] more damage than the bombs themselves," as noted by the Australian coastwatcher D. C. Horton, who also witnessed the scene.[2] The colossal blasts erupting from the dynamite dump, only a few hundred feet from young Jack McCall's location, disintegrated a bulldozer and a group of nearby Seabees. The sounds were deafening, and although the air raid only lasted a few minutes, it felt like hours were passing by. The Forty-Third Division's troops, caught wading through the surf as they left their landing craft, were mercilessly strafed by the marauding fighters.

McCall grabbed his rifle and looked up again through the shredded treetops to see these Japanese fighters—the dreaded Mitsubishi Zero—roaring by, "on the deck," fifty to sixty feet above the harbor. He was close enough to them to see the pilots' grimacing faces, intent on their mission as they strafed the beach, mounds of supplies, and the Forty-Third's hapless troops. The noise was deafening, the humidity was suffocating, and the heat generated by the explosions incredible: more fireballs and columns of acrid and oily black smoke billowed over the battered tree line. Men rushed or staggered about—some in fear, some blackened or bleeding or missing limbs, some in shock, some dying—and pieces of debris, human and otherwise, rained down from the explosions. Over the sounds of aircraft motors, gunfire, and explosions, McCall and his buddies heard another, more disturbing sound: the wails of men in pain, the yells of medics and stretcher bearers frantically seeking out those who could be saved, and the obscenities, curses, and prayers of others watching their buddies dying. During the entire raid, nowhere was the much-expected Allied airpower in evidence. Unknown to those on the beach, rain squalls over Guadalcanal and the Russell Island air bases had grounded the American and New Zealand fighters intended to provide air cover to the troops on Rendova.

More than two hundred Americans lay dead, wounded, or missing—disintegrated either by exploding Japanese bombs or the demolition materials in the Seabees' supply dump, their grisly remains hanging from the battered trees and littering the beach and lagoon. The "all clear" order was yelled out over the staccato popping of clips of rifle bullets exploding in burning

vehicles and the screams of the seriously injured. As one of his own officers yelped out to a group of machine gunners still firing at the retreating
Zeroes—*"Cease fire; cease fire, now, goddammit, or I'll shoot you myself!"*—
McCall gazed around at the debris littering the area, took off his helmet and
ran his fingers through his sweat-plastered hair, and wondered how he had
ever arrived at this condition and how in the hell he would ever survive
it. As he caught the smells of burning rubber, wood, and fabric, scorched
metal and flesh, he realized how utterly scared and alone he felt. He was
as "terrified as a twenty-one-year-old Marine could be," he remarked later.

But as he heard a sergeant yell, "Hey, Pogiebait! We need a hand over
here!" he brushed the sand off himself and grabbed his helmet, ammo belt,
and rifle and leaped out of his foxhole. It was time to get back to work.

As an old man today reflecting on the past—and my days as a young boy
growing up in Franklin—I remember:

The fun of hunting arrowheads along the riverbanks, minnie balls in the
fields and the sheer joy of finding a couple a day.

The hikes to Roper's Knob and a lunch of pork and beans, our own re-
enactment of the Civil War at the "Old Fort" and then a skinny dip in the
muddy Harpeth by the trestle.

My day etching my name deeply in a large flat rock on the Fort, over-
hanging the river, with a hammer and railroad spike—it stayed for at least
40 or 50 more years, before a local historian removed it, and had it sent to a
museum somewhere to preserve the name of a "long gone" Federal soldier!

And I remember when "damn" was a dirty word and only acceptable when
used with "Yankee."

I remember not more than fifteen or twenty cars would ever be parked
around the High School, and school never closed because of snow.

Jack H. McCall, Sr.
April 3, 1997

The valley of the Harpeth River snakes and meanders circuitously
through the green hills of Middle Tennessee, some twenty miles south of
Nashville. For years the river's waters have given sustenance to numerous
peoples. Native American tribes found it to be an excellent hunting ground
and left traces of their presence in flint arrowheads, pottery shards, and
burial mounds found throughout its valley. This part of the Harpeth River's

basin was later found by itinerant European trappers, who bartered pottery and other goods with the local Chickasaw tribe. Shortly after the 1779 founding of nearby Fort Nashborough, the valley was discovered anew by early American settlers from Virginia and the Carolinas who also found it to be an agreeable spot for hunting, fishing, and the cultivation of crops. Duly appreciative of their connections, these settlers christened their settlement after Benjamin Franklin and their county after Hugh Williamson, a Continental general from North Carolina who had been many of the settlers' wartime commander. In time, many of these Native American arrowheads, pottery shards, and other artifacts would be found by a young boy, born in Birmingham on May 1, 1922, but soon transplanted at a tender age to his father's old home place in Franklin, a few hundred yards from the banks of the muddy Harpeth. His name was Jack H. McCall.

In many respects, Jack's hometown was a town marked by history. More to the point, it was a town touched by war and haunted by its aftermath. Andrew Jackson ended a long-running conflict with the Cherokee and Chickasaw tribes with a peace treaty signed in Franklin's Masonic Lodge in 1830, a treaty which, regrettably, helped pave the way for the Trail of Tears deportation of the Cherokees a few years later. One of the bloodiest battles of the Civil War occurred within a few miles of the McCall house; in about five hours on the late afternoon of November 30, 1864, more than eight thousand Confederate and Union soldiers were killed or wounded.[3] In the words of one Rebel veteran, Sam Watkins, the Battle of Franklin was "the grand coronation of death": "My flesh trembles, and creeps, and crawls when I think of it today. Would to God that I had never witnessed such a scene!"[4] Although the Union forces holding the town withdrew to Nashville, the Confederates' victory at Franklin was a Pyrrhic one. The battle decimated the South's Army of Tennessee, which was annihilated as a fighting entity three weeks later at the Battle of Nashville. For months thereafter, the casualties of both sides were cared for in Franklin's churches and private homes, transforming the town into a vast infirmary, morgue, and graveyard.[5] The largest Confederate cemetery of the war was created on the grounds of the Carnton plantation, the final resting place for almost fifteen hundred dead Southerners.[6]

While the Battle of Franklin crippled the Confederacy's last chance for victory in the west, the battle and its aftermath permeated much of the life of the town for years to come. Not surprisingly, as in many Southern towns, chapters of the United Daughters of the Confederacy and the Sons of Confederate Veterans flourished. The local high school adopted the

"Rebel," a grizzled Confederate soldier, as its school mascot. Franklin High's hometown rival, the all-male Battle Ground Academy, erected its campus in 1889 on a portion of the Union breastworks near the Carter House; the entrenchments were still readily traceable many years after the battle.

About two thousand yards behind the McCall home, the squat, overgrown earthwork hump of the Union Army's Fort Granger provided the finest play castle that a young boy, his brothers, and friends could ever have. In the fields around Franklin, limestone-encrusted "minnie ball" musket bullets, buttons, belt buckles, and an occasional rusted bayonet or musket piece could be turned up by a farm plow or hoe. Once, behind the old McCall homestead, Jack was lucky enough to find the rusted, but relatively intact, remains of a Whitney cap-and-ball revolver from the Civil War. And, over it all, surveying the town square and second in prominence only to the hills surrounding Franklin and the town's mighty grain elevator on the banks of the Harpeth, the town's sentinel stood, a granite Confederate soldier overlooking the antebellum courthouse. Its dour stone features were marred by a nick in its hat—caused, it was long rumored, by a gun-toting drunk who had proved to be a menace only to the local statuary but in fact created by an accident during the statue's 1889 erection.[7]

Twenties Franklin was also proud of its latest war heroes, the veterans of the Great War. These included a local lawyer and businessman, Captain Tom Henderson, who, it was reputed, was involved in a plot to kidnap and bring to justice Kaiser Wilhelm II after his abdication and flight from Germany to the Netherlands. "Cap'n Tom" kept mum about the affair for many years, with good reason. He and the other participants, a group of Tennessee National Guard officers, led by their commander, Colonel Luke Lea, the publisher of the Nashville *Tennessean*, came within a hair's-breadth of being court-martialed by General Pershing. The intrepid band of Tennesseans actually infiltrated the Dutch castle where the kaiser was temporarily lodged after his abdication of the German throne before they were apprehended by the nobleman who owned the castle and a squad of Dutch policemen and soldiers.[8] While over a hundred Williamson Countians had served in the military during the Great War, thirty-two of them died.[9] Many others came home wounded, maimed, gassed, or mentally disabled. In late 1941, another war was about to change the lives of its residents again. One of those whose lives would be ineradicably altered by that war was Jack McCall, a recent graduate of the Franklin High School Class of 1941.

Jack was the youngest of the three McCall boys, whose family could trace an unbroken lineage in Williamson County back to its founding. His oldest brother, Albert, Jr., was the quiet, intellectual part of the triumvirate. Robert, the middle brother, was the classic redhead: boisterous, feisty, and fiery tempered at times, and from an early age, unafraid to challenge his parents' authority in very direct ways. Jack was the baby of the family and doted on by his mother, but he was by no means a runt. While he was not afraid to fight when he had to, he always preferred to turn aside another's wrath with a smile or a wisecrack.

Jack loved practical jokes, but as much as he perpetrated them on others, he had the tables turned on him and his brothers almost as often. One of his first recollections of a practical joke was one played on his big brother Al by their grandfather, Robert Lycurgus McCall, who recalled hearing the distant sounds of the fighting at Franklin as a teenager from his home ten miles east of the town. While visiting a gas station down the street from the McCall house one day, crusty old R. L. offered his grandsons what appeared to be vanilla wafers made into an Oreo or Hydrox-like sandwich cookie, only to laugh hysterically as little Al, the first to try the "cookies," tearfully spit his out: liberally sandwiched in between the two wafers was a coating of axle grease. It was a favorite trick of the old man, and R. L. and his "cracker barrel" buddy guffawed every time the joke succeeded.

By the time he reached junior high, certain practical jokes became old standbys for Jack and his partners in crime. A particular favorite, guaranteed to make some of the leading citizens of Franklin turn red, was to tie a billfold on a string with a crisp dollar bill peeking temptingly out of its folds. Hidden behind bushes near the county courthouse or a local bank, Jack would throw the billfold out and see how many bites he could get. When a lawyer or banker reached down to pick up the billfold—*poof!*—it would mysteriously run away. That gag was always good for some laughs at the expense of a few highfalutin "muckety-mucks."

While in certain respects Jack's childhood was idyllic, it was hardly entirely tranquil. The family suffered from the Great Depression and its effects, and Jack and his brothers recalled days when the family went hungry. In a time when the average Southern family remained more or less in one place, A. G. McCall's family moved a considerable number of times—to Birmingham (where Jack was born); to Atlanta; to Lynchburg, Virginia (where the McCall boys befriended another neighborhood kid, Jackie Cooper, soon to be an actor and one of the child stars of the "Our Gang" comedies); and to Murray, Kentucky, their mother Ruth's home. Part of this was due to the Depression's effects on A. G.'s jobs; another part, however, may have been due to a darker side of his character. Although generally a congenial man, A. G. was subject to spells of depression and drinking, his temper could be moody, and his methods of disciplining his sons were fierce. It was, at times, a "spare the rod and spoil the child" kind of household.

Fortunately for his sons, A. G. was well balanced by his wife. Originally a professional milliner, Ruth McCall was also a talented seamstress and quilter and was somewhat artistically inclined. But in a day when few married women, Southern or otherwise, had independent jobs after their wedding days, regardless of the family's situation, she was left to devote herself to homemaking and her boys. Ruth immersed herself completely in these tasks, much as she did later with her work for the local Methodist church.

The McCall boys were imbued very early in their lives with a sense of the family's history, including its military history. One of the progenitors of the family was a Revolutionary War veteran from North Carolina who had acquired his acreage in the county by land grant in recognition of his wartime service. Ruth McCall's grandfather and her great-uncle both served in sister Kentucky regiments in the Confederate Army. A. G. McCall had been called up for service in the Spanish-American War but never made it overseas; a cousin, the owner of Franklin's leading electric store, served on the battleship USS *Tennessee* in World War I; and a distant cousin was an early Army Air Service aviator and US Mail Service pilot who was killed in a flying accident near Birmingham in 1923. Draft or no draft and the horrors of the Great War aside, this was not a family that shirked its military obligations.

As a boy, besides the fun of watching ten-cent serial Westerns and the "Our Gang" and "Little Rascals" comedies at Saturday matinees at the movie theater, the farmland around Franklin offered various treats. These were both of the vegetable and mineral varieties, particularly in springtime and fall as crops were planted and harvested and as the soil was plowed up to reveal the artifacts left by the area's prior occupants. Besides the debris of the Civil War, the tilled fields yielded arrowheads, flint hatchet heads, and other Native American relics, and there were numerous pre-Columbian mounds in the area. Jack and his brothers would occasionally go hunting for these relics with the able help of their next-door neighbor, the Tennessee state archaeologist and the son of one of Nathan Bedford Forrest's officers, Dr. P. E. Cox, an expert on early Native American archaeology who had amassed a sizeable collection of such artifacts.

Despite the eminent Dr. Cox's erudite lectures on Native American life and the Civil War, Jack's mother was concerned that her youngest boy was a little "uncivilized." Like many parents who wanted their sons to have a modicum of culture (and with a brother who was a noted jazz musician), Ruth McCall signed him up for piano lessons. These were provided by Miss Lahatte, an elderly spinster boarding in Dr. Cox's house. Although she could be an unholy terror—Jack recalled getting his knuckles rapped on occasion—Miss Lahatte rewarded good lessons with ginger snaps. These were a big incentive for a kid with a sweet tooth in the days of the Great Depression. Unfortunately, he soon found that the ginger snap rewards were few and far between, as musical skills were just not his forte.

Physical activities, on the other hand, were much more to Jack's liking and talents. By the time he reached high school, football had become a passion, and by their senior year, Jack and his good buddy David Gentry would be co-captains of the FHS football team. High school also brought new illicit pleasures: "playin' hooky"; rolling and smoking Bull Durham handmade cigarettes behind the football bleachers while trying to avoid the wrath of Principal W. C. Yates; and joining several boys in trying to hijack an old Spanish-American War cannon in front of the high school but, in the process, giving it a good push downhill. The cannon rolled some distance until its aged wooden-spoked wheels cracked. In another game effort, Jack decided to run away from home to hitchhike to Florida. Even though the cost of living in the late 1930s was far less than it is today, Jack soon learned that a person could only travel so far on less than fifty cents. He made it as far as the Tennessee-Alabama border before hitchhiking back to Franklin and getting a sound whipping from his royally irate but worried father. Later, his pal "Brutus" Isaacs and he somehow acquired a "flivver," an ancient Model T-esque car. Jack and Brutus treated this jalopy like it was their personal chariot and optimistically painted on the driver's door of the rust-bucket: "DON'T SHOVE, GALS!"

High school also brought out a creative side to Jack. He took up drawing, co-wrote a fight song for Franklin High, and became the publisher and editor-in-chief of *The Daily Blah-Blah*, an underground newspaper that satirized about every teacher, student, and coach imaginable at the high school. Dating and flirting with the girls was another new experience to him, and soon, Jack was popular enough to be elected senior class president. Like his father, whose best talents had always been in haberdashery and managing men's wear stores, Jack was known to his family and friends as

A "real jellybean": high-schooler Jack McCall, circa 1941 (*left*),
and in "Brutey" Isaacs's jalopy (*right*). Slogan on door reads: "DON'T SHOVE, GALS."
Author's collection; photo of car courtesy of Chuck Isaacs.

a natty dresser: a real "jellybean," complete with slicked-back hair and a rakish fedora on special occasions, a fancy stickpin in his tie, and a nicely pressed pocket square always in the breast pocket of his jacket.

Oh, the Class of '41. For teenagers in Franklin, life was fun and fairly innocent. Unlike during the depth of the Depression, jobs were now less scarce, and yet war in Europe was a worry to many Americans. After all, hadn't FDR reinstituted the draft just a year before? Hadn't Bob McCall and four of Jack's class of 1940 buddies joined the Marines?[10] Hadn't a missionary and friend of Ruth McCall been captured and held on the Nazi prison ship *Dresden* for several weeks in April 1941 when a German Q-ship raider, the infamous *Atlantis*, sank the Egyptian civilian steamship she was aboard, the *Zamzam*, off the African coast in April 1941?[11] Yet, despite these harbingers, the storm clouds still seemed far enough off in the summer of 1941.

As summer 1941 turned into fall, there were crops—mainly corn and tobacco—to be harvested, and the extra help was always appreciated by the local farmers. Jack accepted a job as a salesclerk at a dry goods store in nearby Nashville, and he picked up some extra spending money on the side with weekend odd jobs to help Coach Overbey. Someday, he thought, he might even become the first McCall to go to college. He had been a high school athlete, earning letters in several varsity sports, so the University of Tennessee seemed to him to be a good place to earn a college degree. Its academics were good enough, which pleased his parents, but its athletic teams and vaunted fraternity night life were even more of a draw to Jack and his Franklin High buddies. Not this fall, but maybe in the fall of '42, there would be a new, cocky "Tennessee Volunteer" walking the streets of Knoxville. A. G. McCall only shook his head and grumbled to himself about his youngest son going off to become a "college boy."

But in late 1941, fate, in the guise of global events, was about to stop Jack McCall's dating life, his school plans, and his orderly, laid-back, small-town life dead in its tracks for many years—and, quite possibly, forever.

ONE

The Making of a Young Marine:
From Pearl Harbor to Cuba

I volunteered for the Marines about a week after Pearl Harbor, with the
agreement that I would not leave until after Christmas. This being okay,
I had my physical exam then. I reported back and was sworn in New Year's Eve,
the last Marine to be sworn in [during] 1941 in the Nashville office.

I spent the night in the Tulane Hotel, and enjoyed my last night
as a civilian in the festivities of the evening. Early the next morning, Jan. 1st,
we boarded at the Union Station a train loaded with other volunteers
from the east, and bound for Parris Island, South Carolina.

Our introduction and reception in the Marines was anything
but cordial—and our Drill Instructor went to extra efforts to convince us
of our crude backgrounds and stupidity. This being the on-going procedure
along with the hustling, shoving and cussings, we finished "Boot Camp"
in less than half the time usually taken.

On February the 12th, we were railed to Norfolk, Virginia, and boarded
the *William Biddle*, shipping out on Friday the 13th for Guantanamo Bay, Cuba.
En route we had three U-boat attacks, and our destroyer escorts destroyed two.

It may be of interest that this was only 68 days from the "Pearl" attack, and of the
eight hundred men in our first formed Marine unit since war was declared,
80% of them had no military experience. We formed the 9th Defense Battalion.

—JACK H. MCCALL, SR.—

"Yesterday, December 7, 1941—a date that will live in infamy—the United
States was suddenly and deliberately attacked by naval and air forces of the
Empire of Japan." Like so many of his friends, for the rest of his life Jack
McCall could recall exactly where he was and what he was doing on the
day that Pearl Harbor, Hawaii was attacked and when President Franklin
Delano Roosevelt grimly asked Congress to declare war on Japan the next

day. He was nineteen years old and had graduated seven months before from Franklin High. His older brothers Al and Bob had long since moved away from Franklin. Al was working in Baltimore as a draftsman and designer for the Glenn Martin Aircraft Company. Things between Bob and A. G. had gotten so tense and the atmosphere at home so oppressive that, after Bob's own high school graduation, Bob's mother secretly arranged for him to go to California to work at his uncle's store. After a few years there, Bob enlisted in the Marine Corps in 1939 and hinted to his little brother that someday, he might want to consider doing the same thing.

On Sunday afternoon, December 7, 1941, Jack was at home. His mother Ruth had just returned from church, and he was getting ready to do some chores for his dad. Like most Americans (and Franklinites), neither Jack nor his parents had any idea where Pearl Harbor was, so they rummaged around the house to find a map to spot it. Also, like most Americans, they had figured the country would have to fight the Nazis long before it had to fight the Japanese. Jack remembered that, back then, not much respect was given to things that came from Japan: they were regarded as cheaply made and not well put together, like toys. Thus, the fact that *Japanese*-made planes and *Japanese*-made aircraft carriers, manned not by the stereotypically nearsighted and inept pilots but by well-trained and determined aviators and sailors, were good enough to attack the battleships of the Pacific Fleet helped make the surprise attack even more bitter in the minds of some Americans.

Following FDR's address to a stunned nation and his request to Congress for a formal declaration of war against the Japanese empire, the headlines of the next day's *Nashville Banner* screamed the news: "CONGRESS DECLARES WAR: 3,000 CASUALTIES AT HAWAII." A smaller caption reported "*Tennesseans Rush to Enlist in Services*" and noted: "The ringing traditions of the old Volunteer State struck a new note this morning as Tennesseans of all ages thronged Nashville recruiting stations seeking enlistment in the military services of their country. Before noon more than sixty men had applied for enlistment in the Army, Navy or Marines and men were still coming in."[1] After reading the paper and talking with several of his buddies—*Ain't you gonna enlist now, Jack? It's the thing to do, man!*—Jack thought the matter over and figured he knew what he had to do.

With brother Bob in the service, Jack knew that his joining up would greatly displease his parents, but with Bob serving as a Marine, he took little time in making his decision. Jack was reasonably certain that he would eventually be drafted, as he was classified "1-A," the prime draft classification. A lot of his buddies had already been drafted into the Army, and others, like Red Caldwell, had volunteered for the Marine Corps. Still, he thought, why not go ahead and beat the "Christmas rush" and join a crack outfit like the Marines while he still had a choice in the matter? Bob seemed to like it well enough, and in the two or so years he had already been a Marine, it had been good for him; he was already a corporal and would probably be promoted to sergeant soon. Jack thought about it and concluded he was "all for the Marines." After talking it over with some of his pals for a few days, he hopped a lift to Nashville and went to the Customs House on Broadway, where the Marine Corps Recruiting Station was located.

The recruiting sergeant, clad in his dress blue uniform, promised Jack that his departure for basic training would be postponed for a few weeks, during which time he would need to get a physical examination from his doctor. The recruiter knew his man: *Look at it this way, pal; you'll get to spend some time with your family, maybe with your gal, get to say your goodbyes to your mother, and stick around for the holidays. You won't need to shove off until New Year's Day. That's the best deal I can give you, Mac; after all, there's a war on, you know. Now, how about it?* "All right," Jack enthusiastically said, and he signed the enlistment application with his most grown-up signature. He pledged to the recruiting sergeant to return after Christmas to complete the enlistment process, and then back home he went, to break the news to his parents.

After Bob enlisted in the Marines in 1939, Jack had mulled over joining the Marines, and he had shared the idea with his parents at that time. They did not take it well. His father called him a "damn fool" for wanting to enlist in the Marines when it certainly wasn't his time to go yet—couldn't he just get out of high school first and wait it out to see when he'd get his draft notice? Wasn't it enough for Jack that his big brother Bob had already gone out and done the same dumb thing? With Pearl Harbor, though, everything changed, and when he mentioned to his father that he was thinking again about joining up, A. G. took it more in stride.

It did not dawn on Jack precisely what he had done, however, until some days later when, after submitting his physical report to the Recruiting Station, he returned home from work in Nashville one afternoon. As Jack entered the living room, A. G. looked up from his evening newspaper and said: "There's a letter for you on the mantel, son. It's from the government." The Marines had accepted Jack's application, and the letter instructed him to return on the 31st of December for his oath of enlistment and, thereafter, departure for basic training. His mother cried. Jack said that despite all the hard times the family had endured through the Depression and their moves from city to city, this was one time he knew he'd done something to break his mother's heart, and it made him feel sad—but not yet regretful that he had made this decision.

The holidays were filled with farewells to family and friends, and Jack quit his job at McKesson, Berry & Martin on Christmas Eve to celebrate a somber Christmas with his mother and father in Franklin. Brother Bob had sent word that his unit was moving out, but he didn't know where; brother Al, working in war production, reported that his aircraft factory was being camouflaged and that rumors were rampant in Baltimore of Nazi subs and commando parties cruising off Chesapeake Bay. Ruth cried a lot; A. G. was tense and irritable with Jack but did not tell his son off. He knew that these days might be the last he might see of his youngest child. Instead, he barked, "Go do your chores, boy," and Jack sullenly collected his tools to clean the barn and feed his father's prize pigs, now questioning why he had delayed his departure as long as he had.

Late in the afternoon of December 31, 1941, after a difficult goodbye with his parents and in accordance with his instructions, Jack returned to the recruiting station to complete his enlistment. He would be sworn in before departing for Parris Island, South Carolina, the soon-to-be fabled home of the Marines' Recruit Depot. Although many other Middle Tennessee-area volunteers were waiting with him, several had already taken their oaths of enlistment, and Jack was sworn in individually, making him one of the last local Marine inductees of 1941. He was enlisted in the US Marine Corps Reserve, in the Corps "for the duration of the war" as opposed to a "regular" Marine recruit who signed up for a four-year fixed term of enlistment. As they filed out of the Recruiting Station after having sworn their oaths and signed the last papers, Jack and his fellow enlistees began to harbor some doubts as to the wisdom of their actions as the Marine recruiting sergeant, resplendent in his dress blue uniform, grinned broadly and croaked: "Welcome to the Marine Corps. Just you wait: *you'll be sorrrr-ree!*" For effect, the sergeant drew out the syllables in with evident glee.

Early on New Year's Day, after catching a few hours of sleep in the old Tulane Hotel after a night of farewell revelry, Jack boarded a train waiting under a metal-roofed shed at Union Station in downtown Nashville, a few blocks south of the Customs House. The train was soon full of a raucous (if slightly hungover) crowd of other Marine recruits, all headed for Parris Island. As the train pulled away from Union Station, Jack wondered when he would see it again. Because they had enlisted during the holidays, the fresh

Marine recruits arriving in this period would become known throughout the Marine Corps as the "Pearl Harbor Avengers" and the "Christmas Tree Marines." Despite Jack's own mental preparations, including his earlier talks with his brother Bob as to what he could expect, his initiation into the Marines would still be a rude awakening.

As they set forth for their military training, Jack and many of his peers had high expectations to match their high spirits as to the likely length of the war. "I think most of us figured it would last a year at most and that we'd be home by the following Christmas" was Jack's answer when questioned as to how long he thought it would take to beat the Japanese. In the end, it would be four years—and many close calls later—before he made it back home to Franklin.

What Jack also did not fully appreciate at the time was that he would soon be transformed from a young and brash teenager, with the world at his feet, into the world's most unexalted specimen of humanity: the lowly Marine Corps trainee—the "boot."

Boot Camp Days

At Yemassee Junction, South Carolina, the next morning, a miniature but grim-visaged Marine corporal boarded Jack's train. Jack recalled somewhat ruefully years later, "I knew I'd played hell at Yemassee when that little cocky corporal came aboard—he explained how it was going to be." The diminutive NCO loudly and abruptly began the new recruits' initiation into the Corps by bellowing out: "*Now hear this!* You *will* remain on this train car until you are told to dismount. You will not *get out* of this car until I give you the word. You *will* remain in your seats at all times. You *will* keep order. Is *that* understood?" The mob of enlistees quickly fell silent and scrambled for their seats under the withering glare of the corporal. Another group of stone-silent recruits—all from the Eastern Seaboard (enlistees from west of the Mississippi River were trained at the Corps' recruit depot at San Diego)—emerged from a Spartan-looking railside building to line up in single file. Laden with all their suitcases and bags, this somber group now boarded a nearby Parris Island-bound train waiting on a separate siding at Yemassee Junction. Soon thereafter, Jack and the other men waiting on his train followed suit.

A few hours later, the train was greeted at Port Royal, the debarkation point for "Boot Camp," by a line of crisply dressed—and very hostile—Marine noncoms with clipboards tucked under their arms who began bawling orders the moment the train stopped. Upon arrival at Parris Island and after hustling from one clerk's office to another for in-processing, Jack was assigned to the Ninth Platoon of the Marine Training Barracks. As the new recruits ran and plodded from one in-processing station to another, they were greeted by platoons of only slightly less green boots who yelled out the same chilling threat that the recruiting sergeant had made to Jack following his oath-taking ceremony, the words drawn out in the same manner: *"You'll be sorrrr-ree!"* Jack and his peers were double-timed from place to place: to draw uniforms; to draw sundry issue items, known as a "bucket issue" because they were placed in a metal bucket—all other non-combat gear and personal clothing, underwear ("skivvies" in the Marines' argot), toiletries, brushes, and other cleaning gear; and to undergo a quick battery of medical and psychological tests. The "psycho" test was brief in the extreme, consisting of three simple questions: "Are you happy?" "Do you like girls?" "Do you play with yourself?"[2] Finally, after all was complete (and assuming that all three questions were answered to the examiner's satisfaction), the dazed, weary, and fully laden boots were double-timed to the platoon's barracks area by the menacing figures of the two people they would come to hate more than anyone they had ever hated before and (quite possibly) since: their drill instructor and assistant drill instructor.

The members of the Ninth Platoon were lucky in one sense, as their quarters were two-story wooden and brick barracks; these facilities were hardly comfortable, but they were better than the alternatives. For many other enlistees in other platoons, the term "barracks" was an entirely inapt name: in the freezing dead of January and February, several platoons were billeted outdoors in old, ragged tents, while others were billeted in more substantial (but scarcely less chilly) all-metal Quonset huts. For those quartered in the two-man tents, the sleeping arrangements were Spartan in the extreme: each man had a cot, mattress, pillow, one sheet, pillowcase, footlocker, and only one blanket. In South Carolina, which in early 1942 was experiencing sub-freezing wintertime temperatures, the boots fought off discomfort by sleeping in their clothes and wadding newspapers under their mattresses for insulation. The barracks and huts were thoughtfully equipped with small potbellied stoves—not that it mattered much. As the drill instructors or "DIs" said, in time-honored military tradition, "You won't be here to use 'em in the daytime; you can't light 'em up at night because we don't have enough fuel for 'em; you'll just have to polish 'em. Make 'em shine!" As a result, the boots likely had some of the least used—but shiniest—potbellied stoves in the US military by the time they graduated from the rigors of "PI."

Parris Island's other facilities for the care and treatment of the boots were equally spartan and suitable for production-line-type efficiency, so that even the simplest tasks often seemed to be a refinement in cruelty. The recruits' toilet facilities provide one graphic example. While several platoons had latrines in their Quonset huts or permanent barracks buildings, for about ten other platoons, the latrine area, or "head," was an unheated, corrugated-metal building. These were equipped with shower heads at one end. Along one wall, a long sheet-metal trough served as a urinal; instead of providing enclosed individual toilets for defecation, the opposite wall featured a similar trough, covered with simple wooden slats for seats. Another trough was centrally located for washing up and was supplied with small single-faucet, cold-water-only stations and a polished piece of aluminum over each faucet to serve as a mirror. The entire latrine was large enough to handle an entire platoon of boots, roughly sixty to seventy men, at one time; however, because it was also the only latrine for the accommodation of ten platoons' hygienic needs, each platoon had a fixed schedule for use of the head. In the freezing South Carolina winter, with cracks in the sheet-metal siding and no heat, with no hot water for shaving or showering, and with the ever-present DIs relentlessly monitoring their platoon's time in the head between shifts, latrine time was a Spartan experience.

Forget today's advertising images of dress blue uniforms with razor-sharp creases and immaculate, white-topped caps, or even John Wayne's *Sands of Iwo Jima* version of World War II: these new Marine recruits of 1942 were a shabby-looking crew. The Corps' overall supply system rated low in the Navy Department's logistical priorities at this stage of World War II, and with Pacific garrisons under siege or falling, the sartorial splendor of new recruits was not high on the list of the Marines' priority items of supply. Some were outfitted in cotton dungarees; some wore wool; others were in khaki; and even a few were clad in World War I-vintage high-collared tunics and campaign hats, which today would be called "Smokey Bear" hats. Under these circumstances, the term "uniform" took on a completely different meaning. The only thing about their apparel that made the recruit platoons uniform was that they were no longer in civilian garb, and their clothing was, at least, government-issue. Before leaving PI, the uniform situation improved, as attested to by the Ninth Platoon's graduation picture: the new Marines and their DIs resplendent in freshly issued (but temporarily loaned) dress greens, khaki shirts and "field scarves" (neckties), and overseas caps.[3] For their first few weeks, however, they were a motley-looking bunch, much to the self-serving horror of the DIs.

Jack's two drill instructors, Corporal Stallings and Pfc. Story, were "the meanest little SOBs I ever ran into in all my born days." At this stage in the development of Boot Camp, almost all of the DIs were corporals, often sarcastically referred to as "little colonels," who, practically speaking, possessed as much authority over their charges' daily lives as would any true colonel. The assistant DIs were privates first class, often scarcely out of Boot Camp themselves. The boots addressed all DIs—and, for that matter, any other uniformed Marine—as "sir," regardless of their rank. Out of a desire to win the coveted two stripes of a corporal (which would make them officially non-commissioned officers, with the privileges that NCO status conveyed) and to prove their own toughness, the assistant DIs often vied with the lead DIs as to who could be the worst martinets. One of their two DIs was truly despised by all of the boots in Ninth Platoon (they were not yet Marine privates: that esteemed rank could only be earned by surviving Boot Camp). One of Jack's platoon mates, Jim Kruse, remembered this particular DI as being "of small stature" and being one who liked to "take advantage of the situation to curse and browbeat men of larger size, ripping the shirt off one of them."[4]

About the nicest things the boots were ever called by the DIs were "maggot," "shitbird," and "eightball," with the categories of insults only going downhill from there. Depending on each DI's whim, sometimes the sobriquets were all mixed together in a mélange of insults. Thus, a boot could be called a "maggoty shitbird," a "shitbird boot," a "frigging eightball," or a "slimy maggot." The more adjectives and expletives that were strung together and thrown in the face of a cringing boot, the greater the DI's wrath. These combinations were often punctuated at the very end by that hated word, spit out like the worst possible curse to be bestowed on humankind, and capped off with a sneering rictus to match: "*boot!*"

Several examples of the mental harassment inflicted by the DIs on the boots suffice to give an impression of the environment and its goals of breaking down the personal pride and individualism of each boot so that he could be remolded into a Marine. Reveille was at 0400 hours—4:00 a.m.[5]—with police call, cleanup of the platoon area, beginning at 0430. In the pitch-black morning, the boots would line up, ten abreast, on hands and knees and would crawl up the company street running through each platoon's area (itself little better than a sandy path), searching for cigarette butts, twigs, pieces of paper, and other debris. After roll call, morning inspection, and chow, the DIs would inspect the company street. Inevitably, the DI would find something and would mete out collective punishments to the group.

One favorite form of humiliation for mass consumption was saved for the evening, immediately before Taps. A fellow boot at the time who would later become one of Jack's fast friends, Frank Chadwick, vividly recalled the typical nightly scene: "The boots who had screwed up that day had to run through the tent area, yelling, 'I'm a shitbird from Yemassee, the biggest shitbird you'll ever see,' then flap his arms (attempting to fly) and shouting 'Yak, yak' (like a bird). All platoons would have to stand at attention, with [each] DI checking over his platoon. If he thought you smiled or your eyes moved, you joined the single file when they came through your tent area. Very shortly, you had 640 boots running through the Company area."[6]

Each boot was trained to refer to his assigned firearm as a "rifle," never as a "gun." Anyone making that mistake was forced by the DI to step out in front of the platoon, chanting as loudly as possible while clutching his rifle with one hand and grabbing his genitals with the other: "This is my rifle; this is my gun; this [here, the boot would gesture with his rifle] is for shooting, and this [now, grabbing his crotch] is for fun." To help drive the point home further, a DI would occasionally order any offending boot who persisted in calling his rifle a "gun" to sleep with his rifle in his cot. If a young, beardless kid neglected to shave or if a boot had a hint of beard stubble, the DI would condemn him to being dry-shaved by a comrade or, for the worst offenders, having to wear a bucket over his head while another boot dry-shaved him by touch alone.

The peculiar jargon of the Marine Corps also took some mental adjustments to master, as the boots had to quickly learn there was a new name for everything else besides their "guns." Many terms had nautical origins, derived from the Corps' historic role as the Navy's sea soldiers. Left was *port*, right was *starboard*, floors were *decks*, duffle bags were *sea bags*, and the correct answer in the affirmative to a senior Marine was not a mere "Yes, sir" but a smartly rendered *"Aye, aye, sir!"* A jail or prison was the *brig* and the man holding the power to send one to the brig, the unit's commanding officer, was the *skipper*. The origins of other slang terms were more esoteric. A Marine unit's buglers and musicians were its *field musics*, who also doubled as medical orderlies and stretcher bearers in combat. A Marine did not attend church or chapel, he went to the *God Box*, and he drank beer not in a bar but in a *slop chute*. Slackers, goof-offs and other disreputable characters were *goldbricks* and *yardbirds*. Candy was *pogey bait* (of which more, in Jack's case, later).[7] A Marine's khaki necktie was a *field scarf*, and his underwear was his *skivvies*. Marines did not make their camps in the field or jungle; instead, they pitched their tents in the *boondocks*, and the rough leather field boots worn on such occasions were *boondockers*, accompanied by khaki spats or gaiters called *leggings*, and not a cap but a *cover* garnished the head of a Marine. Few of the Marines' names for food were appetizing: coffee was *Joe*, ketchup was *redlead*, a sausage was a *horsecock*, pancakes were *collision mats*, and mustard was *babyshit*. Horseplay was *grabass*; rumors and gossip were pieces of *scuttlebutt*, as distinguished from real information and news, which was *poop*. Hence, any newspaper or bulletin was the *poop sheet* because it provided the reader with the latest "poop."[8]

Instead of being an opportunity to provide some relief from the tension, mail call also soon became dreaded. Anyone receiving a parcel was required to open it in front of the DI, who would first search it for contraband. Assuming it passed muster, the DI would then pass the parcel through the platoon formation, and each boot had to sample the contents. If the contents were food, the parcel would usually be empty by the time it was returned to the recipient. Another favorite ploy of the DIs was to throw the pieces of mail to the boots: if anyone dared move to pick up his mail, he (and depending on the DI's whim, possibly the entire platoon) would be punished for breaking ranks without authorization. Sometimes, the letters remained where they fell on the parade ground for the rest of the morning.

Letters from a sweetheart brought similar abuse and, from the DI's perspective, were excellent fodder for personalizing the harassment, all of which was part and parcel of one of Boot Camp's key goals: to reduce each boot to a lowest common denominator and, from there, to remodel the boots from a bunch of rugged individuals into a team of Marines. If a letter was clearly from a girlfriend—if perfumed or sealed with lipstick, for example—the DI would force the recipient to stand at attention in front of the entire platoon and read the letter while the DI checked to make sure absolutely nothing was left out. As if this was not embarrassing enough, the DI would begin to question the boot, lewdly and graphically, about his love life: did he and his girlfriend make love? (Or, put more bluntly, "Well, *maggot*, did you screw her?") If they had never had sex, what was the boot's problem: was his girlfriend ugly, or, maybe, was the boot "queer?" How, exactly, did the boot and his girlfriend "do it?" Nose-to-nose with a cringing boot, a DI would often leeringly grunt: "So, *shitbird*, did you '69' her?" The sound frequently heard thereafter was the nervous gulp or stutter of an utterly confused young boot, who had no idea that arithmetic was a part of sexual relations and who was desperately groping for any answer that might save him from humiliation before the DI and his peers.

The scatological and sexual slang used by the DI during these interrogations—amounting to a grotesque *Kama Sutra*, provided in a weird kind of Southern accent peculiar to many of the DIs—was often entirely new to most of the teenaged boots. This included Jack, who freely confessed: "I heard more dirty words used in Boot Camp than I ever knew existed—and, you know, I still don't know what some of them mean!" He was not alone. Certainly, in a more circumspect time when Clark Gable's utterance as Rhett Butler of "Frankly, my dear, I don't give a damn!" was enough to get *Gone with the Wind* banned from public viewing in various cities, profanities and vulgarities were generally more out of place than today, and it was possible for young men to leave high school without having a vocabulary as salty as those of today's Americans of a comparable age. As the then-sixteen-year-old New Yorker Frank Chadwick recounted of his DI's blunt and caustic descriptions of certain lovemaking techniques to a platoon of clueless boots: "Most of us had no idea what the hell [the DI] was talking about, and his explanation for us stupid Yankees was hilarious in itself. It was shortly after the first mail calls that no packages arrived; no lipstick or perfume was found on any letters, as everyone wrote home, begging them to just send plain envelopes."

While not immune to female charms, Jack had a bit of a puritanical streak to him, possibly inherited from his good-hearted and God-fearing mother. While well used to "cussing," the DIs' extreme and highly creative use of obscenities and blasphemies dumbfounded Jack at first, and although he adapted to this and could soon swear with the best of them, he never quite forgot this initial shock. Although he had been around farm animals and farm kids all his life and knew something about sex and the facts of life—after all, he was a country boy himself—Jack began to suspect that he had maybe more of a sheltered life than he had thought possible.

The first payday likewise brought little joy to the boots. When enlisting, each boot received a monthly pay of twenty-one dollars, minus five dollars for mandatory life insurance. The boots were shaved bald by the post barber shortly after arrival at PI and later during training for the going rate of twenty-five cents; as the ditty went: "Shave and a haircut; two bits!"

The Corps also required the boots to pay for their bucket-issue goods issued on their first day at Boot Camp. After all these expenses were tallied, the recruits would be "in the hole" on their pay for the next three months.

The first payday only heightened the sense of unreality. Each platoon marched in alphabetical order to a large hall, where each man reported to a very surly paymaster. The paymaster grouchily informed the boot that, although his entire month's pay had been docked to defray costs, it was illegal to work for the government without any pay. Therefore, the paymaster concluded, he had the duty to "pay a bunch of maggot boots" twenty-five cents each. On leaving the paymaster's desk, each boot was next greeted by his DI, lurking near the exit. The DI helpfully suggested that, since he would have no good use for his quarter anyway, a contribution to the Navy-Marine Corps Relief Agency bucket conveniently placed nearby would be a wise use for it. The DI then menacingly hinted to each boot that he wouldn't have the guts to pocket the change. "He was right again," one former boot sadly recalled.[9]

As Jim Kruse's account suggests, the petty harassment of the DIs was not limited to verbal abuse: the DIs had carte blanche to grab, punch, and kick the recruits if and when they deemed it appropriate. Because no officers were generally found in the recruit training areas, by custom if not by rule, any physical abuse that occurred would be meted out by the DIs outside the sight of any commissioned officers. While those born in more recent decades may be horrified to read this, times were very different in 1942. Corporal punishment was still frequently used in school, from first grade to the senior year of high school, and "spare the rod and spoil the child" was still widely followed by A. G. McCall and others as a tool of both parental and educational discipline. Jack and many others like him had grown up in such an environment, and if mere schoolboys were expected to take their licks without crying, young men who had volunteered to become Marines would be expected by their peers and superiors to do likewise—indeed, they themselves expected to do so. A full night's sleep was rare, and a full stomach was even rarer. On the other hand, freezing weather, seemingly endless training and work details, and the perpetual harassment of the DIs were too common. In the space of the four weeks he spent in Boot Camp, Jack lost almost thirty pounds.

Apart from the mental and physical testing, Boot Camp was devoted to learning the School of the Marine (marching and drilling, military courtesy, use and care of the rifle, etc.). The DIs also soon taught the Marines' Hymn to the boots, who bawled it out in something less than perfect harmony but with admirable volume and spirit:

> From the Halls of Montezuma
> To the shores of Tripoli,
> We will fight our country's battles
> On the land and on the sea.
> First to fight for right and freedom
> And to keep our honor clean,
> We will proudly claim the title
> Of United States Marines.

Each DI also relentlessly grilled his boots on their knowledge of their General Orders (as David Slater reminisced: "If a DI came and stuck his nose in your face and yelled, 'What's General Order Number 3?' and you didn't know it, brother, you were in deep doo-doo") and the Marines' chain of command, beginning with the commandant of the Corps. "The Commandant of the United States Marine Corps is General *Holcomb*! That's Thomas A. *Holcomb*, you bunch of slimy maggots. Now, if *anyone* asks *you* who the *hell* the Commandant is, *what* will you tell them?" Corporal Stallings roared. "Holcomb, sir!" Jack, Al Downs, Jim Cruze, and their nervous buddies tentatively responded. "*What* did you say?" "*Holcomb, sir!*" the platoon yelled back loudly. "Like hell, you will, you shitbirds; you'll forget!" the DI cynically growled back.[10]

A primary aspect of their training, perhaps the most critical in terms of combat survival, was basic rifle marksmanship. Regardless of what military specialty one would receive or which unit he would be assigned to serve in after Boot Camp, at this stage of the war, each Marine was expected to qualify as a marksman with the rifle and to be capable of serving as an infantryman. The boots drilled for hours with their bolt-action Springfield rifles, exercising and practicing firing positions ("snapping-in") with them, spending hours on the rifle ranges and even more hours afterward, disassembling, cleaning, and oiling their rifles. The only thing possibly more humiliating than dropping a rifle (which earned the immediate and *very* personal attention of the DI) was to miss not only the bullseye but the whole target completely during qualification shooting. Those not firing or cleaning their rifles—the latter of which, even with the relatively easy-to-disassemble Springfield, was still time-consuming—were put to work policing up the area or were on the firing range themselves, manning the pits under the targets, or "butts." The targets were large paper bullseyes tacked to wooden frames, manually raised and lowered from the safety of the butts. Each boot had fifty bullets—fired in increments from various distances and shooting positions—with which to qualify. The shooters' scores were recorded by the men in the butts, who used pointers to point out the holes made in the targets or, in the case of someone who missed the target completely, raised the hated Maggie's Drawers flag.[11] Moreover, to lessen the dangers posed by so many untrained men with loaded firearms, range discipline was especially harsh, even by PI's rigorous standards.[12]

Despite the discipline and theoretical danger, since a bullet could easily ricochet off the support frames into the butts, range duty was the highlight of Jack's stay at PI. It was one of the very few times that he and his buddies could escape the ever-present scrutiny of the DIs and could "skylark" among themselves in the pits, telling jokes to liven things up or (despite the DIs' order, "No smoking in the butts!") occasionally sneaking an illicit smoke. Qualification day on the rifle range was the last big test as to whether a boot could hack it in the Corps before graduation from Boot Camp, and it was not only a mark of honor to qualify at the highest grades but also a source of additional monetary incentives. Jack ultimately won his qualification badge for his rifle skills, although he'd never fired anything bigger than a BB gun before he joined the Marines. Regrettably, he did not qualify as a "sharpshooter" or "expert," which, besides providing the prestige that such titles brought, also brought an extra five and ten dollars per month, respectively.

Back to the paucity of food. Besides drilling and training, Marine recruits at Parris Island were also "in quarantine" during their four-odd weeks of training. "Quarantine" meant neither talking to *anyone*—not even a bunkmate or tentmate—in public, nor any letter-writing home unless authorized to do so by the DIs (and very definitely, in those days, there was no such thing as telephone calls home). Smoking was prohibited except during strictly limited times; each boot was rationed to one cigarette per day, and once it was smoked, that was it. No departures from post or liberty passes were authorized. After the first couple of weeks, the boots were assigned frequent stretches of guard duty in addition to the grueling training days and hours spent cleaning one's barracks, rifle, and gear. Above all else, there was *absolutely* no unauthorized "pogey bait"—that is, candy.

One evening, while the platoon was undergoing rifle training and temporarily billeted at the rifle range in drafty metal Quonset huts, Jack was assigned to guard a small and strictly off-limits PX-type area, not a place usually frequented by the likes of the flat-broke, starving, and dog-tired boots. He patrolled his "beat" listlessly, when what to his wondering eyes should appear but—wonder of wonders, holy of holies—an intact, unopened box of Baby Ruth candy bars. Manna from heaven! Furtively looking around to make sure he remained unseen, he immediately set to consuming the whole box with relish.

Very early the next morning, the Ninth Platoon was engaged in physical training drills on the rifle range. The boots were put through snapping-in exercises, grueling calisthenics in platoon formation that involved lifting, stretching, and holding their rifles at arm's length for prolonged periods of time as well as moving rapidly on command into simulated standing, seated, and prone firing positions. In the midst of these exertions, Boot McCall collapsed in the ranks, apparently from overexertion or "cat fever" (catarrhal fever, endemic to the masses of shivering boots). Unknown to Al Downs and several others who, on the DI's orders, broke formation to aid him, the shock to Jack's famished system from the candy bars had raised his blood sugar level massively, making him sick to high heaven. In a dazed state, he was carried off to the Recruit Depot's sick bay, where the diagnosis was made and his confession recorded: McCall had overdosed on Baby Ruth bars. Despite his embarrassment (and Corporal Stallings's fury that an entire box of candy had been gobbled down by one who was supposed to be guarding them, not wolfing them down wholesale), word of Jack's fainting spell and its cause spread quickly through the platoon. Hence, Jack earned—the hard way—what would be his lifelong nickname among his Marine buddies: "Pogey Bait" (or, as Jack typically spelled it, "Pogiebait") McCall.

The Ninth Platoon went through PI on what might charitably be called an accelerated program, graduating from Boot Camp in four weeks, much more quickly than its prewar predecessors who typically faced a twelve-week training cycle. The haste of this training cycle, however, was undoubtedly due to the exigent circumstances facing the nation and the Marine Corps more than the platoon's zeal. After a valiant defense, Wake Island and its First Defense Battalion garrison of Marines had fallen, as had Guam, the first American territory to be captured in the war. The Philippines had been invaded, and US and Filipino forces, including the Fourth Marines, were retreating to the Bataan Peninsula and the Manila Bay fortress of

Graduation photograph of Platoon Nine, Marine Recruit Barracks, February 1942.
Jack McCall is in the third row, third from the left, flanked by Jim Kruse (on Jack's
right) and Al Downs (on Jack's left). The DIs, Pfc. Story and Corporal Stallings,
are seated without rifles in the first row, front and center. Author's collection.

Private Jack McCall, wearing a loaned set
of dress blues for a photo after graduation
from Boot Camp, February 1942.
Author's collection.

Corregidor. The British colonies in Hong Kong and Singapore had fallen as well. The Soviets were fending off Nazi assaults on Moscow and Leningrad, throwing their manpower into a costly winter counteroffensive against the invaders, and Erwin Rommel's panzers were on the move again in Libya against Britain's beleaguered "Desert Rats." The situation was grim, and the time was coming for new Marines to face their baptism of fire.

Sixty-three Marine privates, including Jack McCall, graduated from the Ninth Platoon in early February 1942. His graduation picture shows him, "grinning like a possum," standing third from the left in the third row from the bottom, clutching his Springfield at port arms, with his new buddies Jim Kruse and Al Downs to his right and left. Following graduation, the new privates were told that despite the aptitude tests they had taken, all their requests for different military specialties were rejected and that all were assigned—immediately—to the combat units of the Fleet Marine Force. Each platoon's DIs could not help but add, as a parting shot, "If you thought Boot Camp was tough, you idiots, just you wait and see." As Frank Chadwick, at sixteen years old the youngest Marine in one of the Ninth Platoon's sister platoons, recalled: "How right he was, but after Boot Camp we all were new Marines, and nothing could not be done, and we could whip the world." They were no longer boots; even if they were still woefully inexperienced, they were, at least, now Marines.

The majority of the Ninth Platoon, US Marine Training Barracks, and the members of several other newly graduated platoons of the Christmas Tree Marines were about to join the newly formed Ninth Defense Battalion for overseas deployment. At this point, a few words about the Ninth Defense and its kind are in order.

Welcome to the Ninth Defense, Private McCall!

The Ninth Defense Battalion was an example of a type of unit peculiar to the Marine Corps during a short time period, with such battalions' active life encompassing almost the entire span of World War II: never before, and not after, would such a unit be a part of the organization of the Fleet Marine Force. The defense battalion concept partly originated from prewar Marine and Navy studies concerning the defense of coaling stations, forward bases, harbors and naval anchorages, and air stations. In order to better protect such critical but isolated sites, the Marine Corps staff developed the idea of using relatively large, self-contained forces, which could defend islands like Midway, Guam, and Wake. These would have enough artillery and antiaircraft firepower that, if attacked, could drive off the enemy or at least hold their own until reinforcements arrived.[13] Another practical consideration was funding. In the isolationist environment of the 1930s, military spending was rigorously scrutinized, and costly military force projections were anathema. Hence, the likelihood that Congress would support the formation and funding of any military units intended for *offensive* action was slim. Thus, to a large degree, the Navy Department's formation of Marine units officially labeled "defense battalions" would help elicit at least minimal funding for their creation and support. That such battalions might also be strong enough to undertake limited offensive activities was, of course, an additional benefit.

A lack of consensus existed in the Corps, however, as to the potential value of the new defense battalions. One of the strongest critics of the concept was the influential Marine officer Brigadier General A. A. Vandegrift, soon to command the First Marine Division. Archer Vandegrift apparently detested the idea, both as a drain on manpower and scarce logistics assets and as a sideshow that would detract from the formation of all-arms Marine divisions, which he viewed as being the most desirable structure for a wartime Corps. Against his objections, the formation of the defense battalions went ahead.[14] When finally implemented in the 1940-41 period, the nearest US Army equivalent to the Marine defense battalions may have been its coast artillery and field artillery regiments, but even this was an unsatisfactory comparison: there was really nothing else quite like these weird and heterogeneous units in the rest of the US military.

For starters, the size of the Ninth Defense Battalion was much larger than that of the average Marine or Army battalion, with its number of assigned personnel—fifteen officers and eight hundred enlisted men, when fully activated in February 1942; growing within a few months to comprise more than 1,250 Marines—being closer in strength to a small regiment. The battalion's overall structure would initially consist of a Seacoast Artillery Group, a Heavy Antiaircraft ("AA") Group, a Machine Gun Group (later called the "Special Weapons Group"), and a Headquarters and Service ("H&S") Battery. The idea was to create a unit with substantial defensive capabilities—the Seacoast Group to counter enemy seaborne threats; the AA Group to take on high-altitude aircraft; the automatic weapons of the Machine Gun Group to challenge low-altitude airplanes and numerous smaller threats, whether land-borne, seaborne or airborne; and the H&S Battery to provide command and control and logistics (and, in time, armored support from a platoon of light tanks)—but also capable of undertaking limited offensive missions as well, on an as-needed and area-specific basis.[15] As a result, the structure and armament of each defense battalion varied widely, and no common tables of organization and equipment existed between any of the twenty defense battalions in being by 1944.[16] The first eight defense battalions were primarily for static defense and accordingly had little offensive power or mobility. The Ninth Defense would be the first of its kind to receive enhanced mobility and offensive capabilities and would be one of the largest (if not the largest) of the defense battalions.[17]

On February 1, 1942, the headquarters and training detachment of the Ninth was formed at Parris Island under Major Wallace Thompson. Of the fifteen officers and eighteen hundred enlisted men initially forming the Ninth, a trained cadre of more than 150 senior officers and NCOs were veterans of World War I and the Chinese and Central American campaigns of the 1920s and early 1930s.[18] Most of the enlisted were fresh out of Boot Camp, and most of the lieutenants were "90-day wonders" (more often referred to, sometimes less than affectionately, as "shavetails" by their dubious charges).[19] One of the new battery "skippers," then-Second Lieutenant Henry Reichner, remembered his own introduction to his new battery as a fairly perfunctory matter: "Sometime during those first hectic few days at Parris Island, I was taken to part of the Boot Camp and shown a row of tents occupied by newly graduated recruits. 'This row is "A" Battery. Take charge,' were my orders."[20] Likewise, Jack, Al Downs, and Jim Kruse soon found themselves meeting their new CO of H&S Battery of the Ninth's 155mm Group, Second Lieutenant William T. Box, and their new sergeants. Eleven days later, Jack and his "compadres" from his training platoon were loaded on trains and shipped off to Norfolk Navy Yard in Virginia, where the new battalion was forming up en masse. The Ninth's initial complement was a mixed bag: new Boot Camp graduates, freshly out of Parris Island and from across the East Coast; Southerners, Northerners, and Midwesterners; newly commissioned officers; and a core cadre of veteran officers and NCOs.

Their departure from PI was hardly comfortable or speedy, although it was furtive. The Marines were trucked from PI to Yemassee Junction around midnight to shroud their departure, and not even the officers accompanying Jack and his buddies seemed to have a clear idea of their final destination. Once in Yemassee Junction, they were formed up by platoons and marched in files from the trucks to a waiting troop train made up of wooden passenger cars. Each man somehow had to squeeze his seabag, rifle, and equipment into his narrow seating area. Heating in the drafty cars was provided by a single potbellied stove at one end of each car, making for an uncomfortable ride for officers, NCOs, and enlisted men alike. The train coaches were "relics," Lieutenant Hank Reichner remembered. After a near-sleepless, nightlong trip with all shades drawn, the occupants of the train found themselves at a siding at a newly constructed Marine encampment at New River, North Carolina (later to be named Camp Lejeune). Trucks carrying hot chow were waiting, and each Marine was handed a box lunch of liverwurst sausage and an apple to sustain him for the rest of the day. After waiting at a siding all day, the train pulled back onto the main rail line at nightfall and resumed its northbound journey under the cover of night.

The next morning—Friday, February 13, 1942—the Marines awoke groggily to find their troop train drawn up alongside a mile-long pier at Norfolk Naval Base in Tidewater Virginia. The occupants of the train were marched single file to the rearmost car and, from there, straight off the back and up the gangway of a waiting transport ship, the *William Biddle*, to sail through U-boat-infested waters to the US Naval Operating Base at Guantanamo Bay, Cuba. Upon their arrival at the gangway, the new Marines learned that they were officially a part of the Ninth Defense Battalion, Fleet Marine Force. At Guantanamo Bay, according to the orders of the Marine Commandant, the Ninth was to be "trained as a defense battalion, utilizing such weapons at the Naval Operating Base as may be made available."[21] Its secondary mission would be to assist in the defense of the Naval Operating Base from German U-boats, since Guantanamo Bay served as a way station and convoying point for US-bound oil tankers en route from Venezuela and freighters plying the Caribbean. Except for newly issued rifles and personal equipment, the Ninth lacked all of the basic field equipment and heavy equipment—and the advanced training—it needed to be turned into an effective fighting force. The platoons full of newly graduated boots would be joined in Cuba by a large detachment from the Fifth Defense Battalion, the "Polar Bears,"[22] who had been sent to Iceland in 1941 to help the British defend that island from possible German attack.

On "Black Friday," the night of the *Biddle*'s departure, as they left Norfolk, Jack and many of his pals were much more worried about whether they would ever make it back to dry land than whether they would see combat soon. With all personnel on board and manifests checked off, the *Biddle* lifted anchor and moved to the outer Chesapeake Bay to sail after dark. As the ship steamed out of the bay, the sound of gunfire and depth charges were clearly audible: an escorting destroyer thought it had detected a German U-boat. Locked down below deck with all hatches shut and all portholes blacked out, the first "sub attack" induced a real sense of fear in many of the new Marines. The winter seas were choppy, and most of the Marines on board the *Biddle* (by one informal estimate, at least 70 percent of the leathernecks) were seasick—a condition which was not improved by the decision to move a number of the Marines and their gear from one hold to another for organizational reasons. Three U-boat alerts were called during the six-day trip. Escorting Navy destroyers continued to drop depth charges sporadically, claiming two U-boats "kills," although no German subs were actually sunk by these efforts. Several of the more seasoned members of the Ninth were already trained in basic artillery tactics. Those men soon found themselves helping to man the *Biddle*'s 5-inch gun crews.[23] When relieved from their shift on deck, several men reported spotting the prow of a sunken tanker just off the Virginia coast, sent to the bottom less than a fortnight before the *Biddle*'s departure. After this report and as the depth charging continued, nerves began to fray, and several poker games turned into fistfights among the Marines cooped up in the holds and bunks down below. Others, feeling violently seasick from the late winter swells, stayed in their bunks as much as possible and closed their eyes to quell their nausea pangs. Unaware until now of the true menace posed by roving U-boat packs offshore, Jack and many other queasy leathernecks thought to themselves as the blasts of the depth charges reverberated through the holds: "*Damn! Will we be next?*"

After hugging the US coastline, the lights of Havana were spotted on the evening of February 16, and the *Biddle* and her escorts followed along the Cuban coast. In the early morning hours three days later, another landfall was sighted—the rocky promontories surrounding Guantanamo Bay—and Jack and the Ninth's sea-weary "landlubbers" disembarked for what would be an eight-month stay.

TWO

"Where're You Going, Marine?"
The Road from Cuba to the South Pacific

Our time in Cuba was spent in advanced training, much with World War I equipment. U-boats roved the area's seas, and one was rammed by [a] destroyer just out of our bay, its occupants being brought and "brigged" ashore.

Our outfit consisted of 155MM artillery guns, 90MM anti-aircraft [guns], search lights, radar units, and special weapons—of 40[MM] and 20MM guns.

We soon learned that we would be shipping out, and found that we would be joining the 1st Marine Division in the first U.S. offensive of World War II in the Solomon Islands, specifically Guadalcanal.

—JACK H. MCCALL, SR.—

"Where're you going, Marine?"
"I'm off to Sumatra, son:
Killing Christians there, a godless mob,
And it may or may not be my job,
But it will before we're done!"

—MARINE CORPS RHYME,
AS RECALLED BY JACK MCCALL[1]—

Before entering Guantanamo Bay on February 19, the *Biddle* was escorted through a large anti-submarine net. Despite its bright, crystalline blue waters and the exotic trees and blooming shrubs, "Gitmo" Bay displayed a military sense of purpose: barges, small craft, and sub chasers plied the azure waters of the bay, and barracks, camouflaged gun installations, and searchlight positions studded the coast. The Marines' excitement (coupled with their relief to get the hell off the *Biddle*)[2] was palpable. As he gathered up his gear and prepared to leave the *Biddle*, Jack thought to himself: "So, *this* is war!"

On disembarking, the Ninth formed up by batteries and platoons and moved out—mainly on foot—to Defense Point, a craggy promontory overlooking Guantanamo Bay. The point projected well into the bay, and the Ninth's guard posts on the leeward and windward sides of the bay's entrance provided an excellent vantage point for watching incoming shipping and searching for U-boats. Unlike the Army elsewhere, which often hired laborers or contractors to build their barracks and facilities, the first order of business for Jack and his buddies was to help complete their own partially constructed camp. Although some brick and wooden barracks were complete and available, the Ninth's Marines had the chore of finishing some half-finished wooden facilities started by the recently departed Fourth Defense Battalion and Fifth Marines. This work, which began soon after they landed, included setting up latrines, mess halls, guard posts, and huts. No heavy equipment for the unit was yet available, and the task was essentially all labor by hand—moving lumber, breaking rock, and digging holes for fence posts and latrines.

Added to these labors was continued training in infantry tactics, since the battalion would not receive its artillery and heavy equipment for at least three more months. While Boot Camp training had been grueling, the new privates soon learned that there was much that it had not taught them. Parris Island had provided them the emotional armor and toughening up they would need to survive as Marines, but little else in the way of serious combat skills. That was about to be remedied by the Ninth's senior NCOs. One hard-bitten gunnery sergeant, a grizzled veteran of World War I and the Corps' Central American campaigns of the 1920s, held high his copy of the Marines' field manual on basic infantry training, only to throw it over his shoulder, pointedly telling his men that he would teach them everything they needed to know for survival. The Ninth's men also soon learned how to dig—one and two-man foxholes; trenches; bunkers; radio and commo positions; gun pits—as if their life depended on it. Those assigned as artillerymen began receiving their first training in seacoast-defense and antiaircraft work, training in shifts on 6-inch naval guns and obsolete 3-inch AA guns. Despite the long days, full military discipline continued: drills; inspections; periodic forced marches with full packs; personal equipment layouts; etc. One major test for the entire unit was the completion of a fifty-mile forced march with rifle, full pack, and field equipment. The course took Jack and his buddies over salt flats, high ridges, and through a semi-tropical forest. The battalion completed the grueling march within twenty-four hours, although not without its share of blisters, sprained ankles, and bruised and bloodied feet. As Battery A skipper Henry Reichner recalled, it was not only the distance that made this march with full gear so exhausting: "We made well over four miles an hour with packs in intense heat—not enjoyable to those with an overdose of rum or beer."

Among the field exercises, the new hands had their first experience of bayonet and judo training. This was taught by Captain Walter Wells, a tall, cocky, and imposing young officer. He was a former collegiate wrestler at Columbia University and a muscular expert in self-defense who prided himself in his mastery of bayonet drill and hand-to-hand fighting. Jack and his peers had to endure Wells's rigorous (and occasionally terrifying) classes on these tactics. Nevertheless, his awestruck students could surprise "Waldo" Wells at times and could fight back with vigor. Frank Marshall recalled of one of Wells's early bayonet-training classes and the fact that this captain "was a man of supreme self-confidence" in his self-defense skills who "found that the men were reluctant to charge him with bare bayonets as directed. [Wells] finally convinced one class by getting a big fellow . . . irritated enough to lose his temper and charge the Captain full bore with M-1 and naked blade out-thrust. Wells neatly sidestepped, popped one hand on the muzzle and the other up under the butt and flipped the hapless attacker. . . . The man wasn't hurt—just scuffed up a little. . . . Wells gazed at the prostrate Marine for a second and remarked to himself, *sotto voce*, 'Goddam . . . gonna have to watch that.'"[3]

While the Ninth's other officers may not yet have been as intimidating a presence as Waldo Wells in his full stride, they were nevertheless an eclectic group. Before being replaced as battalion CO by Lt. Colonel Dubel in late June 1942 (himself replaced in October 1942 by Colonel David Nimmer), Major Wallace Thompson, the acting "skipper," made quite an impression on many. Jack and others recalled that, unlike several of the battalion's later battalion commanders, Major Thompson seemed omnipresent and omniscient. He was everywhere and into everything, watching training and gun drills, joining the men in their PT exercises, and—above all—inspecting, inspecting, inspecting everything. His subordinate, Lieutenant Henry Reichner, recalled, "It was Thompson who really trained the battalion and gave it its initial spirit. All the others benefitted from his labor and were much more distant, and, if I may say so, more bureaucratic. Am I a Thompson fan? Yes!"

Major Thompson also figured prominently in another episode on Cuba, involving one of the Ninth's most senior NCOs, Gunnery Sergeant Smith. Originally of German extraction, *nee* Schmidt, the "gunny" had enlisted in the Corps during World War I and had changed his name to the Anglicized version. Hence, after service in the Great War and in the Marines' various Central American campaigns between the wars, the gunny already had well over twenty years of service in the Corps at the time of Pearl Harbor. Unfortunately, he had also decided that he had served long enough and that this would be one war too many for him. Gunny Smith decided to wait until after the Ninth was encamped at Guantanamo to tell the major that he wished to put in his retirement papers. Much to his surprise, Major Thompson bluntly told him: "Request denied! In case you haven't noticed, Gunnery Sergeant, there's a war on, and we need every man we can get. You're in this for the duration." By the time the Ninth would finally see action, Gunny Smith would become a legend in the battalion.[4]

Captain Wells's bayonet training was intended to instill a fighting spirit in his men, but at this time, the Ninth's primary adversary was certainly not yet the Japanese or the jungles of the South Pacific. Instead, with German submarines cruising the waters of the Caribbean and the Atlantic almost unmolested, the likely menaces were U-boats, surface raiders, or German naval parties. As torpedoed freighters and tankers occasionally limped into Guantanamo Bay, Jack and the other Marines soon began training in operation of the Naval Base's 6-inch coast-defense guns, practiced anti-landing drills, and manned various lookout posts to watch for enemy submarines. Lookout duty generally meant sharing one's sun-baked post with the local scorpions and large Cuban iguanas, at least one of which fell prey to a trigger-happy lieutenant's pistol. It sometimes meant patrols on horseback around the barbed wire fences separating the base from the Cuban interior; these were installed to help protect the base from sabotage by local Falangists (a Cuban offshoot of Francisco Franco's pro-fascist Spanish party) or from sub-landed German naval commandos. Jack found himself on several horse patrols led by Lieutenant Box. A self-admitted "city boy," Box found the "horse Marine" patrols a bit absurd: "All we had were a couple of guys walking around and a horse, and that was supposed to be good enough! We had three horses to patrol the fence and about 40 or 50 guys, I guess."[5]

Still, these efforts were no mere make-work task: since early 1942, Nazi submarines plied the Caribbean waters, and the survivors of various sinkings would be routinely brought to Guantanamo for medical care and debriefing by the Navy. At least one of these prowling German subs was within close range of Guantanamo Bay and Allied subchasers, and in August 1942, *U-94* became the quarry instead of the hunter. After being depth-bombed and brought to the surface by a Navy Catalina seaplane on August 28, 1942, the U-boat was rammed at full speed by the HMCS *Oakville*, a Canadian corvette, and its surviving crewmen were captured after they scuttled out of the hatches of their sinking ship.[6] According to the "poop" making the rounds of the battalion at the time of *U-94*'s destruction, after the *Oakville* rammed *U-94*, the German crew first tried to shoot it out on the surface with the corvette. A machine-gun battle broke out between the two ships, and only the timely arrival of an American destroyer, the USS *Lea*, kept the infuriated Canadians from killing the sub's remaining crewmen. These twenty-six survivors, in due course, were hauled back to Guantanamo Bay, as it was the closest Allied facility.[7] Some members of Jack's battery were detailed to escort the *U-94*'s sullen crewmen to the Naval Operating Base's brig near Caravetta Point and *Oberleutnant zur See* Otto Ites (the sub's wounded and highly decorated skipper) and a wounded machinist for medical treatment.

The fact that they were now prisoners of war seemed to do little to quash the cocky Nazi sailors' superiority complexes. Despite their arrogance and the proximity of the POWs' brig to the Ninth's obstacle course (which ensured the jeering of the Germans anytime a clumsy leatherneck took a fall during a workout), the Ninth's Marines were able to put them in their place, at least verbally. One Marine officer, Captain Norm Pozinsky, the skipper of the 90mm Group's Battery D, spoke fluent German. Accordingly, Captain Pozinsky was able to serve back at least as many taunts and insults as any sour-pussed *U-bootmann* would send Pozinsky's way. Accompanied by Captain Pozinsky and the ex-German Gunnery Sergeant Smith, the Ninth's guard detachment was lucky enough to escort their prisoners all the way to Miami.[8] Since this was the closest the Ninth Defense had yet come to hostile action at the time, it instilled a new air of excitement and realism to the otherwise drab monotony of drilling, cleaning, standing inspections, policing the area, and guarding the coastline. After more than three months of this tedium, more excitement came as the heavy equipment began arriving in earnest toward the end of May. The battalion's training then began to take a more coherent and focused form.

The heavy artillery core of the Ninth would be comprised of the 155mm Group:[9] two batteries (A and B), each now armed with four 1918-vintage 155mm "GPF" long-range guns, which made up the seacoast-defense portion of the unit.[10] Another large portion of the Ninth Defense consisted of

Batteries C, D, E, and F, making up the 90mm Antiaircraft (AA) Group. Each of these four batteries now had four 90mm AA guns, networked together with searchlights and sound detection teams. Most importantly, the Ninth was issued six radar sets—five SCR-268 fire control sets (each set requiring three operators) and one SCR-270 long-range detection set. Light AA support was provided by Batteries G, H, and I, forming the Special Weapons Group. Its batteries were armed principally with 20mm Oerlikon and 40mm Bofors light automatic guns and water-cooled .50 caliber heavy machine guns. The infantry support firepower of all of these batteries combined was substantial, as the Special Weapons Group's guns could potentially be used to stop a ground attack. Coupled with this already powerful force was the shock impact of a full platoon of eight M-3 light tanks, assigned as part of the H&S Group.[11]

Let it not be believed, however, that much of the Ninth's equipment was well and truly new; it was "new" only in the sense that it had just been issued to the unit: old World War I 155s; old Springfield rifles for many (although quite a few Marines, including most of Battery B, trained in

Some fifty years later, Joe Pratl stands next to a 155mm M1918
GPF heavy artillery piece as originally issued to Batteries A and B
of the Ninth. Courtesy of Joseph Pratl.

Cuba with the new M-1 Garand semiautomatic rifles); out-of-date equipment and field gear. None of the heavy weapons crews had fired a shot yet to calibrate and "live-fire" their big guns.

Part of the reason for the obsolescence and shortage of first-rate equipment may have been due to military-wide supply shortfalls, but part was also directly related to prewar funding issues. As a branch of the Department of the Navy, the Marine Corps was utterly dependent on the Navy for its funding allocations and equipment procurement needs. Before the war, the Corps nominally received about 20 percent of the Navy's manpower and funding allocations, but the Navy earmarked a large proportion of these funds to maintain its own internal programs.[12] Fundamentally, apart from payrolls, uniforms, and subsistence-related budgets, the Marine Corps received little to no funding for major projects or new equipment until after Pearl Harbor, making it very much (as described by one historian) "the navy's poor stepsister."[13] Expanded American rearmament was not statutorily authorized until 1940. As a result, not only the Marine Corps but most of America's armed services were forced to begin the war with a large stockpile of leftover arms, munitions, and other war supplies of Great War vintage. Contributing factors were the prevailing antiwar and anti-interventionist outlook of much of the nation before December 7, 1941, and also the significant reliance on the US Navy in war planning as the nation's first line of defense for both continental America and its far-flung outposts across the Pacific.[14]

Each Marine, true to his Boot Camp basic training, was also prepared to serve not just as an artilleryman, ammo handler, radar crewman, radioman, or tank gunner, but also as an infantryman. These basic training skills would be put to the test in due time. However, the selection of crews for these weapons were made using the most rudimentary vocational testing standards. No special aptitude testing was necessary for a Ninth Defense Marine to end up as an AA gunner, a sound detection expert, a tank driver, or (as did Jack) a water purification expert. The selection process was much more random and sporadic: *We need gunners and ammo handlers for the 155s; you look like you've lifted a few weights in your time; you'll do; get in line! We need radiomen. Anybody here think they know Morse code? Good enough; move along, now; get going!*[15] To form the Tank Platoon, the platoon's sergeants asked which of the Marines assigned to the motor pool had been farm kids who had driven tractors: that was all the job experience needed. Jack was selected and trained to become a "gizmo," in his case, a water purification specialist, as well as serving as a basic Marine artilleryman. When asked if he had studied anything special in high school, his admission that he had taken chemistry classes was probably all his leaders needed to hear: *Good; he'll be able to handle chemicals without blowing us all up.*

By early July, the Ninth was training seven days a week, fifteen to twenty hours a day—though still without "ammo" or test-firing their artillery pieces and tank guns.[16] By this time, though, some additional experience was infused into the battalion by the arrival of a large contingent of veterans of the Fifth Defense Battalion, the Iceland-based "Polar Bears," who were reassigned to flesh out the Ninth and arrived in Guantanamo Bay in June 1942. Despite the rigorous training and tedious moments, life in Cuba had its own vices and, for some, its tawdry rewards.

Caimanera, a town across Gitmo Bay located on Cuban soil, was the local booze and bordello area. Together with another nearby hamlet, the "Brooks Island Resort," Caimanera's red-light district became so infamous and such a source of venereal disease that, in early September 1942, both it and Brooks Island were declared off-limits by order of Rear Admiral George Weyler, the Naval Operating Base's commander.[17] Beer and rum were cheap and plentiful, and the Marines took full advantage of it. The Ninth had three slop chutes around Defense Point—one for officers, one for NCOs, and one for all the enlisted men (EMs)—where beer could be bought by the case and nightly brawls were a common occurrence, at least at the EMs' slop chute. The enlisted Marines would also smuggle in banana cases full of the local brands of beer (*cerveza*), Hatuey and Cristal, forty-four bottles to the case, three cents a bottle. A quart of Bacardi rum would go for twenty-five cents. A private's pay was low, even by 1940s standards: at twenty-one dollars per month, with only five dollars left after all the required deductions, each platoon's members would form tight-knit circles of pals who would pool their meager funds for beer, rum, cigarettes, shaving supplies, and other sundries. When time permitted, they might take whatever leftover money they had and join in high-stakes poker games or frequent Caimanera's seedy establishments. Such pastimes provided an off-duty chance for young men from highly diverse backgrounds to learn more about their fellow Americans. Befitting its seamy reputation, Caimanera was also well known for its prostitutes of various ages and predilections, and their solicitations for business could be heard amid the traffic on Caimanera's streets.[18]

Privates McCall and Downs threw in their lot at the EMs' slop chute with a good-natured Polish American private from Erie, Pennsylvania, John Dobkowski. After a few drinks, Dobkowski taught his newfound buddies Polish drinking songs. Another source of pratfalls was an on-post Chinese restaurant, where Pogiebait, Dobkowski and "Rosie" Downs would occasionally take a break from mess hall fare. While the food was cheap, the biggest source of amusement was provided by the fact that this Chinese restaurant featured fruit pies as dessert. Without fail, someone would buy a pie and with a shout of *"Take that, you bastard!"*, heave it at a buddy with whom he had a temporary grudge. Inevitably, this triggered a pie fight and general free-for-all that lasted until the harried restaurant manager threatened to call in the Shore Patrol, the Navy's police squad, and the pie-encrusted Marines would help clean up the joint in repayment for the damage they had caused.[19]

Quite a few of the Ninth's Marines took advantage of cheap alcohol to unwind from the rigorous training and work schedule. Likewise, so did Jack—once so much so that, after one particularly wild night in "Caimanooch," he consumed one too many *"Cuba Libre"* rum-and-cola drinks, passed out, and missed the liberty boat returning the Marines to camp. Jack's platoon sergeant charged him with committing an "unauthorized absence"—the Marines' equivalent of being absent without leave—a serious breach of military discipline, which carried with it a possible court-martial and potential jail time in a Navy brig. Jack was now in very hot water with Colonel David Nimmer, the Ninth's new battalion commander, who had already cultivated a reputation as being a tough disciplinarian by chewing out the entire battalion en masse on his first day in command. The Colonel was ready to throw the book at him and told him so at a masthead proceeding convened for the imposition of non-judicial (i.e., non-court-martial) punishment. Jack's battery commander, First Lieutenant Bill Box, spoke up on Jack's behalf and told the Colonel that until then, Private McCall had been a model Marine. Lieutenant Box was already well respected among his subordinates, and his willingness to stick his neck out for Jack clinched his reputation as being something other than the average hard-nosed but distant Marine officer. Because Jack got off with only a stern reprimand and a smirk from the Old Man and some additional guard and KP duty instead of brig time or a court-martial, he counted himself lucky, indeed.[20]

Another Marine, Gene Duffy, enjoyed himself enormously in Cuba; so much so one Sunday night that, to the concern of his friends one morning, he had not made it back to post after liberty. Duffy was not in evidence after "Reveille" was trumpeted and the order to fall in for inspection was given. Duffy's battery was led by a Marine Gunner, a former sergeant who was now the Marine Corps' equivalent of a warrant officer—neither NCO nor commissioned officer—and a formidable man. Duly noting Duffy's absence from his formation, the Gunner also observed a group of Cuban day laborers

Downtown Caimanera, Cuba, circa 1942. Author's collection.

passing nearby, carrying lumber and various implements. One of these workers was oddly taller than the average Cuban and was wearing heavy Marine boondocker boots and a sombrero-like hat pulled down over his face. The Gunner sauntered over to the unorthodox-looking laborer and, according to Battery B's Frank Chadwick, asked the man if he could sing the Cuban national anthem. "But if not, *Duffy*," the Gunner muttered, "your ass is in the brig!" The "laborer" peeped out from under his wide-brimmed hat and pensively blew out a mouthful of air. A brief silence followed, and then the miscreant mournfully blurted out, "Let's go!"[21]

The End of the Ninth's Cuban Sojourn: The Voyage to "Destination Unknown"

[By] September it was known that the Battalion would soon be on its way to a Pacific war zone and morale reached a new high. The barracks life in Cuba, with excellent food, comfortable quarters and ample recreation, had become insipid to the officers and men of the Ninth, all of whom had volunteered to fight a war.

—NINTH DEFENSE BATTALION'S OPERATIONS REPORT[22]—

By late September 1942, the scuttlebutt was that the Ninth would not be living out the rest of its wartime days in the balmy Cuban climate. Since August, the First Marine Division, reinforced by the Third Defense Battalion and Marine and Army air units, had been engaged in the fight of its life in a Solomon Islands jungle hellhole called Guadalcanal. Orders were soon cut by Marine Corps headquarters transferring the Ninth Defense to the Fleet Marine Force-Pacific.

On October 4, Jack and the Ninth were on the move again—this time, in preparation for actual combat. The battalion was loaded on three transports, the USS *Kenmore* (a twenty-year-old Presidential Lines civilian liner once called the *President Madison* and now under Navy auspices), the SS *Robin Wentley*, and the SS *Fairisle* (the latter two being civilian-crewed Merchant Marine vessels). The three ships sailed around noontime, accompanied by a fourth cargo ship and a destroyer, en route to "Destination Unknown." Jack had boarded the *Kenmore*, headed for the Pacific Ocean via the Panama Canal.[23] Despite the intended secrecy of their departure, many of the Ninth's Marines were more than a little startled to see parties of Cubans cheerfully lined up on shore, serenading the ships with songs and bidding them adieu. To add to the suspense, as the small convoy sailed through the submarine nets and booms securing the mouth of Guantanamo Bay, the escorting destroyer detected what seemed to be a German submarine and dropped a defensive pattern of depth charges for good measure. *Wham!* The troops below decks were highly perturbed when a series of concussions reverberated loudly off the *Kenmore*'s hull. Sounding much like a giant sledgehammer being slammed against a steel drum, the blasts pitched men out of their bunks and vibrated through the old ship's decks and bulkheads. Having gone through this before on the *Biddle*'s voyage to Cuba was not any more reassuring, and choruses of obscenities, curses and yells of "Jesus Christ!" echoed through the *Kenmore*'s decks until the senior NCOs moved in to reassure and otherwise shut up their clamoring troops.

The heavily defended Panama Canal Zone provided further evidence, if any was necessary, that the unit was headed toward a war zone. Roving Army MPs and naval SPs did not deter a few Marines from making impromptu shore leaves. While the *Kenmore* was temporarily tied up in Balboa, on the canal's western side, one enterprising soul wrapped up his uniform in a waterproof poncho and dropped the bundle over the *Kenmore*'s side. Stark naked, he went down one of the mooring ropes and slipped into the water. Groping around frantically in the dark and smelly brew, he found that his bundle of clothes was rapidly being washed out to sea. Realizing that the jig was up, the Marine decided to surrender himself. After swimming back to the ship, he hoisted himself up onto the accommodation ladder. Still nude and dripping wet, he briskly marched up to the officer of the deck and, undaunted, gave the befuddled OD a snappy salute: "Request permission to come aboard, sir!" With the OD's permission not immediately forthcoming, the Marine bolted past the OD up the ladder and ran for his compartment. Being easily identified, he was caught fairly quickly by the ship's guards, amid the cheers and hoots of his buddies. Meanwhile, several other AWOL Marines had been seized on shore by the SPs. It was an easy matter to apprehend them because the official duty uniform in the Canal Zone was khakis, while the Marines aboard the *Kenmore* were in green field dungarees. When the Navy area commander informed Colonel Nimmer that his SPs had apprehended the Ninth's absent men and planned to escort them back to the *Kenmore*, the Colonel briskly responded that, as far as he was concerned, the Navy could keep them all in the brig; he did not want or need that kind of Marine in his outfit. The *Kenmore* resumed sail without this handful.[24]

After transiting the canal, surrounded by the green jungle and the steel and concrete locks, big guns and fortifications of the Canal Zone, the little flotilla entered the Pacific. It was a sobering thought to most, if not all, of the Ninth's personnel that they still had not test-fired most of their major weapons. They were due to meet up with their ammunition supplies later, and the heavy guns were stowed deep in the ships' holds. The convoy's naval escort dwindled to one elderly, four-stacker destroyer, itself likely a veteran of World War I. Despite this destroyer's presence, long-range Japanese submarines were a possible threat. Hank Reichner remembered: "The

The USS *Kenmore*, circa 1942. Author's collection.

Kenmore was no speedster. The maximum speed of the convoy was about six knots, and at times, when things broke down, we were almost dead in the water." Even so, the small convoy was steaming well out of the range of friendly air cover. The *Kenmore* had some armament onboard—one 5-inch and five 3-inch deck guns, plus various .50 caliber machine guns—hardly enough to deter the skipper of a determined "I-boat," as Japanese submarines were called.[25]

The *Kenmore* was cramped and grimy, and it stank as a result of being host to so many passengers with limited chances to bathe. Jack and the Ninth's Marines and their Navy traveling companions were rationed to limited periods for showering, during which the showers dispensed only salt water. Some men learned the hard way the means of making the best of a proper salt-water shower. As Frank Marshall recounted, the first lesson was to use the right kind of soap: "One young Marine, desperate for a good, soapy shower, believed the rumor that Lava soap was a good salt-water type. He climbed into the shower, tried to lather up his close-cropped hair and wound up with a skull cap of black slime that was insoluble in the sea water."[26]

Likewise, fresh water for drinking was strictly rationed by compartments, each compartment having a limit of only one hour of fresh water or until the "fresh" water (which was yellowish and reeked of chlorination) ran out. With each Marine having two canteens to fill up, the fresh-water supply usually ran out before the time limit was up. Seasickness again plagued many of the Marines, and with nighttime blackout conditions in effect, they were often denied a favorite addiction, cigarettes on deck, for fear of the glow being spotted by enemy subs. The Special Weapons Group's .50 caliber machine guns were lined up on the boat deck, four per side, further constricting what little open-air space was available.

The *Kenmore* had been reconfigured to accommodate two thousand persons, but with approximately fifteen hundred Navy personnel also aboard (including two battalions of Seabees and the crews of eight PT boats, which were lashed to the decks of the *Fairisle* and *Wentley*), the Ninth's twelve hundred-odd Marines had to share extremely cramped quarters. Many leathernecks were billeted in the most peculiar spots imaginable. Several groups slept in the open air on the boat decks or tried to rig hammocks underneath the barrels of the ship's heavy guns. Many others, however (Jack included), were assigned to bunks in the *Kenmore*'s hold, which, as his pal Bob Landon of Battery B recalled, could only be described as a "tragedy." The holds reeked of vomit, sweat, grease, and bilge water. The bunks were narrow, cramped, and stacked four high. Each Marine was expected to stow all of his gear in this assigned space except when he went to sleep, at which time all the men's seabags were clustered in the narrow passageways. The heat and humidity below decks were stifling, and anyone who got the chance to get some fresh air topside relished the opportunity. Those assigned to the topmost bunks felt these effects the worst, one saving grace being that, if someone got seasick, at least those in the higher bunks were spared. Those left without bunks were issued hammocks, which were airier and were slung in the ship's mess area and in the gangways. All hammocks had to be stowed by 4:00 a.m., in time for the cooks to reconfigure the room for mess and to prepare the morning's chow. Mess commenced at 10:00 a.m. and ran until 4:00 p.m., and each Marine could expect one warm meal per day and a box lunch for dinner. Chow was served in shifts, the men in each shift having a different color-coded card, but even with the shift arrangements, chow lines on board the *Kenmore* were lengthy; after waits of several hours, the Marines at the end of the lines could usually expect little food. It was little wonder that the tired old ship was sarcastically renamed the "Killmore" by many of her disgusted passengers, officers and men alike.

With several thousand young men from rival services onboard, the officers were forced to devise ways to keep their troops and sailors busy. The *Kenmore*'s decks and portions of her hull would be sanded, chipped, scraped, painted, and repainted. For the most part, however, the Marines' idle hours onboard were spent playing endless games of cards, cleaning clothes (ingeniously washed by suspending pants or shirts on lines, casting the lines off the ship's side, and allowing the articles to bounce along in the bow waves), tending to gear and weapons, and writing letters. After an outbreak of body lice and impetigo, delousing inspections and mandatory applications of Merthiolate and salves kept the shipboard medical officers busy. When the salves and ointments seemed to fail, the medical officers decreed that all afflicted personnel must shave their pubic areas and then resume the Merthiolate-and-salve treatments. With the outbreak of body lice having been attributed to one of the Marines who had gone AWOL in Balboa and returned unchecked, venereal disease ("short-arm" or "pecker check") inspections—another ample source of humiliation and embarrassment—were conducted by a jaded Navy doctor, who dispensed suitable doses of sarcasm along with the inspections. When a Marine got too close to him during the VD inspection, the old doctor would growl, "Back up, son; I just want to look at it, not marry you!" The officers and NCOs threatened a summary court-martial to anyone found to have contracted a social disease. Fortunately, no cases were detected.

Still, it was not all work, nausea, claustrophobia, and boredom. As the *Kenmore* and her accompanying ships crossed the Equator, Jack and his buddies—"pollywogs" who had never crossed the Equator—had to be indoctrinated into the mysteries of the "briny deep" and the secrets of "Davey Jones's locker." Equator-crossing ceremonies were traditional rituals on Navy ships for generations, and even in wartime, naval traditions had to be obeyed. According to Jack's certificate from the "Ancient Order of the Deep," signed by Davey Jones and "Neptunus Rex" (also known as M. Richardson, Commander, USN, the *Kenmore*'s captain), Private Jack H. McCall, USMCR, "has been gathered into our Fold as a TRUSTY SHELL-BACK, having crossed the equator on board the USS KENMORE bound from Panama to a unknown destination, Longitude—'not given'—Latitude 00 00' 00."

Jack's family often asked him what was involved in his Equator-crossing ceremony. Time and again, Jack's response would be to roll his eyes behind his glasses and say: "You're just a pollywog! Shellbacks are sworn to secrecy never to tell a pollywog what happens." Suffice it to say that the *Kenmore*'s Equator ceremony combined medieval pageant and semi-religious trappings (the grand appearance of King Neptune and his court and Davey Jones before the unworthy pollywogs) with all the worst aspects of a fraternity's Hell Week (getting stripped down to skivvy shorts and being liberally greased with motor oil, blasted with a fire hose full of cold sea water, etc.). Given the rivalries between sailors and Marines, this Equator-crossing ceremony—with the leathernecks outnumbering the swabbies, but having to take their abuse in stride and with swallowed pride—must have been especially rigorous.

Before reaching port the *Kenmore* ran out of fresh food, and her passengers had to begin using boxed rations intended for combat. These rations were nothing to write home about: several Marines later swore they (like so much else, it seemed) were of World War I vintage, with each box consisting mainly of cans of hash, corned beef ("bully beef") or stew, a can of beans, a pack of hardtack crackers, a tin of powdered coffee, and a piece of hard candy. The *Kenmore*'s escorting destroyer, however, was in even worse shape in the way of provisions: it not only ran out of its food rations but also had to maintain continuous watches, which required it to run additional hours for chow calls for its tired and hungry sailors. Believing the

Kenmore to be better supplied than it actually was, the destroyer's captain requested extra fresh food from the *Kenmore*'s master, only to be advised of the sad state of the *Kenmore*'s own provisions. It took some convincing for the destroyer's captain to accept that the *Kenmore*'s occupants were themselves now living on elderly rations, but faced with the reality, the destroyer's crew gratefully accepted whatever could be spared. To add to the stress, the benighted *Kenmore* broke down about one week before reaching New Caledonia. The *Fairisle* and *Wentley* and an additional cargo ship pushed on, leaving the one destroyer to guard the *Kenmore* until she got underway again. The false sighting of a "Japanese sub" by a lookout on the *Kenmore*, resulting in the firing of the *Kenmore*'s stern-mounted 5-inch gun—a tooth-rattling and bone-jarring experience that shook the old ship's fantail—added to everyone's worries as the old liner plied its way towards New Caledonia.

Time: Early November 1942
Place: Aboard U.S.S. Kenmore in mid-Pacific. Officers' meeting in wardroom.
Speaker: Col. David Nimmer

"I have this day received orders for this unit to land in a rear area.
I immediately sent a message in reply, stating that this unit was
combat ready and demanded assignment to a combat area."
(You could have heard a pin drop.)

—CAPTAIN WALTER WELLS[27]—

After thirty-nine days at sea, which Jack recalled as being, on the whole, a "nightmare," on November 11, 1942, the little convoy anchored in the outer harbor of Dunbea Bay, the anchorage of Noumea, New Caledonia.[28] The inner harbor was crammed full of the ships of a task force that was steaming out of New Caledonia for Guadalcanal, while small craft bobbed and weaved on the bay's waters, trying to clear the larger ships. In the case of one thirty-foot sloop, however, these frantic maneuvers were all for naught. As Frank Marshall recounted, "suddenly things went haywire" as the sloop's main sheet went loose.

All hands on the sailboat panicked, since by this time, they were only about 60 yards from the *Kenmore*'s midship and coming down out of control like gangbusters. By this time, [the sloop's skipper] was shouting orders to his crew in frantic Vietnamese—all this to the delight of the spectators on board the *Kenmore*. They began to cheer everyone out of sheer enthusiasm for the welcome comedy relief. Shortly the inevitable happened, and the sloop collided head-on with the unyielding . . . steel hull of the *Kenmore*, lost its bowsprit and headsails and driven by the steady afternoon breeze, began bumping forward along the hull of the *Kenmore*. . . . The applause was thunderous.[29]

A pall would soon be cast on this "comedy relief," however, by somber sights and sounds. As the large task force embarked and the Ninth's far-smaller convoy resumed steam into Noumea's inner harbor, the Marines craned their necks to identify the departing cruisers: the *Juneau*, the *Northampton*, the *Helena*—two of which, *Juneau* and *Northampton*, would lie at the bottom of Guadalcanal's waters before November 1942 had ended. The battleships *Washington* and *South Dakota*—the latter temporarily undergoing repairs—and the damaged aircraft carrier *Enterprise* were also nearby, such ships having been extensively damaged off Guadalcanal. Years later, Frank Yemma, then a private in Lieutenant (soon, Captain) Box's Battery B, recalled a startling incident taking place onboard one of the two mighty battleships: "I seem to think it was the *[South] Dakota* because she seemed to be shot up the worst. The order was given to drop anchor, and they literally did drop the anchor and chain and all—I mean *the whole thing*." "Sweet Jesus, will ya look at that?" Yemma muttered to his equally dumbfounded buddies lining the *Kenmore*'s deck. Another sobering touch was added moments later when several Marines on one of the Ninth's transports, peeking through a telescopic gunsight on the ship's stern gun, witnessed a burial-at-sea ceremony in progress. Yemma clearly heard "Taps" being played from the stern of one of the warships. These manifestations provided more reminders that the Ninth was on the cusp of the combat zone.[30]

New Caledonia was a French colony—originally under Vichy French control but, by fall 1942, under the Free French influence of General DeGaulle and his allies—that served as a major staging area for US troops and supplies bound throughout the South Pacific. Contrary to any notions that they may have had of New Caledonia being a tropical paradise of dusky, exotic Franco-Tahitian beauties, Dunbea Bay was a large, rear-area military anchorage and encampment populated mainly by Navy and Army personnel with a general hostility to "gyrenes." The Army's Americal ("*Amer*icans *In Cale*donia") Division was being organized from Regular Army

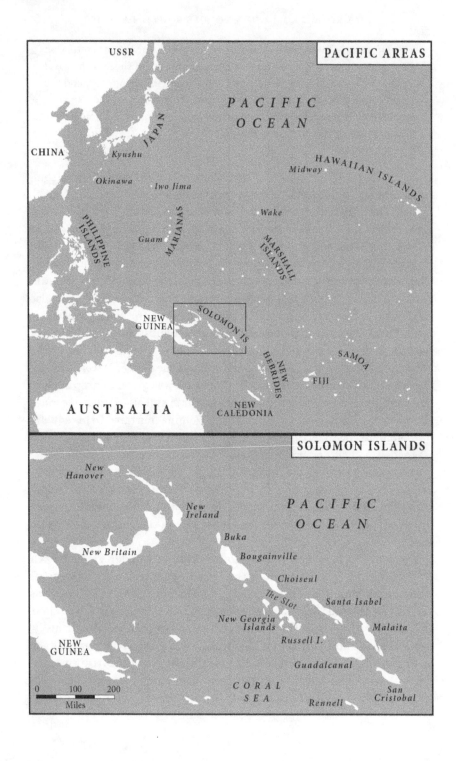

and National Guard units stationed in New Caledonia and was shipping out to Guadalcanal at around the same time that the Ninth's convoy had arrived.[31]

Another new arrival to New Caledonia, Second Lieutenant Christopher S. Donner, a former Stanford graduate student in history who later joined the Ninth in June 1943, noted his first impressions of Noumea: "We loaded into trucks and wound through the wildly colored town, dominated by a large Catholic church and the old French barracks. We looked in amazement at the blacks with their hair bleached to a bright orange. Young, attractive French girls moved through the streets, and everywhere were small statured Malays, the women resembling little dolls. [The] French were almost hostile, the stores charged outrageous prices, wine was $15 a bottle, whiskey $20.... Hard liquor was scarce."[32] While the houses of the French colonists were attractive, the port area was a muddy quagmire, the colonists (the supporters of the Vichy government, in particular) largely despised the Americans, and with combat approaching, there was little time to waste ashore anyway. The Ninth was now assigned to the I Marine Amphibious Corps (I MAC), whose blue shoulder insignia included the Southern Cross, the famed Southern Hemisphere constellation now readily visible to all after crossing the Equator.

It was also common knowledge to Jack and his pals by now that the *Kenmore*'s "Destination Unknown" had a name—Guadalcanal. It was not as if, however, their operational security efforts had been as tight as the Ninth's officers may have desired. To his consternation, Battery A commander Hank Reichner was greeted on arrival in Noumea by his best friend from civilian days, now stationed there by the Navy, as soon as Reichner disembarked from the *Kenmore*. While Reichner had no idea of his friend's whereabouts, the same could not be said for his old pal, who exclaimed joyfully, "There you are, old man! I knew you were coming!" "How did you know that?" Reichner asked suspiciously. "Uh, I'd heard all about it," was his friend's less-than-reassuring response. So much for operational security.[33]

At Noumea, the Ninth's materiel on board the *Fairisle* and *Robin Wentley* were offloaded to other ships because, as merchant ships, they were prohibited at this stage of the war from entering a forward combat area, and—more to the point—their Merchant Marine crews refused to enter the combat area without hazardous duty pay, which was not forthcoming. Also, because it had been "administratively" loaded in Cuba, the *Kenmore* had to be reloaded for combat operations, a task that would require maximum speed and efficiency in disembarking nonessential supplies and cargo and in readying the ship for combat. The working parties followed a grueling four-hours-on, eight-hours-off work routine; all cargo movement was by hand, cargo nets, block, and tackle. Anything deemed to be merely a comfort item was regarded as unessential and was unloaded at Noumea for storage.

For Jack, this process entailed at least one nerve-wracking incident while he, Frank Chadwick, and a group of others were detailed to help unload ammunition in the ship's forward hold. The ammunition had been loaded in no apparent order: 155mm shells were intermixed with other calibers and sizes of shells and small-arms ammunition, and in the course of sailing, some unevenly distributed cargo had tilted and fallen. Worse, the wooden pallets to which the larger shells (the 90s and 155s) were strapped were poorly banded, so that, as shell pallets were lifted out of the hold by the ship's crane, the shells *very* perceptibly moved around on the pallet.

Worse was yet to come. As one pallet of 155mm shells was being hauled out of the hot, dingy and dirty hold, twelve shells per pallet, several of the hefty, ninety-five-pound shells *did* work loose, and they fell back into the hold. They hit several other pallets of shells, which then broke loose, and some shells began careening off the walls and bulkheads. In the dark, the only thing Jack and his buddies could see were the sparks being struck as steel scraped against steel. The little group threw themselves against the bulkheads, convinced they would go up in a fireball; fortunately, probably because none of the shells were fitted with fuses (which themselves were present in the hold, although stored separately, as were bags and cardboard tubes of gunpowder for the unit's big guns), nothing exploded.

As soon as it was apparent that no real damage had been done, the hold erupted in jeers, curses, and obscenities. These were aimed chiefly at the idiot ordnance personnel who had supposedly secured the pallets and shells together in the first place. After venting their frustrations, the ammo detail decided it had earned itself a short break. At this moment, a belligerent second lieutenant appeared at the hold's hatchway, looking down into the dark. He immediately began shouting, "Knock it off down there, dammit! Do you want me to come down there? Get back to work!" The group wasted no time with its response, rank be damned. One of the work party yelled back: "Come down here and say that to our faces, *sir*, if you have the guts to, and we'll throw your ass overboard!" Rank or no rank, the "shavetail" beat a hasty retreat, wisely letting the ammo team continue to catch its collective breath and regroup a little longer, and the unloading process eventually resumed without further incident. Still amazed at their luck years later, Jack said, "It was just a wonder we didn't all get blown up." As Chadwick recalled, "God was with us this day."[34]

While the ship-to-ship loading process was back-breaking work for all involved, some found the laborious process had its own rewards. While David ("Biggie") Slater and a team of Battalion H&S communications men were unloading one of the transports, they found a crate marked "Medical Supplies." They asked one of the battalion's assigned Navy medical corpsmen, who had personally helped pack and load all the Ninth's medical supplies, what it was, but he did not recognize the crate. "Beats me, fellas," the medic muttered; "go ahead and take a look if you like." On breaking open the crate, Slater and his pals were overjoyed to find it held a case of scotch, which—needless to say—Biggie and company "liberated" after destroying the crate to hide the evidence. Fortunately for the Ninth's officers, this same group did not happen to inspect one grim item of supply. Reichner recalled: "Among other items that arrived in preparation for our voyage to God-knows-where were several coffins assigned as part of the battalion's Table of Equipment. Colonel Nimmer solved the problem of maximizing their use by authorizing the packing of a liquor supply in each one for future use!"[35] If only Biggie Slater and his thirsty buddies had known what a treat barely escaped their grasp. . . .

After sixteen days of frenetic activities, the *Kenmore* and an attack transport, the USS *Hunter Liggett*, set sail on November 27, this time filled with a much more somber-minded group of young Marines. Led by Captains Stafford and Box, Battery B remained aboard the *Kenmore* while Jack boarded the *Liggett* with a contingent from the 155mm Group's H&S Battery. An advance party comprised largely of 105 Marines from Battery A had already departed for Guadalcanal six days earlier on the transport USS *Neville*, while Colonel Nimmer and his staff flew from New Caledonia to Guadalcanal for an advance reconnaissance.[36] Where they were going and the grim situation they would face there was no longer secret, and they were going, a more or less brand-new outfit, with old and largely untested equipment.

Apart from some firing of the Special Weapons Group's .50 calibers and a few 20mms at an airplane-towed target at low altitude, performed a few hours after the convoy set sail from Noumea (and about which several veterans gratefully expressed joy at the tow plane's having gone unscathed!); practice gunnery conducted on Guantanamo of the 90mm guns; and (for the 155mm Group) firing drills conducted with the obsolete ex-naval pieces now used as coast-defense guns, several of the Ninth's major weapons still remained relatively untested. Despite their training in Cuba, the knowledge that the 155mm Group had not gotten the opportunity to test-fire its big guns gnawed on the minds of its officers, NCOs, and enlisted men alike.

The battalion was bound for what the Japanese rank-and-file were beginning to call to one another in whispers, out of earshot of their officers and sergeants, "Starvation Island" or *Gadarukanaru*, the "Island of Death"[37]—a place from which, once sent, no one returned, and an island hellhole that, three months into the battle, was something like a tropical Verdun, sucking into its maw thousands of both Japan's and America's young soldiers, sailors, and airmen. It was not for nothing that "The Slot," the narrow waterway separating Guadalcanal and the various islands in the Solomons chain, was called Ironbottom Sound: the sea floor was already covered with scores of Allied and Japanese ships and aircraft, and more victims were yet to come.

As the Ninth's convoy steamed into view of Guadalcanal in the twilight of December 3, 1942, Jack and his fellow Marines and Seabees scrambled out of the ships' innards to line the rails and catch a glimpse of the island's darkened silhouette. Years later, another of the Ninth's leathernecks, Willie Dufour, would remember some "wise guy's" decision to pick this exact moment to play a then-popular record, *Blues in the Night*, with its sinister minor-key opening notes filtering onto the open decks.[38] "Blues in the night," indeed! The sight of the blood-soaked island was enough to give even the most hardened warrior a case of the blues.

Guantanamo Bay had not been war, after all. The real war was finally here for Jack and the Ninth Defense.

THREE

Guadalcanal:
The Fighting Ninth Meets the Island of Death

Our mission [on Guadalcanal], besides seacoast defense,
was to defend the construction of an additional airfield to Henderson.
Air raids, both day and night, were frequent, one of which reached the size
of one hundred Japanese planes. Mosquitoes, malaria, and monsoons
all took their toll, and several men were lost to malaria.

—JACK H. MCCALL, SR.—

For us who were there, or whose friends were there, Guadalcanal
is not a name but an emotion, recalling desperate fights in the air,
furious night naval battles, frantic work at supply or construction,
savage fighting in the sodden jungle, nights broken by
screaming bombs and deafening explosions of naval shells.

—SAMUEL ELIOT MORISON[1]—

And when he gets to Heaven,
To St. Peter he will tell:
Another Marine reporting, Sir;
I've served my time in Hell!

—INSCRIBED ON A MARINE TOMBSTONE ON GUADALCANAL[2]—

If nothing to date had served as a wake-up call to the horrors of warfare, Jack's arrival on board the *Hunter Liggett* to Guadalcanal's waters provided him with a quick and grim reality check. Several major naval engagements had been fought shortly before the Ninth's arrival. In mid-November's Naval Battle of Guadalcanal, while a US naval squadron had crippled the Japanese battleship *Kirishima* (scuttled by her own fleet) and sunk a heavy cruiser, three destroyers, and eleven transports, the US Navy had still suffered a mauling. The new battleship USS *South Dakota* had taken over forty hits.[3] Days before the Ninth's arrival, the Navy had lost the cruiser

Northampton (which Jack and his pals had just seen leaving Noumea a few weeks earlier) and had three other cruisers crippled in the Battle of Tassafaronga on November 30.[4] This vicious naval engagement had delayed Battery A, on board the *Neville*, from coming ashore; that ship and several others bearing reinforcements were forced to wait at anchor off the island of Espiritu Santo, some six hundred miles southeast of Guadalcanal, until the Japanese naval threat cooled down. The *Neville*'s convoy finally set sail from Espiritu Santo on November 27, and the *Hunter Liggett* and *Kenmore* sailed from Noumea on November 28, with both convoys forming part of the Navy's Task Force Sixty-Two.[5]

The oily detritus of Tassafaronga and other recent sea battles still floated upon the water as the *Neville*, the *Kenmore*, and the *Hunter Liggett* sailed into Ironbottom Sound on December 3, 1942 and weighed anchor off Koli Point, near the beaches where the First Marine Division had stormed ashore in early August of that year and where major fighting had occurred in early November.[6] In Noumea's inner harbor, after the reinforcing task force had departed for Guadalcanal, the Ninth's transports had passed the length of the *South Dakota*. This was not long after her battle with the *Kirishima*, and the US battleship rested at anchor with, as Jack remembered, "a hole in her side as big as a school bus." He recalled that he and his buddies stared at the massive hole in the ship's lower forward 16-inch gun turret, wondering what else the Japanese could do if they could wreak damage like that to a steel-plated monster like the *South Dakota*. Jack had one answer shortly: near the *South Dakota*, the carrier *Enterprise* was also anchored in Noumea's inner harbor, similarly undergoing repairs, her forward elevator crumpled and canted upwards from a Japanese bomb. These were sobering sights for a bunch of young Marines heading to the war zone.

Soon after arriving off Koli Point on November 30, the *Neville* briefly ran aground in an area of uncharted sandbanks. Only days later, with the *Hunter Liggett* anchored nearby, the *Kenmore* also ran aground on an uncharted sandbar in shallow water when the ship retired for the night toward the nearby harbor of Tulagi, to the amusement of many of its Marine passengers. "We got to laughing so hard," Frank Chadwick recounted; the *Kenmore*'s captain "became embarrassed and finally asked a destroyer to pass a line to get the ship off the bar." Several hundred of the Ninth's Marines were able to rock the ship somewhat, but not enough to release it from

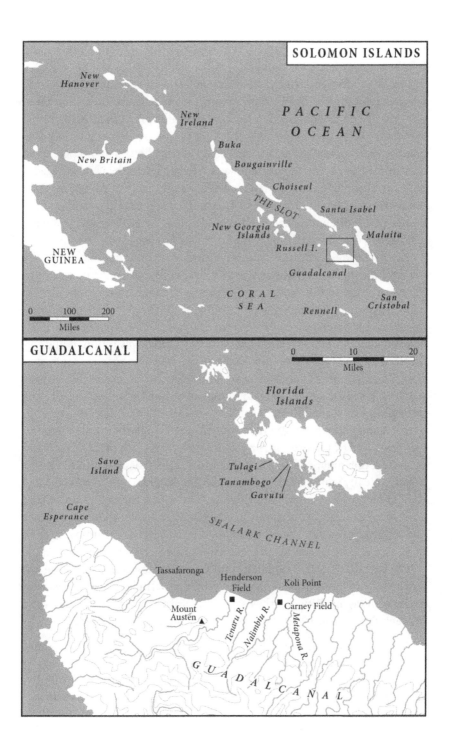

the sandbar's grasp. At high tide, a tug slipped a line onto the *Kenmore* and finally freed it from the sandbar.

Two days after the Ninth's landing, the wake of a Japanese submarine was detected off Koli Point.[7] Several aircraft were dispatched from Henderson Field on Guadalcanal to search for the escaping I-boat. Still aboard the *Hunter Liggett*, Jack watched in horror as a US Navy SBD Dauntless dive bomber arced down out of the blue, cloudless sky, in a near-vertical dive, to bomb the apparent wake of the Japanese submarine as it submerged—only to fail to pull out of the dive and to be caught up in the massive water plume from its depth charge, into Ironbottom Sound. The two-man dive bomber crew did not escape from their airplane's watery grave.[8] "What a welcome to Guadalcanal," Jack later recalled thinking.

The battalion's landings near Koli Point were unopposed. After the nearby fighting in early November, a welter of discarded Japanese equipment still littered Koli Point, and members of the working parties began collecting souvenirs shortly after landing. With the arrival of the *Hunter Liggett* and *Kenmore*, the entire Ninth, minus some 150 Marines in a rear-echelon detachment left behind at New Caledonia, was reunited and[9] officially attached to the First Marine Division. The unit began to set up gun positions and unload guns, ammo, and equipment. It was back-breaking work: many of the supplies had to be moved by hand across the beach. The unloading was accomplished partly by small LCP landing craft—none of which had landing ramps, which would have aided in their unloading immensely—and by twenty-foot prefabricated barges made of steel boxes fastened together and propelled by outboard motors. The Ninth Defense was not organically equipped with the trucks, jeeps, and prime movers needed to haul heavy guns from place to place. Therefore, the lighter automatic guns were generally manhandled into place, and even the larger 90mm and 155mm guns had to be dragged into their positions. The unloading and deployment process took almost ten days before it was completed.[10]

The battalion's role on Guadalcanal was to occupy and defend the flat and heavily foliaged alluvial plain between the Nalimbiu River on the west and the Metapona River on the east. The terrain here was treacherous and presented its own set of difficulties. Frank Marshall recounted:

> The rivers were bordered by jungle so thick that, in some areas, it was not possible to walk erect; pigs and other small animals had made paths, but other than that there were no passages. There was a variety of native thorn that grew up through the branches of the various trees and bushes with a

recurved thorn that tore the clothing and flesh unmercifully. To make one's way through this dense and threatening foliage was a slow job of hacking with machete and axe. Between the two rivers was a flat, grassy plain covered with a variety of high weed called kunai grass [which] grew to a height of about six feet and was quite dense. The soil structure was similar to adobe, being a heavy, rich black soil deposited to a depth of three to four feet. The fact was that this grassy plain three miles wide by ten miles deep was the drainage basin of the two bounding rivers, [a] fact that would become only too apparent in the coming months.[11]

The first night on the Canal was nerve-wracking for all parties concerned. Frequent but false cries of "Condition Red"—the alarm for an imminent air raid—set the tone of nervousness that worsened as the men got their first taste of a jet-black tropical nightfall. Despite the officers' best efforts, fear got the better of some Marines, and their overreactions to the sounds of the jungle would, in Jack's words, "scare the hell out of me." Battery A's Hank Reichner sets the scene:

> To prepare ourselves for Japanese infiltration during the night, we were given the password "SMASH" and the response "AND DRIVE." We bivouacked slightly inshore and set up a rather poor perimeter defense. Many other elements of the battalion were located in the vicinity under similar circumstances. We really did not expect any Japanese attack but everyone's nerves were on edge. Naturally, it took only one blast from one blasted Reising gun [a type of submachine gun used by the Marines] to start things off. For at least an hour the night was punctuated with "SMASHES" and "AND DRIVES" accompanied by incessant bursts of fire and curses. I shouted a few "Knock it offs," as did the Sergeants, but to wander around to seek out any perpetrators of this mess would have been suicide. Embarrassment and calmness settled in and the rest of the night went by peaceably and sleeplessly enough. . . . It was almost an initiation but it did show a certain lack of experience on our part.[12]

The results of these boy-crying-wolf incidents would, in a few weeks, jeopardize Jack's own life when the "Japanese infiltrators" he would see proved to be very real.

Many of the battalion's AA guns were situated about six miles from Henderson Field. This airfield was the home of the "Cactus Air Force" that had been defending Guadalcanal against Japanese aerial onslaughts for the past two and a half months. (In fact, the enemy's construction of Henderson Field had been one of the primary causes for the Marines' landings on Guadalcanal in August 1942.) Battery A and half of Battery B were set up around the Koli Point area, their World War I-vintage GPFs[13] emplaced as coastal defense guns against the "Tokyo Express." The Tokyo Express comprised near-fortnightly raids and resupply runs made by a Japanese destroyer and light cruiser squadron led by its resourceful commander, Admiral Raizo ("Torpedo") Tanaka.[14] Up until the Ninth's arrival, the Marines' prime defense against the Tokyo Express had been almost solely naval in nature, with only a handful of land-based airplanes stationed at Henderson Field capable of launching bombing or torpedo attacks against Tanaka's ships. The Ninth's 155s would add a punch that might deter any close-in bombardments or at least make their outcome more painful to the Japanese. They would also provide some much-needed heavy firepower for the beleaguered First Marine Division and the fresh Army divisions (the American and the Twenty-Fifth Infantry) that were beginning to arrive on Guadalcanal.

Due to the fifteen-mile range of the aged GPFs and the need to site the guns so as to best maximize their effectiveness, Colonel Nimmer decided to place all of Battery A in the Koli Point beachhead area. He split Battery B in half, and H&S Battery—to which Jack belonged, an outfit less than affectionately called the "Ham and Shitheads" by the rest of the 155mm Group[15]—would oversee the Group's operations and logistics. Although officially part of H&S, Jack remained with Battery A and Captain Stafford's half of Battery B at Koli Point. The other half of Battery B was shipped across Ironbottom Sound via the *Hunter Liggett* to the small island of Gavutu. Here, the Japanese had built an observation point and naval gun position atop the imposing Hill 181. This promontory had a commanding view of much of the Sound, the large harbor of Tulagi on nearby Florida Island, and a sweeping vista of the northern coast of Guadalcanal.[16] Gavutu was linked by a narrow three-hundred-foot causeway to a smaller islet, Tanambogo, and both islands had been taken only by a very bloody assault by Marine paratroopers (Paramarines) during the August 1942 landings.[17]

As Battery B's detachment arrived there, three crippled heavy cruisers, the USS *Minneapolis*, *Pensacola*, and *New Orleans*—all survivors of the wild sea fight off Tassafaronga—lay anchored under heavy camouflage netting off Tulagi and Gavutu. The *Minneapolis*'s bow had been blasted away, and the *Pensacola*'s fantail had been smashed by a Japanese torpedo. Their crews were busily sealing up all inner compartments to make the ships seaworthy for towing to New Caledonia for repairs. The camouflage job festooning the battered cruisers was impressive. Frank Yemma of Battery B's Gavutu section remarked: "[A] bunch of sailors [were] on Gavutu when we landed, and I couldn't figure out what the hell they were doing there or why they were there, until I saw this cruiser [the USS *Minneapolis*] with its bow blown off ... there was camouflage over it, and it was very well done because I couldn't see it; just as the light was coming up, I still couldn't see it." Bill Box's other Marines gaped at the damage inflicted to these ships. Encountered so soon after they had witnessed the *South Dakota*'s and *Enterprise*'s injuries, the battered condition of the cruisers again reinforced the true gravity of the American situation on and around Guadalcanal.[18]

The forty men or so on Gavutu, including Al Downs, Frank Chadwick, and Yemma, immediately faced a huge technical challenge: how to manhandle one of the colossal GPFs, plus ammunition and firing equipment, to the top of Hill 181, a rugged, nearly two hundred-foot outcropping covered in jungle trees and vines, without heavy lifting or construction equipment. Shortly after landing, the crews broke out all the axes, saws, and shovels available and began hacking a trail up the slope of Hill 181 through the jungle, using the felled logs to corduroy the trail. Everyone pitched in, and working day and night, after seven full days, the corduroyed trail was complete. Using little more than hand tools, some thirty Marines pushed the massive gun up the hill; using ropes, block, and tackle, the second gun was slowly winched into place near the water's edge. Fifty years later, Box and Chadwick returned to Gavutu and marveled that they were able to achieve this feat, their first assigned mission in the Guadalcanal sector. In retrospect, however, Box also realized how ineffectual his little detachment would have been if the Japanese had ever attempted to retake Gavutu in earnest: "It was pretty stupid, really, since our two guns had only thirty or forty rounds of ammo [apiece]. They put these bodies on an island, so if the Japanese ever came on it, they would have to fight us or they'd kill us—one or the other."

The remnants of the Japanese occupation and the Paramarines' struggle for Gavutu were in evidence in various ways. A small cemetery held the remains of some of the Paramarine dead from August 7, 1942, which Captain Box's section faithfully tended. Near Hill 181 lay an unusual funeral plot built by a unit of Paramarines over the remains of some of the island's prior defenders. As Frank Yemma recalled: "On that Hill 181 on Gavutu, [there] was a cross, and it said 'Here lies five dead Japs, killed by Marines, buried by Marines and whipped by God.'"[19]

To help improve their ability to traverse quickly onto potential targets, A and B Batteries' 155s on Koli Point and Gavutu were positioned on Panama mounts—concrete pads with turntables, on which each GPF's carriage was mounted and on which the entire gun could be turned through 360 degrees. Part of the gunners went to work mixing concrete; setting up wooden molds, the turntable, and the circular metal tracks for each Panama mount; and pouring the concrete, while others filled and stacked sandbags in the sweltering heat and humidity. Each gun position was soon protected by a high wall of sandbags (and occasionally fifty-five-gallon steel fuel drums, packed with whatever filler was readily at hand). Camouflage netting was draped overhead to screen the guns from enemy observation planes, including the despised "Washing Machine Charlie"nighttime raider. To help protect the Marines from bombing and naval raids, large foxholes were dug—around tents, around gun positions, and even in the hospital area next to patients' stretchers and cots, so that each sick or wounded man merely needed to roll off the edge into the hole—and were further walled in by sandbags where possible. Although intended to provide better safety, ironically, these foxholes and trenches dotting the Ninth's position

Men of Captain Box's Battery B detachment on Gavutu. Note the "Panama mount" for the tarpaulin-shrouded GPF and Hill 181, with its Japanese-built observation post, in the background. The Marine on the left, leaning on a shovel, is Frank Yemma. Photo by Leo McDonald, courtesy of David Slater.

generated another peril, as an inattentive person could easily break a leg or sprain an ankle (and more than a few Marines did) by tripping into one in the dark.

Besides adding defensive firepower to protect Henderson Field and the beachside logistical areas from naval and air attack, another of the Ninth's missions was the defense of Carney Field, a new Army Air Forces airfield under construction near Koli Point and some twenty miles from Henderson Field. That the fighting had shifted from the Tenaru and Matanikau River areas along the coast to the western and central parts of the island provided little comfort: as noted earlier, Japanese troops had just engaged in combat near Koli Point the previous month, and their patrols still meandered far across the area.[20] The tropical rain forest and terrain provided these intruders with ample opportunities to work their way through Marine and Army frontline positions and infiltrate into the US rear areas: the dense vegetation masked movements, particularly at nighttime, when the leafy canopy blocked out all moonlight. The Ninth had guards patrolling in watch shifts all night long, with all guards advised to be especially vigilant between 10:00 p.m. and 2:00 a.m. and in the early morning hours just before daybreak.

As one of the battalion's water purification technicians, or "gizmos," Jack was in possibly the most isolated position of the Ninth. This was a small area off the Nalimbiu River, not far from Battery A's guns and campsite and the SCR-268 fire control radar of Battery F, but far enough away that Jack seldom saw his buddies except at chow time or when delivering supplies of purified water. On the Nalimbiu, he set up his equipment and made a small shack for himself and his gear out of a tent and whatever materials he could scrounge. His water purification gear consisted of various hoses and large pumps, sets of filtration units, a large portable canvas tub, and boxes for storing his chemical testing kit. The purified water ("'Putrefied' was more like it," Bob Landon joked) was dispensed from canvas-and-rubber Lister bags. As Battery A's skipper, Hank Reichner, recalled, these bags "can best be described as looking like a huge cow's udder with push-button spigots for teats" jutting symmetrically out of each bag's bottom.

Jack had the reputation for being quite a successful scrounger, which is a useful thing to be in any military unit, but maybe particularly so in an outfit like the Ninth. He was already looking pretty rangy in his faded and ripped herringbone-twill utility uniform and well-broken-in boondockers, which tended to make the wearer's feet resemble those of Al Capp's cartoon character Li'l Abner. To complete the look of an old salt Marine, he added a World War I-model trench knife, complete with evil-looking spiked brass knuckles on the handle, plus his old Marine campaign hat with a hole the size of his thumb in the crown, nibbled out back in Cuba one evening by a hungry rat. (As one of Jack's high school monikers had been "Rathead" because of a stubborn cowlick that refused to be combed down, Jack appreciated the humor of now wearing a rat-eaten hat.) But Jack was hardly alone in his unorthodox appearance. The herringbone-twill fatigues of almost all the Marines on Guadalcanal were sweaty, ripped, and faded from a pristine olive drab to a bleached-out tint of green. Surviving photos of the Ninth's gunners show a motley array of headgear, with everything from World War I-pattern helmets, pith helmets, and campaign hats to a brimmed cap that vaguely resembled a Greek fisherman's hat. Later, a few of the Marines would receive camouflaged overalls, which they called "zoot suits" after the baggily cut civilian men's suits that were a popular style of the late 1930s and 1941. As the chorus of one of their favorite marching and drinking songs concluded: "*The raggedy-assed Marines are on the way!*"

Jack's Nalimbiu riverbank was a prime area for Japanese infiltrators who followed the river down to the beachhead, either to rendezvous with submarines trying to smuggle supplies or reinforcements ashore or to try to steal from or sabotage the Marines' beachside supply dumps. Shortly after setting up the water purification point, he was given a field telephone with which he could stay in contact with battery headquarters. Soon thereafter, shortly after dawn, the battery's switchboard operator received a whispered call: "This is Private McCall. Can the Skipper send a patrol down here? There's Japs all over the place down here!" "Calm down, Pogiebait; you're just seeing things!" was the response. The line was disconnected on Jack's end with a less-than-reassuring "*click.*" A few mornings later, a similar exchange occurred.

Jack, however, needed no convincing from anybody else as to what he was or was not seeing: there definitely *were* Japanese out there, ten- to fifteen-man patrols of them, meandering through the steamy mist and vegetation near the riverbank. This activity continued for several mornings until at last a patrol of the Ninth came down to draw some water from Jack just as a Japanese patrol emerged from the kunai brush beside the Nalimbiu. A firefight ensued, more or less over Jack's head, with him squeezing off a few shots with his Springfield into the bushes. "Now, will you believe me next time?" he recalled saying. As additional proof of what he had seen, the patrol found several trails of blood leading back into the jungle and salvaged some pieces of Japanese equipment, including a small, bloodstained

Japanese "Rising Sun" flag. Jack split this flag in two with a buddy as a souvenir of his close call. From that time on, he saw no more Japanese as close to him on Guadalcanal as he had on that day and the previous days.

Infantry attacks, though, were not the only peril Jack and his pals faced. Despite the American air buildup and the Navy's efforts to keep substantial forces in the area, "Torpedo" Tanaka and the Tokyo Express still periodically appeared to shell the island. While the Tokyo Express's guns sometimes delivered fire close to the Ninth's positions and the airfield construction at Carney Field, the ships outranged the 155s.[21] Even when Japanese shells fell far from the battalion's positions, the blasts from the ships' guns could be seen in the distance. The naval bombardments and battles at sea reminded Jack of heat lightning, and the distant roar of naval gunnery sounded not unlike thunder on a humid Tennessee summer's night.

Also, despite the antiaircraft buildup, Japanese air raids remained a common occurrence. In early January 1943, several large raids occurred, made up primarily of Mitsubishi G3M2 (Type 96) "Nell" medium bombers, which enabled one of the Ninth's AA batteries to make its first kill on January 14. The air raids were frequent and persistent: the 90mm Group alone was in action 117 times from December to June 1943. Thirty-seven of these raids occurred in January 1943 in connection with Operation KE, a final and massive Japanese drive to reinforce their troops and make a last-ditch effort to drive the Americans off the island. In one raid, more than one hundred Japanese planes came over at nighttime, lighting up the skies around Henderson Field with heavy AA bursts and tracers.[22] Because the Marines' primary hospital was near Henderson Field, unless they were in truly desperate shape, the wounded and sick there often felt safer returning to duty rather than being passive sitting ducks adjacent to a prime target.[23] As if the Ninth's AA guns were not enough to defend Carney Field, one of the 90mm Group's battery commanders, Captain Bill Tracy, enlisted the help of some Seabees of the Eighteenth Naval Construction Battalion, engaged in the construction of Carney Field,[24] to construct a complete but bogus 90mm position. This was "armed" with realistic-looking dummy guns to further confuse and distract the Japanese.[25] Despite the presence of several squadrons of fighters on the island, the Allies hardly had air supremacy.

During one massive, nighttime bomber raid in early December, Jack was near the headquarters of Maj. General Alexander Archer Vandegrift, the First Marine Division's commanding general and, at the time, the overall American commander on the Canal. Hand-cranked air raid sirens screeched, the fingers of searchlights began probing the skies, bombs exploded nearby, AA fire became increasingly heavy, and Jack and others without AA positions to man ran to the nearest shelters. What he found was little better than a slit trench, he recalled, with a bottom half-full of water and muck—only to see a glowing cigarette coming from another trench close by. Jack's immediate thought was of his earlier training to the effect that a well-trained enemy airman could see a cigar glowing on the ground from even several thousand feet. He knew *he* didn't want to be hiding next to some moron who had the functional equivalent of a bull's eye painted on his back.

"Hey, you damn idiot, knock off the smoking! Do you want to get us killed?" he yelled at the knucklehead with the cigarette.

"Shut up, Mac; that's the General's trench you're talking about!" a voice roared from another hole.

"*F——k the General!*" Jack yelled back without thinking; then, immediately realizing the court-martial offense he felt certain he had just committed, he felt *very* glad that the night was a dark one and his trench was deep!

On December 4—just the second day that the entire battalion was on the Canal—the radar operators on one of the battalion's five SCR-268 radars set in motion what many of the Ninth Defense's veterans would recall as the battalion's only real "night of panic." The early radars, of which the SCR-268 was one, relied on vacuum tubes and the recently invented cavity magnetron, the first electronics "black box," and the glitches had not yet been fully worked out. It was, after all, suspicion as to the effectiveness of the early radar sets that partly contributed to the success of the surprise attack on Pearl Harbor. In the year since December 7, 1941, the technology had greatly advanced, but errors were still common, and the early radar equipment was particularly prone to atmospheric changes providing false echoes and altering the quality of reception. In fact, similar problems resulting from the inability of early Navy radars to factor out false echoes resulting from landmasses limited its maximum effectiveness in several crucial naval actions off Guadalcanal, and the new technology's teething pains led some Navy commanders to discount its potential advantages, with tragic results as at the Battle of Tassafaronga.[26]

Unlike the Ninth's largest radar, the SCR-270—a collapsible latticework mast set on a trailer-mounted, fourteen-foot, slowly rotating turntable, which was used exclusively for long-range surface surveillance and required a twelve-man crew—the five SCR-268s were used for

Above: a Ninth Defense SCR-268 radar set during the Rendova-New Georgia campaign; *below*: a SCR-270 radar set (in this case, an Army set located near Pearl Harbor at Opana, Hawaii). Official US Marine Corps and US Army photographs.

searchlight direction and AA fire control. Each 268 set required three operators—each one behind an oscilloscope and equipped with hand cranks to adjust the range and altitude readings—for a total fourteen- to fifteen-man crew. These early radar sets generally had an effective range of twenty-two miles, but this particular 268 set's chief, Martin Jones, had performed his own field modifications to increase its effective range to some forty-four miles. As a result, the Ninth now effectively had two long-range search systems, but it would soon become clear that "Jonesy" still had some electronic gremlins to work out in his modified set.[27]

Late on that December evening, as this SCR-268's antenna scanned the skies and over the waters of Ironbottom Sound, its three operators gaped at their oscilloscopes with amazement: there appeared to be at least forty ships approaching. A quick call to headquarters established that no US convoy was anticipated, so there must be only one explanation: a massive visit from the Tokyo Express was imminent. Confirming what Jonesy and the operators saw, the watch officer in the filter room, where all radar data was collected and analyzed, spread the word: *"Condition Black!"* All hands to battle stations! All hell broke loose throughout the battalion area as alert sirens cranked and field telephones rattled. Jack grabbed his Springfield and gear out of his lean-to near the Nalimbiu and scooted for a nearby fox-hole. With many clad in little more than their skivvies and boots, A and B Batteries' gunners raced to their guns, pulling on their helmets, priming shells, removing muzzle covers, and generally getting into readiness for the massive bombardment that was sure to come—but nothing happened. Ironbottom Sound was tranquil, and no flares or gunfire lit the sky. The battalion HQ's signalmen broke out their blinker light to semaphore messages across the sound to Tulagi and Gavutu, inquiring if anything unusual had been sighted, but all responses were negative.

The next morning, apart from the usual oily film drifting up from the hulls of the smashed ships littering its bottom, no trace whatsoever of a Tokyo Express convoy could be detected on the sound. What had happened? It had been a false alarm, but the sleepless night only worsened everyone's jitters. As it was, Colonel Nimmer decided that his headquarters was too exposed and too close to the Koli Point beach. As a precaution, he had the battalion's command post moved further inland.[28] For his part, Jack desperately wanted to drop back into his riverside shanty and sleep, but he found himself lugging tables, tents, and equipment to help move the headquarters.

---❊---

In addition to the periodic naval bombardments and nighttime bomber raids, the Japanese provided a less dangerous, but more persistent, irritant to the night life of the Marines on Guadalcanal. On evenings, even when Japanese air activity was not heavy, either a bimotored bomber or single-engined seaplane would fly over, drop flares or a few bombs, and generally serve as a nuisance. Because its engines grumbled noisily like a washing machine, this airborne pest was variously nicknamed "Washing Machine Charlie," "Maytag Charley," "Trashcan Charlie," or "Louie the Louse." Charlie was the bane of existence of all Marines and Army troops on Guadalcanal because, if nothing else, Charlie ensured that absolutely nobody got a good night's sleep during his midnight and early morning flights. While Charlie was roundly disliked, he was quite possibly even more hated by the Ninth's AA crews. Try as they might, and despite their successes in downing, diverting, or crippling other Japanese planes, Charlie appeared untouchable. One official historian noted: "Charley was a difficult target for the antiaircraft guns since he usually flew high and maneuvered violently when searchlights and guns went into action." Hence, Washing Machine Charlie usually escaped unmolested.[29]

The 90mm Group's ack-ack gunners must have taken an incredible ribbing for their lack of success in downing this highly irritating nocturnal marauder.[30] Night after night, despite a screen of 90mm fire and searchlights and the occasional scrambling of fighters from Henderson Field to intercept him, Charlie just kept on coming. This situation continued until spring 1943 when the Army Air Forces finally began deploying night fighters on the Canal. For the rest of his life, Jack could imitate the sound of Washing Machine Charlie's obnoxiously unsynchronized engines. The sound was, as his impersonation of Charlie can best be recalled, a deep "rum-rum-rum" rumbling sound.

Mother Nature added her own challenges to the dangers and discomforts provided by the Japanese Army and Navy, which for many Marines proved at least as deadly as enemy action. The climate itself was a challenge, even to Southerners like Jack used to ninety-degree summer heat and humidity. The jungle was extremely dense in places, the forest floor a gnarled tangle of slippery roots and vines. As noted earlier, deep under the jungle canopy, nighttime was pitch black, with few breaks in the treetop canopy to let moonlight or starlight shine through. The weather was unremittingly hot and humid, and when rain fell (which was almost a daily occurrence), the result was a tropical steam bath as the raindrops rapidly turned to mist upon contact with the overheated soil, plants, and rotted vegetation. The smell of the rotting plant life could be overwhelming (particularly when combined with the putrid stink of the decomposing dead). In the sodden soil, water pooled rapidly in foxholes and trenches, and the soil liquefied rapidly to create an extremely thick and viscous mud, making it almost impossible for a person to stay dry. The battalion's positions near Koli Point were on a grassy floodplain between two rivers, the Metapona and Nalimbiu, which became swampland in the event of heavy rains or floods. Indeed, monsoon-like rains from typhoons in May flooded the Ninth's entire area. As Frank Marshall recalled: "On May 9th the heavens opened and stayed so through the 10th. In the Solomons, the rain drops must weigh 2 pounds each. This was a biblical rain. This was the rain of Genesis."[31]

Despite the unit's best efforts to build dikes and levees with some Seabees' help (provided in gratitude to Captain Tracy's help in building the fake AA battery at Carney Field), the floodwaters drowned one of the Ninth's Marines, wrecked several Panama mounts, and saturated the gun positions. The monsoon floods also washed Jack out of his area on the Nalimbiu and forced him to higher ground: "I was visiting the guys in Searchlights and my tent was washed away into the bay in a matter of a few hours. I managed to salvage my seabag and rifle in water [that was] waist deep."[32] Combined with a plethora of types of fungus, jungle rot and an especially virulent kind of athlete's foot plagued the already miserable Marines, giving some of them souvenirs of their jungle stay that lasted the rest of their lives.

Wild hogs roamed the jungles of Guadalcanal, sometimes charging the Marines or rooting through encampments and battle sites for anything edible. During the spring's heaviest monsoons, one of Jack's pals, Bill Galloway, and another Marine had found and killed one of these wild hogs. To help stave off flooding, the Marines had piled up a levee of sandbags to keep the water out, but their positions were still open to the flood waters of the Nalimbiu. Few of the Ninth's Marines were country boys experienced in slaughtering hogs. The Kentucky-bred Galloway, however, had learned how to dress one; once this specimen was cleaned and dressed, Galloway and his pals hung it up from a tree near their position, about 250 to 300 yards from Jack's water purification point. The water, however, continued to rise, and the flood soon immersed the hog's head. To prevent contamination, Galloway cut it off. As the water crept up, soon the flood was up to the hog's shoulders. Galloway cut away the shoulders and again rehung the hog. The water continued to rise, and it was obvious that it would cover what was left of the hog. In disgust, Galloway and his buddies cut the carcass adrift and watched it float away in the flood. Imagine Jack's surprise when, after the floodwaters cleared, he went to clean up and reopen his water purification site for business, only to find half of a slaughtered pig in the middle of his gear, clogging up his pumps!

Dead pigs were not the only animals floating in the waters of the Nalimbiu. Large snakes could be found from time to time, and although they were non-poisonous, Jack was deathly afraid of them. Crocodiles also dwelled in the rivers of Guadalcanal, and several lurked near Jack's water point. His buddy Jim Kruse, a clerk for H&S Battery of the 155mm Group, reminded Jack after the war: "I saw many crocodiles in [the Nalimbiu]. Upstream I saw some that were in excess of eight feet in length. In the underbrush near you I saw a lizard that was in the vicinity of five feet in length. I didn't know what it was until I got back to the States and looked it up."[33] The presence of so many large reptiles kept Jack always a little on edge. Jack recalled watching a bored Army machine gun crew across the Nalimbiu that, after spotting and shooting some crocodiles, unsuccessfully "tried to skin one and tan his hide—quite a mess, really."[34]

In one of the Nalimbiu's branches, Jack and the Ninth's sentries were often on the lookout for a particularly large crocodile. After several near-misses, Bill Galloway recalled, Paxton and Prejean, two Louisianans, finally shot and killed the crocodile, which sank to the bottom of the creek. The pair's efforts to retrieve the dead animal with a twenty-foot boat hook borrowed from the Navy failed: the hook could not reach far enough. After several days, however, the crocodile's body floated to the surface. Soon after, it was hauled out by the Cajuns and staked out to several posts. The two were considering whether to dress the dead croc and either skin and preserve its hide or try to cook it when Lt. Commander Miles Krepela, the Ninth's Navy doctor, happened upon the scene. To their chagrin, the pair ended up digging a deep grave to bury the animal on Doc Krepela's orders. While an ample supply of wooden coffins was stacked near the battalion's sick bay, none were required for the crocodile or for its two frustrated hunters.[35]

The local insect life was plentiful: mosquitoes and flies were constant companions, carrying a host of tropical diseases. Local bodies of water were infested with leeches. Giant centipedes and millipedes, often reddish orange in color and up to several inches long, lurked in the rotten plant life littering the jungle floor and in the dark recesses of tents, holes, and personal gear. Their stings were highly painful and poisonous, but what could cause almost as much pain were the infections resulting from the tracks of their paths across bare skin, left by their myriad prickly legs. To Captain Reichner, between a centipede's bite and his own attack of malaria, "it was [the] centipede that put me out of action. As I remember, the critter was in one of my boots and resented my attempt to put it on. The bite hurt like hell, my leg swelled rapidly, and ultimately I spent a night or two in the battalion sick bay, which was just one more tent."

Because of the clouds of mosquitoes, there were malaria, dengue fever, and other jungle diseases with which to cope. In many respects, diseases were a greater hazard for the troops on Guadalcanal than combat wounds. Of the First Marine Division's 10,635 casualties on the Canal from August to December 10, 1942, only 1,472 were gunshot victims; malaria, on the other hand, claimed 5,749 men.[36] This fact is scarcely surprising considering that, even to this day, the Solomon Islands have the world's highest per capita incidence of malaria.[37] In the case of the Ninth Defense, this was absolutely true: malaria struck almost 90 percent of the battalion's personnel—some suffering from multiple relapses—at one time or another, including Jack.[38] Despite the introduction of Atabrine artificial quinine tablets, Jack had recurring bouts of malaria throughout his stay in the South Pacific. Beginning on Guadalcanal, he suffered more than once the raging fevers, sweats, and sudden, deep chills. Dengue fever, which made a man feel like he had acquired arthritis overnight, also plagued the Ninth's personnel.

Jack fared better than many other victims of these diseases, though, some of whom were so severely sickened or crippled that they had to be shipped stateside. One victim was Colonel Nimmer, who was temporarily relieved as the battalion's CO by Lt. Colonel William Scheyer, the battalion's exec, in February 1943 and again, permanently, in March.[39] Two of the Ninth's leathernecks, both members of Battery A, died on Guadalcanal from malignant tertian malaria. This was also called "blackwater fever" from the passing of black urine, a condition caused by a massive breakdown of red blood cells. It was frequently fatal unless properly and aggressively treated, and it inflicted more casualties on the Ninth than did the enemy on Guadalcanal.[40] Malaria was no disease to take lightly, nor was yellow jaundice, a severe case of which resulted in Captain Box being relieved of his Battery B command and being "surveyed out"—evacuated—to a hospital in the New Hebrides for a month.[41] His colleague, Captain Reichner, remembered that one of the two who died of blackwater fever "happened to have a brother on board that we were unable to send home. Because we really had no doctor, I spent most of my time administering morphine and other drugs designed to alleviate the fever. In short, no Corpsman; I was Battery Doctor and Corpsman as well."[42] Thinking of the wretched physical condition of so many of his men due to the rampant disease on the Canal, Reichner later summed up: "At one point, I don't think 'A' Battery could have fought its way out of a paper bag."[43] Despite official hectoring to take quinine and Atabrine, for many—Jack included—it was too little, too late.

The raging fevers caused by serious attacks of malaria frequently induced nightmarish visions and altered all sense of time and space. Biggie Slater provides this highly descriptive account, written in third person, of his own experience with malaria on the Canal:

> Biggie sank to the ground, barely conscious, fever blasting across his shoulder blades. Later, a litter-filled jeep jounced him to battalion sickbay—four large storage tents, cunningly squeezed in among the columns of a few close-gathered trees in a low bog. Biggie was carried to a cot and tucked in the mosquito netting. . . .
>
> Time altered for Biggie. There was a roaring in his ears, icy chills, scalding washes of pain from skull to tailbone. The corpsman took a blood sample and temperature. The man in the next cot raged and scrabbled at his [mosquito] net and groaned and tossed. Someone lifted Biggie's head and teased pills into his gorge. His neighbor cried out again. Night came suddenly—was it the second or the third?
>
> In the tent, the calls became clearer to Biggie. "Corpsman, water." "Corpsman, duck." "Corpsman." "Corpsman." Bedpans seemed not to exist in field hospitals; perhaps marines scorned such appliances. A slit trench was just outside his tent. Biggie . . . stumbled his way to the makeshift head, striking cots and tentpoles as he went. Suddenly, a nightmare: rushing figures tore at the air; one howled, in delirium. Biggie felt the struggle in the dark; four or five vague forms swirled weirdly, just touching him.
>
> Back on his cot, breathing hard, Biggie saw the group bent over his quieted neighbor. "What's the scoop; what's up?"
>
> "Stay in your sack—this guy just died."
>
> Biggie's feverish brain flared. *"Will that happen to me?"*
>
> It didn't.[44]

Likewise, on Gavutu, after having escaped these tropical illnesses longer than many of their buddies, Frank Yemma's battery mates began falling prey during the final construction work on the trail up Hill 181. "One by one we were just dropping like flies, and there was a tent and the guys were in there, just lying there. . . . Those corpsmen that [were in] there, was putting quinine into toilet paper. You had to swallow that. Try that sometime! But that's all they had at the time." Not that the improvised "quinine pills" actually saved Yemma from his own bout of malaria: "There were only five of us left walking down the road, and we're all bragging you know, being very macho about the whole thing. All the other guys had hit the deck—pooped out on us. I got my comeuppance because all of a sudden, I didn't feel good. I had a headache. And they all [said]: 'What's the matter, Frankie?' 'You don't feel good?' 'You're crapping out on us, huh?' Well, of course, I dropped; right down to the tent I went, and I didn't come out of there for five days."[45]

The average Marine had precious little in the way of medical supplies to combat wounds, fevers, and disease. Few effective treatments were available once one contracted malaria or dengue, and medical support was in such short supply that as a postwar historian noted, "attacks of malaria in the Pacific 'were given little more nursing care or rest than the average common cold at home.'"[46] The anti-infection "wonder drug," invented shortly before the war, was sulfanilamide powder. Small packets of sulfa drugs were carried in every man's first aid pouch and in every medical corpsman's bag, together with APC (aspirin with caffeine) tablets, red and blue Merthiolate (similar to Mercurochrome), and a field dressing. The vital anti-malarial drugs were quinine and Atabrine, the latter an artificially produced substitute for quinine. When supplies were available and before Atabrine was readily available, quinine was provided not as tablets but in powdered form. It was often taken by being shaken onto a tiny piece of toilet paper, rolled into a small, tight ball, and swallowed down with huge gulps of water (the latter, of course, courtesy of Pogiebait and his water purification plant), preferably before the toilet paper disintegrated and one got a mouthful of the bitter stuff.[47]

Like many Marines, Jack admitted that he had serious doubts as to the effectiveness of Atabrine, which in addition to turning the taker's skin slightly yellow (leading to the inescapable taunts and jeers and comparison of looking like a Japanese) was rumored to leave men impotent. Hence, close scrutiny was required by each battery's officers and NCOs to ensure that their reluctant troops took it. Sometimes the sergeants lurked with a supply of these tablets at the end of the chow line, actually waiting to pop an Atabrine tablet into each leatherneck's mouth. With almost all of the battalion's personnel contracting malaria during their stay on the Canal, what Atabrine was available had too little effect or was either not taken by the suspicious leathernecks or spit out by them the moment their leaders were no longer looking.[48]

Besides the difficult medical situation, sanitation in the Ninth's campsites was fairly crude. Hank Reichner vividly recalled the rough hygienic arrangements, including one toilet feature that provided certain members of the Navy with a convenient way to harass their rivals, the "gyrenes" of the Ninth:

> Thanks to our helmets we had a ready basin for shaving and washing. Thanks to the Seabees, we had a 55-gallon drum on a short tower to provide us with showers. We urinated into old powder tubes located around the battery area. These gave the place a somewhat distinctive odor and we moved them from time to time. We had two kinds of head (latrine)—the standard four-by-four hole in the ground, and the sea-going head built out over the water [and] flushed by the sea. These last were favorite targets for our destroyers, which would pass close by under forced draft and flush the heads and their occupants into the sea. One skipper's motto was "Run Like Hell, Here Comes Simpson." Instead of airplanes [*author's note*: often stenciled on a Navy warship to indicate its AA victories], he had latrines painted on the sides of the bridge to indicate the ship's conquests![49]

Personal hygiene was even worse on Gavutu, where the only potable water was collected in an open-air metal tank. As Frank Yemma recalled, this tank provided more than the detachment's drinking water—it was also a breeding ground for malaria-spreading mosquitoes: "You could look and see the mosquitoes, the larvae coming up out of the water.... And, so somebody got the idea—said it wouldn't hurt the water—to put a little film of oil on top of the water so [the] larvae couldn't breathe.... And that's what they did. Of course, it tasted lousy."[50]

The personal gear and arms of the Ninth's personnel were a varied assortment. At this stage of the war, many Marines, including Jack, were still armed with Great War-vintage Springfield rifles with old-style long bayonets. Some others had received semi-automatic M-1 Garands. For Marines like those in the Ninth, the bayonet would have been the worst kind of last-ditch weapon, but the bayonets proved useful for mundane tasks, like opening crates and cutting down the stiff and sharp-leafed blades of kunai grass. Officers generally carried .45 caliber Colt automatic pistols.

Several hundred of the Ninth's Marines had been issued Reising .45 caliber submachine guns. More frequently issued to Raiders and Marine paratroopers, the Reising resembled a sawed-off Thompson submachine gun (the "Tommy gun"). Despite their automatic firepower, many leathernecks found the Reising to be prone to jamming and rusting, and it was tricky to maintain.[51] It was a poorly balanced weapon to shoot—it tended to nose upwards when firing ("We often said that's why they were called 'Risings,'" David Slater lamented; "you'd fire ten rounds, and it'd be pointed at the sky"). As the Corps eventually acknowledged the Reising guns' defects, their users were grateful to exchange them in due course for more reliable firearms. Some Marines (including the 155mm Group's executive officer, Major Robert Hiatt) sported the drum-fed, Chicago-gangster-model of Tommy gun.[52] These were not easy to maintain, but they were far more efficient than Reisings. Many Marines tried to acquire other personal weapons—one old-timer, Gunner Brouse, carried a shotgun, while Jonesy, the radar chief, sported an old Colt six-shooter—and knives of all kinds and sizes were exceedingly common. Jack's favorite knife (probably because of the true ugliness of its looks, if not due to its practicality) was a World War I-style trench knife, complete with a built-in brass "knuckle-duster" handgrip with metal points protruding from the knuckles. Many other Marines preferred the more compact and versatile Marine-issue Ka-Bar knife.

The Ninth's experiences on Guadalcanal suggested to its leaders that it lacked sufficient firepower in light automatic weapons; the Reisings helped a little but could not overcome the battalion's lack of good light machine guns. By the end of that campaign and before its future battles in the Central Solomons, the unit negotiated with the Army's XIV Corps—to which the Ninth was attached—to acquire more light automatic weapons, including the Browning Automatic Rifle. Firing the same cartridge as the Springfield and Garand rifles but from a larger magazine, the BAR was more a type of light machine gun than a rifle. It was cumbersome and required a bipod for accurate shooting. Nevertheless, due to its firepower, reliability, and being more portable than the average machine gun, the BAR was a useful weapon to have at hand.

That the Ninth was dependent at this stage on the kindness of the Army for many of these vital weapons was due to shortfalls throughout I MAC for such types of guns and other critical supplies. Those BARs and .30 caliber light machine guns as were available were allocated by the Corps to its primary combat elements, the First and Second Marine Divisions.[53] Many of these logistical difficulties would plague the Ninth Defense's effectiveness well into 1943.

H&S Battery, 155mm Group, on Guadalcanal in spring 1943. Jack is on
the top row, far left; Jim Kruse is in the front row, fourth from right.
Major Stafford and group CO Lt. Col. Wright Taylor are seated
(with open collars) in the center. Author's collection.

In early February 1943, US forces linked up in the Cape Esperance area in
the island's far northwest and pushed toward Mount Austen in the island's
center. By February 9 the heaviest fighting on Guadalcanal wound down
as the Japanese withdrew what was left of their battered forces from Cape
Esperance and other pockets of resistance along the west coast.[54] Batteries A and B had not had a chance to engage enemy ships, and because of
the high altitude of most Japanese air attacks, Special Weapons' lighter
AA guns had not claimed any enemy planes. Still, the 90mm Group's batteries had downed twelve Japanese planes between January and the end
of the campaign, and the Ninth was beginning to earn its sobriquet, the
"Fighting Ninth."[55]

The Ninth's flak gunners got a massive workout on April 7, 1943, as

Admiral Yamamoto launched his last major air operation before his death eleven days later, amassing 350 warplanes to strike out at American airbases throughout the Solomons and New Guinea. On April 7, the Ninth's gunners scrambled to the cry of "Condition *very* Red!" as sixty-seven Aichi D3A1 "Val" dive bombers and 110 Zero fighters hit the Canal. The raiders sank several Allied ships, including a US destroyer, but lost heavily in the process: although American pilots and gunners claimed over one hundred victims, the true number was more like thirty-nine Japanese planes destroyed.[56] Despite their mounting losses of aircraft, the Japanese persisted, launching a last major daytime raid of 120 planes on June 16. Only thirteen of these escaped.[57]

With unbridled pleasure, Jack and his friends watched and cheered as their AA guns and Navy, Army, and Marine fighters chopped up the attackers. Some American planes were always easily recognizable, even in the wildest dogfight: the Army Air Forces' P-38 Lightning with its twin-boomed tail, the Navy's and Marines' tubby little F4F Wildcat, and after February 1943, the Marines' new F4U-1 Corsair with its seagull-like wings, all of which were being stationed in increasing numbers at Henderson Field. Beginning in March 1943, several squadrons of B-25 Mitchell medium bombers and B-24 Liberator heavy bombers of the Thirteenth Air Force joined the growing air presence on Guadalcanal and were based next to the Ninth at Carney Field. Brought in to help in the bombing of Rabaul, the Japanese headquarters and logistics center located some 565 miles northwest of the Canal, the twin-engined Mitchells and the hulking, four-engined Liberators provided an illicit opportunity for several Special Weapons machine gunners to hone their skills as aerial gunners, as they secretly joined the Army Air Force crews on several bombing missions in the Solomons area. Had they been caught doing so by their officers, they would hardly have been heroes, but several succeeded in making some such flights.[58]

A V-Mail Letter Home from Guadalcanal

PFC Jack H. McCall
Batt. B, 155mm GP.
9th Def. Bn., F.M.F.
c/o Fleet P.O.
San Francisco, Cal.

Mr. & Mrs. A. G. McCall
Rt. #1
Franklin, Tenn.
May 9, '43

Dearest Family,

Have been awfully busy lately and have neglected my writing some. Raining to beat the band here and I've been trying to keep my tent intact.[59] I hope all of you are well. I'm fine, still fighting the darned mosquitoes though. I suppose by now Al has already been home? Have you been hearing from Bob alright lately? I hope he's well. They might even hit the States soon, the "lucky stiff." Has Reams[60] ever left Cal.? I wish I could see some of the fellows. Without a doubt some are around here close.

So, Dad's in 4B.[61] Ha. Do you think you could fix a small box with some candy bars and stationery? Gives a guy something to look forward to. Looks like I've just run out of space so will close.

Much love,

Jack

Once again Pogiebait's lifetime love of sweets manifested itself in this V-mail[62] letter home. Packages from home were highly treasured by all and often shared by the recipients. Woe betide the unfortunate Marine who received a package from home only to squirrel it away and have his buddies learn of the fact! Even if moldy or stale when it arrived (which was often the case, as it may have been three or four months in transit), food from home was treasured, precisely because it was from home, and it was a reminder that another, safer world existed somewhere. In short, food parcels from home served as much as a kind of sentimental reality check for the recipients as it did as sustenance, and as a reminder of all of the things they missed about home—clean sheets, a solid roof over one's head, "civvie" clothes, women. Besides the emotional pull, this partly alleviated both the scarcity and the blandness of combat food when field kitchens were not available, as was often the case on the Canal.

Due to supply shortages, the First Marine Division's and I MAC's hungry leathernecks often resorted to eating captured Japanese supplies, particularly rice, during much of their four-month ordeal before the Ninth's arrival in early December. By then the Marines were no longer surviving on the sometimes-weevilly rice (there were bitter jokes about the wormy rice having more protein than other available foodstuffs) and Spam, but after the initial joy of receiving new US-made fare, the novelty of the new rations wore off. Fresh food of any sort was a rarity, as the refrigeration and shipping space it required were scarce.[63]

Most frequently found in the Pacific were K rations, containing ham and eggs (which often acquired a disagreeable olive-greenish hue after being canned for a length of time), canned cheese—the usual lunch selection—or Spam or hash, crackers, instant coffee, candy, cigarettes, toilet paper, and chewing gum. Another variety, less available in the Pacific until later in the war, was the C ration, consisting of a cardboard box holding two cans. One can was filled with crackers, powdered coffee or tea, candy, toilet paper, various condiments, and four cigarettes (preferably Lucky Strikes or Camels, but often of the widely deemed inferior Chelsea brand), and the other was filled with canned food like hash, stew, and the ubiquitous Spam. Another innovation, different from the small chocolate bars found in K rations or C rations, was the Ration D bar. Originally intended as emergency fare if troops were cut off from food supplies or on patrol, D rations appeared at first blush to be large and thick chocolate bars. Because these had been specially hardened to keep from melting—some claimed this was done with paraffin—vitamin-reinforced, D rations tasted far different from any Hershey bar Jack had ever eaten. Rounding out the bill of fare were bulky "ten-in-one" rations, similar to the rations used onboard the *Kenmore*. These may have been the pick of the litter in terms of quantity as well as quality, since (depending on the need) this ration was ostensibly intended to feed either one man for ten days or ten men for one day and contained a wider selection of foodstuffs.[64]

Because of both the shortage and the boringness of foodstuffs on the Canal, the Ninth's Marines actively scrounged for anything edible. Captain Box's section of Battery B on Gavutu had one rare treat—fresh seafood— once. Frank Yemma recalled, "Some of the guys had built a raft. And this big blue marlin was chasing bait coming in. It was on the shoals, and the guys out on the raft happened to see this big blue marlin, so [they] fired all their weapons that they could at it and, sure enough, they got the fish [and] we brought it over to our makeshift galley. . . . [So] needless to say, we had fish for a few days."[65]

Shortage of food was much worse than just a chronic difficulty for the Japanese, who referred to Guadalcanal as "Starvation Island." The Japanese lack of rations was directly traceable to the successful interdiction of their logistics lifelines to the outside world, which had been effectively severed by late 1942. One Japanese officer noted: "It is said if you lose your appetite, it is the end." Another chronicled the final life expectancies of his starving and disease-riddled troops with grimly calibrated precision on the following scale:

> *Those who can stand:* Thirty days;
> *Those who can sit up:* Three weeks;
> *Those who cannot sit up:* One week;
> *Those who can only urinate lying down:* Three days;
> *Those who have stopped speaking:* Two days;
> *Those who have stopped blinking:* Tomorrow.[66]

Years after the war, Jack read *Into the Valley*, John Hersey's report of his combat patrol with a First Marine Division infantry company on the Canal. While he thought much of Hersey's saga was "pretty tame stuff" in comparison with the reality—most notably, the relative softness of language the author attributed to the Marines—Jack noted Hersey's account of a group of Marines talking longingly—not about women, alcohol, politics, or sports—but about *food*, and what would be the first thing they would eat when they got home. "Jesus, what I'd give for a piece of blueberry pie!" "Personally I prefer mince," the dialogue begins.[67]

Jack testified that there was more than a shade of truth to that discussion, particularly given the direness of the supply system on Guadalcanal. "It was all you thought about, for weeks on end," he once recalled. In his few leisure moments, Jack would dream of food and going home. He would develop his own schemes of what would be the first food *he* would eat when he got home—and, as much as it was a favorite dessert, it would not be pie, but something decidedly as unmilitary as could be, as will be seen.

In addition to the seemingly endless search for food, another pastime—what could charitably be called "scrounging"—quickly assumed its role in the life of Jack and his fellow enlisted men on Guadalcanal, even though it was most definitely frowned upon by Colonel Nimmer and his staff. Part of this arose from necessity, particularly as the supply system on the Canal seemed at best to be in shambles. With major shortages of even basic field equipment, and when such equipment was available, finding that it was often almost obsolete gear, the Ninth's Marines were desperate for anything. Partly, too, this arose from competitiveness and from the average leatherneck's quest to do something, anything, to discomfit his swabby and dogface rivals. Faced with the arrival of fresh Army and Navy units supplied with the latest equipment later in the campaign, Jack and many of his buddies often took to making midnight forays to obtain from their non-Marine neighbors whatever could be "liberated." As expected, some of these raids brought out the entrepreneurial spirit in the leathernecks, as Frank Chadwick recounted.

When confronted with one well-stocked, but also well-guarded, beach-side Army supply dump, several 155mm Group Marines found a nearby bell. Guessing (as it turned out, correctly) that it was probably set up as an impromptu air raid alert device, they began ringing a nearby bell loudly, and with loud screams of *"Condition Red!"* they convinced all onlookers that an air raid was imminent. As the soldiers ran into the jungle to seek cover, the Marines grabbed as many crates as they could carry. Once back in camp, they were disappointed to find that the crates contained Army-issue rubberized boots, of little worth for tropical climates because of their tendency to cause feet to sweat and thus to worsen athlete's foot, tropical sores, and jungle rot. At least the wooden crates were themselves put to good use to make floorboards for tents.

A similar foraging opportunity was provided by the arrival of another Army unit to the Canal. As David Slater related:

One day in March '43, when we spotted a convoy approaching Koli Point, our scouts learned it was an Army unit . . . coming ashore right in our area. We all went down to the beach [and] looked with incredulity as they landed and immediately started to string barbed wire *behind us* within the plantation. They also put ashore large stocks of all sorts of gear which our people immediately dipped into, usually, if challenged, claiming they had been *ordered* to transport the stuff to Army depots! I wandered about until I spotted a marvelous inner-spring mattress which I appropriated and began to lug back to the 90 H&S [Battery's] ambulance (I intended to endear myself to Captain Tracy by presenting him with this treasure). Unfortunately, I was almost immediately challenged by an Army officer who asked this raggedy-ass Marine what the hell he was doing with the General's mattress. My explanation, proving unsatisfactory, brought about the immediate command, "Drop it!" However, the battalion [still] did quite well.[68]

Besides scrounging, buying and trading Japanese equipment and supplies provided cottage industries in and of themselves, beginning almost from the day the battalion landed on Koli Point. So did the clandestine manufacture of "Japanese flags" on Guadalcanal. Until curbed (supposedly by personal directive of Army Maj. General Alexander Patch, Vandegrift's successor as the island-wide commanding general on the Canal), this hobby involved taking squares of white silk from abandoned parachutes and using a tincture of red Merthiolate to dye Rising Sun "meatballs" onto the silk. The resulting "Jap flags" were then sold by the Ninth's budding entrepreneurs to gullible Army and Navy personnel or were traded in exchange for hooch or other scarce goodies. Chadwick recalled derisively, "By the end of February or early March, there were more Jap battle flags on the Canal than there were Japs."[69]

Incensed, General Patch's headquarters supposedly announced that any Marine caught in this activity would receive a general court-martial from him personally. Suspecting that, as he was an Army commander, General Patch's threat might not get the attention it deserved, Colonel Nimmer simply said that he, too, expected the trade would stop and added his own promise of a court-martial to any violators. This effectively brought the fake-flag business to a close. As will be seen, though, all the entrepreneurial skills learned on Guadalcanal would stick with Jack and his buddies through the Ninth's successive campaigns.

The Ninth's Next Destination?

Total and complete defeat of Japanese forces on Guadalcanal effected. . . .
Am happy to report this kind of compliance with your orders . . .
because Tokyo Express no longer has terminus on Guadalcanal.

—GENERAL PATCH REPORTING TO ADMIRAL HALSEY,
FEBRUARY 9, 1943[70]—

As the Guadalcanal campaign wound down, the food, pogey bait, and cigarette situation improved greatly. For many months, the Ninth's Marines had counted themselves lucky when they had two cold meals a day, which was usually Spam, rice or K rations, or sometimes orange marmalade (the latter with such eventual frequency that Jack "swore off of orange marmalade for life"). By one estimate, during the campaign, the Ninth's leathernecks ate twice a day about 20 percent of the time and once daily about 70 percent of the time; hence, no food was available for perhaps a tenth of the time. This nutritional regimen was hardly enough to support an active twenty-year-old male in normal times, much less so for one suffering from several tropical diseases and sometimes working fifteen- to twenty-hour days in a humid jungle climate. The only readily available drink was water, usually the iodine-flavored stuff from Pogiebait's water purification shop on the Nalimbiu. This water was warm when poured in after purification, and only got warmer in aluminum canteens. On this sparse and bland diet, coupled with his malaria, Jack lost more weight during his stay on the Canal and was down to 120 pounds (he had weighed about 170 when he had enlisted). By campaign's end, the food situation was moderately better, with fewer meals of rice, powdered eggs, or canned spinach and kraut and more fresh meat. "We had graduated into frozen mutton from New Zealand, Spam and occasional fresh food," Captain Reichner recollected; "I lost a lot of weight, as did most of my Battery. It was years before I could eat mutton or Spam again."[71]

By mid-June, Army units were taking over the Ninth's AA and coast-defense positions. The Army artillerymen's transition was accompanied by the frequent jeers of the leathernecks, who made cracks—not intended humorously—about "Dugout Doug of the Philippines." While Marines generally took a patronizing attitude toward the Army's dogfaces anyway, many (if not all) Guadalcanal Marines had developed an abiding dislike of General MacArthur, believing him personally responsible for abandoning them on the island for so many months without resupply or Army relief. Whenever he was engaged long after the war in an argument over MacArthur's relative merits as a commander, however, Jack often quoted a rhyme that was a special Marine favorite: *"With the help of God and a few Marines/MacArthur retook the Philippines."*[72]

The replacement of the Ninth Defense by fresh Army units, however, could mean one thing: the Ninth would be on the move again. The next set of islands above Guadalcanal was the Central Solomons group, where intelligence since November 1942 had shown the Japanese rapidly building a large airstrip at Munda Point on the island of New Georgia, along with various supporting positions on nearby islands. When completed, this airfield was expected to support several hundred aircraft. Only 170 miles west-northwest of Guadalcanal, the Munda airfield would help the Japanese recapture local air superiority lost when Henderson Field was taken and provide a checkmate to the Allies' possible moves further into the Solomons. As part of Operation CARTWHEEL, a series of Allied offensives designed to eliminate Rabaul, the massive Japanese air, naval and logistics bastion on New Britain, the Commander, South Pacific Area (ComSoPac), Rear Admiral William Halsey, won approval to assault New Georgia, both to seize Munda Field before it became a real menace to Guadalcanal and also to provide a springboard for the reduction and cutting-off of Rabaul and its substantial garrison.[73]

The battalion officially stood down from its defensive mission on June 17, 1943 and began preparing for its next mission. An equipment upgrade was underway as the Ninth's higher command shifted from the First Marine Division to I MAC and then again from I MAC to the Army's XIV Corps.[74] Batteries A and B exchanged their old GPFs for the new-model M-1 155mm fieldpieces, known ubiquitously throughout the US military as the "Long Tom." In keeping with the Marines' penchant for nicknaming everything, these too acquired nicknames. Suspecting the imminent start of a new campaign with the arrival of the new equipment, one Battery A member asked, "Where do you think we'll be taking these guns?" Someone blurted out in response: "Who knows?" Translated into Spanish by Pfc. Gustavo ("Chili Bean") Cervantes, Battery A's sole Hispanic member, this was emblazoned on the barrel of the battery's Gun 3, *Quien Sabe*, and the TD-9 tractor

Quien Sabe, a Battery A 155mm M-1 or "Long Tom," is heaved into position by its gun crew on Rendova, June 30, 1943. Official US Marine Corps photo, courtesy of Col. (Ret'd) William T. Box.

assigned to move it was named in turn, as if in answer, *Quien Cuida*—"Who Cares?" Sensing that his men were on to something good for morale, Captain Reichner encouraged them to name the other three guns. These were dubbed *Sudden Death* (later renamed *Oscar* in memory of Oscar King, one of the men who had died of malaria); *Pistol Pete*, after a Walt Disney character; and *Semper Fidelis*.[75]

As their duties in the New Georgia operation required a major change in the 155mm Group's primary mission from seacoast defense to heavy field artillery work, the group's gun crews received accelerated training in field artillery tactics and gunnery. After completing this difficult training in near-record time—just twenty-two days—the Group's new CO, Lt. Colonel Archie O'Neil, received a personal commendation from Admiral Halsey. Described by Lieutenant Chris Donner as a "slight, dapper individual with flat gray hair parted at the side, a small moustache and a very yellow caste to his skin" (perhaps from too much Atabrine), and with a slight accent betraying his West Virginia roots, O'Neil looked older than his thirty-eight years.[76]

The Tank Platoon had joined up with the rest of the Ninth on Guadalcanal some months earlier, and its training was likewise accelerated. Many of the Ninth's men finally traded in their old Springfields for new semiautomatic Garands (which the old salts—Jack included—never quite got used to, preferring the Springfield's ease of maintenance and reliability in all conditions, even if the Springfield was slower to fire) or the smaller M1 carbines with which, as a non-infantry unit, the Ninth would be largely armed by 1944. The 90mm Group traded in its well-used ordnance to the Army's Seventieth Coast Artillery Battalion in exchange for brand-new 90mm guns with power-operated rammers, remote-control features, and better mobility. Manually operated 20mm guns were remounted in pairs on power-operated carriages, making their ability to traverse and elevate on targets much faster and more efficient.[77] Additional machine guns and BARs were issued liberally; three LVT-1 "Alligator" tracked amphibious cargo vehicles named *Gladys*, *Frances*, and *Tootsie*[78] were issued to the battalion, and another nine LVTs were lent to the unit by the Third Marine Division.[79]

Such improvements, however, did not come cheaply; in exchange for a supply of additional weapons and parts, the new battalion CO, Lt. Colonel Scheyer, traded to the Army all the battalion's movies, PX supplies, and other creature comforts not deemed absolutely essential for combat. Although technically assigned under the command of the Army's XIV Corps for the upcoming operation, "Wild Bill" Scheyer also shrewdly took ad-

Lt. Col. William J. Scheyer, shown here as a colonel in April 1945. Official US Marine Corps photo, Quantico, Virginia.

vantage of doctrinal differences in Army and Marine Corps logistics to procure additional ammunition. His canniness was recognized by an official Army historian: "Loading orders specified three units of fire were to be carried. Since an Army unit of fire for the 90mm guns was 125 rounds and a Marine unit of fire, 300 rounds, [the Ninth] interpreted the orders to mean Marine Corps units of fire and carried the extra ammunition."[80]

With increases in personnel, fifty-three officers, eight warrant officers, 1,371 enlisted Marines, three navy officers, and twenty-four navy enlisted (the Navy personnel serving as "corpsmen," or medics of the Marines) comprised the Ninth by the end of June 1943.[81] To the horror of the all-volunteer old salts, an overload of Army draftees and temporary shortages in volunteers at home required the Marines to begin taking conscripts seconded to the Corps, so more than a few of the new bodies joining the battalion were draftees.[82] In addition, several members of the Tenth Defense Battalion—frustrated by that sister unit's lack of action and its officers' and NCOs' pettifogging spit-and-polish discipline, even in a war zone—applied for and received transfers to the Ninth. Several of these men, among them Joe Pratl and Jack Sorensen, joined Battery A just in time for the next offensive. Pratl recalled his welcome to the Ninth: "The transition for us didn't seem to be a big deal. We were moving so much and working so hard, this change didn't seem so big. The men of the 9th also didn't seem too disturbed as they now put out the welcome mat. Seemed like the 9th had the same chow [as Pratl's old battalion] but their drinks were better, like 190 and grapefruit juice."[83]

When Private Pratl asked where he could find Battery A's CO so he could report in, he was told, "Oh, he's over there." Seeing only a young man clad in shorts, Pratl asked again, "Over where?" "Like I said, he's *over there!*" came the insistent response and gesturing finger. Pratl and several other new arrivals rushed over to meet the skipper, and they passed a tent where a

Battery A's lieutenant Christopher S. Donner is at
the far topmost right corner; standing directly in
front of him is his CO, Captain Henry H. Reichner Jr.
Courtesy of Christopher S. Donner.

Battery A Marine appeared to be drinking a bottle of hooch. Pratl flinched, knowing the blistering response that would have been forthcoming from any Tenth Defense officer. To his amazement, when the drinker said, "Care for a drink, sir?" and held out the bottle, Captain Reichner simply looked at the proffering arm and nonchalantly said, "No, thanks." "He was a no-nonsense and very down-to-earth skipper," Pratl remembered, and Captain Reichner's demeanor immediately won him and his fellow Tenth Defense transferees over.

New officers also joined the battalion. One of these, Lieutenant Chris Donner, recalled his first meeting with Colonel Scheyer and the colonel's tip-off that "something big" was imminent: "He told us that we, as artillerymen, were to have a great opportunity. There was soon to be a push against Munda. We would set our 155's on an island across the bay and hammer the airfield. What could be sweeter? We would be expected to show real leadership as befitted Marine officers."[84]

While not too heavily bloodied by its campaign on Guadalcanal, the hardships the Ninth endured there would serve its personnel well in the months to come. The Ninth's veterans could not recall any comparable Army or Marine unit that had begun such a critical campaign without at least test-firing *some*, if not all, of its artillery pieces. At last the battalion had gotten to test its guns in anger and to train its artillery crews by live-firing in combat, and they had survived and grown in experience with this first test. Wherever the Ninth Defense was going next, it would need all its new weapons, supplies, and men—and more. The next campaign, less well known today than the battle for Guadalcanal, would place Jack McCall and the Fighting Ninth in much more direct danger than he and his buddies had been in previously.

27 June 1943, War Diary of the Ninth Defense Battalion:

> Loading commenced aboard ships assigned to take the 9th Defense Battalion to the scene of the coming operation.[85]

FOUR

A Forgotten Victory:
The Rendova/New Georgia Campaign

June 30, 1943 brought us to another move, the invasion of Rendova and Munda
islands in the New Georgia group and attached to the Army's XIV Corps and 43rd
Army Division. July 2nd, our landing docks, gasoline, and ammunition dumps went
up in smoke as a large Japanese air strike took us by surprise. We lost several men
and had quite a few weapons destroyed. Apparently, this raid was so successful for
them, they planned another for the 4th, which was not to be. Our 90MMs destroyed
twelve bombers and one fighter in less than three minutes with only 88 rounds.
Wa-hoos, fist shakings and screams of delight were heard up and down the coast.

Our 155's shelled both day and night the Munda air field and surrounding
Jap forces, doing great destruction. I may mention also that the island
of Rendova was the haven for a group of PT boats, one commander
of which became a U.S. President, John Kennedy.

After Munda, we secured our 90's, set up positions around the field and on a couple
of smaller islands. Our 155's were located in the Piru plantation and shelled the
island of Kolombangara. One of the Japanese artillery pieces we dubbed
"Pistol Pete," for he would open fire on us every afternoon about dusk, and our
"chow time"; as soon as we returned the fire he would be quiet until the next
afternoon, and we would have cold chow. Soon afterward, an aerial spotter
sighted him and we made short order of him. No more cold chow!

—JACK H. MCCALL, SR.—

No one joked; no one yacked; no one bitched. They just hacked it.

—MARINE COMBAT CORRESPONDENT SAMUEL E. STAVISKY,
ACCOMPANYING THE NINTH ON RENDOVA[1]—

Operation TOENAILS, the New Georgia campaign, was in the planning
stages before the end of the battle for Guadalcanal. It would be an all-
arms effort, combining Navy, Marine, and Army units in a multi-stage
operation to seize New Georgia and its neighboring islands. While one

pre-invasion estimate pegged the number of Munda defenders at four thousand troops, twice that number actually held the area.[2] With approximately fifteen thousand Japanese Army and Special Naval Landing Force (in Japanese, *rikusentai*)[3] troops in the entire New Georgia island group, not counting air units beginning to move in to the Munda airfield—the Japanese had some four hundred aircraft based at Rabaul, within striking range of New Georgia[4]—the US planners decided that several landings would be made on and around New Georgia nearly simultaneously.

A key part of the operation involved seizing Rendova Island, just south of New Georgia, and several other small, adjacent islands for artillery and AA emplacements and PT boat anchorages. Being only eight miles southeast from Munda Point, Rendova's capture would put much of New Georgia—especially the Munda airfield—within range of the Ninth's 155s. With some of the most powerful and mobile heavy artillery assets now available in the South Pacific area, the men of the Ninth Defense learned that their unit was selected to play a crucial role in the campaign.[5]

In recognition of the battalion's wide range of capabilities, the Ninth's orders for the initial phase of the upcoming operation combined both the original defensive roles of a defense battalion with some novel offensive tasks for such a unit. The Ninth was ordered to assist in the capture and occupation of Rendova Island; to provide all-around AA defense to US troops on the island; to bombard Japanese installations and defenses on New Georgia, particularly the Munda Point area and its airfield; to prepare to defend Rendova against attack by hostile vessels; and to support infantry operations on New Georgia with its Tank Platoon.[6] The 155mm Group, in particular, had a critical mission in Operation TOENAILS because of the shorter range of the Army infantry divisions' 75mm guns and 105mm and old-style 155mm howitzers. These guns' shorter ranges required them to be landed on Bau, Kokorana, and Roviana, tiny islets within a few miles of Munda Field, to give them any chance of striking Japanese targets. Once landed, however, it became apparent that the firing tables for these guns had been miscalculated and that few, if any, were emplaced in positions from which they could fire on the Japanese. Thus, the Ninth's Long Toms would be expected to bear the brunt of the heavy artillery support in the upcoming campaign.[7]

Shortly before leaving Guadalcanal, Colonel Scheyer issued his orders of the day on the conduct of the upcoming campaign, concluding with some pumped-up motivational rhetoric: "If any of you have the idea that the Japs are super-men, get it out of your heads. They are fifth raters who

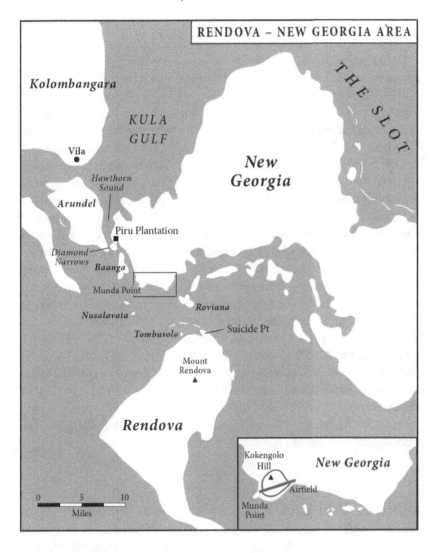

have a mistaken notion that they must die for their Emperor and our job is to help them do just that as fast as we possibly can."[8] Joe Pratl, however, remembered a different form of motivation coming from the 155mm Group's new CO, Lt. Colonel Archie O'Neil, whose "Godspeed address was, in fact, a reaming-out because, like all boys, if you don't keep 'em busy, somebody's going to plan a party"—which, in fact, Battery A did, featuring ample quantities of 190-proof alcohol. Not surprisingly, Colonel O'Neil was furious: "We caught hell," Pratl recalled sheepishly.[9] To top things off, a batch of cans of medical alcohol disappeared, and for some reason, the 155mm Group fell under suspicion, with Battery A's men being the prime suspects. As Hank Reichner recalled: "I issued a strong warning to the effect that I did not expect to have any of the missing cans found in our battery area. Apparently, one was found at B Battery, which then bore the brunt of anger and suspicion by our superiors although they, along with Waldo 'The Beast' Wells, B Battery commander, expressed strong doubts about A Battery." Despite all inquiries, the missing cans were not found before the battalion's departure, leaving Captain Reichner, his junior officers and senior sergeants to wonder if, when, and how they would resurface.

Before embarkation, there was still time for skylarking and some brief comic relief. Jack's Boot Camp pal, Jim Kruse, who served as a clerk on the headquarters staff of the 155mm Group, recalled daring one of their buddies, George Confer, an H&S Battery field music (i.e., a bugler), to play "Reveille" while Colonel Scheyer conducted a final battalion-wide formation on Guadalcanal. After much cajoling, Confer agreed to take the bet. As the battalion formed up, the bugler stepped out of formation unheralded and began playing a jazzed-up and syncopated version of "Reveille" with all of his might. The field music soon froze, however, as Colonel Scheyer and his staff stared him down, and he trembled nervously as the CO asked him to step forward. As the terrified bugler saluted the colonel in front of the entire formation, Colonel Scheyer announced, eyeball-to-eyeball, that he had only one thing to say to Confer: "Don't *ever* do that again!"[10] Enough said; the intrepid field music got the point.

At about the same time that a unit of crack Marine Raiders made their first, stealthy landings on New Georgia, the battalion boarded the heavily camouflaged attack cargo ships USS *Libra* and USS *Algorab* off Guadalcanal late on the afternoon of June 29, 1943. The unit's guns, radar and rangefinders, vehicles, and other heavy equipment were loaded separately aboard four green-camouflaged Landing Ships, Tank (LSTs).[11] After laboring to stow the battery's heavy gear on the LSTs, Jack and others in H&S Battery and the battalion's staff boarded another transport, the USS *McCawley*, known far and wide as the "Wacky Mac." It was also the radar-equipped flagship of the Navy task force commander, Rear Admiral Richmond Kelly Turner. Soon to be familiar to a generation of American soldiers, Marines, and sailors

During rehearsals for the Rendova-New Georgia landings, troops climb
down cargo nets hung over the side of the USS *McCawley,* known as the
"Wacky Mac," to board LCVP landing craft at Nouméa, New Caledonia,
June 14, 1943. Jack McCall sailed to Rendova aboard this vessel.
Official US Navy photograph, file number 80-G-254933.

in both the European and Pacific theaters, the LSTs would receive their
combat baptism in the Rendova landings.[12] Their bulk and slow speed inspired some wags to claim that "LST" actually stood for "*Long Slow Target.*"

The Ninth was slated to land in three echelons, the idea being to get most
of the personnel together with light AA weapons and .50 caliber machine
guns ashore as quickly as possible to set up a defensive perimeter. Next,
half of the 90mm and 155mm guns would arrive in the second echelon, and
the remaining men, vehicles, and guns would follow soon thereafter on the
other "Green Dragon" LSTs after positions had been found and established

for them. Many of the Special Weapons Group's 20mm and 40mm guns were set up on the LSTs' decks to augment the little ships' own defensive firepower.[13] The invasion convoy's voyage from Guadalcanal to Rendova was only about 175 miles, but the transport fleet sailed in complete blackout, escorted by destroyers and several cruisers, while lookouts were posted to keep watch for Japanese aircraft, submarines, and warships.

After their experiences on Guadalcanal and in the lead-up to boarding the transports, tensions were running high among the men, and reports that Japanese air attacks were expected at any minute heightened the expectant atmosphere. Still, there were many who looked forward to some action. As Battery A's commander, Hank Reichner, noted: "Our biggest morale problem on Guadalcanal had nothing to do with meager and lousy food, the weather or lack of mail. Simply stated, we were anxious for a real fight with the enemy. Many of 'A' Battery's Marines pled with me [during the Guadalcanal campaign] for a transfer to a Marine infantry unit." With some of its men dubbing themselves the "lost battalion" due to their lack of action on the Canal,[14] the thrill-seekers among the Ninth's leathernecks were about to get their wish. As Colonel Scheyer noted: "The prospect of closing with the enemy was all that was needed to supply morale."[15]

The voyage to New Georgia created sensations different from those the men felt during the *Kenmore*'s approach off Guadalcanal because most of the men thought that they now had a clearer degree of awareness as to what they would face upon landing. Thus, the inklings of what was to come either heightened or lessened one's doubts and fears, depending on each individual's makeup. For most, a great worry was that of letting one's buddies down, and personal fear was suppressed as best as possible and kept to oneself. Battery B's Frank Yemma recalled having something of a panic attack as he heard depth charges going off around his LST during a submarine alert en route to Rendova: "I was down below deck and, all of a sudden, these depth charges started going off, and it just shook the hell out of that LST. Well, I tell you, I went up the gangway, and there was some sailor who was just ready to batten down the door as I was going up, and I tell you . . . I just pushed my foot right against that door because he was ready to close it. And I hit him with the door, and I knocked him out, cold as a cucumber, but I said 'They're not going to lock me down below.' I was going to get out on deck in case we got hit! But anyway, he survived the hit; [the sailor] just was stunned."[16]

For others, pre-invasion fear was much worse than a mere case of the jitters, with one Marine's fear or nightmares apparently leading to him becoming the Ninth's first casualty of the campaign well before the convoy reached Rendova. Frank Chadwick remembered, "We were on a ship going to Rendova.... There was a guy sitting on gun watch. We'd been through some air raids. It was nighttime. He stood up and said, 'I've had enough of this,' and he dove overboard and was gone. We didn't even stop."[17] In a memoir written shortly after the war's end, Lieutenant Chris Donner vividly recalled the same incident (which occurred aboard his LST) and the hubbub that followed:

> It rained that night, June 30th. I slept fitfully until near 2:00 a.m., when I dressed and reported to the bridge for watch. There was some excitement among the personnel topside. Ten minutes before my arrival, one of our radar operators for the 9th Defense, a boy who had been in my Replacement Company, had jumped overboard. He was one of those sleeping on deck.... Suddenly the boy jumped up from his cot and fell on the wet deck. He rose again and vanished over the guard wire into the dark ocean. The Skipper, who had been summoned to the bridge, figured that the unfortunate lad must have been caught by the screw, for on an L.S.T. there is a propeller near each side of the blunt stern.[18]

For most Marines, suicide or self-inflicted wounds were simply not serious options. No matter how truly scared one might be, each man's ability to "hang in and take it" was regarded as a matter of pride and self-respect. The highest contempt of Marines was reserved for cowards and "goldbricks," and no Marine wanted his buddies to contemplate that he might fall into one of those despised categories. When one's own personal survival—not to mention the survival of one's squad or platoon mates, or the battery or battalion as a whole—was at stake, teamwork and trust were critical commodities. Practically speaking, too, there was just nowhere to run in the Pacific if one was scared or sought to avoid duty—no rear areas, no civilian homes or farms in which to hide, unlike the European environment—and the result would mean ostracism, or much worse, from a host of pissed-off young Marines.

In the case of the Ninth's officers, they, too, had ample reasons to feel tense in addition to the concerns of combat. As one of only two Marine units to participate in the initial phase of Operation TOENAILS—the other being the crack First Marine Raider Regiment—the Ninth Defense was very much under the scrutiny of I MAC's and the Fleet Marine Force-Pacific's leadership. An I MAC senior officer, Lt. Colonel Edward H. Forney,[19] was accompanying the Ninth, serving both as a field artillery adviser to Colonel Scheyer and as General Vandegrift's official observer of the battalion's performance. Another senior observer was Colonel John W. Thomason, a famous Marine veteran of World War I who was best known for his writings and illustrations of trench life in that war, representing the FMF-Pacific's headquarters. Accompanying the Army's Forty-Third Infantry Division and slated to land beside the Ninth on Rendova was the Second Marine Division's observer for the operation, Lt. Colonel David M. Shoup. Though little known to many outside the battalion's senior leadership, Colonel Shoup would become very well known throughout the Corps in only five more months, and he would enter the pantheon of American military heroes as the intrepid CO of the Second Marines on Tarawa.[20] Much was at stake in this operation besides the taking of Munda Field; Operation TOE-NAILS would be a test of inter-service cooperation, as well as for Marine amphibious planners and others backing the defense battalion concept as to how well these "defensive warfare" units could be turned to offensive tasks.

Rain squalls and fog shrouded the hulk of Rendova Mountain as a group of Navy cruisers and destroyers began a brief but savage bombardment of Rendova very early on the morning of Wednesday, June 30, 1943.[21] As the phosphorescent tracer shells of the bombardment faded away, the landing parties prepared to board the landing craft for the assault. The previous night's traditional send-off dinner aboard the LSTs—pork chops, with plenty enough for seconds[22]—had long been digested, and the men nervously munched on whatever rations they had available as they waited to board. Already sweating profusely in the humid early morning air and with some fighting nausea, each battery's officers and NCOs went up and down the ranks, checking the serviceability of their platoon members' equipment and asking them whether or not they had contraband. Diaries and personal journals were strictly forbidden (although some Marines kept them in secret) for fear that, if captured, these might provide Japanese intelligence with useful information—not necessarily from a purely military standpoint, but enough to get an idea of morale in the unit and on the home front, and possibly enough to give the detested "Tokyo Rose" extra fodder for her radio shows.[23]

Each battery's cadre shook down the enlisted Marines for Japanese souvenirs carried along from the Canal. Scuttlebutt had made the rounds as to what the Japanese did to Marines and GIs who were captured with Japanese letters, photos, flags, or souvenirs on their persons, and it did not take much hectoring by the junior officers or NCOs to make the point. When Jack's turn came on the deck of the *McCawley*, out on the transport's deck went most of the artifacts he had scrounged or traded on the Canal: parts of a Japanese officer's Nambu pistol, some items of Japanese insignia, and—worst of all—his prized trench knife with the built-in brass knuckles. "What the hell do you think the Japs will do to you if they catch you with that thing, Pogiebait?" Not much imagination was required for Jack to get a pretty good mental picture of the consequences, and he did not like it. Over the side of the Wacky Mac it all went, with one exception—the half Japanese flag Jack had won on Guadalcanal. That artifact stayed hidden in the lining of his helmet. Then, at about 6:35 a.m., over the rails went Jack and his buddies.

Jack recalled that the Rendova landing was the first time he'd had to go down a cargo net into a pitching and yawing landing craft. This task was itself a difficult and risky process: the mass of sixty to seventy pounds of rifle, ammo, and equipment weighted down the wearer, while the landing craft bobbed unevenly beside their transports. A real sense of timing was necessary to negotiate the process with any measure of safety. First, each man had to let go of the net at the exact moment that the swells lifted the landing craft up and beside the ship. If one's timing was off, he would drop a considerable distance and crash onto the steel floor of the landing craft or onto his angry (and often seasick) buddies below. Otherwise, he might fall between the landing craft and the ship, to be drowned or crushed between the two vessels' sides. Fortunately, Jack timed it just right and let go so that his feet felt nothing but the hard, bobbing floor of the landing craft—not that he had too much choice in timing his jump, since he could feel the boot of the Marine hanging on above him beginning to step on his helmeted head!

With several dozen nauseated Marines and their equipment now packed tightly into the landing craft's well, its Navy coxswain pulled the landing craft ahead and then away from the *McCawley*. It was a relatively brief trip from the ship to shore, but it felt like an eternity. Smoke and flames were coming up from the edge of the Lever Brothers plantation beside the narrow stretch of beach; the tops of many coconut trees[24] had been shredded in places by the naval shelling, and the surrounding ground was littered with coconuts. The sound of small-arms fire was audible and coming from the near distance. The beach at Rendova was very narrow and the treeline was near the water. Rifles, pistols, and submachine guns at the ready, the Marines at first clustered among the roots of mangrove and coconut trees

Laden with vehicles and equipment, one of the LSTs transporting the
Ninth Defense approaches Rendova Harbor early on June 30, 1943.
Official US Marine Corps photograph, courtesy of Col. (Ret'd) William T. Box.

and swamp grass along the edge of the beach before a chorus of yells and
curses from their NCOs prompted them to get up and move a few yards.
Sodden from head to toe and hunkered down near the foot of a large beachside palm tree to get his bearings, Jack was now entering a world of utter
chaos and pandemonium unlike anything he had ever encountered before.

The Ninth Defense was not supposed to be leading the charge on Rendova,
yet it was. Specially trained assault units of the Army's 172nd Infantry

Regiment, Forty-Third Infantry Division, called the "Barracudas," had been assigned to take the beach before the Ninth landed. The sequence of landings of the Army and Marine troops had somehow gotten seriously off-schedule, however, and it was now the Ninth's artillerymen who were landing well ahead of the Barracudas' infantrymen. Instead of coming ashore at Rendova Harbor, most of the Barracudas had landed eight miles north, leaving the harbor still occupied by some Japanese *rikusentai* naval troops. The main Rendova landing force, including Colonel Scheyer and his leathernecks, was ignorant of this mistake and expected to make an unopposed landing until the irascible Admiral Turner confronted them with urgent orders, moments before they disembarked: *"You are the first to land! You are the first to land! Expect opposition!"*[25] D. C. Horton, a coastwatcher who witnessed the Rendova landings, wrote: "The coxswains of the Army landing craft, thinking that the beaches were clear, vied with each other to get their troops ashore first. This happy state of affairs soon ceased and all became confusion tinged with not a little dismay as the first troops were met with machine gun fire from the Japanese. It was realised, somewhat belatedly, that the Barracudas had not cleared the beachhead and that the incoming troops would have to fight for it."[26]

Out of sequence or not, the Ninth was already approaching the beach and was going to have to take it by itself. The battalion's men had to revert quickly to their infantry skills first learned in Boot Camp and on Cuba. Several firefights broke out between the first parties from the 155mm Group and the misplaced Barracudas and Rendova's Japanese defenders, with several Japanese troops being killed. The Ninth Defense had drawn its first blood in the New Georgia campaign.[27]

Once he was certain that the beachhead was secure and after his recon parties had driven off or killed Rendova's two hundred-odd Japanese defenders,[28] Major Robert Hiatt, the 155mm Group's exec, decided it was time to unload the heavy equipment. Although an Army combat engineer battalion had been slated to land behind the Ninth and help it set up, the engineer unit's commander refused to land until he was certain that Rendova's beachhead was fully secure. In frustration, aware that the tiny harbor was clogged with landing craft awaiting the chance to unload and depart, and watching supplies, guns, and equipment stack up on the beach, Colonel Scheyer requested that a Seabee unit land ahead of schedule to assist in beach clearance.[29] As a line of Marines held the edge of the beachhead and fanned out, all other available hands began unloading the various craft and helping the Special Weapons Group build gun positions up and

An LST disgorges troops and Long Toms of the 155mm Group at a former
Lever Brothers pier at Rendova Harbor. Official US Marine Corps photo,
courtesy of Col. (Ret'd) William T. Box.

down the beach. The 90mm Group's personnel began staking out sites for
their guns and radar sets, and recon patrols from A and B Batteries began
to move inland to look for good positions to emplace their Long Toms.
Working parties cut and blasted down trees to clear positions and provide
unobstructed fields of fire for the big guns. To add to the urgency, Japanese
air raids were again reported as being expected at any minute—radar on
nearby ships detected incoming Japanese aircraft, probably coming from
Rabaul, the massive Japanese air and naval base located some four hundred
miles away on New Britain Island off New Guinea's northeast coast. Scheyer
and Hiatt were furious with the Army engineers. Time was running out:
ships and landing craft were backing up in Blanche Channel, and equipment and supplies waited to be unloaded. As Scheyer requested, members
of the Navy's Twenty-Fourth Construction Battalion, the Seabees, soon
began coming ashore, and they pitched in and helped with the unloading
and digging-in process.[30]

As the Marines and Seabees poured ashore, clogging the beachline, it was a chaotic scene. "Since we had been expected to saunter ashore, all the first echelon gear had also come along—seabags, tents, etc.—and was dumped in a huge mound off to the left of the initial landing zone on Rendova. That became my vantage point to survey the hectic scene of wild activity of boats coming in with people and gear, destroyers rushing back and forth, dive bombers whacking New Georgia, dogfights in the sky, and an occasional Zero roaring by. I thought I was in a movie," Dave Slater recollected.[31] Some Seabee bulldozer crews found themselves under sporadic rifle fire from a few remaining Japanese defenders, while other Seabees hacked down coconut trees to improvise coconut log-corduroyed roads to fight the mud that was already beginning to slow down the deployments. The Seabees' game efforts met with mixed results at best: "The spinning wheels of ordinary trucks and jeeps were soon throwing the logs in all directions as the trucks and jeeps sank into the mud. The Seabee bulldozers than had to be used to pull out the imbedded vehicles: the bulldozers were lashed to large coconut palms for traction before painstakingly winching each truck or jeep onto the semisolid ground beside the putative road."[32]

Captains Hank Reichner and Walter Wells,[33] the respective COs of Batteries A and B and competitors at almost everything, were themselves equally peeved at the situation. Despite their and their NCOs' incessant hustling, cursing, and urgings, the two batteries faced struggles similar to those of the Seabees in getting their eight Long Toms off the beach. Rendova's trails were little better than wide footpaths. To improve the trails enough to enable Long Toms and vehicles to move down them, Batteries A and B and the Seabees had to cut, hack, and blast with dynamite some six hundred coconut trees. To add to the two battery commanders' woes, it began raining again, and the slimy muck created by the incessant downpours bogged the guns up to the hubs of their wheels. Every spare body in the 155mm Group (Jack included), every Caterpillar TD-9 prime mover (similar to the Seabees' bulldozers, but without the blades), and every LVT Alligator worked to heave the guns out of the mud and trundle them to their designated positions at an agonizingly slow pace. Battery E, one of the 90mm Group's batteries, somehow managed to get its own large AA guns in position and in operation on nearby Kokorana Island at Rendova's northern tip (but without its vital fire control equipment, which had been unceremoniously dumped on Rendova) by 4:45 p.m.[34] During the initial reconnaissance of Kokorana by a 90mm Group detachment earlier that morning, an errant group of Barracudas materialized: as neither side knew there were other Americans on that island, it was only by the narrowest of margins that the two groups avoided shooting each other.[35]

In the afternoon, despite the failure of several early-morning Japanese air attacks and during a break in the rains,[36] one Zero fighter made it through to Rendova, flying the length of the beach at near treetop level. "Will you look at that? What guts!" one Marine turned to Jack and exclaimed, half in awe. Every Special Weapons' light AA gun available began firing at the Zero, accompanied by every Marine or Seabee who could lay his hands on a weapon. Somehow the plane escaped unscathed.[37] The Zero pilot's lucky getaway did not seem to be a good omen.

Later that evening the monsoon-like rains resumed, and the rain came down for hours. Rendova's water table lay naturally close to the surface, and drainage ditches were carved throughout the old Lever Brothers copra plantations. Despite these drainage ditches, it took little time before the area became a quagmire. Marines slipped and fell in the mud, as deep as four feet in some places and aptly described by one of the official Marine histories as a "slimy gumbo" and in the Ninth's after-action report as "almost impassable . . . swamps."[38] The LVTs *Frances*, *Tootsie*, and *Gladys* were put to good use, since the caterpillar-tracked amphibians were about the only vehicles that could negotiate the mud. Even using Caterpillar TD-9 tractors and the sturdy Alligators, it still took teams of thirty or forty mud-smeared men and two tractors to wrestle each big 90mm and 155mm into position. Several of the battalion's trucks and jeeps had to be written off; their engines and drive trains, overdue for an overhaul after Guadalcanal, burned out in the fight with the slime, and the TD-9 "bulldozers" at times sank deeply into the glutinous mess. Still, Battery A was in position by 1800 hours that evening, and Battery B deployed its four fifteen-ton Long Toms into position in eight hours, firing registration shots to start getting the ranges to targets in the Munda area soon thereafter. Colonel O'Neil, the 155mm Group's new CO and a West Virginia mountaineer,[39] was then able to report all guns ashore, and the group was officially placed under the control of Brigadier General Harold Barker, the Forty-Third Infantry Division's artillery commander and the senior artillery officer present.[40]

While Battery A set up its four 155s for firing, a peculiar thing happened. As one of the gun crews cleaned its Long Tom in preparation for its first shot, a rammer staff inserted from the gun's muzzle clinked against something metallic. Fearing a live shell in the gun's barrel, the rest of the crew froze as the ramrod squarely tapped the metallic item again. The crewmen gingerly pressed the ramrod home once again. With the gun's breechblock open, a row of large tin cans fell to the ground. It was the missing medical

Battery B's gunners face a tough pull with this Long Tom and its
tractor mired in glutinous mud. Official US Marine Corps photo,
courtesy of Col. (Ret'd) William T. Box.

alcohol, in pristine condition and in plain view of both battery skipper
Hank Reichner—who, only days before, had fervently sworn to Colonels
O'Neil and Scheyer that *his* boys hadn't filched the stolen alcohol—and
Colonel Forney, I MAC's official observer. "Colonel Forney observed with
a wry smile and said: 'Von Reichner, I knew you bastards had that alcohol!'
Fortunately, we had other things to do, and I never heard about the matter
again," Reichner noted thankfully.

The first night ashore on Rendova was a fearful one for many, even for
Jack and those who had already experienced the pitch blackness and noises
of tropic nights on the Canal. Colonel Scheyer's pre-invasion orders and
each battery commander's own instructions to his men stressed the importance of not resorting to unwarranted gunfire but of challenging intruders with the correct password and then using bayonets, knives, and rifle

butts in night combat. Nevertheless, there were still frequent outbreaks of random gunfire, with some startling results the next day. "Cattle could be heard rustling about," Joe Pratl remembered, "and a group of farm lads said cattle don't move unless they are prompted by Jap infantry trying to find their way in the dark."[41]

Those rumors, coupled with the sounds of movement in front of their hastily dug foxholes, were all that was needed to prompt a fusillade of wild shooting in the 155mm Group's sector. Frank Yemma of Battery B picks up the tale: "There was a lot of firing that night . . . [and the] next morning, they found steers—*cattle*. It seems that the British or the Australians [who had lived there had] let the cattle go when the Japanese got there, and I don't know, about four steers came down through the jungle, and everybody opened up because they didn't know what the hell it was, hearing all this commotion!" Unfortunately, one of Battery A's platoon sergeants in charge of guard duty, who had left his foxhole to check the perimeter's security, wandered out in front of his platoon's positions at about the same time that the cattle stampeded through the area. Sergeant Cox was shot during the random fusillade. His body was found the next day, "his face swollen to an unrecognizable shape, a bullet having pierced his windpipe." Ironically, after having repeatedly told his sentries to fire only if their challenge went unanswered, Sergeant Cox failed to reply with the password and was shot as he tried to run away. It was a sobering reminder as to the reasoning behind Colonel Scheyer's and Captains Reichner's and Wells's orders.[42] However, this accident would not be the only "friendly fire" incident during Operation TOENAILS.

Black Friday: The Japanese Strike Back

The next day, July 1, Jack, Jim Kruse and all available hands began unloading the Ninth's second echelon off two Green Dragons as quickly as possible. While the 155mm and 90mm Groups' members unloaded *LST-354* and *LST-395*, other members of the Special Weapons and 90mm Groups improved their AA positions.[43] To Jack's and Jim's frustration, their platoon sergeant who frequently suffered from migraine headaches, with perfect timing, came down with one such massive headache during the unloading of the LSTs. In the midst of activity, he disappeared. "Where the hell's your goddammed Platoon Sergeant?" a more senior NCO yelped at Pogiebait and Kruse, who could only unhelpfully stammer back, "Uh, Gunny, we haven't seen him lately." Much to their disgust, their absent sergeant was soon found lurking aboard a Green Dragon from which, despite all entreaties and curses, he would not move until his sick headache had abated. In a matter of days, he was evacuated from the island. *What a hell of a way for that bum to get out of this place, Pogiebait!* Kruse commented to Jack. *Well, look at it this way, buddy,* Jack rejoined, *at least he's out of our hair now.*[44]

Because of the high-water table and muck, the leathernecks had to build up their positions rather than digging into the rain-sodden soil. They created high protective berms and revetments made of sandbags, coconut logs, sand-and-coral-filled 55-gallon steel fuel drums, and mud-filled wooden ammo crates. In this way, the 90mm Group began to set up its radar, searchlights, and aerial target acquisition equipment. Adding to the hubbub, radar on the nearby Navy ships once again detected Japanese aircraft en route from Rabaul. The men toiling on the beach and offloading the boats witnessed a squadron of B-25 "Mitchell" medium bombers flying over Rendova to bomb Munda Field early that afternoon.[45]

Jack was helping manhandle one of the big guns out of a Green Dragon when one of its bow doors dropped with a sudden jolt and caught his uniform. The LST had not landed directly on the beach but rather where the water was deep, and Jack was pulled under the clamshell door. In the haste and confusion of unloading, he feared nobody would see him as the weight of the steel door dragged him down. He began to panic, and the time he was underwater seemed like minutes. Jack seldom discussed this incident, although he admitted later it was the most frightening experience he had ever had: "I thought I was going to die." At last he was able to break free and come to the surface, his lungs near to bursting, pulled out by some fellows who noticed his thrashing underwater. One of his sergeants said, "Why don't you go onboard and take a break, McCall?" Jack gratefully accepted the sergeant's offer, and he meandered onboard the LST.

As Jack's pals continued to unload the two Green Dragons, the first of several major Japanese air raids began. Without warning, a low-flying group of Zeroes skimmed over the treetops and dropped several small bombs at the Green Dragons, including the one that Jack had just boarded. One bomb landed on the ship's left side, across from Jack's position on the right-hand side. The blast lifted the LST out of the water, throwing Jack and others to the deck. The second bomb landed at its fantail, and its explosion lifted the LST's stern high and slewed the ship around. The two successive blasts "rang the bells" of those nearby who were otherwise uninjured by metal fragments from the bombs and shards of debris from the LST. As the first wave of Zeroes departed, Jack thought, *"Damn, that was close!"* But it was not over yet.

Frank Chadwick, who was helping serve a 40mm AA gun on an LST's deck, ran to get additional clips of shells from the LST's ammo locker near the bow. He reached the locker precisely at the time the bombs fell, and the concussion knocked him to the deck. As a second wave of Zeroes came over Rendova, strafing the beach and blasting a nearby Special Weapons' 40mm position, Jack and the slightly stunned Chadwick had ringside seats. They watched as the gunners cleared their dead and wounded from the smashed site, righted their guns, and resumed fire at the second wave of attackers. After the attack, Chadwick realized his dungaree jacket had been peppered with holes from tiny bits of shrapnel from one of the bombs. Two Special Weapons .50 caliber gunners shot down the battalion's first confirmed AA victim of the new campaign, a fighter strafing the beach around 1400 hours that afternoon. However, in doing so, the Ninth suffered its first true combat fatality, as one of its gunners was killed in the Zero's strafing run.[46] The unloading drill was to be continued the next day, July 2, with *LST-342* and *LST-398*, the last remaining Green Dragons.[47]

On Friday, July 2, Jack joined the 155mm Group's gunners in unpacking powder and shell fuses to set up an ammo point. In the midst of intermittent showers, a group of newsreel cameramen and combat correspondents set up their equipment to film the beginning of the bombardment of Munda Field. Chris Donner noted that "a small group of Army officers had gathered near [Battery A's] Number Four gun to give the opening of fire the atmosphere of a spectacle," while "a large number of Seabees" labored around the coral peninsula to build a more durable access road. Nearby, the 155mm Group's headquarters staff set up an observation post for their fires in a 150-foot casuarina tree.[48] By midday, Batteries A and B began that day's mission, firing registration shots at Kokengolo Hill, a large hill overlooking Munda Field: "The first rounds from 155[mm] Long Toms in the Pacific began to crack out of the muzzles," Donner proudly remembered.[49] Yet, during these first few days on Rendova, Japanese air raids were frequent, vicious, and deadly. Jack vividly recalled the most severe air raid of the Rendova landings on July 2, during which Zeroes again strafed the beachhead with near impunity. The Japanese airmen concentrated on hitting the ammo and supply dumps sited on a small peninsula jutting into the harbor.

Around 1:35 p.m., not long after another extremely intense line of rainstorms had drenched Rendova, a formation of twenty-four medium bombers and forty-four fighters flew over Rendova Harbor in perfect formation from the direction of Rendova Mountain. From their appearance and the direction of their approach, many onlookers quickly concluded that these were Allied planes, with several identifying them to the benefit of their buddies as being friendly B-25 Mitchell medium bombers, much like the ones they had seen the previous afternoon.[50] Biggie Slater of the 90mm Group recalled watching "a Sea Bee working party of a hundred or so led by a young lieutenant unloading and maintaining road capabilities. He saw the planes and reassured his men that they were our B-25s, these being two-engined, twin-tailed (as were the planes [overhead])."[51] Unknown to the men on Rendova, however, all Allied aircraft on Guadalcanal and the Russells were grounded that day because of the heavy periodic rainstorms.[52]

Down at the beachside ammo point to procure more shells for Reichner's guns, Captain Bill Box and Lieutenant Donner stopped an idle truck driver. Just as Donner asked the driver to pitch in and help, "a 40mm began to set the air throbbing with its fire, and I heard the guns of a plane open up. I caught sight of the truck driver, now out of the cab, diving into the ground; others followed, and I instinctively went along."[53] Nearby, while the crews of the LVTs *Frances*, *Gladys*, and *Tootsie* still argued over the identity of the aircraft, a bomb landed near *Gladys*, wrecking the valuable Alligator and killing one of her three crewmen while wounding the other two. Two other bombs simultaneously fell near *Frances* and *Tootsie*, damaging one of the vehicles and scattering their crews.[54] The "Black Friday" attack was on.

Private Frank Yemma was caught in the open as he watched the incoming raid:

> Just as we got out on the [beach], I heard these planes, and I looked up and there was no camouflage on them. *None*. They were silver. I remember that very well. They looked like commercial aircraft. I said, "What the hell?" I kept looking. Then I could see the Rising Sun on [them]. I said, "Oh, my God," and here they come, the bombs. . . . I dove up under the gun, [under] the trails of the gun. . . . Because [the driver towing a heavy gun] pulled it in under the palm trees, thank God, I [was able to dive] under the gun, and there was debris flying all over the place. And it didn't last very long. . . . But, anyway, I wasn't five minutes ashore, and the Japanese welcomed me that way.[55]

Packed on a narrow stretch of Rendova beachline "less than a mile long and 500 yards deep,"[56] the conditions were ripe for a slaughter.

Drums of gasoline and diesel, boxes of ammunition, and the Forty-Third Infantry Division's casualty clearing station were all hit, and five tons of Seabee demolition materials exploded in brilliant flames. Jack recalled that it was absolute pandemonium. Caught in the open without foxholes, on the hard coral of the small peninsula, the Seabees took the brunt of the attack, surrounded by drums and crates of fuel and ammo. The colossal explosion of the Seabees' gelignite dump on a peninsula jutting into Rendova

Harbor arguably "[caused] more damage than the bombs themselves."[57] In the detonation of the Seabees' nearby explosives dump, a bulldozer and several Seabees disintegrated as they, too, were blasted sky high. The sounds were deafening, and although the air raid only lasted a few minutes, it felt like hours had passed.[58]

Not long before he had been pressed into ammo-hauling and stevedore duties, Jack had set up his water purification gear on a stream near the beachhead. When the air raid began, he remembered, he was crouching low in a shallow foxhole, shooting away (like almost everyone else around him, it seemed) with his rifle at the Japanese planes flying low over the beachhead. He recalled his amazement that no US planes were in evidence anywhere, and he cursed to himself, "Where in the hell is our air force?"[59] His rifle kept jamming, but at least shooting it gave him the feeling of doing something useful. Besides, because the Zero pilots flew their machines extremely low to the ground during this attack, the 40mm and 90mm guns were practically useless: the Japanese fighters came in at treetop level, anywhere from fifty to ninety feet above the beach or lower. As Jack remembered: "One got so low, I could see the face of the pilot. He was grinning away under his helmet and goggles, and I could see his machine guns blazing. If I had a rock, I probably could have hit him; he was that low." Jack also recalled that this pilot's antics—and his incredible lowness to the ground—so stupefied him that he stopped firing and gaped in amazement as the plane machine-gunned its way along the length of Rendova Harbor. Of this air raid, Frank Chadwick recalled similar details: the Zeroes were painted in a brownish-greenish camouflage, and the canopy hoods were opened back so that the pilots' helmeted and goggled faces could be easily seen. Within ten minutes, the raid was over; not a single attacker had been downed.

The Japanese aviators' attention to the area of Rendova Harbor near Battery A's positions earned it the nickname "Suicide Point." Between them, all three branches of service took over two hundred casualties during the Black Friday air raid. Four of the Ninth's men were killed, one was declared missing in action, and twenty-two (including Chadwick) were wounded.[60] The wounded also included one of Australian coastwatcher D. C. Horton's native scouts, hit by bomb fragments as he and two others frantically tried to paddle a native canoe out of harm's way.[61] Of course, the fear caused by the Japanese air raid was not confined to the enlisted men or the Solomonese and Fijian scouts. One of the Marines' other casualties was Lt. Colonel Shoup, the Second Division's observer assigned to cover the Army's Forty-

Suicide Point ablaze on July 2, 1943, after the Japanese air raid. Official
US Marine Corps photo, courtesy of Col. (Ret'd) William T. Box.

Third Division to learn firsthand about amphibious operations. Although
only lightly injured, Shoup wrote vividly in his diary of the pandemonium
and terror of that raid: "Air raid at 1335—*terrible!* No warning. Right in
bull's eye. Estimate 300 casualties. All HQ hit badly. Gross sights—arms
and legs moving all directions. . . . Nearly crapped out myself."[62] The fact
that a man as trained and disciplined as David Shoup—later to be the only
surviving recipient among the five Medals of Honor issued for the bloody
fighting on Tarawa—felt "nearly crapped out" as a result of the July 2 raid
is testimony to the savagery of this air strike.

At least twenty-five bombs had struck Battery A's area, and two Long
Toms were damaged. Four leathernecks died when three bombs hit Captain Reichner's battery positions. An unexploded sixty-kilogram bomb
wedged itself between the gun trails of one of Battery A's 155s, Gun #1,
and dented one of its recoil cylinders in the process. The "dud" bomb put
Bill Galloway's Long Tom out of action for seventy-two hours, both to

One of Battery A's guns, temporarily incapacitated due to an unexploded
Japanese bomb, July 2, 1943. Courtesy of William Galloway.

allow bomb-disposal personnel to remove and defuse the dud and for the
damaged gun to be repaired.[63] Adding to an already bad situation, Battery
A's gunpowder reserves had been set ablaze in the attack, as had a vehicle
loaded with small-arms ammo, the heat of the flames "cooking off" rifle
bullets that spewed in all directions. Several of the battalion's few motor
vehicles, including at least one of the precious Alligators (all three being
damaged to some degree) and a massive Caterpillar prime mover, were
smashed beyond repair. The battalion's surgeon and assistant surgeon, Navy
Lt. Commander Miles Krepela and Lt. Nathan Gershon, had their work cut
out for them and their Navy corpsmen. Even Navy Lt. Jake Goodwin, the
battalion's Navy dentist, provided first aid on the beach.[64]

The medical help, however, came too late for some men. Emerging from
a water-filled ditch full of red ants not far from Suicide Point, Biggie Slater
of the battalion H&S Battery observed firsthand some of the human costs
of the raid:

Out of the smoke and dust tottered two men. One, his left arm shredded, leaned heavily on the other. A corpsman leaped up and relieved the second man of his burden. He walked on toward Biggie, who saw he was covered with blood.

Biggie pointed. "Hey, Mac, is that your buddy's blood, or yours?"

"I don't know, his, I guess."

As the man passed, Biggie saw the pencil-sized splinter projecting from the man's chest, and he called out, "Corpsman, corpsman."

"Mac, you're hit."

The man looked at Biggie and then down at himself. He breathed pink bubbles.

"Gee, gee. Oh!"

His eyes rolled. He fell. He died.[65]

The July 2 air raid was the first and bloodiest of more than 150 air raids the Japanese would undertake during the course of the Rendova/New Georgia campaign.[66] The Japanese surface fleet added to the chaos by shelling Rendova later that evening. Led by the cruiser *Yubari* and nine destroyers, this flotilla fired several volleys of shells at the beachhead, but without much material success. The Japanese ships escaped, challenged only briefly by a small group of PT boats that failed to inflict significant damage on the retreating enemy vessels.[67]

Even after the dead and wounded had been evacuated, the Suicide Point area remained a gruesome scene for several days. Staff Sergeant Sam Stavisky, the Ninth's assigned combat correspondent, described it as looking "like the face of the moon."[68] "Down at the point the holocaust had taken a heavy loss of life and created a mess of burned supplies, wrecked small boats and water-filled coral craters," Lieutenant Chris Donner recounted.[69] His skipper, Captain Reichner, also recalled: "While we were hard hit on July 2, the Army infantry landing from the LCIs and SeaBees were hit much harder. Bodies, body parts and body remnants were all over the place, on the ground, amid fallen trees and floating in bomb craters. Many of the survivors were totally demoralized and appeared mentally deranged. The stench after a day or so was pretty bad, and body after body began to float to the surface of the water-filled bomb craters. Pathetic piles of soldiers' gear were everywhere, sad memorials to those who gave their lives on Suicide Point."[70]

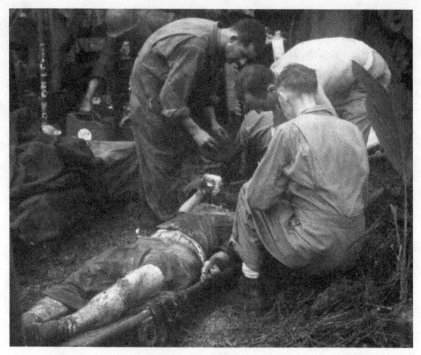

"Air raid at 1335—terrible!" Dr. Krepela's navy corpsmen assist a
casualty of the Suicide Point air raid. Official US Marine Corps photo,
courtesy of Col. (Ret'd) William T. Box.

Despite the turmoil and grisly remnants of July 2, all of the Long Toms
were soon back in position and lobbing their ninety-five-pound shells across
the narrow stretch of water separating Rendova from New Georgia. The
eight Long Toms administered a severe pummeling to enemy forces, both
in support of the Army's July 2 main landings on New Georgia at Zanana
Beach and on Munda Field itself and adjacent Kokengolo Hill.[71] As one
historian noted: "Munda's fate was sealed in an instant" when the Ninth's
Long Toms began their bombardment of the field: "Had any aircraft been
there [which, in fact, was the case], they would have been blown to oblivion
in a moment."[72]

Frank Yemma recounted the spectacular effects of some of Battery B's
first shots at Munda Field: "The only thing we actually saw—because with
field artillery, you never see your target, what you're hitting, but [we] saw
all this black smoke going up—[we] had hit an ammunition dump. That's

what we were shooting for, and we hit our target . . . and we could see that from Rendova, we could see the smoke going up on Munda so, for once, we knew that [we had hit it]."[73]

The success of their July 2 air raid, and the clear dangers presented by the 155mm Group's efforts to the continued occupation of Munda Field, inspired the Japanese high command in Rabaul to launch an even heavier air raid with the goal of putting the Ninth and the other American units on Rendova and the Army's New Georgia beachhead out of action. Whether Vice Admiral Jinichi Kusaka, the commander of the Southeast Area Fleet in charge of the Rabaul and Solomons area, had a sense of historical irony in terms of planning this next raid is unclear, but the date his staff selected for it was July 4, 1943.

The Fourth of July Raid

One of Jack's peers in the 90mm Group, Edmund Hadley, would later recall, "I will always think of July 4, 1943, as the day the planes fell."[74] On that day, the Japanese Eleventh Air Fleet at Rabaul dispatched another raiding party of one hundred medium bombers—of both Japanese Army and Navy aviation units—and numerous Zero fighters to finish off the work of July 2. As before, the primary targets of the raid were Rendova's beaches and supply dumps and the Ninth's heavy artillery positions. This time, they would be in for a major surprise. Contrasted with the Murphy's Law-esque glitches that had plagued the Ninth's air-defense network earlier, Frank Marshall wrote of the "glorious 4th": "This was one day that Murphy wasn't working."[75]

Besides the rainstorms that had thwarted Allied air cover and the fatal airplane misidentifications, another reason for the major Japanese success on July 2 was that the Ninth's radar screen was offline, partly due to a terrible error: its newest SCR-602 radar had broken down, and its largest radar, the gasoline-powered SCR-270 in Battery E used for long-range target acquisition, was out of commission from a true snafu. The precious 270 set had been foolishly refueled with diesel fuel from a drum mislabeled as gasoline, and a mechanic, attempting to clear the fuel stoppage during the July 2 raid, was electrocuted.[76] The bombers' flight path compounded the problem, since the incoming raiders' approach from around Rendova Mountain had shrouded them from detection by the five smaller and shorter-range SCR-268s.

July 4 dawned bright and sunny on Rendova. By noon all the defects in the Ninth's radars had been remedied, and shortly after 1300 hours, huddled over the big radar's oscilloscope, the SCR-270's crew reported: "Incoming bogies, at about 15,000 feet!" Around 1335 hours, "Condition Red" was again sounded across the island as the fully operable radars detected and tracked a massed group of over eighty Japanese aircraft heading generally towards Rendova.[77] "Aw, hell, here we go again!" the leathernecks fumed and griped as they hastened about.

First in were the fighters, arriving over Rendova at about 1430 hours. Much as they did on July 2, a wave of sixty-six Zeroes dived down to roar in at treetop heights. This time, however, Special Weapons' automatic weapons were ready; these light guns' rapid fire downed one Zero and dissuaded the rest from completing their low-level strafing runs. Thinking back on July 2's fiascoes, Frank Marshall of the Special Weapons Group noted: "It was refreshing to be able to get in a punch now and then." Still, it was not an unmitigated American success. A Special Weapons officer, Lieutenant Joe La Cesa, was killed from the concussion of a bomb near a 40mm position at Suicide Point, as was another group of Forty-Third Division dogfaces. In addition, three more Marines were wounded, and much equipment was shot up, including a pair of LCIs, before the Zeroes left.[78] Pogiebait sought out the nearest foxhole and spent the raid firing fitfully and futilely at the attacking Zeroes with his rifle.

Of the one hundred-odd Japanese bombers dispatched from Rabaul, only sixteen broke through the Allied fighter screen. Because they flew from a westerly direction—that is, from New Georgia and over Rendova Mountain—many of the Americans again made the same initial mistake they had on July 2, once again assuming these were American B-25s on a raid.[79] The presence of so many nearby Zeroes, who were obviously making no efforts to attack the "friendly" bombers, rapidly convinced them otherwise. The bombers came in at a much higher altitude than the Zeroes and were in perfect formation, flying level and straight, at an altitude of about 12,500 feet,[80] "just like they were a bunch of migrating geese," Jack remembered. This height was well within the effective range of the 90mm Group's guns. With all the Group's radars and AA fire control equipment again fully operational, the 90mm guns' aiming would be dead on the targets.

At 1410, a Special Weapons 40mm gun led off: "Within a few seconds the enemy planes became the target for every antiaircraft weapon on the island, joined in happy futility by a number of weapons with insufficient range or destructive power for such employment."[81] Never mind the ineffectual fire of the peashooters: the powerful 90mm guns of the Ninth had

A 90mm AA gun and its crew in position after the July 2 and 4 air raids.
Note the coconut-log and sandbag revetment. Official US Marine Corps
photo, courtesy of Col. (Ret'd) William T. Box.

the range and capabilities to do the job. While only one of the 90mm Group's
batteries, Battery E, was fully operational, its four guns were enough. In
the words of Captain Bill Tracy, Battery E's commander on neighboring
Kokorana Island, "Opening bursts were right on target. . . . The flight entered a large cloud. Pieces of plane were noted falling out of the cloud."[82]
Despite the lead bomber's rapid destruction with Tracy's first burst of
fire, "the formation flew straight ahead, closing its ranks and remaining a
beautiful target."[83] With each gun averaging five to six shells per minute,
Tracy's four big guns put up a withering volume of fire.[84]

Like an aerial Charge of the Light Brigade, with little if any time to
respond to the devastation being wrought, not a single Japanese bomber
broke ranks to take evasive action; all flew straight into the 90mm flak
bursts. One bomber after another literally disintegrated in the bursts or
fell earthward in flaming pieces. "Even as bits and pieces of aircraft came

plummeting and fluttering down, the formation continued to close up, presenting a marvelous target," David Slater recalled. Of the sixteen bombers in the formation, only four escaped, all to be finished off by American and New Zealand fighters scrambled from the Russell Islands, a small island group thirty-five miles northwest of Guadalcanal. With only eighty-eight shells and two to three minutes of firing time, Captain Tracy's battery had destroyed twelve bombers, and Special Weapons' gunners had claimed one Zero, setting a world record for the largest number of aircraft destroyed by antiaircraft fire with the least amount of ammunition expended.[85] The victory was immediate and total and was readily observed by many of the Americans on Rendova and the neighboring islands.

The CO of an Army field artillery battalion of 155mm howitzers[86] supporting the Thirty-Seventh Infantry Division was one of these witnesses. Based on a small island off New Georgia, Lt. Colonel Henry Shafer had a rare vantage point from which to watch the entire spectacle:

> [He] saw sixteen bombers fly out of the west and proceed right over his head in a superb stepped-up vee-of-vees formation. . . . Shafer could not yet identify the insignae [sic], but since the bombers paid his battalion no attention, he swallowed in pride and comfort, convinced they were Americans. The bombers continued in a gentle curve from Segi [on New Georgia] and made straight for Rendova. . . . Then Lieutenant Colonel Shafer and his gunners had a ringside seat to an incredible spectacle. Antiaircraft shells from Rendova and Kokorana [where Captain Tracy's Battery E was stationed] blossomed blackly within the bomber formation, and Betty after Betty fell away in flames. None of the remaining warplanes veered from its initial heading until only two [sic] were left. The antiaircraft fire ceased as the last two bombers flew out of range—right into the guns of waiting fighters, which destroyed them.[87]

As the Ninth's history records: "That day cheers were heard all over Rendova 'like a "Babe" homer in Yankee stadium,'"[88] or, as Jack recalled, "Wahoos, fist shakings and screams of delight were heard up and down the coast." Lt. Colonel Scheyer celebrated the occasion by helping to stencil a fresh line of miniature Rising Sun flags down the barrels of Battery E's 90mm guns, twelve red flags for twelve kills. It was a textbook example of precision antiaircraft gunnery. It was perhaps also a textbook example of how *not* to conduct a bombing run under AA fire.

After the air battle, some Marines were puzzled by the Japanese pilots' behavior. Granted, the entire action had lasted only a few minutes, but

Lt. Colonel Bill Scheyer (squatting on box) and Battery E's captain Bill Tracy (stooping, far right) help stencil victory marks on one of Battery E's 90mm guns after the July 4 victory. Official US Marine Corps photo.

despite the brief elapsed time, it seemed clear that the bomber flight could have used a more spread-out formation and still have inflicted damage on Rendova. As David Slater recalled, "The flight of bombers was flying in a diamond formation: four bombers in small diamonds—each group of four being corners of the squadron diamond."[89]

A more open formation may have reduced the effectiveness of the bombing run somewhat, but why was such a formation not adopted? After all, it was ultimately fatal for the bombers to have remained in this lemming-like formation. What had driven the Japanese pilots and bombardiers to maintain this highly ineffectual flight plan? In truth, it may have been just plain and simple lack of training and combat experience, which by mid-1943, because of increasing losses of skilled pilots and airmen, was becoming a major problem for the Japanese naval and army air forces.[90] In a formation like the one used at Rendova, the better-trained aircrews could lead and direct the rest of the formation with greater ease, while the less experienced ones could tag along at the rear in a sort of aerial "follow the leader." This greatly simplified command of a bomber squadron, albeit with a fatal consequence: once enemy AA gunners located the flight and got the precise range and height, the entire formation was that much easier to bracket and hit.[91] To Jack and most of his buddies, though, no lengthy or technical explanation was necessary: "They were crazy. It was just suicide to fly like that!" If the Japanese pilots' behavior seemed foolhardy, the existence of the Ninth's secret weapon indeed made this kind of formation flying suicidal. That secret weapon was, of course, radar.

While still fairly primitive in 1943, and while searchlights and optical telescopes would continue to be used for the rest of the war, the battalion's radar helped make the July 4 victory complete.[92] Once the enemy's altitude, approximate speed, and distance were fixed by the radar operators, this data was provided to the 90mm Group's central fire control station, or filtering room. It, in turn, relayed the data to each 90mm battery's CO or fire control officer and, at nighttime, to the huge searchlights of Battery F. The fire control officer translated this information into the correct elevation and deflection for the 90mm guns. Once radar had gotten the guns on

One of Battery F's six searchlights. Official US Marine Corps photo, courtesy of Col. (Ret'd) William T. Box.

target, however, and so long as the weather was good or distances to the targets were favorable, the rest of the target tracking was all done visually. Hence, AA fire was not yet purely an automated system that removed human effort and skill from the equation.[93] The shells' fuses would be set to explode at the correct altitude, and each twenty-two-pound shell, with its brass cartridge case, would be hefted into a cradle connected to the gun platform. Next the shell would be pushed by a mechanical ramming arm into the breech, and the sliding breechblock would be closed for firing.[94] Within seconds after the battery began firing, the oily black puffs of flak bursts would be seen around the target.

The various models of radar, coupled with the loading and aiming features of the new model 90mm guns the Ninth acquired as it left Guadalcanal, undoubtedly helped Battery E rack up its world record. While these improvements in technology cannot detract from the gunners' skill and courage, they did give the gun crews an edge in speed and accuracy that was better than with optical, searchlight, or sound-ranging equipment. While it was optimal to destroy as many enemy bombers as possible, simply forcing the enemy away from choice targets like the ammo and supply dumps of Suicide Point was also a goal of AA gunnery. Hence, the Ninth's AA crews could claim a twofold victory: the destruction of as many aircraft as they downed on that fourth of July, and the successful defense of a critical area. That fewer than ninety shells were needed to accomplish this feat was, in a sense, a bonus.

The Ninth's AA gunners of the 90mm and Special Weapons Groups claimed forty-six Japanese aircraft kills during the course of the entire New Georgia campaign, and at least eighty Japanese air attacks were recorded in the first twenty days of the fighting on Rendova and New Georgia.[95] To many observers, however, the battalion's performance during the July 4 raid was its finest hour, and it redeemed the frustrations of the July 2 raid. Witnessed as it was by so many onlookers (sailors and Army dogfaces as well as Marines), it was a tonic for the hard-pressed US forces and helped bolster the confidence of many. In the years to come, Jack, Frank Chadwick, Al Downs, Jim Kruse, Bill Galloway, and other veterans of the Ninth would celebrate each Independence Day by calling each other on the telephone to remind each other of what they had lived through on that notable July 4 of 1943, when the "bombs bursting in air" were very real indeed and the "red glare" was more than the plumes of skyrockets.

————◆◆————

One last, puzzling historical note exists as to the identity of the Japanese medium bombers used in the July 2 and 4 attacks. Various records, including the Marines' own official history of the campaign, have identified the bombers as being of the Mitsubishi G4M2 Type 1 "Betty" model. These sources also note that when the Japanese bombers were first spotted on both days, they were misidentified not by one but by many individuals and groups as American B-25 Mitchells, likely partly due to a squadron of those having been spotted in flight over Rendova to bomb Munda on July 1.[96] The same official Marine history reported: "Inexperienced ground troops, lacking sufficient training in aircraft identification, stood in open-mouthed admiration of the 'friendly B-25s.'"[97] Unseasoned troops were not, however, the only American personnel to think these hostile bombers were American B-25s. Even several comparably better-trained AA gunners and officers made the same mistake. Both the Betty and Mitchell were twin-engined, low-wing-position medium bombers of roughly the same size and bomb capacity, with a partly glassed-in "greenhouse" nose for their bombardiers. Still, there was one critical and relatively easily identifiable difference, even in the haste and stress of combat: the Mitchell had a twin-rudder tail assembly visible from almost all angles, while the stubbier Betty had a single rudder at its tail. Adding to the confusion: although frequently identified in reports and by eyewitnesses as Bettys, the raiders were in fact an entirely different type of Japanese bomber.

The Imperial Japanese Army often used another model of heavy bomber made by Mitsubishi, the Ki-21, codenamed "Sally" by the Allies, which was also very similar to the Betty.[98] Like the Betty, it certainly had the range to fly the 770-mile circuit from Rabaul's and New Britain's airfields to Rendova and back. Postwar records indicate that the Japanese Army Air Force's Fourteenth *Sentai* fielded eighteen Ki-21s from Rabaul to attack the newly landed American forces on Rendova "without loss and [with] unusually accurate results" on July 2. The same unit's records indicated that it sent seventeen Sallys, escorted by Japanese Army Nakajima Ki-43 "Oscar" fighters and Japanese Navy Zeros, to attack the Rendova beachhead on July 4, where they were met by heavy antiaircraft fire and fighters, with significant losses—all of which tracks the Ninth's account, but for the identification of the raiders as Bettys.[99] In terms of record-keeping after the fact of the July 2 and July 4 raids, it may have been easier to simply call all the Japanese raiders "Bettys" instead of breaking them down by type. The Seabees' officer was certainly not alone in making what, in his unit's case, was a fatal error. Other witnesses, including Hank Reichner and the

Friend or foe? Comparative aircraft recognition silhouettes.
From top left: a Mitsubishi Nell; a B-25 Mitchell; a Mitsubishi Betty;
and a Mitsubishi Sally. Author's collection.

Army FA officer, Lt. Colonel Shafer, fell prey to this initial misidentification as well.[100] Hence, two errors of aircraft ID occurred: the mistaking of Japanese bombers for friendly Mitchells, and the mistaking of Japanese Sallys for their Betty siblings.

Aircraft recognition errors cut both ways, however. During one of the early Japanese air raids on Rendova, Jack vividly recalled watching two planes zoom low across the beach near Suicide Point, engines screaming loudly. Recognizing the lead plane as a Zero, several Battery B gunners, including Jack's friend "Zombie" Jones, decided that they would not let this one get away. The gunners furiously peppered the airspace in front of them with automatic weapons fire. Unfortunately, Zombie and company failed to "lead" the Zero—that is, firing far enough in front of the enemy plane for the bullets to hit it in a timely manner—and the bullets riddled not the first plane but the second one, which turned out to be a US fighter in hot pursuit. Zombie, Jack, and their buddies watched dumbstruck as the American pilot barely managed to bail out before his fighter plummeted into Blanche Channel. Soon thereafter, the American aviator "hit the bay and came out mad as hell," as Jack remembered; he also remembered it took a lot of diplomacy (and the presence of several Marines, who were more heavily armed than the pistol-packing aviator) to keep the battered, half-drowned, and thoroughly infuriated pilot from making his own "friendly fire" casualties out of Zombie and several other Marines.

After that incident and several other near-misses on other members of the notoriously profane VMF-214, the "Black Sheep" (which several leathernecks remembered brought forth torrents of obscenities from the squadron's pilots and Major Gregory "Pappy" Boyington himself over the battalion's air-to-ground radio sets), one Battery E vet, Jerry Morris, noticed an American flag stencil in an odd place. It was prominently placed on the barrel of a Ninth Defense AA gun next to a row of similarly sized red "meatball" flag stencils. "Only in the Marines," Morris laughingly recalled, "could you get away with that."[101] Many friendly-fire incidents, however, were no laughing matter, such as the shooting death recounted earlier of the Battery A's sergeants on June 30.

The Ninth's Marines were certainly not the only US branch of service to be cursed by friendly-fire casualties during the Rendova-New Georgia operations. Navy PT boats figured in the most embarrassing Central Solomons mishap. This involved the assault transport USS *McCawley*—Jack's transport to Rendova, the Wacky Mac herself—which was also Admiral Turner's flagship as CO of Task Force Sixty-Two, the Navy's task force for Operation TOENAILS. Not long after Jack disembarked from it, the radar-equipped *McCawley* was the victim of a Japanese bomber strike during the first day's landings. Still smoking from its damage and under tow by a US destroyer, the Wacky Mac made for Blanche Channel on the evening of June 30. As she entered the channel, a PT boat, mistaking the *McCawley* and her escort for a Japanese convoy (even though the ships clearly made no efforts to take evasive action), launched a spread of torpedoes and sank the *McCawley*. It was not until their boat returned home that the jubilant PT crew learned the "Japanese ship" they had sunk was Task Force Sixty-Two's flagship.[102] As will be seen, the Army would also suffer more than its fair share of fratricidal shootouts in the jungles of New Georgia, leading in part to the coinage of a new medical term: *combat neurosis.*

When the Army began landing on New Georgia proper, elements of the Ninth Defense—most notably, the Tank Platoon and elements of Special Weapons—were detached to support Army operations on New Georgia. In many respects, the Tank Platoon's activities were a pioneering effort

Captain Blake and a Tank Platoon member with a captured Japanese flamethrower, which doused Blake's M-3 tank but failed to ignite.
Official US Marine Corps photo.

in terms of the Marines' use of tanks in true jungle fighting on such a scale. The Tank Platoon's eight light tanks (beefed up by an additional four M-3s on loan from other Marine units) saw vicious and sustained action in support of Army infantry attacks, and the tanks' crews faced attacks by small groups of desperate but determined Japanese troops armed with flamethrowers, magnetic mines, and Molotov cocktails. By the end of the battle for New Georgia, all of the platoon's M-3s had either been destroyed or deadlined for major repairs.[103]

The Special Weapons Group's detachments set up light AA and machine gun points on Zanana and Laiana Beaches, the latter being about two and a half miles from Munda Point, close enough to hear the detonations of the 155mm Group's shells landing on the nearby Japanese defenders.[104] The 155mm Group's guns on Rendova, lined up within a few yards of each other amid the coconut groves on the island's northern tip, were now somewhat better protected by coconut-log and sandbagged revetments and loosely shrouded in camouflage nets. The group was earning itself the nickname "Murderers' Row," and the Long Toms' shelling of Munda Point would continue almost unabated for the rest of July.[105]

Around 5:00 a.m. on July 9, the 155mm Group joined in a massive and extensively coordinated assault on Munda Point, later described as "one of the heaviest artillery barrages of the Pacific war."[106] Over 5,800 shells were fired in one hour between the Ninth's Long Toms and the smaller 105mm and 155mm howitzers of three Army artillery battalions. A group of destroyers offshore fired another 2,344 shells, and then fifty-two TBFs and thirty-six dive bombers—"virtually every machine that could carry a bomb"—finished off the job.[107] One of the defenders of Munda Point serving in an antitank and AA cannon unit, Probationary Officer Toshihiro Oura, wrote grimly on July 10: "The artillery shelling's accuracy has become a real thing. We can never tell when we are to die."[108] But for all this mighty outpouring of explosives and sweat, the Forty-Third Division advanced only four hundred yards and still suffered sizeable casualties in hand-to-hand fighting.[109]

At about the same time, in a desperate bid to reinforce New Georgia's defenders, the Japanese Navy dispatched several major convoys much like the Tokyo Express-style runs of Guadalcanal. One such attempt was made on July 6, but in the ensuing Battle of Kula Gulf, they succeeded in moving only 850 of 2,600 troops from Kolombangara closer to Munda and lost two destroyers in the process while sinking the American cruiser *Helena*.[110] The fireworks at sea were readily visible to the 155mm Group's exhausted gun crews on Rendova, who, far out of their Long Toms' effective range and bereft of ship-to-shore communications, could only guess helplessly whose side was ahead. "We watched the tracers zip through the darkness over Kula Gulf and saw the bright explosions as ships were hit," Chris Donner observed. "All we could do was hope that our forces were winning."[111]

One week later, late at night on July 12, Jack and his buddies were able to watch from their foxholes what looked from a distance like tropical heat lightning and sounded like very loud thunder. It was, in actuality, ships' gunfire again, as an American task force intercepted and broke up another Japanese convoy in the Battle of Kolombangara, with the Japanese losing the cruiser *Jintsu*. These naval battles were the closest the Ninth's men had come to watching a major naval battle unfold since Guadalcanal. Several Japanese warships, including the *Jintsu* and several destroyers, broke through the US naval cordon, steamed within range of Rendova, and opened fire. Due to poor weather conditions and faulty target-spotting, the shells overshot the beachhead by approximately two miles and fell inland.[112] Still, it was close enough for Jack and his fellow leathernecks to hear the explosions and be thankful that they had been spared from the horrors of an accurate naval bombardment.

Although Pogiebait had been saved from this threat, the Japanese resorted to using another old ploy from Guadalcanal. Shortly after the Naval Battle of Kula Gulf, those nocturnal pests, Louie the Louse and Washing Machine Charlie, returned to make life miserable for the troops on Rendova. Lieutenant Donner wrote:

And now began the night activity which began to wear us down. The Japs began to harass the beachhead by small, intermittent air raids, six or seven throughout the night, which kept us jumping or rolling into foxholes because no one knew where the next load of bombs would drop in the darkness. Each time the sky above the harbor would light up with fireworks as the unwelcome "bogies" and "washing machine Charlies" were caught in the searchlight beams. We came in the next ten days to expect the first warning just after darkness had claimed the sky. The last cigarettes and pipes of the evening would go out, and we would crawl into our holes as we heard the unsynchronized drone of the Nip motors. Very few of these were shot down, for they had no definite bombing run to carry out. Whenever they felt like letting go, down came the stick. We became proficient at estimating the precise point at which the bombs landed. Almost everyone was reduced to sleeping below the deck level during that period, in order to get more than snatches of sleep.[113]

While the Allies were already beginning to win daylight air superiority over Rendova and New Georgia by mid-July, the nocturnal pests owned the night for weeks to come, much to the regret of Pogiebait and his sleep-starved, grimy, and malaria-ridden buddies.

Wantuck and Rothschild: How the Ninth
Helped Save the Day on New Georgia

About July 15, with the Army's Forty-Third Infantry Division ashore in force on New Georgia and advancing to Munda Point, elements of the Ninth Defense were redeployed from Rendova toward New Georgia and other small islands. Although not widely known to Jack and the rank-and-file, its officers now knew from their daily briefings and interactions with higher headquarters that the campaign was not progressing according to plan. "By this time, it was evident that the Army attack at Munda had stalled badly," Lieutenant Chris Donner remembered. "We knew, too, that the Marine Raider Battalions, over at Kula Gulf, were being badly hacked up by overwhelming numbers of Japs because of the delay. Theirs was to have been a swift move to cut off the retreat from Munda, but the 43rd Division couldn't force the Nips to retreat."[114] On top of this, several large Japanese units had disappeared: a counterattack was seemingly in the works.

Since early July, part of Special Weapons had been posted at small-caliber AA positions along New Georgia's coast, with a large detachment under Lieutenant John Wismer emplaced at Zanana, the Army's beachhead for the July 2 main landings. This position helped provide air defense for a rear-area command post of the Forty-Third Division, an antitank platoon from that division's 172nd Infantry Regiment, and rear-echelon logistics units; however, to call this a "rear area" was a misnomer. Numerous Japanese patrols still infiltrated the area, and one of Lieutenant Wismer's patrols killed four Japanese troops in mid-July.[115]

In fact, by this time, elements from two Japanese infantry regiments were moving rapidly through the coconut groves and marshes toward the Zanana beachhead. An experienced and well-trained unit, the Japanese Thirteenth Infantry Regiment had been ordered to move from the island of Kolombangara to Bairoko Harbor on New Georgia to strike the right flank of the US XIV Corps, held by the Forty-Third Division. The Japanese regiment moved its three battalions one at a time under cover of nightfall, in barges and small boats, over the course of several evenings beginning on July 9. Amazingly, despite the presence of a nearby screen of PT boats, these barge convoys were undetected by the Americans, and the entire Japanese Thirteenth Infantry Regiment and part of the 229th Infantry Regiment then slogged through trails and swamps to their jumping-off points near Bairoko. From start to finish, although this activity took almost a week, the disappearance and movement of most of two enemy regiments apparently escaped the attention of XIV Corps' and the Forty-Third Division's intelligence staffs. The Japanese assault groups were fully reassembled in their jumping-off positions in the marshes of the Barike River, southeast of Munda Field, by July 15. Late on July 17, several US patrols reported spotting a column of several hundred Japanese moving eastward.[116]

As he reported to the Forty-Third Division's rear-area command post on July 17, passing by the division's and XIV Corps' rear-area elements, Lieutenant Wismer noticed that the Corps' right flank appeared to be undefended. When he questioned a senior Army officer as to why this was the case, the officer assured him that the flank was made up of impenetrable marshland. The Allies' prior experiences with the Japanese army should have reminded those members of the corps and divisional staffs who relied on harsh terrain to thwart Japanese attacks that this was a false hope: as the Marines had learned on the Canal and as British, Dutch, and Australian troops had learned to their cost in Malaya, Singapore, and the East Indies, "impassable" swamps, too, could be negotiated by dedicated troops. Lieutenant Wismer chose not to trust solely to this officer's judgment. On the night of July 17, he spread his fifty-odd Marines out and put considerable effort into setting up and improving the detachment's defensive perimeter and observation points. He cut back his AA gun crews to half strength, and the Marines freed up by this reorganization dug foxholes on a small knoll 150 yards off the edge of the beach. Several of Wismer's detachment volunteered to beef up their already considerable defensive armament by scrounging some broken-down machine guns from a nearby Army Ordnance small-arms collection and repair point, and they further scrounged some ammo belts to feed the newly acquired guns.[117]

As night fell, the seasoned troops of the Japanese Thirteenth Infantry Regiment began to infiltrate the rear areas of the Forty-Third Division. Around 9:00 p.m., this regiment's Second Battalion attacked the XIV Corps' command post area, and launching a bayonet charge, its Third Battalion attacked Wismer's and the Forty-Third Division's Zanana Beach positions. The first Japanese onrush toward the Zanana defenders was driven back, to the apparent surprise of the attackers who had believed they would strike an essentially undefended position. Loud screams and yells and the explosion of grenades and 50mm "knee mortar" shells signaled the onset of a more determined charge. Several of the soldiers and Marines broke and ran, and the first defensive line began to collapse.[118]

Let Lieutenant Wismer tell the rest of the story: "At about nine o' clock approximately 100 Japanese came into the draw and started to set up mortars. We held our fire at the last moment before they started firing in order that the greatest concentration of enemy troops would be present. Upon opening fire, we drove back the Japanese into the jungle. They regrouped and made a banzai charge. The forward positions were overrun and individually we made our way back to the gun positions on the beach, where we prepared to defend against the next charge. To our surprise, it did not materialize."[119]

The reason why a final charge was absent was largely due to the guts of two of Wismer's enlisted men. As Wismer's force fell back to make its final defensive stand alongside their 20mm and 40mm AA guns and machine guns near the beach, Private John Wantuck and Corporal Maier Rothschild volunteered to the lieutenant to stay up front in one-man foxholes near the center of the collapsing defensive line. They took the brunt of the Japanese attack, with each manning one of the scrounged machine guns. Between Wantuck's and Rothschild's fire and that of the light AA guns on the beachhead firing over their heads, the Japanese attack broke up, but it was not until it was almost dawn that Lieutenant Wismer's party finally found Wantuck and Rothschild.

Wantuck's corpse was bullet-riddled and slashed by bayonets and grenade blasts. Rothschild was found under a bush, alive but wounded and supposedly still screaming bloody murder after hand-to-hand grappling with a sword-wielding Japanese officer, whose sword Rothschild had barehandedly deflected before killing the officer. Army and Marine investigators determined that, between them, Wantuck and Rothschild had killed some twenty Japanese, wounded twelve to fifteen others, and eliminated a 90mm mortar and its crew, which was deploying to blast the Forty-Third Division's nearby rear CP out of existence. In the entire area of the Japanese Thirteenth Regiment's attack,[120] over one hundred Japanese bodies were found.[121]

For their bravery, Major General Hester, the Forty-Third Infantry Division's commander, recommended Wantuck and Rothschild for the Medal of Honor; however, in order to be eligible for this, the highest US military decoration for bravery in action, there must be two credible, living eyewitnesses to the purported act of courage that was "above and beyond the call of duty." Because Rothschild was the only living American witness,

John Wantuck (seated) and Maier Rothschild
(standing, with clip of 40mm shells) at Zanana Point
before the attack. Official US Marine Corps photo.

because no other witnesses were available who could provide independent, eyewitness testimony as to their actions, and because the Marine Corps preferred to "take care of its own," Wantuck and Rothschild ultimately received the Navy Cross. In late 1944, a Navy destroyer was commissioned in Wantuck's honor, and memorial services were held in his hometown of Elmira, New York. Lieutenant Wismer, a West Pointer who opted to become a Marine instead of an Army officer, was recommended by the Army commander for a Distinguished Service Cross for his own heroism and tenacity in holding the beachhead, but the Marine Corps apparently failed to act on the recommendation. Apart from a chewing-out from several Marine staff officers for leaving his forward positions and for trying to "play infantryman" when he should have been focusing on AA tactics,

Wismer received no official recognition from the Marine Corps for his own role in the defense of the Zanana beachhead.[122]

Jack recalled that Rothschild was already something of a loner long before the events of July 17 and that he had the reputation of being "a man with a past" (he was, in fact, a former Wall Street employee).[123] Moreover, Rothschild was older than the average enlisted Marine, and was one of the few Ninth Defense enlisted Marines who had seen some prior service in the Corps before the war. Rothschild had "adopted" Wantuck, who was just seventeen years old and was regarded by some as being a little slow. There was apparently a suspicion that Rothschild had put Wantuck up to helping him scrounge the machine guns and setting them up in the first place. Those who knew Wantuck well believed it was not an act that would have naturally occurred to him unless somebody else had suggested it, as he was fairly naïve and otherwise would not have known any better. It was also a risky act, since the .30 caliber machine guns they manned were tripod-mounted, water-cooled M1917s. To be effective, this model required at least two men to keep the weapon served with ammo and the barrel's cooling jacket full of water; when the coolant ran out, the gun often quickly overheated and jammed. Neither gun, of course, was likely in pristine condition anyway, having been junked and left at an Ordnance Corps collection point. Under the circumstances of the attack, Wantuck's and Rothschild's machine guns must have jammed quickly in the heat of the frenzied firefight. Jack also admitted that, since Rothschild was one of the relatively few Marines of Jewish extraction in the Ninth, that too tended to set him apart from the typical gentile Marine. Whether due to his background, the death of Wantuck, or his own personal terrors faced in the Zanana Beach jungle, Rothschild became even more withdrawn. Unlike some other Marine heroes, he seemed reluctant to make much of being a Navy Cross recipient when he could possibly have done so to return home on War Bond tours or recruiting duties.

Not long after the war, Rothschild broke contact with his fellow Ninth Defense veterans, and after treatment in a VA hospital, he disappeared completely. Jack and his friends never heard from him again. Like Wantuck, Rothschild was undoubtedly a casualty of the New Georgia campaign.

The casualties inflicted by Wantuck's and Rothschild's efforts and by their detachment's 40mm guns, their guns firing at maximum depression, had stopped the one battalion of the enemy's Thirteenth Infantry cold, and its survivors withdrew into the nearby swamps. That regiment's other infiltrations, however, proved to be more successful: its troops caused havoc throughout the Forty-Third Infantry Division's positions. In the inky blackness of the New Georgia night, suspecting that Japanese snipers lurked everywhere, some Americans completely lost their fire discipline, firing or throwing grenades at everything that moved. A number of casualties in the Forty-Third Division resulted from GIs shooting one another. The psychological state of many troops of this division was already less than good and led to similar incidents shortly after landing. The events of July 17 and 18 further jeopardized the division's overall morale and combat effectiveness.

Other elements of the Japanese Thirteenth Infantry and 229th Infantry Regiments were also sowing confusion behind American lines. Their patrols had succeeded in cutting communications lines between XIV Corps' forward command post and the Forty-Third Division's main CP. These served as the nerve centers of the Corps' and Division's key operations, the locus for the signals, engineer, and logistics staffs, and the divisional CP was soon under direct attack. At least one casualty clearing station was overrun, and several of the patients, doctors, and troops helping to evacuate the casualties were massacred.[124] In the words of the Army's official history of the campaign: "[The] Japanese . . . launched simultaneous raids against the engineer and medical bivouacs and the 43rd Division command post at Zanana. . . . The attacks against [the] bivouacs were easily beaten off, but at the command post the raiders' first onslaught carried them through the security detachment's perimeter and into the communications center where they ripped up telephone wires and damaged the switchboard before being chased off."[125]

While all available soldiers in the area, including cooks, signalers, and supply troops, were cobbled together to form a hasty defensive perimeter, there was a likelihood that a determined Japanese assault could seize or wipe out Corps and division headquarters, thus crippling or further delaying the chance of an Allied victory on New Georgia. Fortuitously, the force's senior artillery officer and Colonel Scheyer's nominal boss during Operation TOENAILS, General Barker, was visiting the Forty-Third's Division's forward CP when the CP was cut off and surrounded by the Japanese. Realizing the enormity of the crisis, he requested emergency artillery support from all available Army and Marine artillery.[126] Captain James R. Ruhlin, a Forty-Third Division field artillery officer stationed in the CP, found one telephone line that was still functioning. Ruhlin,

General Barker, and a private manned that telephone and began calling for fire support from a foxhole as the Japanese attack raged around them.[127] An urgent call for artillery fire was soon placed over the surviving phone line to all available artillery units in General Barker's command, which included the Ninth. Thus, Colonel O'Neil and Major Hiatt at the 155mm Group's headquarters control post had to plot a fire request for Batteries A and B to provide protective fires for the Forty-Third's CP area.

If the 155mm Group's CO and his exec felt nervous about their new mission, it would have been understandable. Neither of the Group's batteries had ever practiced nighttime firing as a field artillery unit before. After some hasty experiments, however, the Old Man and the exec were satisfied that by hanging lanterns on the aiming stakes used to align the guns,

Colonel Archie O'Neil (on left, with pipe) and
Major Hiatt (on right, with telephone talker and
headset) plot a fire mission for Batteries A and B.
Official US Marine Corps photo.

the 155mm Group could provide accurate fire support. Flashlights were quickly converted into makeshift lanterns and attached as markers to the aiming stakes. Within fifteen minutes of the call for fire, all hands were tumbling out of their foxholes, lean-tos, and tents, clad in little more than their skivvies and boots, and the big guns went into nighttime action.

General Barker and Captain Ruhlin, in their besieged CP, provided excellent forward observer support by directing artillery fire over the unsevered telephone line from the CP. For four hours, Army and Marine artillery blanketed the Japanese attacks with shells, sometimes only one to five hundred yards from the Forty-Third's campsite. Like their brethren at Zanana Beach, the battered Japanese survivors pulled back into the nearby marshes and rain forests. Depleted by its losses, the Japanese Thirteenth Regiment regrouped in the swamps and marshes and moved back to Bairoko Harbor and thence back to Kolombangara from whence it had set forth nine days earlier.[128]

Elsewhere on New Georgia, no longer exulting over the long-anticipated counterattack of his countrymen, Toshihiro Oura recorded in his diary entry for July 19 how it felt to be on the receiving end of one of the Ninth's bombardments that same evening:

> Last night's [July 18th's] shelling was terrific. The road that runs to the rear of the east side of the Field Defense HQ is the infantry's route of advance. The enemy appears to have observed this by air and are concentrating their fire in this sector. This concentration of fire is just over our dugout. Since it has only one entrance, the air is stuffy, and the sounds of the explosions cause ringing in our ears. There were explosions of several shells 15cm in diameter and 70cm long [i.e., 155mm shells]. It is really more than I can bear. The men were really scared, and they all ran into my dugout. I had to take them out mercilessly and assign them to other dugouts.[129]

The 155mm Group's nighttime mission of July 17 and 18, 1943, was hazardous, and not only because this was a first-time undertaking. Sometime during the lengthy shoot, a squadron of Japanese bombers was over Rendova. Spotting the Long Toms' muzzle flashes shining like torches through the dark jungle canopy—as Jack recalled, these seemed bright enough to "turn night into day"—the enemy raiders flew in to attack Batteries A and B. This brought parts of the Special Weapons and 90mm Groups into action: their flak was enough to deter the raiders, and the 155mm Group was able to continue its fire mission unmolested. The Ninth's actions on two fronts—Lieutenant Wismer's stand at Zanana and the 155mm Group's nighttime bombardment—helped save both the Forty-Third Division and XIV Corps from imminent destruction, thus salvaging the American foothold on New Georgia.

Had Wismer's detachment not been precisely where it was and not held its ground as fiercely as it did, the Japanese Thirteenth Regiment would have likely overrun the Forty-Third Division's rear area. Even if it were temporary, such a move would have severed the division's ability to resupply and reinforce its forward elements and would have required its combat troops to stop their offensive momentum and double back to secure the rear area. Had the XIV Corps' and Forty-Third Division's CPs and their respective staffs been captured, killed, or otherwise stymied, the effect—both as a practical matter and from the standpoint of American morale—would have been devastating for the duration of the Central Solomons campaign. Not only would the central planning staff for that campaign have been eliminated in one stroke, but the detailed plans for Operation TOENAILS could well have fallen into Japanese hands. Had that occurred, the effects would have been incalculable. Suffice it to say that it certainly would have made the course of a bitterly fought campaign even more difficult, time consuming, and bloody to all involved. The evenings of July 17 and 18 had been, as Wellington said of Waterloo, a "damned close-run thing."

On to Munda Point and Kolombangara; The End of TOENAILS

The day is set and we are ready. Be alert, and when the enemy appears, shoot calmly, shoot fast, and shoot straight.

—LT. GEN. A. A. VANDEGRIFT[130]—

Japanese imperial headquarters admitted today in a Tokyo broadcast recorded by the Associated Press that the American offensive centering around New Georgia Island in the Solomons was continuing on a scale of considerable magnitude although it insisted all attacks were being repulsed with heavy casualties.

—ASSOCIATED PRESS, AUGUST 5, 1943[131]—

Soon after the Japanese counterattack, the redoubtable Admiral Halsey, the South Pacific area commander, issued orders to stabilize and strengthen the American presence on New Georgia. Concerned by the report of Major

General Oscar W. Griswold, XIV Corps' CO, that the Forty-Third Infantry Division was "about to fold up," and with an especially high number of the division's troops in two of its regiments suffering from combat fatigue, "Bull" Halsey resolved to dispatch massive reinforcements. Accordingly, he ordered his senior army corps commander to "take whatever steps were deemed necessary to capture Munda."[132] The rest of the XIV Corps began arriving to reinforce the battered Forty-Third Infantry Division. The Army's Thirty-Seventh Infantry Division, another National Guard division, was also soon bogged down around Munda. It, in turn, was followed by elements of yet another Army unit, the Twenty-Fifth Infantry Division under Major General J. Lawton ("Lightnin' Joe") Collins. The latter division had seen combat in the final months of the fight for Guadalcanal and was a particularly well-led and well-trained unit. Elements of Admiral Halsey's headquarters and the crusty old admiral himself joined them.

The desolate landscape around Munda Field testified to the grim effectiveness of the 155mm Group's work. Official US Marine Corps photo, courtesy of Joseph Pratl.

Despite their July 4 repulse, Japanese army and naval air forces continued to bomb and strafe around Rendova, and the Rendova/New Georgia
installment of Washing Machine Charlie's antics featured several nighttime
raids both by small seaplanes based at Kolombangara and bombers launched
from Rabaul. By one battalion estimate, approximately three thousand
90mm rounds were fired by the 90mm Group one evening alone, without
apparent success. On August 1, a Japanese air raid attacked Tombusolo, an
islet next to Rendova, where part of the Special Weapons Group had been
deployed to protect a Navy PT boat anchorage. PT Squadron Nine was
stationed there to intercept Japanese barges, canoes, and small coastal convoys shuttling supplies and troops to and from New Georgia and its sister
isles. Despite furious ack-ack fire, Japanese "Val" dive bombers destroyed a
PT boat, blasting its plywood hull into planking.[133] (It was from this same
anchorage one day later that, under the command of Navy Lt. (j.g.) John F.
Kennedy, *PT-109* began its fateful mission in which it was rammed by the
Japanese destroyer *Amagiri*, with Kennedy helping to save the lives of his
surviving crewmen.[134])

July 23 was the day of the last entry in Japanese Probationary Officer
Oura's war diary, which reflects the progressive deterioration of his and
his troops' spirit. That morning's entry begins: "*Battle Situation*: Nothing aside from annihilation. No cooperation from the Navy. If I were to
compare the complete cooperation of the enemy, it would be like the war
of a child and an adult. Our mountain artillery positions were knocked
to pieces by enemy tanks. We are encircled, so they say, and about to be
overrun. Consequently, all we can do is to guard our present positions."
His final diary entry is brief and full of foreboding: "There are signs that
I am contracting malaria again."[135] Like Toshihiro Oura—whose name was
not listed among the relative handful of prisoners taken in the capture of
New Georgia—the Japanese forces' days on New Georgia were numbered.

As Army infantry units and Captain Blake's light tanks began closing in on
Munda Point, Batteries A and B shifted their fire missions in early August
to other Japanese targets. In mid-July, Battery A moved from Rendova to
nearby Tombusolo to resume its old seacoast-defense mission over Rendova's western approaches,[136] while Jack remained behind with H&S Battery
and Battery B on Rendova itself. On July 29, General Noburo Sasaki, the
Japanese area commander, began withdrawing his forces from New Georgia

"Under new management": Munda Field, New Georgia's prize, photographed from Bibilo Hill in August 1943. Official US Marine Corps photo, courtesy of Col. (Ret'd) William T. Box.

to nearby islands. After five weeks of savage fighting, Munda Field fell on August 5, 1943,[137] with the Tank Platoon's surviving tanks in the thick of the fray. Two days later, the bulk of the Ninth began shifting from their positions all around New Georgia and Rendova to concentrate around the Munda Point area, where the AA components' principal mission would become the defense of the airfield. Battery B was moved to Kindu Point, near Munda, to resume its old seacoast-defense role.[138]

The move to Kindu Point involved some combat. The hills surrounding Munda Field were studded with log bunkers, caves, and revetments and had been used as Japanese command posts, bombproofs, and supply areas. Bibilo Hill, a prominent feature overlooking Kindu Point and most of Munda Field, had been the last stop in the savage fighting for Munda and was only finally taken with the support of flamethrowers and Captain Blake's Tank Platoon, plus tank reinforcements from another defense battalion's tank platoon.[139] Because stragglers were likely hiding in the caves and numerous coconut-log bunkers studding Munda Point and Kindu Point, Battery B resorted to sealing up as many of the bunkers, caves, and tunnel entrances as possible with TNT blocks. Enough Japanese holdouts remained to make this a risky undertaking for Battery B's ad hoc powder monkeys, who, lacking Bangalore torpedoes or explosive satchel charges, had to improvise their own techniques for bunker-busting. Frank Chadwick recounted to historian Eric Bergerud: "When we moved out to Kindu Point after the capture of the airfield . . . [we] must have killed sixty or seventy Japs in pillboxes or trenches. We burned them out with [quarter-pound] blocks of TNT. We approached positions like this carefully. We had air-cooled .30-caliber machine guns. We also had a 20mm antiaircraft cannon on a wheeled mount. You'd just lay down a field of fire into those pillboxes, and someone would crawl up with a . . . block of TNT with a hand grenade fixed to it."[140] Amazingly, nobody from Battery B was killed or seriously injured in the process of leveling these last dugouts, tunnels, and log-roofed bunkers around Munda and Kindu Points.

Next, Seabees moved into the Munda Field area shortly thereafter with bulldozers, rock crushers, and steamrollers to pave out the battered surface of the runway. To Jack's amazement and happiness, one of the Seabees he met on New Georgia would turn out to be a familiar face from Franklin. Watching an open-air movie one night, Jack was nudged in the dark by a person who whispered, "Hey, buddy, can you spare a match?" The voice sounded oddly familiar, and by the light of the match, Jack recognized Reams Osborne, his hometown next-door neighbor and pal from Franklin High, whose general whereabouts Jack had kept up with in his correspondence with his parents. By August 13, the runway was patched well enough for Army Air Force and Marine air units—including VMF-214's Black Sheep—to redeploy from the Russells and Guadalcanal to Munda Field.[141]

With the battalion's elements now more or less together for the first time since Cuba, it was like a reunion: Al Downs, reassigned from Battery B to the 155mm Group's H&S Battery, to which Jack and Jim Kruse belonged, had hardly laid eyes on his Boot Camp pals since they landed on the Canal. They were able to get enough guys together for an occasional poker game and scrounged-up bottle of rum or whiskey. Jack and his buddies enjoyed watching the buildup of American aircraft, particularly the inverted-gull-winged Corsairs of the Marine fighter squadrons. The Corsairs were especially welcome due to their ruggedness, the ease with which they could be recognized and distinguished from Zeroes, and—as a matter of Marine Corps pride—because they were flown by Marine pilots.

Jack opened the New Georgia branch of his water purification plant up for business on a stream running near Munda Point, positioned so that he could watch and hear Army and Marine fighters coming and going from Munda Field and, sometimes, see PT boats en route to their harbor off Rendova. The wreckage of a Japanese antitank gun, and (until finally covered with quicklime and buried) the reek of its dead gunner, was near his new site. Not far away were the carcasses of wrecked Zeroes and Betty bombers. Jack resumed his hobby of scrounging around in the area, and soon he had found and "liberated" from abandoned Japanese positions near the airfield a complete Imperial Navy sailor's blue uniform (probably abandoned by a *rikusentai* member); a painted and lacquered tin case of Japanese cigarettes, emblazoned with the red stripes of the Rising Sun flag (although, suspecting they were poisoned, he never dared to smoke one); and a Japanese pocket knife. He also made a fine ashtray from the brass cartridge case of a Japanese 70mm howitzer shell. Raiding an abandoned bunker near Munda Field, Jack emerged from the bunker's stygian darkness with a Japanese helmet, only to look inside and find the stinking remains of part of its prior owner's head and brains. Nearly retching, he threw the helmet as far away as he could. Although that gruesome outcome curtailed his souvenir collecting for a while, he soon began undertaking a lucrative, if highly dangerous, hobby: deactivating Japanese grenades to sell to newly arrived Seabees, Black Sheep pilots, and aircraft mechanics at Munda Field.

At first blush, Japanese grenades looked generally like a small version of the standard American Mark 2 "pineapple" grenade, having a serrated but more cylindrical steel body and a handle with a metal cotter pin at the top. Beyond this, the activation procedures for the two grenades were vastly different. Instead of simply pulling the pin, letting go of a safety lever attached to the grenade's top, and throwing it like the US version, the Japanese model was activated by pulling the pin and smacking the stem of the fuse hard and squarely on the user's helmet or boot heel, a rock or tree. One then had to throw it as quickly as possible: the fuse was highly erratic and could go off within two to three seconds after the pin-removal/base-striking procedure took place.[142] Somehow, Jack learned how to unscrew the fuses and soak each grenade in a helmet full of kerosene to loosen up the explosives packed in the grenade's steel body. Given the inherent instability of the Japanese grenade's fuses or the possibility that some "son of the Emperor" may have jury-rigged one to do in a "Yankee dog" like Jack, it was a minor miracle that he did not blow himself up in the process.[143]

The wreckage of imperial hopes: a grounded Zero fighter in its Munda Field
revetment (*top*), and the remains of a Japanese antitank gun and its dead gunner
(*bottom*). Jack recalled that this wrecked gun was very near his location on
Munda Field. Official US Marine Corps photos, courtesy of Joseph Pratl.

Jack had been in place only a few days when he was reminded that this island had not yet reverted to being a tropical paradise: on August 15, Japanese long-range guns sporadically began shelling Munda Point from nearby Baanga Island. These guns were reputedly British-made pieces for naval and coast-defense use, perhaps taken from the British garrisons at Hong Kong or Singapore. They were roughly equal to the Long Toms in range and the duo was collectively nicknamed "Pistol Pete" by the Ninth's Marines.[144] Jack remembered that the most hateful thing about Pistol Pete was its (or, more accurately, their) sense of timing. As far as Jack could tell, Pistol Pete seldom hit anything militarily significant in the Ninth's area, other than holing some tents with shrapnel and riddling some fifty-five-gallon drums of fuel.[145] However, Pistol Pete usually began to fire around chow time, forcing all hands to drop their food and run for cover for anywhere from ten to thirty minutes. The shelling usually began in the vicinity of Battery B's positions around Kindu Point, and the shells were walked, in gradual increments, from there to Munda Field.[146]

Consider for a moment the psychological effect this had on the Marines. The move of the bulk of the Ninth Defense to Munda meant that the battalion, as a whole, could regularly get hot food for the first time in months. Because the combat situation on Munda was more stable than either on Guadalcanal and Rendova, mess tents and field stoves could now be set up. Pistol Pete's dinnertime shellings were less than a major bombardment, but more than a mere inconvenience. They were dangerous and, moreover, just enough to get a hungry Marine really steamed up. Therefore, they were far worse for Pogiebait's and his buddies' morale than any of Tokyo Rose's radio ravings.

Once Pistol Pete had finished a bombardment—and since only two of Battery B's guns were positioned to return counter-battery fire onto Baanga—General Barker's staff assigned the job of destroying Pistol Pete not to the Ninth but to a battery of Army 105mm howitzers. These smaller fieldpieces would return fire, but their shooting was fruitless because Pete's positions on Baanga were well camouflaged and could not be successfully located, plus the lighter 105mm howitzers lacked the range and power of the Long Toms. The Army's first bombardment seemed to silence Pete—that is, until the next chow time for the Ninth, when the latest nuisance shelling began and chow was ruined once more.[147] An Army attempt by elements of the Thirty-Seventh Infantry Division to storm Baanga on August 10 with a lightly armed raiding force was repulsed in view of Battery B's Kindu Point positions, as hidden Japanese machine guns opened up on the assault party's landing craft. The sodden survivors of that failed raid were rescued

A damaged photo of one of the Ninth's twin tormentors, Pistol Pete, after their
capture on Baanga Island. Photo taken in September 1943; Mount Rendova is
in the background. National Archives and Records Administration.

by a tough group of native scouts from the First Fiji Commando, a British
Commonwealth unit comprised wholly of Fijians.[148]

Pistol Pete carried on from August 16 to 19 before spotter airplanes
sighted the guns' positions by their muzzle flashes during a bombardment.
Colonel O'Neil finally got the authorization he needed to blast Baanga with
his own Long Toms whenever Pete struck again. Between air strikes and
vigorous bombardment of the island, Pistol Pete was finally silenced for
good around the middle of August, with elements of the Forty-Third Division dispatched to occupy the island on August 19.[149] The meaning of Pistol
Pete's demise was simple, even if a bit macabre, to Jack and his buddies:
"No more cold chow!"[150]

Jack did not have much time to settle down on Munda Point before he
was moved again. Due to ammunition-related issues, General Barker had

ordered the 155mm Group to fire only observed missions (that is, fire missions whose results could be directly watched by forward observers) for several weeks beginning on August 3. With fresh ammunition supplies supposedly eliminating the dangers posed by out-of-date and decrepit stocks, by the end of August, Colonel Scheyer felt confident enough to recommend to XIV Corps that his 155mm Group resume its field artillery duties, including indirect-fire missions.[151] The Corps' staff agreed, believing that the capabilities of the Ninth's Long Toms "made them ideal weapons for bombarding Kolombangara from the shores of Hathorn Sound and preliminary reconnaissance showed that the best site for them would be on Piru plantation just north and to the east of [the] Diamond Narrows." With the Japanese forces in the area now largely bottled up on Kolombangara, its harbor of Viru, and adjacent islets, the die was cast for another move of Jack and his buddies in the 155mm Group.[152]

So, on August 29, Battery A began moving to Piru Plantation, an area temporarily used earlier as a logistics base by the First Marine Raiders, who were now advancing through the island's northern jungles. Bill Box, now on the 155mm Group's staff and helping provide site reconnaissance for Major Hiatt, recalled: "[We] hiked from Munda using a native guide . . . through jungle most of the way. I remember that I was scared. I remember I was glad to see that open area with the supply parachutes left by the [Marine] raiders!"[153] Piru Plantation looked across a seven-mile stretch of water to the craggy heights of Kolombangara Island, where the bulk of the Japanese forces in the area—about ten thousand estimated as being there in early July, just before the invasion—were now positioned. Battery A's Long Toms began the siege of Kolombangara on August 31. Two days later Battery B joined in the shelling after another eventful arrival.[154] Captain Wells's Long Toms arrived by boat on September 1 at a small coral pier that was approximately one foot above the waterline and about six feet wide. While the battery's officers and senior NCOs left to select their gun positions, Japanese artillery began to bombard the pier area. The sailors manning the landing craft, undoubtedly feeling like sitting ducks, threatened to leave but were coerced into staying, and the bombardment stopped as suddenly as it had begun.

Unfortunately, Battery B had already been hammered before reaching Piru. Because of a shortage of landing craft, Battery A had departed for the plantation first; while Battery B waited beachside with its guns and gear, a Japanese scout plane flew overhead early on the evening of August 31. It apparently sighted Battery B's guns and equipment, as sporadic air raids began on the beach around 10:00 p.m. and lasted until dawn. While the battery lost some equipment, its men, the precious Long Toms, and ammunition fortunately remained intact. To add to the dangers, pieces of shrapnel from 90mm AA shells from the Ninth's own guns rained down on the beachside positions. Hence, Battery B's gunners spent the night in foxholes and bomb craters, hiding from both Japanese bombs and fragments of their battalion's own ack-ack shells. Frank Chadwick and another member of Battery B's Gun #2, who had been assigned to guard the gun from Japanese infiltrators, were nearly killed by an exploding bomb, its blast deflected by the trunk of a coconut tree. Despite these attacks, Battery B was in operation at Piru on September 3, and its four Long Toms soon joined in besieging Kolombangara.[155]

Jack's water purification point at Piru was situated on a freshwater creek just off the beach. This new site took advantage of a coconut log-lined well that the Japanese had dug, which provided an ample supply of fresh water requiring less purification. Jack's site was two or three hundred yards directly in front of the barrels of Murderers' Row, close enough to get the full effect of the noise and vibrations of the 155s when they fired. The sound was deafening, particularly when all eight Long Toms were firing in battery, more or less simultaneously so as to maximize their effectiveness. To make matters worse, Japanese artillery on Kolombangara had now identified the 155mm Group's positions at Piru as the source of much of their discomfiture and would, from time to time, fire counter-battery barrages to try to silence the 155s. "They fired at us, and for every round they threw at us, we threw five back. Nothing spectacular. We'd fire, and they'd fire," Frank Yemma remembered.[156]

Either of the effects of being beside a battery of 155mm monsters in action or being in the midst of an enemy bombardment was enough to ring your bells. Now, Jack had to contend with them *both*, sometimes simultaneously. The Japanese shelling was among the worst of experiences. Frank Chadwick testified as to this period of action: "You'd be in your hole, look out, and see the flashes and count them; you'd see the smoke, too. And then the artillery would come barreling in like a freight train. I used to peer out and think to myself: there's one, two, three, four: now let's see where they're going to hit. The shelling lasted about half an hour. They never got us, but shells landed to the left, in front, and behind us."[157]

155mm Group gunners at Piru Plantation prepare to bombard Kolombangara and chalk a suitable slogan on a ninety-five-pound shell before firing. Official US Marine Corps photo, courtesy of Col. (Ret'd) William T. Box.

Jack was, therefore, truly between a rock and a hard place, with occasional Japanese shells exploding nearby and the Long Toms essentially firing over his head. This situation lasted for several days before Jack finally decided, in the middle of a barrage by both 155mm batteries on September 17, 1943,[158] that he had just about enough. His head pounded terribly, and no mere APC caffeine-and-aspirin tablet would stop this headache: his ears rang, he was deafened, and he wondered if he might be suffering from a brain concussion. Even if it meant abandoning his post without his sergeant's permission, Pogiebait decided to take a break, leave his hole, and head back to the 155mm Group's positions. The efforts required to load and fire a Long Tom were considerable, and this process would have afforded Jack some time to evacuate his foxhole between firings. The Long

Tom was loaded by setting the shell's fuse; next, the hefty shell was placed on a two-man cradle (when time permitted; when it didn't, which was often, one of the gunners simply heaved the shell by hand into the breech himself), manhandled up to the gun's breech, and rammed hard to set the shell's rifling bands into the rifling grooves inside the gun barrel. Then, depending on the desired range, several silk bags of gunpowder (usually three bags of basic gunpowder and three bags of "super-charged" powder) were rammed directly behind the shell, without a brass cartridge case being used to hold the powder. The gun's breech was sealed, the lanyard was attached to the primer, and the gun was fired with a pull of the lanyard. Once a fire mission was completed, five or six members of the twelve-man gun crew would take a TD-9 or TD-18 tractor and an Athey trailer—a weird-looking, Caterpillar-tracked caisson used to haul ammunition—and locate the nearest supply point to secure more ammunition while the rest of the 155's crew cleaned and performed post-firing maintenance on the gun.

A point left unstressed in the official histories—yet one with a major impact on the Ninth's effectiveness—was the vintage and quality of the unit's ammunition, especially the gunpowder and fuses used for the explosive shells. While the 155mm M1 gun was a great improvement over the World War I-era GPFs, the ammo supply was often unreliable and was described in the Ninth's after-action report as "the most serious problem faced by this battalion during the campaign."[159] For starters, the supply of shells became highly limited. Captain Box, as ammo officer, reported that some shells left behind on Guadalcanal as unserviceable (some, allegedly, were World War I vintage) were salvaged when ammo stocks began running low. Ever since Guadalcanal, not only the quantity but also the quality of the ammunition posed the weak link in this chain. Because of defective M-51 fuses, some shells would explode prematurely. As a result of a premature muzzle burst, which occurred on July 10 and was the first indication of the severity of this problem, the 155mm gun crews took to ducking down in the gun pits whenever their guns were fired.[160] Adding to their woes, some shells appeared to be leaking contents from their base plates.[161] Other shells would be safely fired but would not explode on target: the fuses were duds, leading to some excitement as the Ninth's gunners occasionally had to remove and discard on New Georgia their own unexploded ordnance fired only days before at the enemy.[162] Similar problems cropped up with the gunpowder supply. Due to the age and deterioration of the powder (combined with rough handling in transit from stateside arsenals, which cracked open many storage tubes and exposed the gunpowder inside to rain, making it worthless),[163] spontaneous combustion sometimes occurred, and the bags might burst into flame, with the gunners frantically separating the burning bags from the intact ones to prevent a massive explosion. In fact, before the move from Rendova to New Georgia proper, these defects were so severe that Battery B had to suspend its fire missions on August 3. (As noted earlier, Brigadier General Barker, the operation's overall artillery commander, had limited the entire 155mm Group to shooting only observed missions for a time beginning in early August. Considering that this suspension coincided with XIV Corps' final drive on Munda Point—when all guns available would have been needed to support this offensive—one can surmise that these ammunition problems posed more than merely trivial concerns.)[164]

Ammunition issues did not just affect the Long Toms. The Special Weapons Group had experienced severe problems with defective Army-supplied 40mm shells, a problem only rectified when that group obtained Navy-manufactured batches of ammo.[165] Likewise, the Ninth's 90mm Group faced similar problems with "short" fuses, with several AA gunners being killed and wounded from metal shards. Of two twin brothers serving in the same 90mm gun crew, one was killed in this manner as a fuse exploded prematurely, detonating the shell. With the much-publicized loss of the five Sullivan brothers (all serving on the USS *Juneau*, sunk off Guadalcanal in November 1942) in mind, the survivor of the twins was soon thereafter transferred home.[166]

Returning to the event in question: Sergeant Bill Galloway of Battery A, who had survived the July 2 air raid after his gun, *Semper Fidelis*, was immobilized with a dud bomb between its trails, watched Jack as he jogged back to the 155s' firing positions. Galloway and the others in his gun crew yelled, "Hey, Pogiebait! Where's the fire?" "Where the hell you're going?" "You're leaving your post!" Jack yelled back in response, "My head hurts too bad! I'm going to lay off for a while. I'll go back out in a little bit," and he kept on going. Galloway just shrugged, and he and his gun crew prepared to load and fire another shell. Like some of the other shells in the 155mm Group's ammo supply, this one was oozing a substance near its base plate, but Galloway's gunners took rags and wiped off the shell so as not to lose their grip while lifting it. The usual loading-and-firing procedures followed in short order.

When the lanyard was pulled, a roar blasted the position: the defective shell was a short, and the liquid seeping from it was its highly explosive filler. It had likely ignited in the gun barrel when the Long Tom was fired, and the shell exploded shortly after leaving its barrel. Fragments of steel—both from the shell and from *Semper Fidelis*'s barrel—were strewn in various directions. Sergeant Galloway and several others were wounded by shards of metal, with Galloway carrying a half-inch piece of steel in his lung for the rest of his life,[167] and the massive gun carriage itself was peppered with steel fragments. Jack's water purification gear, on the other hand, was a wreck: his pumps and filters were riddled, and water sluiced out of his holding tank as if it were a colander. Jack and his buddies could only shake their heads in wonder: if he had not spontaneously decided to take his impromptu break, he certainly would have died or been horribly wounded.

Pogiebait McCall was a lucky man, indeed!

Another practical challenge facing the 155mm Group during the Central Solomons campaign was that of effective fire direction and observation. The Japanese forces on New Georgia and Kolombangara were often concealed in well-sited and camouflaged log bunkers and revetments. Because many Japanese troop movements were made at nighttime, it was extremely difficult to spot their positions. The 155mm Group's exec, Major Bob Hiatt, gave the problem considerable thought and came up with some tentative solutions in the hope that they would improve the accuracy and results of the group's fire missions. Major Hiatt was one of the newer additions to the Ninth, having joined the battalion shortly before the Rendova landings. A field artillery specialist, he was responsible for the site reconnaissance for Batteries A and B each time they relocated to a new position. He was also in charge of the group's Fire Direction Center.[168]

For a time, the Ninth "enlisted" a Marine aviator, Captain Lionel Pool of Marine dive bomber squadron VMSB-142, to serve as an aerial observer attached to help the 155mm Group's gunnery,[169] but more aerial observers were needed. One of Major Hiatt's answers was to co-opt a Navy torpedo bomber squadron based in the nearby Russell Islands, to which—after having lost another aerial observer recruited by Hiatt, a Lieutenant Craig, to being shot down three times (he survived)—Hiatt detached two members of his staff, Lieutenant Donald V. Sandager (described by Hiatt as a "quiet, efficient field artilleryman") and Sergeant Herschel Cooper, to become aerial forward observers.

Their first missions were hardly rousing successes. The Navy TBF pilots resented the nerve-wracking and dangerous work of flying low-

Major Robert C. Hiatt, photographed as a lieutenant colonel on Okinawa in 1945 as he tests a pair of captured Japanese Nambu heavy and light machine guns. Official US Marine Corps photo.

level reconnaissance with a pair of half-crazy Marines, who kept telling them: "Fly lower; I can't see anything!" The Avenger pilots assigned to fly Sandager and Cooper were usually the lowest men on the totem pole for any particular day's missions. The task of flying the two FOs was also frequently rotated—a different pilot every day—which complicated matters considerably. For instance, because of the turnover in pilots, neither Sandager nor Cooper could simply say, "Take me where we went yesterday." Instead, the two FOs had to brief their new pilots in exacting detail daily as to what routes to fly and where to look for possible targets or for Japanese AA positions to avoid. On one mission, Sandager found the Avenger torpedo bomber to which he had been assigned to have no parachute for him. When Sandager challenged the TBF's pilot, the pilot brusquely responded that it wasn't his problem: he had *his* parachute, and if Sandager wanted his own chute, well, he'd just have to find one on his own. Sandager responded by drawing his .45 pistol, placing it near the pilot, and slowly telling him that if it were necessary to bail out, he knew who would be wearing the parachute. After that altercation, parachutes were made available to the two Marines.[170]

While his aerial FOs experimented with perfecting their duties, Major Hiatt devised another plan that he hoped would improve his fire direction capabilities. "Turret Top" Hiatt seemed to have a thing for using trees as observation platforms, despite the risk that enemy artillerymen often preregistered their guns on tall objects such as trees or towers for the very reason that they made such excellent observation posts (OPs). On Rendova, his reconnaissance party found the highest tree on the island and, at the behest of Colonel Forney, converted the 130-foot tree to an OP equipped with a Japanese battery commander's three hundred-pound telescope with lenses much superior to the standard-issue Marine telescope.[171] On New Georgia, the exec's penchant for treehouse OPs was soon again in the forefront, both near Munda and at Piru Plantation.

On a large hill northwest of Munda Field, Major Hiatt found a colossal banyan tree, wide-based and some seventy feet tall, which he decided would make an excellent OP, notwithstanding that the tree was in an area that was still largely Japanese-held territory. Only a short distance away, the hill steeply dropped off into a one hundred-foot cliff overlooking the Diamond Narrows channel. The major ordered the 155mm Group's communications section to cut notches into the massive trunk to support wires for field telephones and to nail wooden slats to its side to form a primitive ladder to its top. (As water boy for the group, when he was not lugging around 155mm ammunition or Lister bags full of water, Jack sometimes found himself carrying around wooden boards, nails, and tools, although to what purpose, he had no idea.) At the top of the tree, the unit's carpenters built a small platform, which was then equipped with the captured telescope, a compass, a map table, a field phone, two rickety seats, and simple belts to strap down the observers in case of high winds.[172]

Climbing the tree was itself a chore. The wooden rungs were often slippery and not well placed, so each observer would take off his boots and climb barefoot, locking his toes around the lower rung and pulling himself up to the next one. Under the best of conditions in daylight, while trying to be as inconspicuous a target as possible for an eagle-eyed Japanese sniper, it often took considerable time to climb to the top. With the ever-present fear that a sniper would spot the observers and pick them off as they made their journey to the treetop OP, the climbers had a real incentive to hurry up their ascents.

When an observer reached the top, however, he was greeted with an incredible vista: the "treehouse" offered a commanding, 360-degree view of Kolombangara and Arundel, the Diamond Narrows between New Georgia and Arundel, and much of New Georgia itself. On a clear day, the observers could scan pretty far in any direction, viewing cloud-covered peaks on the farthest islands. On most days, the view was magnificent, but the observers would quickly remember that they were there for a more serious purpose and would get to work, calling in on the field phone to Major Hiatt at the Fire Direction Center to get his orders for target sightings. The area surrounding the tree was heavily jungled. A small trail had been hacked out of the foliage to the tree, and a small campsite was made in a clearing at the foot of the tree for a guard party. While the observers took their turn manning the treehouse, the others stayed under cover and guarded the trail.[173]

After several days of manning the OP tree, the observation crew got a case of the jitters when they heard unexpected sounds of movement coming up the trail; those on the ground got ready to defend the tree. The approaching patrol turned out to be Army infantrymen, several of whom were Guadalcanal veterans.[174] The patrol leaders, a lieutenant and sergeant, stepped forward to ask the Marines what in the devil they were doing there. After hearing the OP crew's explanation, the Army lieutenant announced that the area was just being secured from the Japanese and that his patrol's assignment was to drive the enemy to the east. "You know, don't you, that you're behind Jap lines?" the lieutenant told the observers. He was amazed to hear the Marines reply, "Yessir, we know that." Frank Chadwick recalled the lieutenant's response after the leathernecks made him an offer to climb to the treetop platform: "He looked at the tree and said if he had been ordered to climb the tree or face a court-martial and be shot, he'd tell them to shoot him. He told us that he had learned to respect the Marines on the Canal and New Georgia and thought we were a very courageous group, but he [had] changed his opinion. He now thought we were all crazy. We took this as a compliment."

When Batteries A and B moved to Piru Plantation, Major Hiatt set up yet another OP. This one featured a massive mahogany tree near the beach[175] and, alternatively, a fifteen-foot-tall collapsible metal tower[176] placed within yards of Jack's water purification station. One of the major's reasons for choosing this particular site could scarcely have made Jack feel secure about his water point's location: Hiatt reportedly selected this tree because, besides its being just the right height, he noted that the tree was in an area of the plantation that the Japanese on Kolombangara would usually shell first before shifting their fire further inland to the Long Toms' positions. Hence, the OP tree—and Jack's—general location was a hot spot, although it was less an immediate object of the Japanese gunners' attention than the 155s' firing positions further back.[177]

Between the Japanese guns on Kolombangara and nuisance raids from Washing Machine Charlie, life for the Long Toms' crews became more unpleasant. As the Marines' official history of the campaign admitted, things at Piru Plantation rapidly degenerated into a grudge match. Each side resorted to various ruses to lure its opponents out to take a drubbing by heavy artillery:

> For the men of the 155mm Group, the war soon took on the semblance of a personal fight. Each night the Americans heard the starting sputter and ensuing drone of a Vila-based seaplane that circled overhead to drop a small load of bombs. Several projectiles, fired at irregular intervals by cleverly concealed enemy coast defense guns, usually followed this raid. These nuisance tactics robbed men of sleep but inflicted little damage and no personnel casualties. By day the Japanese had a most annoying habit of shelling the Americans while at mess, resulting in spilled food and ruffled tempers. Whenever boats landed near the Marines' best observation post (the tree near the beach), their opponents would lay in a couple of rounds to make that area untenable.
>
> Naturally a battle of wits ensued. Since the enemy could not hide the gun flashes, the Marines returned the fire to silence the hostile pieces. The foe met this gambit by setting off powder charges at different points every time they discharged their weapons. But cool-headed Americans detected this ruse when they noticed that they were receiving only one shell for every three or four flashes plotted.[178]

Fed up with interferences to their chow calls and the waste of hot food lost in diving for cover every evening, Colonel O'Neil's and Major Hiatt's observers now spent their mornings looking for signs of cooking fires on Kolombangara. Whenever a wisp of smoke was sighted anywhere on the neighboring island, a salvo or two of 155mm shells followed. When the Japanese responded by concentrating their fires on the OP in Pogiebait's new neighborhood, Major Hiatt had his gunners vacate the post, and he began to rely more heavily on Sandager's and Cooper's aerial spotting reports. Between his two aerial observers in the Avengers and other observers in Higgins boats now plying the waters off Piru, the Long Toms began to saturate large portions of Kolombangara with highly accurate fire.[179] In the Marine Corps' later analysis, "Experience at Munda [proved] that

From left to right: Captains Bill Box, Norm Pozinsky, and
Hank Reichner at Piru Plantation, late summer 1943.
Courtesy of Col. (Ret'd) Henry H. Reichner Jr.

when spotter planes adjusted fires, the 155mm guns' effectiveness was
greatly increased."[180]

To thwart Japanese gunners attempting to down the observation planes
and dive bombers hitting Kolombangara, the 155mm Group learned to coordinate its fire missions before the Dauntlesses and Avengers struck. It
became apparent that each preliminary bombardment only tipped off the
Japanese that an air strike was imminent. Whenever the big shells began to
fall, the enemy AA gunners would hide; whenever the shells stopped falling, the same flak crews raced back to their weapons, and nine US Navy
bombers were lost over the course of several days as a result. In response,
Major Hiatt's gunners tried a new tactic. The Long Toms would fire a preliminary barrage, ostensibly warning the enemy that an air raid was imminent. "Three minutes later, after their opponents had time to man their
guns, the 155's again would pour it on, catching the Japanese in their open
emplacements. Then, upon completion of this second bombardment, the
planes would attack." This new ploy worked well enough, and the Navy's
aircraft losses to enemy AA fire ceased to be a problem.[181]

Japanese counter-battery fire from Kolombangara toward Piru continued sporadically from mid-August until early October. Knowing that the

Japanese were fully prepared to make the seizure of Kolombangara another bloodbath like the fight for New Georgia, Halsey bypassed Kolombangara to land his forces on Vella Lavella, the next island in the Central Solomons chain, on August 15. This move shrewdly cut off Japanese reinforcements to Kolombangara; made the seizure of Bougainville, the next island on the agenda, easier to achieve; and made the taking of Kolombangara superfluous.[182] Faced with a cut-off garrison, the Japanese withdrew what was left of their men from Kolombangara around October 3. By that date, XIV Corps' commanding general, General Griswold, had already declared success in the New Georgia area on September 23, and he now issued orders decreeing Operation TOENAILS to be an American victory.[183]

Still, no shortage of enemy targets existed for several weeks after "victory" had been pronounced by General Griswold. Because its defenders hid in their bunkers during daylight hours, the only Japanese typically seen on Kolombangara during the daytime was a motorcycle courier. He was spotted on his rounds at various times on successive mornings by a reconnaissance plane or by the crew in the OP treehouse. With the courier's route across Kolombangara established after several days of observations, Major Hiatt decided that this individual courier would be the group's next target. Henceforth, every morning during the courier's usual departure time, all eight 155s opened fire along his suspected routes. Somehow, with all the luck of Washing Machine Charlie, the courier miraculously escaped death by these bombardments, although it was reported that, after being blown off his motorcycle near a small bridge, he quickly dusted himself off, retrieved his motorcycle, and resumed his rounds otherwise unscathed. One Battery B gunner remembered: "We always said that the courier had a lot of courage, and we all bet that this was one Jap that was never constipated."[184]

On October 3, while spotting over Kolombangara in his Avenger, Lieutenant Sandager observed large Japanese forces evacuating Vila, its main harbor: he was witnessing the withdrawal of Japanese forces off the island, amounting to 12,400 troops. This evacuation was completed by October 7, which effectively marked the end of combat in the New Georgia area.[185] As the Long Toms' targets disappeared from Kolombangara, Jack and Battery B were moved—yet again—from Piru Plantation to Roviana Island, southeast of Munda Point and due south of Zanana Beach, to resume the old seacoast-defense mission. These moves were accompanied by more administrative changes: Bill Box once more took charge of Battery B, while Walter Wells took over as CO of the 155mm Group's H&S Battery. At the same time, Battery A moved from Piru Plantation to Nusalavata Island to perform similar tasks. Colonel Scheyer, who had been with the Ninth through its toughest days to date, was relieved as CO on November 3 by Colonel O'Neil, who, in turn, was replaced by Major Hiatt.[186]

Before leaving for his new job with I MAC headquarters, Scheyer saluted the effectiveness of the Long Toms in routing the Japanese:

> For the first time in this war the enemy had been driven from his base by bombing and artillery fire. At Kiska [in the Aleutians] it was bombing and ship's gunfire. At Kolumbangara [sic] it was bombing, Army artillery fire and the 9th Defense Battalion Seacoast that turned the tide. I am proud of the job that you did.
>
> Years from now you can look in the mirror and say, "I was there and I did my job—WELL."[187]

The Ninth's after-action report for New Georgia included an observation as to the men's overall health and welfare during the grueling campaign: "The officers and men of the Ninth in general survived their second campaign in better physical condition than might reasonably have been expected."[188]

General Griswold, XIV Corps' commander, issued a letter of commendation to the Ninth, crediting (if in something of the usual understatement of military bureaucracies everywhere) the battalion's "effective antiaircraft protection" and "essential counter battery fire" as having been vital to the success of the New Georgia campaign.[189] What was more, in appreciation for the Ninth's work, Lightning Joe Collins of the Twenty-Fifth Infantry Division saw to it that the battalion was awarded the Army Distinguished Unit Citation. In turn, Maj. General Collins personally thanked the battered veterans of the Tank Platoon and Captain Blake for the tankers' share in making victory possible on the Munda Trail.[190] To cap off the praise, the former CO of their old outfit on Guadalcanal, A. A. Vandegrift, now a three-star general and I MAC commander, passed on his personal thanks to Colonel Scheyer: "Please tell your officers and men how proud I am to belong to the same outfit they do."[191] Given that General Vandegrift had originally fought so hard against the formation of the defense battalions and other special Marine units—plus the fact that he was regarded as being a Marine's Marine—the general's compliment was high praise, indeed. It was Vandegrift himself who reputedly first referred to the battalion as the "Fighting Ninth" after Guadalcanal; again, quite an honor from one originally opposed to the defense battalion concept.

For many years, the fighting on and around Rendova, New Georgia, and Kolombangara has remained a largely forgotten chapter of the American war in the Pacific. While much less well known than the Guadalcanal campaign and the Marines' bloody fights at Tarawa, Peleliu, and Iwo Jima, for instance, Operation TOENAILS was a bitterly fought campaign with well over three US divisions and sizeable naval and air forces being engaged for more than two months to occupy islands that were supposed to have been taken in less than half the time by a substantially smaller force. Jack and many of his fellow veterans would undoubtedly have bridled at Professor Eric Bergerud's assessment that the campaign was a "tactical victory for the United States, but a strategic failure" because even though it had cleared the Central Solomons of the Japanese, it had cost the American forces dearly:[192] almost one thousand dead and another thirteen thousand casualties from wounds or disease, out of a force of thirty thousand. Of the dead, 811 Army troops were killed in action, followed by 132 Navy and forty-eight Marines of the Ninth Defense and the Fourth Marine Raiders.[193] Sickness and casualties also plagued the Ninth, which coped with the evacuation of 142 of its men—some 10 percent of its effective strength—during the month of July alone.

Also, by requiring Admiral Halsey to commit his strategic reserve for the Bougainville operation, TOENAILS had the effect of delaying the latter campaign. The campaign's veterans would doubtless, however, have agreed with author Bergerud that the New Georgia area was "one of the worst pieces of real estate in the South Pacific."[194] Still, without the ultimate occupation of New Georgia, it is questionable whether the Bougainville operation would have succeeded. If nothing else, New Georgia and its environs were a valuable testing ground for new tactics that succeeded on Bougainville and future operations, so in that sense, Operation TOENAILS did provide a "pattern for victory" in the Pacific, as coastwatcher D. C. Horton titled his study of the campaign.[195] As another student of the battle for the Central Solomons has written: "The importance of the New Georgia campaign's central event—the land drive to capture the Munda air base from its Japanese builders and defenders—resides not so much in a feat of American arms at a trying time but rather in the age-old and enduring lessons encountered in turning merely trained soldiers into veteran warriors."[196] By the campaign's end, Jack and the Ninth's leathernecks definitely regarded themselves as "veteran warriors."

As the fighting moved away from New Georgia, a new and very welcome piece of scuttlebutt ran through the ranks of the Ninth. The battalion had served in combat areas without interruption since landing on Guadalcanal in November 1942, sixteen months after leaving the US for Cuba. Wasn't it about time for a hard-charging unit like the Fighting Ninth to get some R&R? The unit's quartermasters began circulating uniform requisition sheets, including—it could not help but be noticed—orders for winter-weight green uniforms.

Could leave and a break in Australia or New Zealand be far away now? It seemed so close, and the uniform-resupply orders seemed to confirm that such were where the Ninth was now bound. To add to the evidence, XIV Corps headquarters had promised that the winners of the Corps' round-robin softball tournament would be granted leave in New Zealand. After winning eight of ten games, the Ninth captured the Island Softball League's pennant, though not without a rocky start:

> Opening day arrived. By luck-of-the-draw, the Ninth's team, the only Marines among twelve teams, was to play the first game. By luck of the coin toss, the Ninth was at bat at the first pitch. The Polack [Stanislaus Pacholski, the team's pitcher and self-appointed manager] stood respectfully at the plate as Major General Wing of a National Guard division [the Forty-Third Infantry, in fact; Leonard F. Wing was General Hester's successor as its division commander] stepped up to make the first ceremonial pitch.
>
> The General, a figure more suited to smoke-filled back rooms than to war, delivered. The ball left his hand in a weak arc; it slapped down about halfway to the plate and dribbled erratically toward home. The first-base coach, a hard-bitten gunner, stared. The batter stood rigid. The umpire shouted, "Strike One!"
>
> The Polack went mad. "'*Strike One,*' my ass!" he yelled, ceremony or no ceremony, General or no General. He hated being behind in the count. The General and his aides retired in good order to his car and left the game to the enlisted men. The Polack went on to win.[197]

It seemed like an eternity had passed since Jack and his buddies had seen anything resembling civilization. Most figured that they hadn't seen "civilization" since leaving Norfolk in February 1942. With few or no women or nurses in the combat zones around Guadalcanal and New Georgia— apart from a few Red Cross girls on the Canal later in 1943 and some air-evacuation nurses occasionally flying into Munda—the lack of female companionship was pretty well apparent to all. Christmas was spent around

Munda Field, which had now sprouted semi-permanent tents, shacks, and corrugated-metal Quonset huts. There were no turkeys or trimmings for the holidays. Such as it was, the chow—ten-in-one rations of dehydrated eggs, potatoes, and potted ham—was at least plentiful and edible, and occasionally, beer and Coca-Cola were now available. (For the lucky ones, these drinks might be chilled by a pilot thoughtfully flying up to ten thousand feet to provide some impromptu refrigeration for the drinks—for a price, of course.) Meanwhile, in some rear area, Navy LCIs and transports were being mustered to ship the battalion out to its next station. Jack had the pleasure of seeing old pals more often, like Chadwick, Downs, and Kruse, whose sections had been detailed to other parts of Rendova and New Georgia during the last few months. It began to feel like the old gang was together once again. Occasionally, he would get permission to visit his hometown pal Reams Osborne in the Seabees' camp near Munda Point.

Jack and his pals remembered New Year's Day 1944 as being ushered in by the Ninth in spectacular fashion: it seemed like every Special Weapons' gunner had found a machine gun and loaded it with a belt of tracer bullets. The midnight sky around New Georgia was brightly lit by cascading flares and tracers. Those not participating in this impromptu fireworks show took cover from falling debris and spent bullets and cursed the boys in Special Weapons for all they were worth.

Would the New Year bring an even bigger present from Uncle Sam, a chance for romance and some hijinks in the lands of the kangaroos, the Diggers, and Cobbers? In late December 1943, everything—the new uniform orders; the shipping schedules; XIV Corps' promise to the New Georgia Pennant winners—indicated that such would be the case.

Guess again, friend.

FIVE

"R&R": Brief Interlude in the Russells

In January '44, we were told that, after our 14 months in the combat zone,
we had certainly earned some rest and recreation. We filled out requisitions
for winter weight uniforms, and we all felt sure that we were headed for
either Australia or New Zealand. Wrong, it was the Russell Islands, about
half-way between Guadalcanal and New Georgia. More drills and training,
but with a twice a week ration of beer and Cokes.

—JACK H. MCCALL, SR.—

"Somewhere in the Pacific"

Somewhere in the Pacific
Where the Sun is like a curse,

And every day is followed
By another slightly worse;
Where the coral dust blows thicker
Than the shifting desert sand
And the white man dreams and curses
And prays for a better land.

Somewhere in the Pacific
Where a girl is never seen,
Where the skies are never cloudy
And the grass is ever green;

Where the flying foxes' chatter
Robs a man of blessed sleep;
And there's not a drop of whisky
And for beer the briny deep.

Somewhere in the Pacific
Where the nights are made for love,
Where the moon is like a searchlight
And the Southern Cross above
Sparkles like a diamond necklace
In the beautiful tropic night;
'Tis a shameless waste of beauty
I cannot hold you tight.

Somewhere in the Pacific
Where the mail is always late,
And a Christmas card in April
Is considered up-to-date;
Where we never have a payday,
And we never get a cent,
But we never miss the money
'Cause we never get it spent.

Somewhere in the Pacific
Where the ants and lizards play,
And a thousand fresh mosquitoes
Replace the ones you slay;
Take me back to dear Massachusetts,
And let me roam that dell,
For this God-forsaken outpost
Is a substitute for Hell.

—ANONYMOUS—

Imagine the disgust and disappointment of Jack and the Fighting Ninth's men when, after New Year, they learned that they were not heading for Australia or New Zealand, but instead to Banika, in the Russell Islands. "What a raw deal!" Jack recalled thinking at the time. His buddies likely would have been more vocal and graphic in their responses to this news—particularly had they learned that some of their own officers secretly favored this choice. Radio and communications specialist Biggie Slater, one of the voices of Duke Radio (the Ninth's headquarters call sign), learned this by overhearing several of the battalion's officers: "The *real* reason we didn't go to [New Zealand] or Australia was the upper echelon's perception that the battalion would [go berserk there]; witness its predilection for places of ill-repute and boozing *a la* Caimanera. Thus, the decision was that, in order to keep this crowd of unpredictable liberty hounds together as a fighting unit, it would be best to keep them away from 'civilization.' So, 3rd Amphib [i.e., III Amphibious Corps, formerly named I MAC] was cooperative."

The differences between the choices of R&R venue were so stark as to be scarcely worth comparison. The Russells were a small group of islands in the Solomons, sandwiched in between Guadalcanal (from which they were only sixty miles) and the New Georgia group. Other than the fact that the islands were in a quiet sector far away from the current combat zones around Bougainville and Cape Gloucester on New Britain, there was little to set the Russells apart geographically or climatically from any other part of the Solomons. Like those islands, the Russells had similar stands of coconut trees, rainy seasons, and the much hated, glutinous mud on every road and track; mosquitoes and outbreaks of malaria; and centipedes, land crabs,[1] rotting jungle vegetation, and the other flora and fauna of the Solomons. Due to a shortage of transport prohibiting the movement of the entire unit all at once, from mid-January to early February 1944, the battalion sailed by batteries from New Georgia to Banika.[2] This was one of the two largest islands in the Russells (the other, neighboring Pavuvu, was the R&R venue for the 1st Marine Division after its fight on Cape Gloucester). The anonymous poem "Somewhere in the Pacific" effectively summed up the attitude of many of the Ninth's leathernecks, Jack included, when they landed on the Russells and surveyed their new home. At least it was something of a break, the first real stand-down in well over a year.

When the Ninth first landed on Banika, the unit was ordered to bivouac next to a swamp and an aviation fuel supply dump. The camp's existence

"Don't you think I know what a swamp is, boy?" Confirmation of Jack McCall's protestations to the author that the Ninth was originally encamped on Banika in a swamp. Photo by Harry Jones, courtesy of David Slater.

was literally threatened by the fact that fuel had leached into the soil through the water table. This fact became abundantly plain when Gunnery Sergeant Smith (née Schmidt), now one of Biggie Slater's senior NCOs, got an idea that all that was needed to dry up the marshy soil of their new campsite was to dribble some kerosene on the ground where each tent would be planted, light a match, and burn the ground dry. Seconds after Smith dropped his match, the surrounding ground exploded into flame as if it had been torched by a flamethrower, and a large pyramid tent nearby went up in flames. Further, with so many men already suffering from the residual effects of malaria and dengue fever, the presence of a large swamp next to the campsite sent Colonel O'Neil "over the top." O'Neil demanded permission from the island's garrison commander to relocate to a higher and drier area. His request to move the battalion was finally granted,[3] although not before more of his men came down with fevers and chills.

The Russell Islanders, who could be seen from time to time, were much like the natives of Guadalcanal and New Georgia, being Melanesian rather than Polynesian in extraction. Despite the unwanted intrusion of the war into their lives, they were friendly and appeared to tolerate the Americans' presence on their islands. The mail, supply, and hot chow situations were much improved, and the supply of pogey bait, PX goodies, and Coca-Colas was not exactly endless but was more reliable than on Guadalcanal and New Georgia. The battalion also received several official, if limited, beer rations during its sojourn on Banika.[4] There were the occasional Army and Navy nurses , Red Cross workers, and a traveling USO show to spice up life. Also, while there was still hard work to be done, the facilities were much less primitive than on the Ninth's earlier Pacific locations: when there was time off on the Russells, there were at least places to go, movies to see, and homemade baseball diamonds to enjoy along with volleyball courts, ping-pong tables, and a small battalion library.[5] Still, when asked what his R&R was like on Banika, Jack responded with one word: "Tedious." He and others found themselves often engaged in disposing of rotten coconut husks, which festooned the ground around the Ninth's campsites and emitted a pungent stink, as well as being frequently turned into stevedores to move supplies at a nearby Marine logistics depot.

Although there was a small chapel with organized services on Banika Island where the Ninth was now posted, church religion did not play a high role in those days for many of the battalion's personnel. Happy as they may have been to have and use their personal Bibles when times were rough on Guadalcanal, Rendova, and New Georgia (and Jack admitted thumbing through a "bulletproof" Bible his parents had given him on quite a few occasions and saying the Lord's Prayer to himself when the time seemed right), organized religion and attending the "God Box" were not primary leisure-time activities for many young Marines. The Ninth Defense's men were no exception, with one frustrated Navy chaplain suggesting that not mere chaplains, but heathen-converting missionaries, were what the Ninth Defense really needed.[6]

The average Marine's seemingly cynical attitude toward religion may have partially resulted from the DIs' attitudes manifested at Parris Island. But, in times of combat, whether or not they admitted it to their buddies, many otherwise religiously lackadaisical and worldly Marines might well find themselves clutching rosary beads or, like Jack frequently admitted doing prior to the landings on Guadalcanal and Rendova, reciting to himself the twenty-third Psalm or the Lord's Prayer. The Ninth officially provided its men during their Banika sojourn with chapel facilities, offering both Protestant and Catholic weekly services, described to higher headquarters as "much needed facilities for religious services."[7]

While my father and others among the Ninth's men whom I interviewed seldom mentioned the battalion chaplain, he did make an impact on at least one of the unit's officers, who wrote home to his wife on several occasions about him. Like the Ninth's medical and dental officers and pharmacists' mates (corpsmen), the chaplain was Navy personnel, attached to the battalion. Lt. (j.g.) Budde F. Janes was a young Presbyterian minister who joined the Ninth in 1943 on Guadalcanal, having graduated from Navy Chaplain's School in late December 1942.[8] Of the unit's "padre of the sea," Lieutenant Chris Donner (who was Catholic) wrote his wife Madge that Chaplain Janes "gave a very appropriate sermon in the village church" for Mother's Day 1943 on Guadalcanal, adding: "There are masses for the natives [which given the Solomons' experience as a British colony, were typically Episcopalian/Anglican services] and others for the Catholic servicemen." More appreciatively, perhaps, Donner noted to Madge on Guam: "We do have a library of several hundred volumes, gathered from here and there by the Chaplain. The latter, about whom I have written before, is now a very busy individual. Besides his religious duties and the literary efforts, he is writing a novel, directing athletics, and acting as steward of our liquor mess. Did I mention that he used to have a prosperous church and attractive home in Santa Cruz near Palo Alto? In addition, the Battalion now has the services every Sunday of a Franciscan monk, from whom I was (last Sunday) and will be able to receive the Sacraments."[9]

Outside the official religious channels, others took to singing hymns, with Battery A's Sergeant Smiley Burnette particularly noted for organizing frequent gospel sessions. Hank Reichner recalled a few of his men's gospel sing-alongs on Guadalcanal: "Our chief recreation at night was to sit around the gun pits singing a few Baptist hymns, such as 'When the Roll Is Called Up Yonder' while watching the battalion searchlights pick up Japanese planes so our fighters could shoot them down. The hymns testified to the fact that 'there are no atheists in foxholes' and also to the religious upbringing of many of the Marines." After a few sessions like this, Smiley Burnette helped to unofficially organize an a capella barbershop quartet, which acquired a sizeable following, including men from other batteries and nearby units. Smiley's little choir sang all the old Protestant favorites, full of longing for God, family, and home, for a time of rest and peace, and for the simplicity of "that old-time religion." Their favorites included "Amazing Grace" and the poignant "The Old Rugged Cross." As Jack's H&S Battery pal, Jim Kruse, later reminded Pogiebait, it was not just the rarity of gatherings like these that made the 155mm Group's musical quartet special: "They were good, too. I found it amazing that these guys could sing so well together with no musical accompaniment."[10]

Reichner also remembered that, aside from the hymns, "we also sang lustily [other] ditties." One of the most popular of these earthier numbers, sung to the tune of "Bless Them All," could sometimes be heard as Jack and his buddies set off and returned from work details, or as they sat around in camp, commiserating as to their lot in life over some beer or manufactured hooch. The song lambasted everything from the low promotion odds of the Christmas Tree Marines to the leathernecks' favorite nemesis, "Dugout Doug." One can bet that upon reaching their "vacation hideaway" in the Russells and finding that it was hardly New Zealand or Australia, this song was roared out with a newfound appreciation:

> F—k them all, f—k them all,
> The long and the short and the tall.
> There'll be no promotion, this side of the ocean,
> So cheer up my lads, f—k them all.

> They sent for MacArthur to come to Tulagi
> But Douglas MacArthur said no.
> He gave as his reason, it wasn't the season,
> Besides, there was no USO!

Group photo of Battery A, taken in spring 1944 on Banika.
Courtesy of Dr. Christopher S. Donner.

F—k them all, f—k them all,
As off to our foxholes we crawl.
There'll be no promotion, this side of the ocean,
So cheer up my lads, f—k them all.[11]

Horseplay, "Skylarking," and Morale

The Marines of the Ninth Defense seldom suffered from a lack of diversions in their rare free time. Softball and baseball were always popular pastimes, and poker, red dog, acey-deucey, and crap-shooting were favorites as well. Given the relatively few legitimate outlets to spend one's newfound cash, the winner of each game could do little with his earnings except buy cigarettes, candy, or PX supplies; trade it for Japanese loot or liquor; send some home for safekeeping; or go for broke in another card game or game of chance. As noted earlier, the trade in Japanese gear was always a fruitful source of amusement and sometimes cash.

The Ninth had its share of fishermen, several of whom developed novel ways of fishing. Off Rendova and New Georgia, impromptu fishing parties would take advantage of the amphibious LVT Alligators to wade into deeper waters and cast their lines. Fishermen less patient with the traditional methods of the sport would shoot fish with their rifles, while some true daredevils, including Jack's Battery A pal, "Tojo" Whalen, went "TNT-fishing." The equipment of choice for this novel aquatic sport required quarter-pound TNT blocks, hand grenades, or small-caliber Japanese shells jury-rigged to explode underwater. TNT-fishing could be almost as deadly to the fishermen as it was to the fish, but it produced a large haul of dead and stunned marine life that floated to the surface. Unfortunately for one Ninth trooper who carried his love of grenade-fishing to the Russells, he had forgotten that Banika was not the combat zone, and any large explosion there could likely trigger an alert. His efforts at grenade-fishing one afternoon started an island-wide panic, with trigger-happy soldiers and Marines suspecting the Japanese were attacking. For his pains, the hapless fisherman was almost court-martialed.[12]

Another Marine who frequently indulged in this dangerous pastime was Gunnery Sergeant Smith of the 90mm Group's H&S Battery. As David Slater remembered, he did so not without injury to himself and to a bystander after one TNT-fishing trip:

Well, the Gunny, who lived in my tent and was usually drunk, came back from such an expedition in the possession of two blasting caps (used to detonate TNT blocks). These were wrapped in paper, which the Gunny absent-mindedly threw into the trash can (a topless 5-gallon tin that originally had held coffee). Then, after a last drag on his cigarette, he threw that, too, into the trash.

Nearby, as I sat on my cot, engrossed in writing a letter, I heard two pistol shots (or so I thought). I immediately hit the deck and looked around. There was the Gunny, with a stunned look and a bloody foot next to the shredded can. I suddenly felt stinging all along my left side, from armpit to ankle (I was wearing only shorts and shoes). Looking, there were bloody spots galore. I had been peppered by tin shreds. Our nearby comrades then hustled us off to Battalion sick bay, where the Gunny was repaired, and the corpsman gleefully tweezered numerous splinters out of my hide.[13]

While beer was more frequently available in the Russells, black-market alcohol—sometimes filched from Navy or Army Air Forces officers' supplies; sometimes flown in from Australia and New Zealand by AAF crews; sometimes navy "grog" saved up by an Aussie or New Zealand sailor—was also available, if sold at exorbitant prices (often thirty or thirty-five dollars per pint).[14] Other frustrated entrepreneurs took to brewing their own hooch. This was a popular hobby wherever GIs were stationed, and the Ninth Defense was no exception. Even Hank Reichner sheepishly admitted to a certain pride in his unit's distilling efforts: "On the lighter side, some of our people teamed up with a great [Seabee] outfit and managed to build a portable still. I guess we probably turned out the best corn whiskey in Guadalcanal until the troops got in the mash one night and got rather ill."[15]

One highly potent blend was known as "torpedo juice." This earned its name as it was often made by mixing alcohol found in the propellant tanks of aerial torpedoes (or when available, pure grain medical alcohol, 190 proof) with whatever fruit juice happened to be handy, which was often grapefruit juice. The resulting concoction was also called "jungle juice." "Lord knows how many aerial torpedoes dropped from TBFs didn't travel five feet," David Slater wistfully recalled. John Hall, an enterprising Baltimorean in Battery E, was proud of his batch of "raisin jack," a highly popular form of hooch distilled from fermented raisins and sugar.[16] As will be seen in a later chapter, however, the consequences of consuming wood alcohol or other non-potable fluids could be grim—a fact that seldom deterred the battalion's truly dedicated drinkers.

One didn't have to be an alcoholic to find solace in hooch, however, and while the unit was out of the line, many of the Ninth's officers turned a blind eye to their men's occasional drinking. Hank Reichner recalled that his tentmate and Battery A exec, George "Doc" Teller, was an excellent junior officer and sidekick who could often produce the goods whenever the situation called for a good, stiff drink. "We were often visited by our friends from the infantry and managed to help them relax with our small supply of booze allocated to us from the battalion coffins. This supply dwindled and Doc saved the day, drawing on his experience as a medical student. At that time, he had learned how to make 'noodle soup,' a mixture of medical alcohol and lemon extract—a deadly combination. One drink was enough!"

As was the case with units of all branches of service, nicknames were common. These were awarded due to some personal foible or goof-up, physical appearance, overall attitude, or any similar distinguishing characteristic. (When left with no other alternative, "Mac" would always suffice, as in "Watch it, Mac!," "Up yours, Mac!" or "Semper Fi, Mac!") One of Jack's pals, a bantamweight boxer named John Whalen, was nicknamed "Tojo" due to his small stature; he was the butt of many jokes about his just passing the minimum height requirements to be a Marine. Al Downs was called "Rosie," the name of his hometown sweetheart back in Pittsburgh. An ardent and unreconstructed Kentuckian, Bill Galloway was labeled "Rebel"; Charles Jones was "Zombie"; David Slater was "Biggie"; Robert Hausen was "Hercules," or "Herc" for short. A beardless kid like Bill Sorensen or Frank Chadwick, both underaged, were often called "Chick" or "Chicken," short for "spring chicken." In contrast, any married Marine or anyone older than twenty-five was likely to be called "Pop" or "Pappy." This was, after all, largely a young man's war.

Regardless of their efficiency or bravery, even the Ninth's staunchest officers and NCOs had nicknames—sometimes used to their faces but usually not, depending on the particular officer and his disposition on any given day. Any commanding officer was the "Old Man," although he was never called this to his face. Captain (later Major) Walter Wells, Bill Box's successor as Battery B commander and later the exec and CO of the 155mm Group, was known to all as "Waldo," and sometimes by his friend Hank Reichner as "Waldo the Beast." A real straight-shooter, Wells would accept being referred to by his nickname by his enlisted Marines, although most of them knew their limits and when not to take liberties with this privilege. Chadwick recalled: "Wells was a good Marine officer: he was a man you either loved or hated, no middle ground, but most loved him. He was respected and no one crossed him, no matter which group you belonged to."

Wells's perspective was similar to that of General George S. Patton, Jr.: he believed that to get his men to remember, he had to give it to them dirty and loud. The general attitude of Battery B's Marines toward their new skipper can best be described as ranging from grudging respect and admiration to intense fear and dislike.[17] For his part, Jack got along well enough with Captain Wells—or, at least, never got on his bad side—without having to engage him in the obnoxious rites of "earbanging," the currying of favor with a superior officer. In his own way Jack respected Captain Wells, but secretly he feared the captain a little, too.

Battery B's outlook toward its new CO, compared with his predecessor, was a study in contrasts. Depending on his disposition, Captain Box was "Sweet William" when in a good mood or "Wild Bill" when in a bad mood and "on the warpath." Most of the men recalled Captain Box as generally being of an engaging and sunny disposition, sincere without being perceived as overly familiar or weak in any way. Battery A's leathernecks expressed similar feelings of pride and loyalty toward their Old Man. Captain Hank Reichner was known on Gitmo by his subordinates as "The Little General" and, in later years (due to his double-H initials and his family's German origins), as "Hammering Hank, the Horrible Hessian."

The balding and ruddy Bob Hiatt was called "Turret Top" and "The Lobster" (especially the latter when angered). One pudgy lieutenant in Battery B was called "Jelly Belly."Green second lieutenants were "shavetails"; gunnery sergeants were "gunnies"; any lesser degree of sergeant was, naturally enough, "sarge"; and corporals (possibly due to their arrogant attitudes as DIs at Parris Island) were "little colonels." While the enlisted men's ability to get away with calling some of the officers and NCOs by their nicknames to their faces was certainly not common for all Marine or other military units, in a real sense, it reflected the high degree of camaraderie that existed between all ranks in a unit like the Ninth and the "no chickenshit" kind of attitude that permeated it from the top down.

The personality and geographical mix in the Ninth was highly varied as well. As boots, many young Marines were naïve and gullible; although they may have fancied themselves young "men of the world," their DIs usually quickly proved them otherwise. In a society where newspapers, radios, and movies had neither yet permeated society in a homogenized way nor created a mass culture such as that of today's United States, regional differences still abounded and were often highly noticeable. Many of the Ninth's enlisted men were from the North and Northeast, although there was a large contingent of Southerners—Jack being just one of several native Tennesseans in the battalion. The shared rigors of Boot Camp had helped break down many of the regional and ethnic differences, and Jack found some of his closest buddies to be guys not from the deep South, but from places like Indiana (Kruse), Iowa (Hausen), New York (Chadwick and Whalen), Pittsburgh (Downs), and even Poland (Dobkowski). Whether Catholic, Protestant, Jewish, or Greek Orthodox, they made up a big, raucous, disjointed, and sometimes dysfunctional family. As Chadwick opined: "The Marine Corps was like a brotherhood, you looked out for each other. It's hard to describe. You'd be playing cards; you'd get into an argument, get up, slug each other, and then get down and start playing cards again."[18]

Of course, neither the Ninth nor its subordinate elements were truly a family. As surrogate fathers and big-brother figures, most of the battery commanders were roughly the same age as their enlisted men and were often ten or more years younger than many of their platoon sergeants and gunnery sergeants. There were no maternal aspects to this existence, and few fathers and brothers are ever forced to order their sons and siblings to die—or to watch them die miserably. Too much sentimentality was a liability from a leader's perspective, but most of the Ninth's officers successfully negotiated the fine line between caring for their men and requiring them to make the maximum sacrifice when necessary.

Even at this stage of the war, the Ninth's leathernecks were, in the main, a high-spirited crew, despite their lack of real leave time and the tough conditions they faced. Practical jokes and goof-ups ran rampant, including some that truly backfired. Frank Chadwick recalled one stunt that he and his tentmates played on one gullible Battery B Marine.

The man in question was convinced that he was experiencing a nervous breakdown. For several weeks, every time he went to take a shower and emerged from the shower, his uniform and towel were nowhere to be found. He would sprint back to his tent, stark naked, only to find his dungarees, underwear, and boondockers neatly laid out on his cot. The Marine would mumble, perplexed, "How in the hell did my stuff get here?" "Aw, come on! Don't you remember walking out of here just like that?" his tentmates and neighbors would retort, grinning and winking stealthily at one another. After weeks of this bizarre, recurring behavior, the leatherneck finally got a referral from Doc Krepela to see a Navy psychiatrist. It was with mixed amazement and disgust that the practical jokesters soon found their prank had backfired: the psychiatrist agreed with their tentmate's opinion as to his failing sanity and prescribed immediate departure from the combat zone for a long course of treatment in the rear area.

Of all the field-grade officers of the battalion, the one we will call Lt. Colonel "Baker" served for a time as the 155mm Group's CO and was widely regarded as an odd but humorless martinet by the battalion's enlisted men. His own junior officers were hardly any fonder of him, secretly referring to him in their own personal code as the "TORSO"—"The Original Revolving Son of a Bitch." Baker was known for four things: his habit of frequently scratching himself, no doubt from an acute case of jungle rot (earning him yet another nickname, "Scratchy Ass"); his habitual wearing of khaki uniforms in lieu of the typical olive-green dungarees, even in a combat environment like Guadalcanal; his penchant for collecting "girlie" magazines and "pin-up" pictures of nude women (which would have hardly been noteworthy if he had been an enlisted man but, in a time before *Playboy* and other such magazines were common, even the lowest enlisted men took notice when a field-grade officer indulged in this kind of behavior); and his dog, which he had "promoted" to sergeant and which he took with him on his morning strolls down the beach, during which he would expect military courtesy to be rendered not just to himself, but to his dog as well.[19]

His patience sorely tried by his superior, one day on Guadalcanal, Captain Reichner was discussing the TORSO with Battery B's skipper at the time, Tom Stafford, on a field telephone. When Major Stafford made a comment about Colonel Baker, Reichner spluttered without a second thought: "Him—that old bastard!" Unknown to both officers, however, "that old bastard" had tapped into the conversation from the 155mm Group's switchboard. This became immediately apparent when a new voice interjected: "*Reissh-ner*, I may be a bastard, but I am not old! *Come down to my tent!*" And so, Reichner dutifully trooped down to Colonel Baker's tent to accept his reaming-out.

Hearing rumors that Colonel Baker's sanity was being widely questioned, Colonel Scheyer, Baker's nominal superior on the Canal as battalion exec, put the question bluntly to Reichner. Faced with a direct question, Reichner mustered an equally direct answer: "Sir, I believe that Colonel Baker has lost his mind." Colonel Scheyer naturally reported this to Colonel Nimmer, who confronted Colonel Baker with the reports he had received. Incensed, Baker somehow explained his way around his weird follies but, of course, naturally wanted to know the sources of these opinions. Colonel Nimmer identified Baker's subordinate Reichner as one of the sources—thus once more proving the truth of the old military adage that *merde* rolls down-hill. By now, Colonel Nimmer, too, was angry with Reichner, who some-how evaded his wrath: "He was furious, as he felt that my remarks about [Baker] were disloyal. Only by some divine intervention was I not relieved of my command. I suspect Lt. Colonel Scheyer was my guardian angel. As I did not initiate my remarks, but rather responded to questioning from a superior officer, I felt that I was blind-sided."

Reichner figured that with these slip-ups, he had given Colonel Baker all the ammunition he needed to court-martial him or wreck his budding ca-reer with an unfavorable efficiency report. With a creeping sense of dread, Reichner took a call in Battery A's CP several weeks later from Colonel Baker, who dryly said over the field phone, "Come down to my CP, *Reissh-ner*. I want to show you your efficiency report." To Reichner's amazement, Baker had given him all "excellent" ratings with one exception: a "fair" for loyalty. "I guess he figured there must have been some truth to what I had said, after all," Reichner surmised. Unfortunately, and with a regrettable sense of timing, Reichner chose to point this out to Colonel Baker at the end of Baker's review; "'Get the hell out of here,' said he, and I fled back to my tent for a couple of 'noodle soups' with the realization that any further promotion for me was a questionable bet. With all this, though, he and I stayed on pretty good terms." "I guess he thought I was as crazy as he was," Hank Reichner ultimately concluded.

Doc Krepela's Antics

Besides being a gifted combat surgeon, Lt. Commander Miles Krepela, the unit's Navy doctor, was widely regarded as being one of the battalion's leading comedians and a fair judge of separating the truly sick from the malingerers. On one occasion near the end of the Guadalcanal campaign, he was visited by an especially wan-looking Marine. "O.K., son, what's the problem here?" Doc Krepela asked with his best bedside manner. "Doc, I just think I'm cracking up. I don't think I can take it anymore," the Marine sighed. "Well, what do you think will make you feel better?" Dr. Krepela asked skeptically. "If I could get a pass to New Zealand, I think I'd feel a lot better; but, you know," the Marine said, visibly perking up at the thought, "if I could only get leave to get shipped back over the water, stateside, I'm sure they could cure me there." Without a word, Dr. Krepela stood up, unbuttoned his fly, and prepared to "take a leak" on the dirt floor of the pyramid tent serving as his office. "What are you doing, sir?" the incredulous Marine exclaimed. "Well, if that's all that it takes to get you back to the States, I'm going there with you!" Doc Krepela responded. "Forget it, sir; you're crazier than I am!" the newly cured Marine yelled, as he ran out of Doc Krepela's sickbay.

On the other hand, Frank Chadwick recalled having a severe case of jaundice and being ordered to see Dr. Krepela, who promptly had Chadwick deliver a urine sample. The glass vial was soon filled with a ghastly smelling, yellowish-brownish liquid, which Doc Krepela held up admiringly to the light. "Oh, my! Look at that beautiful color!" the doctor exclaimed in awe, as he turned the vial around in the light like a prism or kaleidoscope. "Have you ever seen such a perfect color? I've never seen anything like this in my life! This is just beautiful!" "Oh, Lord, what are you talking about, Doc?" Chadwick uttered in fevered amazement. Doc turned around at Chadwick and winked: "Aw, quit your squawking; I'm sending you straight to the hospital. That's what you wanted to hear anyway, right?"[20]

While often fondly remembered for his antics, no veteran of the Ninth questioned the dedication, competence, or bravery of Doc Krepela, his deputy lieutenant Nate Gershon, or their staff. The medical team's collective performance on Rendova—particularly in dodging exploding fuel and ammo supplies on Suicide Point to rescue wounded and dying Marines, GIs, and Seabees after the July 2 air raid—was almost unanimously regarded as heroic. Despite having the chance to move the Suicide Point dispensary to a higher and safer ground, Doc Krepela successfully argued to keep it in its position, which made it easier to transport the wounded over the muddy trails and easier to move the casualties onto evacuation boats. Because of the dispensary's proximity to ripe targets for Japanese airmen, in the Black Friday air raid, one of Krepela's pharmacist's mates was felled by flying shrapnel.[21] Although many of the Ninth's men recalled the fact that their Navy dentist, Lt. Jake Goodwin, was forced to ply his trade with a foot-operated drill, others recalled his superhuman efforts at lifesaving after the Suicide Point raid, as the dentist was pressed into service as a first-aid man and battlefield surgeon alongside Krepela and Gershon.[22]

Doc Krepela was widely regarded as being something of a miracle worker among his charges for his creative responses to several other life-threatening incidents. On one occasion on New Georgia, he gingerly removed a live Japanese high-explosive shell with a hair-trigger fuse from a Marine's leg, and he also repaired the smashed skull of another Marine who had been brained by the recoil of a 155mm gun.[23] The number of men who survived deadly attacks of malaria and dengue fever is proof alone of the successes that Miles Krepela, Nate Gershon, Jake Goodwin, Goodwin's successor Robert Wiethoff, and their largely unsung Navy corpsmen and pharmacist's mates worked in the jungles of the Pacific. As one of Krepela's corpsmen said to Sergeant Sam Stavisky, the Ninth's assigned combat correspondent on Rendova and New Georgia: "When a Marine goes down, a corpsman goes up."[24]

Camp Life in the Boondocks; "Scrounging"

Life in the Marine Corps, according to one joke of the period:

Question: What's the difference between the Marines and the Boy Scouts? Answer: The Boy Scouts have adult supervision.

Even in the rear areas of New Georgia and Banika, the more refined campsites of the Ninth lacked most of the basic creature comforts. The ever-present tropical humidity tended to rot the canvas tents, and a coating of mold and mildew would frequently blossom if left uncleaned for any length of time. The Marines' clothes, leather and canvas equipment, and boots would likewise deteriorate rapidly; in some cases, men's underpants and trousers literally rotted off their bodies. As a result of the damp tropical climate, many men in the Solomons suffered from trench foot, athlete's foot, and other fungal rashes infesting their crotches and underarms—the "creeping crud." This was usually treated by various tinctures, liberally swabbed on the victim by a bored and disgusted corpsman. The campsites themselves were studded with sandbag-revetted foxholes and trenches (often half-filled with rainwater) that served as bomb shelters from Pistol Pete's and Washing Machine Charlie's depredations. The roads and trails were more frequently than not mucky quagmires, and quite a few jeeps and trucks that entered the Ninth's campsites under their own horsepower left under "Marine power" at the end of a tow rope during the rainy seasons.

To conjure up a reasonably accurate depiction of the Ninth's campsites around Munda Field, one can picture the following scene:

A collection of faded olive-drab tents is seemingly ensconced in a field of mud and beaten-down elephant grass. The entire area is surrounded by lush green foliage—giant banyan trees and coconut palms—but is covered overall with a tropical miasma, and a heavy afternoon rain has done little to cool down the atmosphere; in fact, if anything, it now more closely resembles a continual steam bath. A one-lane, more or less circular trail meanders around the circumference of the tents and awnings. One knows that this is the Headquarters, 9th Defense Battalion because a circular sign proudly proclaims the fact to the world at the entrance to the campsite, along with another sign noting it as the home of Duke Radio, "Duke" being the Battalion's call sign.

The ubiquitous 55-gallon steel drum is everywhere in evidence and is put to every conceivable use: as supports for vehicle and generator revetments and Biggie Slater's half-underground, corrugated metal radio shack; as garbage and mess hall slop cans; modified as grills, burners and stoves; and cut in half as latrines; and, occasionally, for their intended use, filled with diesel or gasoline, for topping off the Ninth's vehicles. Elsewhere, five-gallon tin cans, originally filled with coffee grounds—the Corps' true lifeblood, preferably never consumed in any way other than jet-black and scaldingly hot—are as omnipresent and omni-functional as the large steel drums, serving similar uses but on a more intimate scale. A few of Pogiebait McCall's Lister bags full of purified water, each looking just like "a huge cow's udder," as Captain Reichner once described them, hang from tripods and tree limbs.

Palms and colossal banyan trees stud the hills and rises overlooking the camp. In places, the tumid smell of mud is overpowered by riper odors: slop from the Battalion's mess hall and semi-empty marmite cans of half-warmed, leftover Spam; the stink of the latrines, not yet burned off by the day's unused powder bags from the Long Toms; the pungent carcasses of hundreds of crushed land crabs and other New Georgia fauna; and, not far from the mess hall, the sinister reek of human death: the smells of decomposition from corpses and skeletons of Munda's dead Japanese defenders in a bulldozed cemetery—many of them killed in fact by the Ninth's bombardments—and whose outraged skulls, bones and limbs jut upwards from the overturned earth towards the damp tropical skies. A few radio antennas and field-telephone lines vie with the trees for altitude.

And—if the observer looks more closely—scattered among the tents, trees and bushes and hidden in the tall grass, one might notice various pieces of non-Marine issue equipment. Several jeeps on the edges of the perimeter, away from the CO's tents, seem to bear traces of fresh Marine-issue forest green paint, but in places barely covering a lighter and browner coat of original Army-issue olive drab camouflage.

The Ninth's scroungers have been hard at work.

The Ninth's battalion headquarters area on New Georgia, near Munda Field.
(Photo by Harry Jones, courtesy of David Slater)

Although the Ninth had a well-deserved reputation for combat discipline
and efficiency, it had also had quite a reputation for scrounging from
the Army and Navy and for its off-duty life. As has been seen, the often-
doubtful logistics situation on Guadalcanal helped to encourage these activities. This wilder, seamier side of the Ninth's existence continued into
the Central Solomons campaign, despite the battalion's augmentations and
supplies of new equipment at the end of the fight for Guadalcanal.

As a result of their depredations on one Navy medical supply dump on
Guadalcanal, in which the Marines used their five-finger discount to help
themselves to a supply of alcohol, the 155mm Group's officers and Army
MPs conducted a fruitless shakedown at dawn for leftover hooch. Battery

A had hidden its stash in a hole under a tent's main tentpole (and as we have seen, later secreted it in a Long Tom's barrel). Battery B wrapped its leftovers in a blanket and hung it in the battery's head. Frustrated by its failure to nab the offenders, island command forced the battalion to break camp one week early and live in beachside pup tents until boarding for Operation TOENAILS commenced. Orders were posted that any member of the Ninth Defense found outside this impromptu quarantine zone would be subjected to a court-martial. After the Central Solomons campaign, with the Ninth scheduled to leave New Georgia but well recalling its prior marauding activities on Guadalcanal, that island's Army commander allegedly refused to let the battalion be stationed there ever again, with one apparent consequence being that it was sent instead to virgin territory in the Russells instead of returning to Guadalcanal at the end of Operation TOENAILS.

Similar troubles arose on New Georgia at campaign's end. With a colorful band of characters like VMF-214's Black Sheep stationed nearby, it was inevitable that brawls and thefts would occur between these two units. One confrontation between a group of Marine gunners and the aviators over stolen hooch almost resulted in a shoot-out. Several Army units nearby began to lose large amounts of their gear, including several jeeps. David Slater recalled: "Legend has it that we had guys who could change an Army jeep into a Marine Corps jeep in an hour. A fast repaint and stenciling of U.S.M.C. ID did it." The culprits were identified when an Army MP unit recaptured one of the jeeps with a Marine nestled behind its wheel. The battalion now incurred the wrath of New Georgia's island commander, again an Army general, who had a new guardhouse built in which he jailed the arrested Marine, and on which a sign was posted, decreeing it to be "A Brig for Marines (9th)." As Chadwick recalled: "He soon had more Marines in the brig. We felt lucky because we finally received our shipping for the Russells, or our whole battalion would have been his guests."

Their arrival in the Russells did little to dampen the Ninth's light-fingered miscreants. After having been ordered to pitch camp on Banika next to the fuel-filled swamp, Colonel O'Neil finally convinced the island's Army commander to authorize a relocation to higher ground. It took about a month to build the new bivouac area and complete the relocation. Afterwards, with little to do but clean equipment and brush up on training, someone in the chain of command decided that the 155mm Group had an ample share of potential stevedores, and work parties were assigned to help unload ships and move cargo. This detail lasted for several weeks, until a supply officer noticed that too much cargo was vanishing. In one instance, a truckload of potatoes and salted mutton disappeared without a trace while being "unloaded" by a squad from the 155mm Group. While on another work party, Jack and Chadwick spied several forlorn-looking wooden crates labeled "Planter's Peanuts." Needless to say, several crates did not reach the new supply depot.

Back at the Ninth's base camp, Jack, Chadwick, and their buddies eagerly broke open the crates to find not peanuts but an even more welcome and tradeable treat: cigarettes, dispensed in increments of fifty or one hundred to a can: "We had enough cigarettes to last the whole Battalion a hundred years." Best of all, the cans were perfect form fillers for the standard Marine-issue horseshoe backpack; as David Slater reminisced, "Heavy smokers would have more cigarettes than gear in their packs." With so many young men already hooked on the habit, the US military distributed tobacco rations liberally, as much as anything to boost morale and soothe nerves. Accordingly, cigarettes were supplied in huge quantities, often for free.[25] Where food in the Pacific lacked taste or was otherwise in short supply, the spicy taste of tobacco substituted for food and helped curb the appetite. Jack had already started smoking before the war, but the war hooked him for good. Pogiebait McCall may have had only a few vices, but this one would get him in the end.

Why did the battalion's penchant for scavenging go on to these extremes? It invariably seemed to the average Marine that not only did the Army and Navy have superior logistical systems, but the quality, quantity, and diversity of things in these services' supply systems were vastly better than what was available in the Corps' logistics base. Part of this may have been due to a "strictly business" attitude on the part of the Corps' logisticians. As opposed to the Army and Navy, which generally took more care to supply their respective troops with creature comforts, most Marines (until 1943) had volunteered for this and, as such, were likely expected to tolerate a higher level of personal discomfort. Also, in much of Marine planning, the Corps' logistical structure was geared directly toward combat and combat support items—strictly beans and bullets, at the general expense of beds, beer, and "baloney." The infusion of the crusty and rambunctious "old breed" Fifth Defense Polar Bears into the battalion on Cuba may also have affected the younger Marines' attitudes at an early date:

> We *learned* from the contingent of "Polar Bears" [David Slater recalled] that came down to Gitmo on the *Merak*. This was a rough crew: quite a few old Corps types, flotsam and jetsam of the Depression. [Upon] our arrival at Cuba, [Colonel] Nimmer had us take up a formation on the parade ground—I

still see it in my mind's eye as though it were yesterday—and proceeded to ream us out as the scum of the earth hardly worthy of his command (and here quite a few of us were innocent young boots). He had perused the record books of the Polar Bears the night before and discovered that they were a rather tarnished bunch. However, he magnanimously announced, he would expunge their derelictions and allow them a new leaf in the 9th. (Fat chance!)

As far as the Ninth's enlistees could tell, the battalion and group commanders officially took a dim view of their men's acquisitions made outside the standard channels of supply, and the Ninth's COs would periodically remind their subordinates of the consequences of theft and the need to maintain good supply discipline. Nevertheless, knowing full well the unit's unfulfilled requisitions and dire needs for larger pieces of equipment not found on an authorized table of organization—trucks, jeeps, LVTs, etc.—the

David ("Biggie") Slater exiting one of the battalion's communications tents near Munda Field. Photo by Harry Jones, courtesy of David Slater.

COs themselves actively sought to loan, scrounge, or borrow such equipment. Before the New Georgia campaign (besides his creative ammunition accounting method, as we saw), Colonel Scheyer and the battalion's supply officer signed temporary hand receipts to borrow nine additional LVTs and extra machine guns from the Third Marine Division.[26] Given the sometimes shaky supply situation, it is probably not at all surprising that the battery and group commanders might have turned a blind eye or dropped subtle hints to their NCOs and junior enlisted when the latter took to their own sources to beef up the unit's supplies and gear.

In May 1944, as the Ninth packed its gear and marched to its pre-invasion quarantine area for its next field mission, the Russell Islands Command's quartermasters would have been amazed to find the quantity and variety of "borrowed" gear left behind in the battalion's bivouac area. With good reason, Colonel Scheyer, on his departure from the battalion, reputedly said that if he ever faced combat again, he hoped it would be with a unit as great as the Ninth, but he also hoped he would never, *ever* have to command an outfit like the Ninth in a rear area again!

Attitudes toward Women and Sex

If a poll were taken of the Ninth's young men as to what was most noticeably lacking in the Pacific, it would have been female companionship. There were few native women (except for the brief sojourn on New Caledonia, some of the inhabitants of Banika, Guadalcanal, and New Georgia—who generally were not viewed as objects of romantic interest but frequently were hired through bartering goods or food by some members of the Ninth to help with laundry or menial chores—and later on Guam) to open up any opportunities for romance or sexual release. With the general absence of women in this sector of the South Pacific and the high testosterone levels of a bunch of young Marines, it was hardly surprising that things would get out of hand too often when an attractive young woman appeared in the area.

During the Ninth's stay in the Russells, the unit had its first USO show of the entire war.[27] The unit's carpenters had built a stage and amphitheater for showing movies, and a traveling USO Camp Show featuring Ray Milland and three beautiful starlets staged a two-hour show to the lusty roars, catcalls, and applause of the sex-starved leathernecks. After the show, the USO troupe was invited to the battalion's officers' club for drinks and some banter. Unfortunately, during an interval when the lights went out, one of the actresses felt herself being groped, and she began to scream loudly. As the lights came back on moments later, still screaming,

Jack (wearing cap) with several Ninth Defense buddies
and two Red Cross "donut girls" on Banika, early 1944.
Author's collection.

the irate and tearful actress slapped the officer nearest her—who happened
to be none other than Colonel O'Neil. Upon hearing her accusation, the
red-faced (for more reasons than one) CO apologized to her for his officers'
conduct and promptly closed down the party. An officers' call was held the
next morning, in which the colonel angrily demanded to know who was
responsible. Unsurprisingly, the guilty party did not reveal himself. The
enlisted Marines never found out precisely what the colonel did to his
officers in response to this misbehavior, but for several days afterwards,
the battalion's officers were noticeably close-mouthed and downcast over
the incident.

In April 1944, not long before the battalion's departure from the Russells,
a similar incident occurred but on a larger and much more serious scale.
The Seabees had completed a hospital on Banika, Mobile Hospital 10 or

"MOB 10," and Navy nurses were assigned to the island to staff it. Shortly after the nurses' arrival, a group of Navy medical officers took some of them for a jeep tour of Banika. Unfortunately, the day they had chosen for their tour was a Sunday, when many of the Ninth's personnel usually took their semi-weekly showers. Since no women other than the indigenous Russell Islanders were generally found on Banika, the battalion had not had good cause to enclose the open-air showers. In the Russells' tropical heat, with uniform requirements being relaxed at best, "our crew was practically a nudist colony," David Slater recalled. It was well after Reveille, and many of the Marines were showering or doing their laundry in nothing more than their skivvies when a cry of "*Women!*" arose from the far end of the road. That one-word yell, at full-throated volume, was all it took to provoke a stampede.

Within seconds, a large pack of semi-naked Marines ran down to the road, wolf-whistling and yelling. The leathernecks in the open showers turned around to give the nurses and their escorts a show of unanticipated full-frontal nudity. Some of the Marines hollered crude comments at the highly embarrassed MOB 10 nurses, who tried to hide their faces and turn their heads. Whether out of apparent solidarity with the others or pure perversity, some of the otherwise semi-dressed Marines themselves dropped their trousers and skivvies and joined in the flashing and heckling of the nurses and doctors. In a cloud of dust and with an angry honking of horns at the catcalling mob, the convoy rapidly left the area for the hospital.

In a matter of minutes, some of the battalion's officers and NCOs descended on the group, raising hell. By day's end, screens or tarpaulins enclosed the showers and latrines. An order was then posted to the effect that because they had abused the lax dress privileges of the Russells, the Ninth Defense's Marines would now be required to dress in full dungarees at all times. The reports of the enlisted men's lewd behavior toward the nurses, plus long-standing allegations of their piracy of supplies, may have hastened a decision to expedite shipping schedules so as to get the battalion redeployed from the Russells as soon as possible. Still, to the more warped minds and wits of the Ninth Defense, the men's rancid conduct toward MOB 10's nurses was somehow viewed as a cause for sick humor.

Although absent from the Ninth's postings in the Pacific, the mere existence of women Marines was an additional source of grousing and gossip, often obscene, among the old salts, Jack included, who occasionally griped in later years: "I joined the Corps before there were women or dogs!"[28] Despite their service to country and Corps, the 18,460 members of the

Marine Corps Women's Reserve who served during the war were the victims of much harassment from many of their male counterparts. (Some of the women, however, gave back as good as they got and came up with their own profane and colorful nicknames for their male colleagues.[29]) Some male Marines viewed the presence of women in the Corps as a diminishment of their manhood; others argued that it would lead to a corruption of the Corps' traditions and fighting spirit. Despite his own grousing, Jack's views on this subject would shift later in the war. The near-constant loneliness and the lack of female companionship was alleviated to some degree on Banika by contacts with a few American teachers, Red Cross girls, and missionaries (but with precious few dates).

There were apparently few incidents of homosexual activity. This may have been attributable to the attitudes of the majority of the Ninth's Marines themselves, but it may also have been curbed by the absolutely savage treatment meted out to those few caught engaging openly in such activities. In 1944, which was still several years before the issuance of the Kinsey Report and later psychological studies, homosexuality was regarded as neither a behavioral proclivity nor a preexisting psychological condition. It was deemed to be a form of mental sickness, and a particularly vile one at that. In civilian life, the prescribed medical treatments for homosexuals were grim enough; in the military of the 1940s, they were ruthless.

Years after the war, Jack, who was noticeably prudish about discussing sexual matters of any kind in front of his family, recalled to his wife Pat the fate of two men caught *in flagrante delicto* late one night aboard the *Hunter Liggett* shortly before the Ninth's landing on Guadalcanal. They were hauled out in their skivvies and left on deck in a fenced-in area. They were fed only bread and water, and they were left in the open to sit there, all day long in the sun, as an object lesson of sorts. Some people threw things at them; others spat at or cursed them as perverts. "They were treated just like animals." Of this incident, Captain Reichner remembered the following line as he censored one of his battery member's postcards home afterwards: "They caught your artist friend eating meat at midnight and he is now in the brig."[30]

Once ashore on Guadalcanal, the 155mm Group's commanding officer, Colonel Baker, devised a similarly grim punishment for these two. Frank Chadwick recalled:

> He had them pitch their shelter halves in a small barbed wire area. They were given a canteen of water per day, one meal and [were] not allowed to wash. . . . They were dirty and beginning to smell very bad [by the time that

the] chaplain heard about it and came over for a visit. He informed [Colonel Baker] that this [was] crude and disgusting and gave him one day to either court-martial them or put them back on duty. The chaplain came back the [next] day and found nothing had been done. He informed him that he was not going to bother the Battalion C.O. but send a wire directly to Admiral Halsey [then serving as the area commander for Guadalcanal and the Solomons], who he knew personally, and let him deal with the problem. Needless to say, the two Marines left the Canal the next day for New Caledonia. No one ever heard what happened to them but the [battalion] C.O. kept close reins on [Colonel Baker] thereafter.

The 155mm Group's muster roll for January 1943 reveals the fate of at least one of the two men, who was a member of the "155s." In terse and cryptic language, under the column "GENERAL COURT MARTIAL PRISONER," accompanying remarks indicate that the prisoner was awaiting transportation to the US Naval Prison at Portsmouth, New Hampshire—the naval version of the Army's military prison at Fort Leavenworth—for five years' confinement after conviction by a general court-martial effective January 26, 1943 for "Scandalous Conduct tending to the Destruction of Good Morale (Oral Coition—one specification)," having also been reduced in rank from a private first class to private. The muster roll's remarks also indicate that, following imprisonment, the man would be dishonorably discharged—an act with long-term consequences for one's future odds of employment in postwar America. Perhaps also adding to Jack's and several of his buddies' reticence and overall discomfort as to the situation was the fact that the Marine in question was one of their old Platoon Nine Boot Camp classmates from Parris Island.[31]

Sex was a frequent subject of discussion, whether telling dirty jokes, bragging about one's female conquests, or commiserating with the recipient of the dreaded "Dear John" letter. Skinny-dipping, communal showers, the traditional silliness of Equator-crossing rituals, and playing "grabass" were all deemed permissible, too, and few seemed to think there was anything prurient or objectionable about such activities. In some respects, it was a more naïve time, and teenage and college-aged boys could do such things without fear of being labeled unusual. Homosexual behavior, however, was one social taboo that even wartime did little to break down, and the treatment to be expected from one's peers if caught experimenting in that fashion would have undoubtedly been even more vicious, in many cases, than the semi-official treatment inflicted by Colonel Baker. Not that the official punishments themselves were any more tolerable. There was certainly no "don't ask, don't tell" policy in effect in the military in those days. Anyone caught engaging in such acts would risk, at best, a court-martial and dishonorable discharge, with the stigma attached thereto and a life-long impediment against many jobs in the civilian work force, or, at worst, incarceration—either in a military prison or in a mental ward.

Regardless of how one felt about the offense in question, Jack later admitted to his wife that he thought the punishment administered was "a hell of a way to go."

The Haunted Finger: Attitudes toward the Enemy

One cannot disguise the overall deep and abiding hatred shared by many (if not most) Marines toward their adversary. To a very real degree, the feelings of Pacific veterans toward the Japanese often differed both qualitatively and quantitatively from the feelings of many GIs in the European Theater toward the Germans and Italians. This difference animated many aspects of the Pacific War and helped create an even more savage war than existed, in many respects, in the Allied campaigns against the Axis powers in Western Europe and North Africa.

To be fair, this is only a generalization: certainly, many American troops and sailors despised the Germans. On a more personal level, many of Jack's fellow Franklin High School friends came to do so for a variety of reasons. One met and married a young German Jewish refugee whose family fled Germany shortly after the *Kristallnacht*, just before the Nazis' war on the Jews reached its most murderous proportions. Two schoolmates, Jimmy Gentry and Fred "Brutus" Isaacs, young US Army sergeants, helped liberate the Dachau and Buchenwald concentration camps, respectively, in spring 1945, and they would bear witness to the horrors they saw there for the rest of their lives. Jack himself would have added personal cause to hate the Nazis: Jimmy Gentry's big brother and one of Jack's closest schooltime friends, David Gentry, an Army Signal Corps lineman, was killed by the Germans in Italy. By and large, however, feelings of anger toward the Germans tended to be directed either at leading individuals like Hitler and Goering or, more amorphously, to organizations like the Nazi Party, the Gestapo, and the SS.[32]

This was manifestly not the case in the Pacific: again, as a generalization, the enemy was largely defined as being all Japanese people. There were undoubtedly deeply racial overtones on both sides. For the Japanese, this involved some resentment of the Americans dating as far back as

Commodore Perry's 1853 forcible opening of Japan to foreign trade, one of the first episodes of "gunboat diplomacy," bolstered by the anti-Asian immigrant hysteria of the late 1800s and the 1920s, and in certain circles, a contempt for Americans as racist, ill-disciplined, and avaricious materialists.[33] For Americans, jingoistic newspapers and magazines had deprecated Asian people since before the turn of the century. There were also reports of Japanese brutality during the 1930s, which may have influenced some of the Marines in their prewar teenage years. These included reports of the Rape of Nanking in 1937; the sinking of the US gunboat *Panay* by Japanese aircraft in the Yangtze River that same year; reports of Japanese gas attacks on Chinese civilians; and, hitting much closer to home, the brutal 1942 Bataan Death March, in which thousands of US and Filipino POWs—including several Middle Tennesseans—would suffer and perish en route to prison camps. These views were strongly reinforced by the Marines' training and by wartime propaganda—"The only good Jap is a dead Jap"[34]—which almost constantly used the epithets "Jap" and "Nip" in daily speech and in writings of all kinds. Added to this was the popular press's own contributions in newspapers, magazines, movies, and animated cartoons. Many of these did not blossom until after the Christmas Tree Marines had been inducted and shipped off to the front. Even so, some of this propaganda was available at a very early date in the war.

The local evening newspaper, the *Nashville Banner*, printed a poem of great savagery on its front page on the day after Pearl Harbor. Placed next to a photograph of Roosevelt's request to Congress that very day to declare war and under the headlines "CONGRESS DECLARES WAR: 3,000 CASUALTIES AT HAWAII," the free-verse poem, composed by *Banner* editor-in-chief James G. Stahlman, may have typified much of what appeared elsewhere in the popular press in the days and weeks to come, all of which helped set the tone and which reflected the anger and desire for revenge felt by many Americans after Pearl Harbor. This piece of doggerel also reflects some remarkably prescient comments about the nastiness of the war that was about to come to the Pacific:

At last we're at war.
At war with Japan.
We didn't want it.
We tried to avoid it.
We sought peace.
At the very moment

When Jap bombers swooped low
To murder Americans
On duty
On our ships,
Our air fields,
Our foreign stations.

We stood by too long.
We were too patient.
We trusted the dastardly Orientals too far.
We were just a bunch of saps.
So the Japs pounced down,
But they'll bounce back.

This isn't going to be child's play.
We're in for some tough fighting.
But not a circumstance compared
With what is coming
To the Sons of the Rising Sun.
No! Sir! They've asked for it.
Now let 'em have it.
Total war.
All-out war.
No quarter.

Let's make it what they started.
Let's track them to their holes.
Let's sink their fleet
If it takes our last ship,
Our last sailor,
Our last shot.
Let's blockade their population into starvation.
Let's bomb their cities to shambles.
Let's give them what they asked for.
Let's blast
And shoot
And bomb
And burn.
Let's put the dirty yellow beasts
Where they belong.

This is the opportunity of the ages.
Japan has defied the world.
Let's wipe her from the face of the earth.
It can be done.
It must be done.

There's been nothing compared with her perfidy,
Her bestiality,
Her trickery,
Her lying,
Her deceit.

Japan is doomed.
Let's make that doom sudden,
Absolute.
Let's hasten the day
When the sun will set
On the land of the Rising Sun.
To Hell with the slant-eyed Son of Heaven.
To Hell with his seventy million little yellow devils.
That's my ticket.
I hope you like it.
Let's get going![35]

The *Banner*'s hymn of hate was hardly alone in expressing these sentiments. Jack once recalled that, after Pearl Harbor, it seemed that every time he heard the words "treacherous," "deceitful," "yellow," "cowardly," "dastardly," "back-stabbing," or "sneaky," the word "Jap" was almost certain to follow. To what degree the *Banner*'s headlines and Stahlman's poem helped to influence Jack's decision to join up, I cannot say, but Jack preserved the headlines and the entire front section of the December 8, 1941 *Banner* in his scrapbook for years afterwards.

Still, it was not necessarily a question of "pure" racism, blindly applied to all Asian peoples. Many Marines, Jack included, harbored no particular grudges against Asians in general, and many harbored sentiments in favor of the Chinese, surely as oppressed a group of humans as existed in the 1930s and 1940s. More than a few American churches had sponsored missionaries to the Orient. Pearl Buck's novels of Asia were bestsellers in the interwar period, and after the massively destructive 1923 Tokyo earthquake, American churches, humanitarian groups, and relief agencies contributed tons of supplies to the Japanese. Many young Marines like Jack, who were fairly naïve and who had not traveled far from home until they left for Boot Camp, probably could not have distinguished between a Japanese, a Chinese, a Korean, and a Filipino unless somebody had pointed out their differences. For many Marines, the feelings of anger toward their enemy were not preexisting but acquired.

One piece of hard evidence occasionally cited by Jack and some of the Ninth's Marines that many claims of Japanese barbarity were not necessarily just "war stories" occurred after the battalion's arrival on Guadalcanal, where some heard of the "Goettge massacre." In autumn 1942, the First Marine Division's chief intelligence officer, Lt. Colonel Frank Goettge, led a patrol to investigate a beachside area where a number of Japanese wounded had allegedly been abandoned by their own forces. This patrol was ambushed and surrounded; the sole survivor, who feigned death and escaped at high tide, claimed that he had seen Japanese officers and men killing the prisoners and wounded of Goettge's patrol.[36] Generalized talk about the Goettge massacre was just another stimulus for the very hard feelings directed toward the enemy. The overall attitude about the Goettge patrol's fate can be summed up by Frank Chadwick: "We all talked about it some, sure, but we all figured Goettge was just a do-gooder. We figured we wouldn't make the same mistake he did."

The scuttlebutt was that a Marine must never let himself be taken prisoner by the Japanese. The Marines' pride in neither surrendering nor ever leaving a dead or wounded Marine behind on the battlefield assumed a new, darker meaning, as it was widely suspected that the Japanese would torture and kill any POWs or mutilate the dead. The general expectation was that the Japanese soldier, in turn, would likewise never let himself be taken prisoner and would fight to the death. In time, tales would also circulate on Guadalcanal that because they were starving, the Japanese would resort to cannibalism—a tale that, in some dire circumstances, was later proved to be true in certain instances on New Guinea and in the Bonin Islands.[37] The grim fate of Wantuck and Rothschild, in the Ninth's own experience with an all-out Japanese infantry assault, hardened these attitudes and imbued many members of the unit with distrust and an almost fanatical hatred of the enemy.

The Tank Platoon's discovery on the Munda Trail of a pair of dead Army medics, apparently shot down as they attempted to rescue wounded GIs, hardened the hearts of Captain Blake and his tankers who, only moments before, had pitied a mangled and dying Japanese antitank gunner whom they had just shot. That even a literate and educated man like Robert Blake (an erstwhile reporter for the *Cleveland Plain Dealer*) could be moved to such bitterness and fury was representative of what the sheer hatred and violence of the Pacific War was doing to men's minds:

> In a glance the story tells itself. These two medics had heard the wounded scream and crawled out to bring them in. They got as far as this, when the Jap machine guns caught them and they too lay and bled and begged for help, until death came for them at last. . . .
>
> The full impact of the crime the Japanese committed strikes me. . . . *How I wish that I had shot that wounded Jap, hollowed out his skull point blank with my forty-five, or better, ripped him open with my pocket knife!* I grit my teeth. I will kill them, kill them, kill them, a thousand lives for every one of ours! And if compassion ever tempts me, I will think of that field of blackened American corpses, of the dead gunner and his mate, of the riddled stretcher bearers, and of the wounded who lay and bled, and knew no help could come, and died in agony, forsaken, and alone.[38] [*Emphasis added.*]

Jack himself admitted: "We couldn't understand them. It was like they were crazy people. They were fanatics, and the only way you could stop them was to kill them. Life just didn't have the same meaning to them as it did to us." The concepts that the Emperor Hirohito was the living incarnation of the sun goddess *Amaterasu* and that Japanese soldiers who died bravely in combat would essentially be deified were religious principles so unlike the Judeo-Christian ethics of the average American as to be very difficult for the typical Marine, GI, or sailor to comprehend in any way other than by simply deciding that the enemy was, in essence, "crazy."

The environment of this kind of war itself undoubtedly also contributed to hatred on all sides. In Europe, while many of the ordinary American creature comforts were lacking, the cities, towns, and villages roughly approximated what one might expect of American urban and rural life in the 1930s and 1940s. There, a GI had a reasonable chance of possibly finding such comforts and maybe even inhabitants with whom he could relate. This was scarcely the case in the South Pacific: the climate and terrain were far removed from anything that Jack and most of his counterparts had ever experienced; tropical diseases were rampant; and the natives were frequently in hiding and, when seen, were often regarded as childlike and backward by the majority of both the Americans and Japanese. The overall environment tended to reinforce a "backs to the wall" sense of isolation and deprivation—in the words of the poem, "For this God-forsaken outpost/ Is a substitute for Hell." This attitude could just as easily be applied to the average Japanese soldier, as well as to the average Marine.[39]

Both sides' pre-combat military training and indoctrination, of course, amplified their mutual hatred. While the Marines undoubtedly had ample cause to despise Boot Camp, the brutal training and abuse meted out to Japanese conscripts in all branches of that nation's military made many of PI's rigors seem pale by comparison. Robert Edgerton wrote:

> Derisively called 'less than a penny' (the price of their draft-notice postcard), [Japanese] soldiers and sailors were hazed, sworn at, slapped, beaten and forced to complete degrading tasks. They had no privacy, and any form of protest was a capital crime. An officer or NCO who lost his temper might actually beat a recruit to death. One [Japanese] soldier wrote this: 'One year's army life has drained the humanity out of everyone. Second-year privates treat us first-year privates as though we were their slaves or rather machines. . . . Were a second-class private to discover that I had written a letter like this in the toilet, I would probably be murdered.'[40]

In consequence, relatively few prisoners were taken by either side in the Pacific War. Perhaps more so than in Europe, flame weapons were extensively used: both backpack-carried and tank-mounted, flamethrowers became a staple of island fighting, and their first extensive usage by American troops was against the Japanese on New Georgia. Despite home-front criticisms of their barbarousness, they continued to be extensively used in the Pacific. Likewise, napalm bombs were also used against the Japanese.[41] There may be some grim irony in tracing the increasing use of flame-generating weapons, from the flamethrower roasting of Japanese troops in bunkers and caves in 1944 to the firebombing of Tokyo and the atomic incinerations of Hiroshima and Nagasaki in 1945,[42] as a literal embodiment of the American press's exhortations in 1941 to "send the Japs to Hell" and to make their doom, in the *Banner*'s words, "sudden" and "absolute."

Even the dead on both sides were often savaged. There were reports of mutilations of dead Americans by the Japanese, but such atrocities were not limited to the Japanese. Jack and others recalled seeing American ghouls who collected Japanese body parts, including those who pried gold fillings out of the mouths of the dead.[43] Some Navy personnel decorated a boat landing on Guadalcanal with a row of skulls hung from a rope. Enemy graveyards, such as one near the Ninth's headquarters adjacent to Munda Field, were sometimes desecrated. At least one Ninth Defense Marine carried around a Japanese skull that he scavenged from this graveyard after its bulldozering on command of a Ninth Defense major, until he was finally forced by another officer to dispose of it. With a few exceptions, this type of ghoulish behavior was more common among rear-area or new troops who had not seen prolonged combat than among seasoned frontline troops who had gotten a bellyful of death and its residues. While such behavior was hardly an accepted norm, it may not have been an illogical extension of the war of unremitting savagery being waged in the swamps, jungles, and coral atolls of the Pacific. Appropriately, the unit's distinctive insignia carried by many of the Ninth's vehicles and on the turrets of the Tank Platoon was the number "9," fashioned into a death's-head.

While hate in all its forms was a significant aspect of the Marines' attitude toward their enemy, many leathernecks—Jack included—had to admit to some grudging respect for the Japanese soldier's courage and resourcefulness. Plenty of hard evidence of these traits could be found in the actions of the submarine commander off Koli Point; the tenacity of the Japanese aircrews in their raids over Guadalcanal and Rendova; the lonely stubbornness of the motorcycle courier on Kolombangara; in the desperate charges at Zanana Beach; and in the human-bomb attacks on Captain Blake's tanks. The ability of the average Japanese soldier to survive on little or no rations, for weeks at a time, was impressive to the Marines, as was his ability to improvise bunkers and equipment from various available means. Admit-

The Ninth's unofficial insignia.
Author's collection.

Taken by a Ninth Defense Marine from a Japanese cemetery on New Georgia, this skull was carried around as a souvenir until an officer forced the Marine to bury it. Grisly souvenirs like this were not altogether uncommon sights among Marines and GIs in the Pacific. Photo by Harry Jones, courtesy of David Slater.

tedly, it was also easier to hate an enemy who was seldom seen when alive, who was not directly seen when being targeted for destruction. Such an enemy usually came into notice only in an antiaircraft weapon's gunsight or when found as a corpse. In time, though, several experiences on Guam would add some doses of compassion to Jack's and some of his comrades' views toward the Japanese as human beings and not merely as a faceless and monstrous enemy.

Still, some of what Jack may had seen or heard discussed on Guadalcanal and the Central Solomons resurfaced about twenty-five years later in the form of a fairly sick practical joke that he played on his family. One Halloween, he called his two small children into the family kitchen. When the entire family was assembled there, he eagerly announced, "Hey, I've got a war souvenir I've never shown you before. You want to take a look?" In one hand, he cupped a small, nondescript white cardboard box, its lid partly ajar. As he took off the lid, he solemnly pronounced: "It's a finger I cut off a dead Jap on Guadalcanal—and look, there's some dried blood on the cotton. Hey, wait a minute: *it's still moving!*"

As his two children screamed wildly in fear, the haunted "Jap finger" began wiggling around on its bed of cotton. It scared the daylights out of both of his small children. As we ran to hide, tears rolling down our faces, tears rolled down *his* face, too—of laughter. Our mother berated him, and Jack quickly and sheepishly admitted to his two distraught children that he had painted his own index finger with yellowish iodine and had cut a hole in the bottom of the box to fake his souvenir. "See? It's all okay, honey. It's not real!"

As far as Jack's practical jokes went, the haunted finger was one that was hard to forget. As the war in the Pacific went, however, there were undoubtedly quite a few soldiers and sailors for whom such "souvenirs" were very real, indeed.

Gyrenes, Dogfaces, Seabees, and Swabbies: Attitudes toward the Corps' Sister Services

The Marines, of course, were long noted for their rivalries with the Army and Navy. The "swabbies" of the Navy were often the butt of the Marines' hazing for their "luxurious" life on board ship, with three good meals a day, frequent treats of milk and ice cream, and reasonably comfortable conditions compared with the rigors of field duty. The treatment meted out to the sailors paled, however, in comparison to that directed at the Army, which most often took the brunt of the leathernecks' worst abuse.

From Boot Camp days onwards, Marines were taught that they were something special, volunteers who fought because they had the guts to do so, as opposed to mere draftees who went into the Army because they had to[44] or National Guardsmen who had (it was claimed) joined before the war just to dress up and show off for their neighbors. The Marines, fairly or not, often blamed the Army for their logistical shortfalls instead of the Navy Department, which actually exercised the power of the purse over Marine logistics and procurement. Many Marines despised General Douglas MacArthur, "Dugout Doug," whom they personally (if wrongly) blamed for the abandonment of the Fourth Marines on the Bataan Peninsula and the First Division's isolation and starvation on Guadalcanal.[45] Likewise, the Ninth's Marines harbored feelings of contempt toward several of the Army units they were assigned to support, regarding them as rank amateurs at best or, at worst, dangerous to be around. These feelings of distaste were often reciprocated.

As noted earlier, the Army's Forty-Third Infantry Division garnered a good deal of disrespect from the leathernecks. Its lack of basic combat skills on New Georgia had shocked many of the Ninth's Marines, but the Ninth's dislike of this particular division predated Operation TOENAILS. As Hank Reichner remembered of his battery's encounters with the Forty-Third on the Canal: "We referred to [this] division as (General) 'Hester's Happy Hustling Housewives.' We had also developed a custom of barking like dogs whenever a convoy passed by or on other appropriate occasions. Of course, they referred to us as 'Bellhops.'"[46] Around the end of February 1943, however, there were fewer opportunities for jeering and brawls between the Housewives and the Bellhops, as large elements of the Forty-Third left Koli Point on Operation CLEANSLATE to capture the Russell Islands before the New Georgia campaign. The hellholes of Rendova and New Georgia only deepened this mutual disrespect.

The differences in morale, basic military skills, and tactical effectiveness between the Ninth's batteries and the component units of the Forty-Third Division were perhaps not necessarily as simple as the gulf between the Marine Corps' ethos driven in and reinforced by Boot Camp (although that certainly may have been a part of it, as far as the outlook of the Ninth's men goes) and that of the newly activated National Guard outfits.[47] After all, part of the cadre of the Forty-Third's officers and NCOs were long-term soldiers with more than a bare modicum of experience. Before arriving on New Georgia, the Ninth had gotten its combat blooding on Guadalcanal. In all fairness to both the Forty-Third Infantry and its sister National Guard division on New Georgia, the Thirty-Seventh Infantry, both were sent into largely unprepared for the environment to be faced on New Georgia. The location for their introduction to war was a brutal one, too: "Halsey gave the 43rd Division an extremely hard objective on one of the worst pieces of real estate in the South Pacific. *It was one of the last places on earth to send a unit for initiation into the World War II charnel house.* After reconstruction and leave, the 43rd and 37th returned to action in the Pacific [and when sent] back into action they served very well."[48](Emphasis added.) Both divisions ultimately learned their trade; however, the first impressions they made died hard with the Marines.

Distrust, however, was not necessarily directed at all Army soldiers or units equally. For other Army divisions with a Regular Army core or the more experienced and better-led National Guard units—e.g., "Lightning Joe" Collins's Twenty-Fifth Infantry Division or the Seventy-Seventh Infantry Division—the Marines developed a grudging respect. The Ninth's encounters with the Twenty-Fifth Infantry Division on both Guadalcanal and New Georgia were more favorable because the leathernecks considered the Twenty-Fifth to be a more professional outfit and one that would be less likely to get you killed from its troops' inexperience or sloppiness. The Twenty-Fifth "Tropic Lightning" Division evidenced "a combat edge far superior to other Army units" in that sector.[49] In the later Guam campaign, the Marines of the III Amphibious Corps would be so impressed with the performance of Major General Andrew Bruce's Seventy-Seventh Infantry Division that many Marines on Guam would nickname the New York-based Organized Reserve division—in the highest token of respect a Marine could award to an outfit of Army dogfaces—the "77th Marine Division."[50]

In contrast to some of the ship-borne elements of the Navy, Jack and many of the Ninth's Marines formed a deep, abiding appreciation for the Navy's Seabee engineering battalions, particularly the older members of those units. The Seabees had been instrumental in helping the battalion disembark at Rendova, and when let down by the Army engineers' refusal to come ashore, Seabees helped the Ninth's artillery groups build positions and lug their guns into place. The average Seabee appeared to the average young Marine to be much older than he was, and a lot of good-natured teasing took place between the Ninth's Marines and the Seabees to that effect. (One frequent joke was that the Ninth's young leathernecks ought to always be nice to the older Seabees, since most of them were probably some Marines' fathers!) Still, the Marines did not necessarily apply the same warm feelings toward the younger Seabees. Jack and many of his pals often viewed those Seabees closer in age to themselves with some suspicion. Pogiebait sometimes wondered if such men had volunteered for the Seabees with the expectation that Seabee life would be an escape from the rigors of combat.[51] Events like the Suicide Point air raid of July 2, 1943, however, proved that service in the Seabees did not provide an immunity from all the dangers of modern war.

On the other hand, the Seabees so frequently contributed to the assistance and comfort of the Ninth that it was tough for even the crustiest and most cynical Marine not to be appreciative. Before the 155mm Group's departure from Banika, it broke camp and was essentially placed in quarantine near the island's pier areas in flimsy tents. A passing Seabee officer remarked to several Battery B Marines that he was looking at a lot of Marines who would be going on board the nearby ships and not returning. When the Marines informed the Seabee that they were part of those same Marines and that their camp was torn down and mess equipment stowed, the Seabee officer ordered his mess hall to feed the waiting leathernecks.

Besides feeding a battalion-sized contingent of its own personnel, the Seabees' mess hall was now also supplying several hundred Marines with chow three times a day for several days. Frank Chadwick recalled: "They went out of their way to see we were taken care of. It was the best food we ever had in the Pacific, and we always thanked God for the Seabees. They were older than we were, and most probably did not have to be in the service at that time, and they treated us as family members."

The Experience of Combat and Attitudes about Combat, Casualties, and Death

Leaving aside combat with the enemy in all its forms, the battalion's preparations for combat were often in themselves a war against time and the elements. Just getting a unit the size of the Ninth Defense offloaded from its transports and landing craft to its battle stations was a massive undertaking in itself.

As already noted, the movement and positioning alone of the Seacoast & Field Artillery Group's 155mm guns required substantial labors. Designed for the static warfare of the Great War, with heavy cast-metal wheels, the group's original GPFs needed exhaustive manhandling to simply drag them in and out of their positions. The GPFs were most effectively positioned for seacoast defense when used with Panama mounts. The preparation of these gun mounts required even more labor in making and pouring concrete and—when ready to depart—in blasting or cracking the guns loose from their concreted turntables. The introduction of the M-1 (Long Tom) model was a vast improvement over the GPFs, both in terms of maintenance and mobility when one had decent roads or trails. The Rendova landings were accompanied by intermittent but torrential rains and glutinous mud. Whatever advantage was gained in off-road mobility was canceled out on Rendova by the need to lug this even heavier model of 155mm gun around by teams of men and bulldozers through the morass. Besides the eight Long Toms, the Ninth's officers and CO also had to contend with the siting and emplacement of eight light tanks, twelve 90mm, sixteen 40mm, twenty-eight 20mm, and thirty-five .50 caliber AA guns, as well as many smaller machine guns, radars, water purification gear, sound detectors, searchlights, and listening posts. Organized for area protection, the Ninth Defense occupied a much wider piece of terrain than the typical twelve-gun Army field artillery battalion of the lighter and more mobile, but less powerful, 105mm howitzers. This dispersal over a broad area led to another difficulty for the Ninth's unit commanders. In modern military terms, this difficulty is referred to as "command, control, and communications," or "C3" for short.

Reduced to its essence, the C3 problem is one of being able to oversee and direct the daily operations and combat performance of a particular unit. In the case of a unit as large as the Ninth, whose positions would be spread out and networked over an area of up to thirty square miles, this simple-sounding concept encountered a high degree of complexity in practice. How can the battalion CO ensure that his AA groups provide maximum coverage without leaving gaps through which enemy planes can penetrate? Further, how can the CO achieve this seamless web of defense without risking friendly fire casualties to US aircraft landing during an air raid or to friendly ground troops if duds fail to explode or shell fragments fall onto their positions? How will the junior commanders set up their defensive perimeters to prevent infiltrators if batteries are in positions separated by several miles from one another? How will neighboring units receive word if enemy intruders are spotted? Each question like this absorbed massive amounts of time and planning, both before and after the unit's deployment. In the early days of the battalion's existence, the unit had few radios—although it had early-model TBY "walkie-talkie" radios, these proved to be low-powered and unreliable—and had to rely extensively on EE-8 field phones and couriers to get messages to and from its various subordinate headquarters. Radios were used sparingly and only in an emergency to reduce the risk of compromising communications security.

To a large degree, each group was already a semi-autonomous entity and self-sufficient, operating in the field much like a mini-battalion. (This aspect may explain why lieutenant colonels and, in a pinch, majors were assigned command of each of the battalion's subordinate groups.) This mode of operation permitted a certain amount of flexibility and ingenuity. Before Operation TOENAILS, for instance, the Special Weapons Group's new CO had formed his entire group into gun teams, blended from the group's individual batteries and armed with a mission-specific mix of 20mm, 40mm, and .50 caliber guns.[52] These gun teams functioned more like miniature task forces instead of batteries or platoons as officially organized on paper.

If C3 problems occupied much of the time of the battalion, group, and battery officers, similar problems arose in the ranks. Spread out as the battalion was in a combat environment, holding a unit formation to pass on orders and information would be disruptive and perilous. These difficulties were magnified at nighttime. As noted earlier, the tropical darkness had an utter stillness and a darkness unlike anything Jack or his peers had experienced. Terrified as one may have been of the dark, getting out of a tent or foxhole to seek out a buddy or pass on information was not a likely action: witness the fate of Battery A's sergeant who died during the first night on Rendova. At best, in a landscape covered with razor-sharp kunai grass, foxholes, fencing, ditches, and latrines, a stumble in the dark under such conditions might lead to breaking or spraining a leg or ending up covered in stinking mire. At worst, one could get his head shot off. To help provide early warning of intruders, the leathernecks fell back on the World War I doughboys' trick of filling empty ration cans with pebbles and tying them to strands of wire, so that any movement through the wire would set the cans to rattling.

A pressing fear that sometimes bordered on panic among some troops in jungle combat was the threat of snipers and enemy infiltrators—"one of the great bugaboos of the Guadalcanal campaign," in one historian's words.[53] It was not for nothing that Colonel Scheyer's orders to the Ninth Defense before it embarked upon Operation TOENAILS stressed "a few words of caution" about this particular matter: "Every unit, including the 9th Defense, when it landed on Guadalcanal, imagined it heard Japs and a good battle started in which our own men were shot. Bear in mind, always, that nighttime is the time for knife-fighting. Do no promiscuous shooting at any time, save your bullets for the Japs. It may be possible that one or two Jap snipers will fire at us from coconut trees, [but] that doesn't mean that every tree has a Jap in it."[54] In hindsight and in light of the coming campaign in the New Georgia area—witness the various "friendly fire" incidents—these proved to be wise and prophetic words. In the pitch blackness of the jungle at night, there tended to be a "shoot first—ask questions later" mentality, which needed to be curbed immediately. This was necessary both to thwart friendly fire and to prevent such firing from giving away one's own position if, in fact, there were Japanese patrols or snipers actually nearby.

The mere fear of snipers and infiltrators also tended to have a terribly demoralizing—in some cases, paralyzing—effect. On New Georgia, the Forty-Third Infantry Division suffered heavy casualties resulting from friendly troops' attacking one another over supposed snipers. Episodes of chaotic behavior known as "jitterbugging" (so-called after the frenzied 1930s' dance craze) or the "jungle jitters," often involving nighttime friendly fire shootouts, were widely reported throughout elements of that division. Speaking of one jitterbugging incident in one especially affected regiment of the Forty-Third, the 169th Infantry, the Army's official historian of New

Georgia writes: "Some men knifed each other. Men threw grenades blindly in the dark. Some of the grenades hit trees, bounced back, and exploded among the Americans. Some soldiers fired round after round to little avail. In the morning no trace remained of Japanese dead or wounded. But there were American casualties: some had been stabbed to death, some wounded by knives. Many suffered grenade fragment wounds, and 50 percent of these were caused by fragments from American grenades.... The regiment was to suffer seven hundred [casualties] by July 31."[55] Chris Donner wrote: "We were amazed by the number of psycho cases being evacuated from the 169th Regiment. They told wild tales, accompanied by fearful gestures, of Japs who came after them at night with long metal pincers to pull them out of their foxholes."[56] This kind of frantic behavior only strengthened the aversion that many of the Ninth's Marines felt about that particular Army division.

In fact, the first clinical diagnoses of war neurosis, later named "combat fatigue" (for which Lt. General George Patton would become infamous in the "face-slapping" incidents in Sicily only a few months later), were identified on New Georgia, with 360 soldiers from the Forty-Third being evacuated for psychological treatment less than two weeks after the initial landings. The only immediate answers for such massive, unit-wide instances of jitterbugging available at the time were training, adjustment, and the relief of the officers responsible for the men involved in such behavior. In particular, it was found that training to combat the perception that the Japanese were "supermen" helped make a difference in curbing the onset of such "mass nocturnal delusions and their natural consequence, panicky nocturnal fratricide"; but, after the rash of incidents during the first two weeks of the fighting on New Georgia, incidents of jitterbugging ceased to plague the Forty-Third Division as mysteriously as they had started.[57]

In certain respects, the Marines' pre-combat training and combat leadership appear to have been head-and-shoulders superior to that of some Army units and helped keep the Ninth's casualties relatively low.[58] This does not mean, however, that even proportionately better-trained Marines were immune to the fears and stresses generated by combat, as reported to Eric Bergerud by one of the Ninth's men: "Air attacks, bombardments, and most combat is over very quickly.... Most guys weren't scared before things took place. We were awfully young, you know. During the chaos, you're so damn busy you don't really think. The training takes over. You're conditioned to act in a certain way.... Afterwards, everyone starts to shake. You break out those cigarettes. You kind of lose it, really."[59]

As far as fears of death went, the classic view of youth—*"It can't happen to me; I'm too young to die"*—was just about the best psychological defense available. As Frank Chadwick further recalled: "Most of us felt it will never happen to me. You knew people were killed and wounded all the time, but deep down you thought it would happen to some other guy. So we worried more about our buddies. You made yourself believe that nothing could happen to you, that you had to worry about your friends. It wasn't logical, but it would have been a lot harder to go on brooding about it."[60] Another potential defense against worrying about death was the very unreality of the situation, perhaps best captured by a sentence frequently used by many of the Ninth's veterans as to certain memories or vignettes of combat: "It was just like watching a movie" (much as Jack McCall often said of the July 4 raid) or, in David Slater's similar phraseology, "I thought I was in a movie."[61]

"Just like a movie." War in the Pacific was, of course, nothing at all like a movie, and no Hollywood production could adequately depict war and its horrors—particularly, its smells. Still, Jack, Chadwick, Lieutenant Donner, Slater, and Yemma, among others, recalled watching incidents that had a certain movie-like quality to them. There were instances that—at the time, and not merely in veterans' hindsight—frequently gave one the sense that he was watching a gigantic panorama being played out in front of his eyes, instead of something happening in real time. For young men in their late teens and early to mid-twenties, these sights and sounds bore no resemblance to anything they had ever witnessed before. In so many respects, certain situations did have an air of unreality that helped place some mental distance and the appearance of safety between the onlooker and the stark danger that was actually happening.

One of the best examples of this phenomenon, and one witnessed by a large number of men simultaneously, was the July 4, 1943 bombing raid. Years later, this air raid and its aftermath were described by so many of the Ninth's veterans as being "just like a movie" or "better than a movie"—the words often used by Jack, Chadwick, Slater, and Yemma, among others— and onlookers had "ringside seats." None of the onlookers had ever seen anything like the awesome destruction of the Japanese bomber squadron in about three minutes, complete with pyrotechnics and sound effects. It was natural that young men raised in the 1920s and 1930s, America's first generation of children raised with Saturday movie matinees, might mentally equate these sights into a spectacle worthy of Cecil B. DeMille. Like miniature comets, the Japanese bombers were smashed to fragments

Wreckage of a single-engined aircraft (top) and a Mitsubishi Betty bomber near Munda Field. Official US Marine Corps photos, courtesy of Joseph Pratl.

and cartwheeled to earth in pieces—wings, fuselages, and bloody scraps of people. Unlike most of its sisters, however, which simply disintegrated when hit, one particular bomber "[tumbled] to earth end over end, like a model that was built wrong."[62]

The Japanese bombers' fatal and fiery end resulted in "[w]a-hoos, fist shakings and screams of delight," as Jack recalled, and "cheers . . . heard all over Rendova 'like a "Babe" homer in Yankee stadium.'"[63] No matter that the bombers' occupants had met gruesome ends—ripped open, disembow-eled, and bleeding from shards of metal and glass and exploding ammuni-tion belts; roasted alive by aviation fuel; or disintegrated as their planes' remains plummeted into Rendova Bay or onto the surrounding islands. Japanese aircrew did not normally carry parachutes, so their chances of escape were practically nil. With an enemy as depersonalized as the Japa-nese, however, and so soon after so many of the Ninth's own personnel, GIs, and Seabees had met such violent and gory deaths as they had on July 2, the deaths of enemy airmen hardly mattered—except that killing more of the enemy might improve one's own chances of coming home alive. Hence, the sight of the enemy's aircraft being reduced to so much falling and smok-ing scrap metal was seen by many of the leathernecks as only improving their own chances of getting through the war alive. Of course, as also noted previously, it was much easier to kill the enemy without remorse if he was viewed as something impersonal—like an airplane, bereft of humanity—or simply not seen at all. In some respects, the sights they witnessed on July 4 did not, at the time, seem so much like death to the Ninth's onlookers as like a giant, ghastly, yet enjoyable, fireworks show.

Death was everywhere on the Pacific's battlefields. It lurked everywhere on Guadalcanal: in a medical tent, as David Slater lay next to the artillery-man who died of malignant tertian malaria; in the Japanese bones, skulls, and teeth pocketed by rear-area scavengers; and under the roots of a tree where a Marine had buried his buddy with words from the book of John carved in its bark: "For God so loved the world. . . ."[64] Death was omnipres-ent on Rendova's beaches and at Suicide Point during the July air raids and on New Georgia as the Tank Platoon assaulted Japanese bunkers in sup-port of the drive to take Munda Field. Often, the casualties were American troops. Captain Blake recounted the lonely death of one soldier on New Georgia, ambushed and separated from the rest of his unit on the Munda Trail, just as the fighting came to its end:

> Late that night, from far ahead came an anguished cry for help and a splat-tering burst of machine-gun fire. The cry faded out. All who heard it knew

what it was. But no one will ever know the horror of the death that man died, lost, alone and forsaken in the jungle darkness.

The next day we found him on the trail, face down in front of an abandoned machine-gun position. The campaign was over. He had been the last man to die. And he came so close to coming through alive. I cannot get him out of my mind.[65]

Death in the tropics was seldom clean and was never as choreographed as Hollywood depicted it. The fates of many of those killed in the July 2 air raid on Suicide Point were quick, spectacular, and grisly in the extreme, as Japanese bullets and bombs detonated a huge cache of Seabee explosives, the explosion of which left body parts strewn in every direction. Many fatally wounded in combat, however, seldom had the luxury of dying as immediately or (one suspects) as painlessly from their wounds; certainly, Captain Blake's nameless dogface who fell on the Munda Trail died a lingering death, alone and abandoned until it was too late to save him. Death from malaria was, relatively speaking, cleaner than death in combat, but the process was almost as traumatic for those watching the feverish gibbering and screams of a man dying from disease as it was to see a buddy take a bullet in the head, chest, or bowels. Decomposition set in rapidly in the tropics, as did flies and maggots, and the stench of rotting flesh quickly pinpointed the presence of the dead, overpowering the otherwise omnipresent stink of naturally rotting jungle vegetation.

The smell of death wafted around Munda Field for weeks after the battle. The putrid odors emanated from the bloated corpses of its defenders, several of whose bodies lay unburied for days near Jack's position and in the helmet Jack had found with portions of its owner's head still reeking inside. Jack recalled, "You could sense when death was near"—even if it was not your own death that was imminent. This frequent proximity to death throughout the Guadalcanal and TOENAILS campaigns hardened the Ninth's Marines in countless ways, even permeating their casual conversations and sense of humor with a grim edge.

By the time they had reached New Georgia, many of the Ninth's Marines, like Biggie Slater and his pals, could casually eat their chow and discuss whether a decomposing leg sticking out of a hillside pile of churned-up earth was Marine or Japanese in origin:

The leg, showing halfway to the knee, was highlighted by [the] sky and seemed to be kicking against it. Down below, the men explored their rations and discussed the leg.

"Hell, it's a marine—the shoe is G.I."

"Yeah, sure looks like it; are there leggings?"[66]

Bummie, a Brooklyn cop before the war, deadly aggressive under the influence of liquor or adrenaline, was sentimental and concerned about the man—if there was one—attached to the leg.

"Let's put up a marker for Graves Registration."

Two sticks were tied together and the men climbed to the crest of the ridge, Bummie carrying the cross. They gathered around the leg, examining the shoe. The color wasn't right. Doggie brushed dirt from the leg; it was wrapped in puttees.

"Goddam Jap," said Bummie as he threw down the sticks.[67]

Similarly, Jack later recounted to his brother Al that the remains of a leg were thrust out of the ground next to Munda Field in the abandoned and bulldozed Japanese graveyard adjacent to the battalion HQ's mess hall and some of Jack's Lister bags. A notice was tacked to its decaying foot: "HERE LIES A MAN WHO ATE AT THE 9TH DEFENSE'S MESS HALL!"[68] Humor acquired its own peculiar and pungent flavor in such an environment, where the relationship between life and death was often starkly visible in even the most mundane activities.

The terrors of a Japanese artillery bombardment have already been noted; the impact of Japanese air raids was similar. While Washing Machine Charlie and Louie the Louse were usually more of a nuisance than a real menace, these nighttime raiders occasionally dropped "daisy cutters," small but deadly anti-personnel bombs that scattered shrapnel low to the ground. Taking cover under a truck or vehicle did not offer much protection from a daisy cutter blast, since their fragments whizzed along at knee level and could hit a man cowering under a vehicle.[69] Japanese bombs also made a distinctive sound as they fell. As Biggie Slater remembered, "Quite often their casings had riveted parts, and the protrusions disturbed the air in ways that (at least as I heard it) caused a sort of warbling, whooshing sound."[70]

No matter how much one wanted to ignore Charlie's noisy motors and go back to sleep, the Ninth's Marines could never be fully sure whether Charlie might only drop empty sake bottles tonight, flares, or the dreaded daisy cutters. The Marines frequently faced multiple air alerts in one night, sometimes as many as six or seven per night, spaced as little as an hour apart. Each time the call of "Condition Red" went forth, off to the bomb shelters or foxholes they would dash, or to the AA, radar, or searchlight position if in crewing the 90mm or Special Weapons guns, another night's precious few hours of sleep lost in the process.[71] Real sleep was, under the best of circumstances, a rarity. In the South Pacific war zone, what passed for sleep was, in David Slater's words, an "axe-edged delicate balance between life-restoring unconsciousness and life-preserving alertness."[72]

Major air raids on the Canal and in the Central Solomons campaign were on a magnitude far above Charlie's and Louie's nocturnal incursions. Chadwick fell prey to the Japanese raiders that bombed Jack's LST in the July 2, 1943, raid on Suicide Point. He was floored by a blast only a few yards from Jack as he was running to get more 40mm shells from the ship's ammo locker. Jack was flattened by the same concussion that downed Chadwick, but apart from bruises and a ringing in his ears, Jack was unhurt. Chadwick, too, escaped that raid uninjured, but in another Japanese air strike later that day, he was wounded:

> I heard this terrific noise and felt an intense heat. The concussion bounced me around and I could hear the shrapnel flying all over. And then I was sitting there thinking, "What the hell happened?" You don't think very clearly after a bomb goes off, and I didn't really understand what was going on. I started getting this pain in my leg, reached down to rub it and my hand was all red. I think, "Christ, I've been hit." A numbing effect sets in. You start to get the shakes fast unless a wound is very serious. At that moment the second bomb landed and knocked me silly. It blew out a tooth and injured my mouth. The first thing I knew I was spitting out four or five teeth. I looked down and saw my wrist bone sticking through the skin. But it didn't hurt. . . . The doc [doubtless, the intrepid Commander Krepela or his staff] set my wrist bone, snapped it back into place, and put a splint on it. Then it hurt like hell.[73]

Seeing combat and getting wounded was not enough to guarantee a leatherneck a medal. In comparison to its sister services, the Marine Corps seemed to be notoriously stingy in awarding decorations and medals. For instance, only sixty-eight Purple Hearts were presented to the Ninth's combat casualties, even though the battalion had suffered casualties much higher in number. If the victims had been in an Army unit, they doubtless would have all been awarded this medal. Despite his wounding on Rendova, Chadwick was not among the unit's Purple Heart recipients. Likewise, despite taking steel fragments from the 155mm explosion at Piru, Bill Galloway received nothing, a situation that was rectified only many years after war's end. When each Ninth Defense member asked whether or not he was entitled to that medal, he was essentially told that, unless the nature of his wound was clearly documented in his medical records, no Purple

Heart was authorized. As Chadwick reminisced: "While all other services, especially the Army, awarded medals very easily, the Corps awarded very little, and many so deserving received no decorations. The philosophy was that all Marines were volunteers, and you were expected to do your duty. Therefore, any award [issued by the Corps] was well earned and deserved."[74]

Jack himself believed that, for his length of service and clean record, he was entitled to receive the Good Conduct Medal, as was, in fact, reflected in his discharge papers. All of his postwar inquiries as to his eligibility for this medal, however, resulted in denials. In his later years, Jack would semi-humorously grunt when faced with his Army lieutenant son, who had already received several medals and ribbons in only three years of peacetime service: "What a jellybean! A peacetime Army 'shavetail,' earning more medals than a combat Marine! It just figures." Even those making the ultimate sacrifice might be short-changed, in the eyes of many of their surviving buddies: after all, Wantuck and Rothschild only received Navy Crosses, not the Medal of Honor, for their deeds. Although, as noted before, there were certain valid reasons why these two were deemed ineligible (e.g., lack of eyewitnesses), many of the more jaded leathernecks just chalked it up to the way the Corps typically conducted its business.

The lack of promotions and delays in those that were granted were a similar cause for dissatisfaction, especially for the Christmas Tree Marines. Jack was promoted from private first class to corporal late in 1943, and despite his record of good conduct, he held that rank until he left the Corps in fall 1945. The lack of timely promotions, and its effect on morale, was duly noted by the Ninth's officers, who were themselves often disappointed by the lack of credit their Marines received for their efforts. "One of the most galling things to me," Hank Reichner noted after the war, "was the lack of promotions among the Christmas Tree recruits. It was even more so when new arrivals with less service were Corporals, etc. We were forgotten."

Despite whatever fears they may have secretly harbored, few of the Ninth's Marines "broke down" or resorted to self-inflicted injuries as a way out of the war. This means of escape was more common in some other units or taken by many engaged in the worst aspects of the European Theater. Nevertheless, the Ninth's personnel were not immune to wartime psychological stresses, and the unit had its victims: recall the Marine who leapt overboard from Lieutenant Donner's LST on the way to Rendova. In another case, Biggie Slater watched a 90mm Group member "crack up" three days after the Rendova landings: "A young guy stood up from his hole [and] shoved a .45 into his mouth. He hesitated long enough for a bunch of us to swarm over him and take the pistol away. He was surveyed out—as I recall, he was only about 17 and probably a [field] music (they carried side arms)."[75]

Still, the esprit de corps, the gung-ho attitude instilled in them, partly helped to keep the Ninth's Marines together as a team. There were other possible reasons, though, why this cohesiveness was the rule for this unit and others like it in the Pacific. As noted previously, in the jungle and un-like France or Italy, escape in the Pacific was far less convenient: there was nowhere safe to run and hide. "You never wanted to let your buddies down," Jack recalled. This was cultivated not just from loyalty's sake or from self-respect. It was also frankly due to a certain amount of self-preservation. As Frank Chadwick explained: "We had a saying that 'it takes more guts to get up in the front line and run than it does to stay there.' [Y]ou're afraid if you let them down that every one of your buddies is going to be right there on your ass."[76]

Preparing for the Next Offensive: Into the Central Pacific

After five months on Banika, the Ninth got word in May that it was to be redeployed for a new offensive, now in the Central Pacific. For Jack and the Ninth, it would be an entirely new sector of the Pacific and an entirely new kind of war. General MacArthur's and Admiral Halsey's forces had been bludgeoning their way through New Guinea and the Solomons, respectively. While those campaigns were being waged, the Central Pacific theater in 1943, under the primary control of Admiral Chester Nimitz, had been the scene of additional battles, including Tarawa and Makin. Influencing the course of this campaign were other battles of an intramural nature between the US military branches and their leaders. Halsey and the South Pacific area (including the Solomons) were subordinate to Nimitz and his forces— the Navy being the predominant branch—based out of Pearl Harbor. Vying for resources, logistics, and political capital to support his own vision of how to win the war in the Pacific via his own area of operations, of course, was Douglas MacArthur and his Southwest Pacific Area, headquartered in Australia. Although not entirely a US Army operation, the Army's leader-ship was paramount in MacArthur's command. MacArthur and Nimitz's superior, the US Navy's commander in chief Admiral Ernest J. King, also distrusted each other intensely.

Not only was the Central Pacific area another steppingstone to Japan (and one in conflict with MacArthur's own vision of moving upon Japan via the Southwest Pacific and the Philippines); the Navy's strategy in this area was also intended to draw Japan's fleet and air power into areas where the US Navy would be on its chosen field of action. Seizure of the Gilbert Islands, the Marshalls, and then the Marianas would provide the Allies with other options as well, from which they could support the recapture of the Philippines or strike into Formosa and China. Following the occupation of the Gilberts in November 1943, including the bitter fight for Tarawa, Nimitz turned next to seize the Marshalls in early 1944. The wide and deep lagoons of its coral atolls made excellent air bases and anchorages for Nimitz's next goal—the Mariana Islands.

After occupying the Marshalls in February 1944, the attentions of Admiral Nimitz and his staff focused on seizing the Marianas. This island group, including Saipan, Rota, Tinian, and Guam, made up the first element of Japan's inner defensive ring. They dominated the west-central Pacific, sitting athwart the lines of communication from Japan and the Ryukyu Islands in the north to New Guinea in the south and the Philippines and Formosa (Taiwan) in the southwest. While the Twentieth Air Force—the American air force tasked primarily with the bombing of Japan—had already deployed its new B-29 Superfortresses to Chinese bases, Japanese counteroffensives there threatened those bases' security. The occupation of the Marianas would provide an excellent location for Nimitz's fleet against Japan's home islands as well as another potential springboard for the liberation of the Philippines.[77]

The Marianas would also provide a more secure and easily supported base for the growing B-29 armada, the Twenty-First Bomber Command, than did the B-29s' existing Chinese airfields. From the Marshalls, the B-29s could accommodate the three-thousand-mile round trip from the Marshalls to the Japanese main islands and back with a full bomb load.[78] Admiral Nimitz and the Chief of Naval Operations, Admiral King, had long pushed for taking the Marianas over the opposition of General MacArthur and other Army leaders. Now, the introduction of the B-29 gave them an unexpected ally in the Army Air Forces' commander General Henry "Hap" Arnold, a longtime critic of the Navy's operational plans.[79] Arnold's support cinched the deal, and I MAC (renamed III Amphibious Corps in April 1944) and an Army division were tapped to support the recapture and garrisoning of the Marshalls.[80]

For many older Marines, there was a personal significance to the retaking of Guam. An American possession since 1899, many old-breed Marines had once been stationed there, and there was a deep and abiding affection between the Marines and the island's inhabitants, the Chamorros. Tactical exercises concerning Guam had been a Marine officers' training problem in their classes at Quantico since 1936, and those officers who were familiar with Guam's terrain knew it could be a tough nut to crack.[81] There were also underlying matters of national pride and humanitarianism at work, which, while secondary, preyed on the minds of some of the planners. As the first US territorial possession to have been seized by the Japanese, Guam's recapture would have immense symbolic value, not just to the American people, but also to those in other Japanese-occupied countries who hoped for liberation. Furthermore, while not generally known to most of the rank-and-file participants in the upcoming landing, the conditions of Guam's largely pro-US citizenry were becoming increasingly desperate.

Despite receiving relatively benign treatment (at least by the standards of conduct in other occupied territories in the "Greater East Asia Co-Prosperity Sphere"), by late 1943, the island's populace became subject to increasingly savage treatment by the Japanese occupants. The island was renamed *Omiya Jima* ("Great Shrine Island"), and Guam's schools were closed. Christian services were forbidden, and one priest, who was especially vocal in protesting the Japanese authorities' treatment of his flock, was tortured and beheaded. Several mass murders of civilians were perpetrated for no apparent reason other than for terror and intimidation. Many thousand Chamorros were relocated by the *Kempetai*, the Japanese military secret police, to concentration camps during summer 1944, where they worked under brutal conditions.[82] Others were shipped to labor camps in Japan, where their treatment was, if anything, likely worse than that of the miserable citizens left encamped on Guam.

The fate of the Guamanian people after the Japanese invasion was shared by one family connected with Jack's own family: the Johnstons, whose father, William, was a Franklin-born boy who had settled in Guam after being posted there as a Marine in 1909. Before the war, Bill Johnston served as Guam's commissioner of public works, and his Guamanian-born wife, Agueldo, was the principal of Agana High School. All this changed after the Japanese landings: Johnston was arrested, and the Japanese closed down the school system and confiscated a small movie theater the Johnston family owned. In June 1944, Bill Johnston was seized by the *Kempetai*; Agueldo and her seven children were herded into a concentration camp. Unknown to them in their captivity, the family's home in Agana had been leveled by pre-invasion bomb strikes.[83]

As American bombers soared overhead on their pre-invasion bombing runs in mid-summer 1944, the Johnstons and other inmates of the concentration camps studding Guam were heartened that liberation would soon come. The historian and wartime Marine William Manchester recounted the song the Guamanians composed as they waited for liberation:

Oh, Uncle Saum,
Oh, Uncle Saum,
Won't you please come back to Guam?[84]

All this, of course, was unknown to Jack and his buddies, who had not yet been briefed on the precise nature of their next mission, although the increased tempo of their activities assured them all that something big was imminent.

In their Russell Islands backwaters, the pace of training and personnel reshufflings picked up as Pogiebait and the Ninth's men readied for their next operation. The battalion bade farewell both to Captain Blake and his intrepid tankers, who were transferred to form a III Amphib Corps tank battalion, and to the first contingent of its Marines to be shipped home.[85] Under the so-called "5% Plan," for those Marine units that had been in the Pacific theater for at least twenty-four months, 5 percent of its personnel who had been overseas for such period were subject to rotation stateside. As a result, orders were cut for the return home of two captains (one of the two being the much-admired Captain Bill Box), a warrant officer, and sixty-five enlisted men.[86] One of those EMs lucky enough to get his rotation orders was Jack's longtime buddy, Al Downs. Their friendship went back to the Ninth Platoon at PI, when Al was one of the witnesses to Pogiebait McCall's "christening." While Jack was delighted that Al was going to get home to his fiancée Rosie and thus might survive the war after all, it was still a letdown and a loss of a good friend to have around.

Before Al's and the other short-timers' scheduled departure in mid-March 1944, Jack and Al played a farewell game of poker with their buddies. Whether from a parting lucky streak or an unbeatable poker face, Al's luck held, and he netted $70 from the pot. With half of his winnings, Downs bought a watch. With the other $35, he tracked down and bought a fifth of Australian rum, but he and Jack and Al were only able to rummage up one lukewarm bottle of cola. In a flashback to their "good old days" on Cuba, where the beer and rum flowed freely, the two buddies split their rum-and-cola and exchanged tales about what they had been through together. They drank last toasts to salute Al's great luck in making it through the war to that point, and to the hope that all of them would be able to get home again, in one piece.

As had occurred on the Canal before the beginning of Operation TOE-NAILS, the battalion began receiving new pieces of equipment—notably, new radars, the first of their kind to be received by any American unit in the South Pacific—and the training schedule picked back up in preparation for the next offensive. The 155mm batteries were put to work test-firing their renovated Long Toms at towed sea targets; the AA gunners fired at airplane-towed targets; and the radar crews plotted intercepts and calibrated their new sets.[87] By April 1, Colonel O'Neil declared the Ninth fully combat ready.[88] Then came the order to break down the battalion's camps and move beachside into pre-invasion quarantine.

As much as many of them dreaded going back into action, nobody was exactly heartbroken to be leaving Banika. Mimi Canu, a veteran of the Ninth's Headquarters Battery, summed up the feelings of many: "[The Russells] were a pain, always the same kind of working party to pick up coconuts, getting our gear repaired, waiting to go to New Zealand for a rest, even was told when [we would go there], but the army never showed up to relieve us."[89] But, as the editor of the Fighting Ninth's newsletter philosophized, some fifty years later, about the battalion's sojourn on Banika: "What the H___, you can't winnem all."[90]

After staying beachside in quarantine for days, beginning on May 10, the Ninth was moved by batteries to a small fleet of waiting transports (the USS *Harry Lee*, *Polk*, *Francis W. Parker*, and the USAT *Sea Fiddler*) and several LSTs.[91] Jack found himself bunking aboard the *Sea Fiddler*, a grimy Army transport. Conditions on this ship were scarcely an improvement over those on the dreary old *Kenmore*. Harry Jones, a fellow denizen of the vessel, described the *Sea Fiddler* as being "a remarkably dirty ship with some kind of green algae growing in various corners" and commanded by a Dutch captain whose command of the English language was less than perfect: "As his English was poor, he was pretty incomprehensible and, being generally ignored, tended to extend his remarks. All I ever translated was 'You men. . . .' [We] were fed only twice a day and then mostly Spam sandwiches from stores *we* had brought aboard. Chow lines were very short on that ship!"[92]

In the midst of a heavy storm (and more seasickness), the convoy steamed to the Purvis Bay anchorage off Florida Island, near the battalion's old stomping grounds on Guadalcanal and Gavutu.[93] There, it linked up with a larger fleet of Green Dragons, transports, and destroyers and sailed to Eniwetok in the recently captured Marshalls chain.[94] The battalion was now attached to the Marines' First Provisional Brigade, itself part of III Amphib Corps under Lt. General Roy S. Geiger. Besides the Ninth, the provisional brigade was made up of the reconstituted Fourth and Twenty-Second Marines, plus various headquarters and support elements.

The sight that greeted Jack and company as the battalion's transports and LSTs entered the atoll of Eniwetok was an amazing and awe-inspiring one, which left very different impressions from those the Ninth's Marines had developed when they entered New Caledonia's and Guadalcanal's waters in 1942.[95] Although primarily assigned to serve as an occupation force once Guam was recaptured, the battalion would also support the landings and seize various key objectives on Guam. It was also part of an on-call, floating reserve for the first landings in the Marianas on Saipan, which was defended by a large, well-armed, and fanatical Japanese detachment. Given those missions, the issue of "whether we would be around to see it [i.e., the war's end]," was a considerable question.

Jack, too, wondered how much longer this war was going to last and whether he himself would be around to see the end. From what he had experienced, though, one thing was clear: whenever and however it arrived, the end would be messy, indeed.

SIX

Operation FORAGER:
The Invasion and Occupation of Guam

> The [Guamanian] prisoners' morale soared. Their confidence in the United States
> was intact. In fact, it had never waned. During the first two weeks of the war they
> had expected the Marines back by Christmas. Chagrined then, they nevertheless
> continued to follow grapevine reports of struggles on other islands with high
> hopes. A surviving testament to their loyalty is a crude U.S. flag, sewn in Yono
> concentration camp. There are but twelve stars and nine stripes—the seamstress
> had no more cloth—but it is all the more stirring for that.
>
> —HISTORIAN AND FORMER MARINE WILLIAM MANCHESTER,
> IN *GOODBYE, DARKNESS*[1]—

A Voyage "From Tedium to Apathy" and Back

From Eniwetok, the fleet for the Marianas invasion, Operation FORAGER,
steamed for the southern Marianas, about one thousand miles away. The
task force's initial goal was to seize Saipan, the headquarters and logistical hub of the Japanese war effort in the Central Pacific. Located north of
Guam, Rota, and Tinian, Saipan's capture would theoretically make the
seizure of those islands simpler. Saipan's liberation and occupation, however, was anything but simple: its capture became a bloodbath.

The Marines' First Provisional Brigade and the Ninth Defense were
designated as "floating reserves" for the Saipan landings. As part of decep-
tion operations for the invasion, the Fourth Marines were to simulate a
landing on the eastern side of the island. When the mock landings came
under fire, the Fourth's landing craft and LVTs turned tail and returned
to the main body of the fleet.[2] With many of the Japanese forces now redeployed facing east, the genuine landings took place on Saipan's southern
beaches the next day, June 15, yet these were still bitterly contested.[3] The
Ninth's ships and LSTs lay at anchor off Saipan for several more days, and
III Amphib's staff informed Colonel O'Neil that, in the event the Second

Marine Division had any major difficulty breaking out of its beachhead, the Ninth Defense would land to reinforce the breakout attempt. The Second Marine Division's breakout off the beaches succeeded, and the Army's Twenty-Seventh Infantry Division then came ashore. (Later, both divisions would encounter *banzai* charges and massed suicides of Japanese soldiers and civilians once they moved inland.[4])

Accordingly, the First Provisional Brigade's floating reserves, including the Ninth Defense, were released, and the provisional brigade's miniature armada steamed back across the one thousand-odd miles it had already traveled to the Marshalls.[5] Jack and his pals were overjoyed to see Eniwetok's blue waters after being cooped up aboard the transports and LSTs for weeks. Water and space had been as scarce onboard the "tubs" as on the old *Kenmore*, so the battery commanders had authorized their men to string up tents and tarpaulins on deck in an effort to provide some kind of shade. A coral atoll surrounded by deep-blue water, Eniwetok was beautiful in a tropical-island way that the Canal, Rendova, and the Russells had never been, and getting ashore promised to be a real break after days afloat.

This was a hoped-for blessing that failed to materialize. With the exception of some work details sent ashore to draw fresh rations and other supplies and engaging in some landing exercises and drills on its local beaches, the Ninth's men did not set foot on Eniwetok during their offshore sojourn. Most remained on their cramped, stinking transports and LSTs. III Amphib's chief of staff, General Silverthorn, later claimed that despite their lengthy confinement shipboard, the Marines "suffered no debilitating effects from such long captivity."[6] This statement flies in the face of Jack's experience and those of most veterans of the Ninth. The heat was oppressive, and the tropical sun beating down on the steel hulls and sides turned the transports and LSTs into floating pressure cookers for many of their hapless inhabitants. The battalion's history noted the "intolerable heat and scant opportunity for bathing," summing up the health consequences: "All of the men had prickly heat rashes and various types of skin disease." These ailments, however, remained largely unalleviated because of the lack of fresh water for showers or even salt-water baths.[7]

Soon enough, another massive convoy formed up near the lagoon with orders to join Task Force Fifty-Three and commence operations to recapture Guam. After ten days off Eniwetok, this flotilla (minus the USS *Harry Lee* and the third echelon, which remained at Eniwetok) set sail back the way they had come, some fifteen hundred miles, to the southern beaches of Guam. Finally, on July 20, 1944, the first echelon of the task force sighted the coast of Guam. Pogiebait and his buddies sensed that, for the first time in over two months, they were finally about to be back on dry land.[8]

In all, Jack and the Ninth Defense spent some nine weeks aboard their grimy little fleet. The bone-wearying boredom of the battalion's voyage resembled that of the USS *Reluctant*, the fictitious Navy supply ship operating in the Central Pacific depicted in Thomas Heggen's 1946 novel and the later Broadway play and movie *Mister Roberts*, as it sailed "on its regular run from Tedium to Apathy and back" with "an occasional trip to Monotony" and a one-time voyage "all the way to Ennui, a distance of two thousand miles from Tedium."[9]

Ironically, when the poop circulated that they would be landing with the First Provisional Brigade on the southwestern beaches of Guam to support the Third Marine Division's drive against 18,500 Japanese defenders, many of the Ninth's Marines were not as sobered by the news as they normally might have been. Indeed, some of them were ecstatic—soon their days of being "web-footed Marines" would be over! Chadwick satirically recalled of their oceanic roaming: "We now had more time at sea than most sailors."

"W-Day": The Ninth's Landings on Bangi Point

The Ninth Defense's assigned missions on Guam in support of the First Provisional Brigade were similar to its prior duties on Rendova and New Georgia; this time, it included beach security, removal and demolition of Japanese booby traps, obstacles, and mines, and the grim but necessary duty of graves registration.[10] The 155mm Group's service as heavy field and coast-defense artillery, however, was no longer part of its mission on Guam, as the battalion was in the process of transitioning to a strictly antiaircraft defense unit. The battalion was divided into three echelons for the invasion: the first, an advance party under Colonel O'Neil, included much of the H&S Battery and the Special Weapons Group (twenty-seven officers, 349 men); the second and largest, now under Colonel Baker, consisted of the rest of H&S and both the 155mm and 90mm Groups (forty officers, 1,013 men); and the third, a small rear echelon (four officers, 149 men), remained for the time being at Eniwetok. The battalion was scheduled to land on the southern beachhead in the area of Bangi Point and would then move due north toward the coastal village of Agat.[11]

While not as bad a snafu as the initial Rendova landings had been, the Ninth's landings had their share of problems. First, the unit was scheduled to land the first echelon at 9:00 a.m. Despite thirteen days of air and sea bombardment by Rear Admiral Richard L. ("Close-In") Conolly's task force—after 28,761 naval shells had blasted the island in what was reputedly "the best bombardment of the war"[12]—the provisional brigade's and the Third Marine Division's landings were held up by stiffer resistance than had been expected. Consequently, disembarkation of the battalion's first echelon did not commence until 10:30 a.m. on "W-Day," July 21, 1944. Coming ashore several hours after the initial combat landings, the Ninth's first echelon had to wade approximately a quarter mile before hitting the beach. Unknown to the invasion's planners, sharp coral reefs and outcroppings in the waters off Bangi Point extending from one side of the beach to the other would have ripped the bottoms out of many landing craft had they continued their run-in at low tide. This failure of intelligence was even more surprising given that since 1899, Guam had been an American protectorate and key naval outpost.[13] Jack and his buddies would soon directly face the life-threatening consequences of this intelligence gap.

With the landing delays, the Ninth's first echelon encountered low tides when they finally deployed for landing. Slogging ashore with personal gear, weapons, and ammo, they passed landing craft, LVTs, vehicles, and debris from the initial invasion force, many of which were still burning. They also passed a number of corpses, both American and Japanese. The loss of many landing craft, especially the prized amphibious LVTs,[14] in the first wave of the Guam invasion hindered the battalion's and other units' ability to assemble and get to shore rapidly. All the while, Japanese snipers continued a desultory fire at the Ninth's Marines.

For Jack—who was assigned to Battery B, now under the command of "Doc" Teller—and his buddies, the basic landing drill was much like what they had faced on Rendova: a hearty and traditional early-morning pre-landing breakfast of coffee, steak, eggs, and fried potatoes, then assembling by squads, platoons, and batteries for the landing and, for those on board the transports, down the treacherous rope cargo nets into the pitching and rolling landing craft or LVTs. As they waited and watched the Fourth and Twenty-Second Marines' landings during the early morning, many of the Ninth's Marines "scanned self-made maps and sketches and followed the progress of the battle by radio reports and field glasses," according to Marine correspondent Sgt. William Allen, who was assigned to follow the landings alongside the Ninth's headquarters element.[15] As several blood-covered Marine infantry casualties from the earlier landings were hauled on board the transports for aid by Dr. Krepela's staff around noontime, however, combat correspondent Allen noticed a change in the disposition of many of the onlookers: "For the first time during the day some of the Marines hardened. They had crowded around to watch the wounded brought aboard and what they had seen was not pleasant. They quietly walked away."[16] For the boys of the Ninth, it was a sobering experience. They now knew that they would participate in something that many of them dreaded, after hearing the tales of the bloody invasion of Tarawa the previous year and of Saipan only days before: an assault landing under direct enemy observation and fire.

In his personal effects, Pogiebait carried a pocket-sized Bible, its cover encased in a sheet of brass inscribed *"May This Keep You Safe from Harm,"* which his parents had sent him as a wartime Christmas present. While his part of the Battalion prepared for landings on Bangi Beach, and as he watched from the *Sea Fiddler*'s railing the landing craft bringing back the first casualties, Jack pulled out of his pocket the "bulletproof" Bible his parents had given him and said a few prayers to himself.

At least on Guadalcanal and Rendova, the landing craft and LVTs had more or less gotten everybody directly onto the beach. Off Gaan Point and Bangi Point, the unforeseen reefs forced the landing craft to disgorge their loads of men far from shore. These coral barriers required the troops to wade in from the edge of the reefs, well within rifle or machine gun range of any defenders who had not yet been killed or scattered. Because it lacked knowledge of the reef's existence and scope, Close-In Conolly's bombardment force had done little to blast holes through the reefs for the landing craft to pass safely through to the beachline. Worse, due to the damage already inflicted on the first waves, the resulting lack of sufficient LVTs required many of the men to stagger ashore through the surf in full battle gear. The amphibious versions of the ubiquitous two-and-a-half-ton cargo truck, the DUKWs or "Ducks," were rendered impotent as the trucks' rubber tires were slashed to ribbons on the sharp edges of the reef.[17] Even with the benefit of prior experience—or maybe because of it, since the old salts now knew what to expect—the Guam landings were much more terrifying than those on the Canal or even Rendova.

Laden with seventy-odd pounds of gear, ammunition, and weapons,

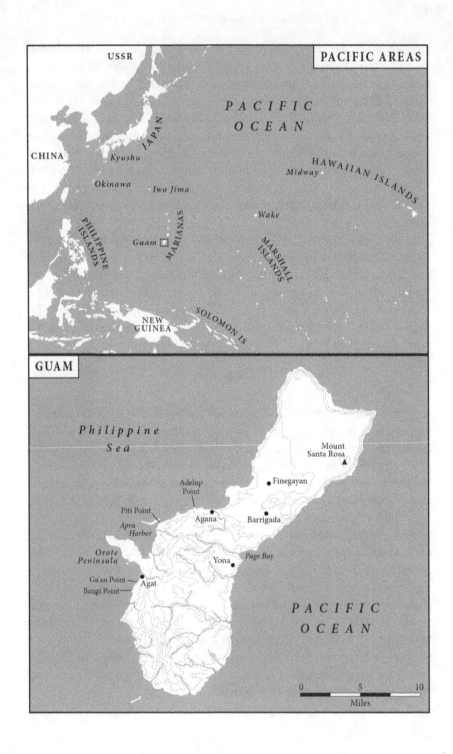

PACIFIC AREAS

USSR

CHINA

JAPAN

Kyushu

Okinawa

Iwo Jima

PACIFIC
OCEAN

HAWAIIAN ISLANDS

Midway

Wake

PHILIPPINE
ISLANDS

Guam

MARIANAS

MARSHALL
ISLANDS

NEW
GUINEA

SOLOMON IS

GUAM

Philippine
Sea

Mount
Santa Rosa

Finegayan

Adelup
Point

Piti Point

Agana

Barrigada

Apra
Harbor

Orote
Peninsula

Yona

Pago Bay

Ga'an Point

Agat

Bangi Point

PACIFIC
OCEAN

0   5   10
Miles

anyone falling down in the surf had to fight hard just to get back on his feet and keep from drowning. The sharp coral sliced and bruised the hands and knees of anyone who fell. Everyone trudged cautiously through the waist-high waters to avoid stepping on underwater mines or obstructions or into a deep hole or tidal pool. Even though three combat regiments had already landed, the small geysers of water sporadically plinking upwards reminded everyone that this was definitely a hot beachhead.

Since much of the sniper fire seemed to come from two small islands just off Bangi Point, Colonel O'Neil called for a detachment to wade out to the islands (the landing craft still blocked by low tides and the reef) and deal with the snipers. As the detachment neared the first island, the leathernecks—both in the surf and further ashore on the beach—craned their necks at the sound of an approaching motorboat. The boat roared out of a cove on the second small island and made at full speed for the Orote Peninsula, about two miles to the north. The startled Marines opened fire, but the hundreds of rounds had no apparent effect on the Japanese occupants, who were seen landing the boat and running pell-mell onto the rocky shore of the peninsula. While the Marines' enthusiasm was excellent, their marksmanship was lousy: each of them would have earned the embarrassment of the despised "Maggie's Drawers" flag had they been back at PI. "There was a lot of kidding, short-lived, about sending everyone back to the rifle range," Frank Chadwick ruefully recalled.

During the initial landings and for most of their stay on Guam, the leathernecks were delighted to encounter almost no Japanese aircraft, a fact that lessened the primary duties of the 90mm and Special Weapons Groups considerably. In mid-June, as the Saipan invasion began, the naval forces encountered what would be the last major direct engagement between the air arms of the US and Japanese fleets. In the Battle of the Philippine Sea, the US Navy inflicted a crushing defeat on the Japanese Combined Fleet and the Japanese Naval Air Force, sinking three carriers and—depending on who does the counting—destroying between 270 and 476 aircraft in the process for a loss of only twenty-nine American planes. This lopsided victory, the "Great Marianas Turkey Shoot," effectively eliminated Japanese air power in the Central Pacific and the Philippines.[18]

The absence of Japanese air power over Guam was, at least, one blessing for which the Ninth's men were deeply thankful. Unlike Rendova, the beach was still taking some shelling from enemy mortars and small field guns. For the moment, the area held by the Ninth on Bangi Point was much smaller than the area it held down on Guadalcanal or Rendova, but that

was of little comfort: more of the battalion massed in one place just made
a better target for the Japanese. During that first night on Guam, the area
near the battalion's perimeter was hit by a brief but massive counterattack.
Flares exploded overhead to illuminate the area and huge shells—this time,
US naval ones—fell, some as close as two hundred yards from the men in
the Ninth's frontline foxholes. Fortunately for them, the brunt of this attack by the Japanese Thirty-Eighth Infantry Regiment fell on the Fourth
and Twenty-Second Marines and not on the Ninth.[19]

Next morning, the larger, second echelon landed, with Jack joining in as a
participant. Except for the fact that fewer Japanese shells and bullets were
pinging around them, little had changed since the preceding day to make
the second echelon's landing any less treacherous than that of the first. The
formidable coral reef barriers remained intact and continued to prevent
the LCMs and LCTs from taking their occupants closer to the beach. Like
the earlier waves, Pogiebait and the Marines of his echelon had to step off
their landing craft at the reef's edge. Unlike the first waves, however, since
there were no available LVTs waiting to ferry them the rest of the way,
this group had to wade through about twelve hundred yards of surf and
water to reach the beach.[20] Jack recalled sloshing through the chest-high
surf as American shells rocketed overhead, "sounding like a freight train,"
to explode several miles away onto Japanese targets. As the high tide began to roll in, Jack plunged into a tidal pool over his head: encumbered by
seventy-odd pounds of equipment, he had visions of drowning. The same
panicky feeling that he had felt on Rendova when he was trapped under
the LST's door erupted, but somehow he clambered out of the deep pool
and staggered to dry land.

The scenes on the beach offered little respite or comfort from the terrors
of the surf: one day after W-Day, the Bangi Point beach was still a wreck.
Despite efforts at clearing the beach, battered American equipment and
some dead bodies littered its shore or floated in the tide.[21] With most of its
men now ashore, the battalion began the laborious process of moving in
Special Weapons' light AA guns. Jack and his Battery B mates cursed and
groaned as they strung barbed wire, dug foxholes, and manned the Ninth's
outer defensive perimeter in the Guamanian summer heat. The 90mms
and 155mms remained on board the ships lying off Eniwetok, at least for
the moment, as did the battalion's last echelon.[22]

With many Japanese beach defenders now stranded on the Orote Peninsula north of Agat, the First Provisional Brigade was ordered to turn
north on July 23. The Twenty-Second Marines were told to lead the way,
followed by the Fourth Marines, with the Army's Seventy-Seventh Infan-

The scene on the beaches near Bangi Point encountered by the Ninth's men.
Official US Marine Corps photo.

try Division to hold the areas previously occupied by those two regiments. This move was intended to cut off the Orote Peninsula and seize the major Japanese airfield there.[23] As Army units moved in, including an antiaircraft battalion, the Ninth Defense was tasked with defending a much smaller perimeter than it had first held. The new perimeter stretched from Agat to Bangi Point, the latter being a small peninsula jutting out about one thousand yards south of Gaan Point. To protect this area, however, the Ninth would have to run frequent infantry-style patrols and help drive Japanese stragglers north toward the Ninth Marines (an infantry regiment of the Third Division, not to be confused with the Ninth Defense Battalion) and the Seventy-Seventh Infantry Division. Fortunately, firefights were few, as most groups of Japanese encountered were small and fled rapidly. Amazingly, many of these stragglers did not seem to be equipped with weapons, which was later explained by the fact that many were Imperial Navy service troops or Korean forced laborers from the Japanese navy yard at Piti. Although these live-to-fight-another-day tactics may have annoyed the Ninth's officers, few of the enlisted leathernecks were troubled. "We were not dismayed that they did not stand and fight but fled. As combat goes, this was a relief, as we would rather chase them than stand there and get shot up," Frank Chadwick recalled.

At least, the Ninth was spared from the desperate charges launched against the Twenty-First Marines and Ninth Marines and from the fighting in the ridges and hills around Guam's capital, Agana. This fighting included relatively rare attacks by Japanese tank units. Wild rumors abounded that many of the Japanese defenders who had launched some particularly frenzied charges on the Twenty-Second Marines and the Seventy-Seventh Division's dogfaces were out-of-their-minds drunk. These rumors were soon confirmed: supply stashes around Orote contained huge stockpiles of booze—beer, sake, and scotch—"enough alcohol in its godowns to intoxicate an entire army," as First Provisional Brigade member William Manchester recalled.[24] To the disgust of Jack and many of the Fighting Ninth's parched mouths, however, most of the contents of these hooch depots fell into the marauding and appreciative hands of the no-less-drymouthed infantrymen of the First Provisional Brigade and the Third Division.

By the end of July, with the Japanese flushed out of the areas around Gaan Point, Bangi Point, and Agat, those elements of the battalion not providing security or manning foxholes were clearing the beach of obstacles, debris, and mines. The Bangi Point beach had been strewn with mines of various types, including a peculiar kind of hemispherical anti-ship mine, but oddly, many of the mines' fuses were not activated. The reason may be found in the fact that the Japanese had impressed local citizens as forced laborers to lay mines and obstacles. This Japanese use of slave labor had backfired: the Chamorros frequently planted the mines without removing the fuses' safety pins.[25] Without their Long Toms to man and maintain, both batteries of the 155mm Group were put to work blasting holes and removing mines, wrecked vehicles, and occasionally dead bodies. After a week or more of lying unburied, the corpses were in an advanced state of decomposition and stank to high heaven in Guam's heat and humidity.[26]

From Agat to Agana

The First Provisional Brigade's headquarters directed Colonel O'Neil to march the battalion from its area around Agat to assume the defense of the island's largest airfield near Agana. This next slog required a twenty-mile road march from Agat to Agana on a very dusty and narrow winding road about the width of a single truck. Moving in two columns down the side of the road, with jeeps and other vehicles taking up the middle of the road, the Ninth began this march around dawn on or about August 3.

A street scene in a Guamanian town, showing signs of heavy combat, summer 1944. Official US Marine Corps photo.

For Jack and the majority of the rank-and-file slogging along the edge of the road, this latest march was miserable. Clouds of dust churned up by the unit's trucks and jeeps soon coated the faces, mouths, exposed arms, and nostrils of the sweaty, tired leathernecks, and flies and mosquitoes alighted on the men's bare skin. En route, the battalion passed the northern sector landing area of the Third Marine Division, an area studded with high cliffs and well-emplaced Japanese gun positions. The western beaches had not yet been fully cleared of the detritus of battle, and Jack and his buddies marveled that anyone could have made a landing there and survived. It took the Ninth about ten hours to complete its march to Agana in one hundred-degree heat. The battalion reached the city's outskirts around dusk, and its men immediately began digging in.

Agana was a wretched sight. The capital of Guam and the home of over half of the island's prewar population of some nineteen thousand people, most of its one and two-story buildings and homes had been pounded to piles of shapeless rubble, in large part from the Americans' pre-invasion bombing and shelling and also by the Third Division's recent push through the city. Agana Cathedral, the Church of San Antonio, the Bishop's Palace, government buildings, and the central plaza and heart of Agana, the once beautiful Plaza España, were all battered or smashed outright.[27] The fighting had left hundreds of Chamorros homeless, and the Japanese themselves had concentrated many more in the labor camps in the southern and eastern corners of the island. One refugee camp near Agat alone would accommodate and feed over 12,100 civilians.[28] One such refugee was a teenager, Vincente T. ("Bennie") Blaz, who would later act as a local guide for several of the Ninth Defense's patrols. Later in life, Bennie Blaz would become a Marine Corps brigadier general and a US congressman for the Territory of Guam.

Biggie Slater recounted an incongruous moment in the rubble of Agana, as well as one ego boost for the capital city's liberators:

> Guam was American. Biggie and his comrades knew it with certainty when they saw the smashed soda fountain in the rubble of Agana's main street. The counter marble had burst from a shattered building: syrup pumps and seltzer taps drew cheers from the files of men moving past.
>
> [Despite the destruction, the] Guamanians seemed happy to greet the new conquerors, even though twenty thousand Japanese still remained, hemmed in on the northern part of the island. They showed their joy in homey, hospitable ways. Within a few days of the initial assaults, a Chamorro impresario

The dusty march to Agana. Unidentified unit. Official US Marine Corps photo.

organized a troupe for entertainment of the troops. The revue had a smash
hit finale: "Mr. Sam, Sam, dear old Uncle Sam, won't you come back, please,
to Gu-a-a-m."[29]

The final song, of course, was the plaintive tune composed by the Chamorros
as they languished in the *Kempetai*'s concentration camps and dreamed of
their day of liberation. Jack and the 155mm Group, however, spent little
time in the debris of Agana and basking in the happiness of its now-freed
citizens. Battery A was next assigned to clear an area of cliffs to the northwest of Agana, and Battery B was ordered to mop up a nearby airfield on
its northeastern outskirts while the rest of the battalion was tasked with
sweeping the central part of Agana.

"Mopping-up." "Sweeping." The words made the difficult work of patrolling and hunting down the enemy sound so easy and hygienic, as if they were the commonest of kitchen chores. Jack and his brethren came to detest these euphemisms, for they cloaked the harsh reality of the situation. In the case of Battery B, this mopping-up would become substantial and bloody work, as Major Wells and Captain George ("Doc") Teller, Bill Box's successor in April 1944 as Battery B's commander, received intelligence reports that the Marines of the 155mm Group might be up against a much larger force of fifteen hundred or more Japanese. Granted, the enemy was starving and low on materiel, but so was the Japanese on nearby Saipan where they claimed at least fourteen thousand American casualties in less than one month's time under similar circumstances.[30] It was with some trepidation, then, that Batteries A and B began their grim work of patrolling, as the timing and circumstances seemed ripe for a desperate *banzai* attack.

The day after the battalion arrived on Agana's outskirts and before the Ninth again moved out, the Third Marines swept through the Agana air-field area with little resistance. Battery B moved into the airfield area later that evening, setting up a base camp, digging foxholes, and stringing up a barbed wire perimeter. Time was of the essence: the Seabees were waiting for the airfield to be cleared of Japanese stragglers before they could begin grading and improving it to provide the eight-thousand-foot finished run-way needed to accommodate the huge B-29s.[31] Colonel O'Neil bluntly told Wells, Teller, and their officers that only two days could be spared for the mopping-up operations. At least, that was the plan. In practice, it would take Pogiebait and his buddies over twice that long to clear the area.

Patrolling Around Agana

The perimeter of Agana airfield was thickly wooded and entangled with vines, providing excellent cover for its defenders. The airfield itself was a wreck: smashed aircraft, fuel stores, and huts littered the runways and adjoining landscape. Although the majority of the remaining Japanese (ap-proximately ten thousand of them) were hemmed up in the island's north around Finegayan, Barrigada, and Mount Santa Rosa, substantial numbers of them remained outside the better-defined northern pockets of resis-tance, eking out a meager existence by raiding US units' supplies. On its first patrols, Battery B began encountering some of these small groups of Japanese, which varied in numbers from four to twenty men. Unlike the splintered groups encountered near Agat, these were more organized and fully armed. Again, however, most of these small groups chose not to open fire with their weapons, instead scattering when challenged and taking cover in the dense thickets. From the reports flowing into the battery and 155mm Group CPs, the initial estimate was that Battery B was up against some twelve hundred Japanese. It was soon apparent, however, that the actual enemy forces were fewer since many of the defenders were moving from one sector of the airfield to another and were being double-counted. Fortunately, when firefights broke out, the enemy's infantry tactics were largely uncoordinated.

The battalion's work in this respect was tough and often grim: in the first few weeks of its patrols, which would last for months, several hundred Japanese were killed in brief but rapid firefights, often at close range in the jungle and underbrush. Still, the mopping-up was far from complete and two days behind schedule when Colonel O'Neil arrived at the airfield to give his 155 Group subordinates a dressing-down for the delays. The colonel was not about to go hat in hand to the First Provisional Brigade's hard-pressed commander, Brigadier General Lemuel C. Sheperd Jr., and ask him for help. The pressure was on to increase the group's patrols by day and by night. After two more days of running patrols, the surviving Japanese defenders withdrew to the northeast and out of the Ninth's sector, into an area between the two US divisions in the campaign.

The Seabees finally arrived by mid-August with all their heavy equipment to begin the reconstruction and expansion of the airfield to accommodate the colossal B-29s that would soon be based there. The Ninth did not move from the area, however, since the lightly armed construction engineers still required its presence for perimeter and AA defense. Battery B's patrols continued, although fewer and fewer Japanese were found around the airfield as the days passed. After several more days, an Army MP battalion arrived to provide security for the airfield and to relieve the 140-odd weary leathernecks of Battery B from their patrolling duties. Jack and his peers thought they had earned a respite from the hard work that Battery B had been carrying out since the opening days of the campaign. They soon found out how sadly mistaken they were again to expect a break.

Patrolling brought hazards of various sorts. Not long after Battery B had begun its patrols around Agana airfield, shortly after dawn, a host of weary Marines were standing in line at the base camp for hot chow served from marmite cans. Near the end of the chow line, Jack and Frank Chadwick heard a commotion behind them. Four figures stood at the end of the line in uniforms that looked like the faded olive-drab herringbone fatigues of the Marines, but their footwear was radically different from anything American: black, split-toed rubber shoes, called *tabi*, which looked more like goats' hooves than boots. They were unarmed, but they were clearly Japanese infiltrators. Jack, Frank, and several others quickly leapt out of line and pulled the Japanese with them. It was clear from their emaciated condition that the men were starving, and in desperation they had crept into the chow line, hoping to get some food and pass themselves off as Marines in their greenish uniforms.

As they wrestled with the starving prisoners, a green "shavetail" lieutenant, who had joined the Ninth in the Russells as a Battery B platoon leader and whom Jack habitually referred to as "Jelly Belly," ran over to see what was happening. He was already heartily disliked by his subordinates and tended to bring out the worst in them. When confronted with the POWs, Jelly Belly griped about how this situation would spoil his breakfast. The lieutenant had just violated two of the cardinal rules of military leadership: a good officer eats last, and no matter how difficult a situation he is faced with, a good officer keeps his composure in front of his peers and subordinates. More damnable was his apparent concern about his own personal welfare over the more serious concern that they obviously had these—and undoubtedly other—Japanese infiltrators roaming freely around camp. This lieutenant had lost the respect of his subordinates, and now they smelled blood. When the lieutenant agitatedly asked, "Well, what the hell are we going to do with them?" he received an answer from one exasperated Marine: "No problem, *sir*. We'll just take 'em over there, over to the bushes, and shoot 'em. Then, *sir*, we can all have a quiet meal."

Despite the bloodthirstiness of this answer, the lieutenant's Marines had no intention of following through on the threat, as they were aware of the consequences, both legal and practical. Rather, it was delivered as a test of Jelly Belly's backbone, to "pull his chain" and gauge how he would respond. He had been found lacking: "We knew we couldn't do this," Frank Chadwick recalled, "as [Major] Wells would have a fit and we would all pay for it. . . . The more [the lieutenant] got excited, the harder we pushed the issue [until] we reached the point [that] he was screaming at us and was going to run up to find the Major. We knew we had pushed him to the limits, and we didn't want to face the wrath of Major [Wells]. We calmed him down, got Wells, called the MPs and intelligence to pick up the prisoners.

From that day on, the lieutenant was always nervous and a little scared as to what the men under his command would do."[32] This lieutenant had good reason to be afraid of his men and, moreover, Major Wells. Eventually, after learning from BAR gunner Chadwick and his assistant gunner Carl Diterando of a particularly idiotic order that Jelly Belly gave to a patrol, Wells "chewed out [Jelly Belly], told him to get his gear and get his ass out of camp," as Chadwick related. Major Wells also supposedly called Colonel O'Neil and told him that if the colonel sent this officer back to Wells, Wells "would shoot him on sight." "We never knew where he was reassigned to, but he never rejoined us," Chadwick concluded.

While patrolling around Agana, the Ninth began encountering more of the native Chamorro people, who, with the Japanese withdrawing, came out of hiding to barter with the Marines for food, clothing, and fuel. The Marines soon found that the Chamorros had one item well worth any bartered rations or blankets: potent concoctions called "tubâ" and "agi."

Tubâ (or "tupa," as it was sometimes called) was a kind of wine made from fermented hearts-of-palm sap. Agi (or "aggie," short for *aguayente*) began as a thin, milky fluid, which was extracted from the flowers and shoots at the top of coconut trees. This juice was allowed to ferment for four to six days, during which time it congealed in thickness and acquired a high alcohol content. Although it could be drunk in this form (as tubâ), it was often further distilled into a near 180-proof, clear drink, which could be turned into an especially nasty variety of torpedo juice. Chadwick remembered: "We'd pour this in our aluminum canteens, add lemon powder to kill the taste. The alcohol reacted with the aluminum, and the canteen got so hot you could not hold the canteen in your hand. One or two sips of this and you didn't know which end was up. We realized we couldn't handle this and continue our patrols, so most everyone dumped the contents."

Not all the alcoholic liquids on Guam were as drinkable as these concoctions, however, and the consequences of drinking some of them were far worse than what Chadwick and others faced in their experiments with tubâ and agi. In one effort to keep a particularly obnoxious party going after all the usual varieties of hooch and jungle juice had been consumed, a mess sergeant of the Ninth and four others were poisoned by drinking denatured alcohol salvaged from Japanese stores. As a result, the five died in considerable agony, as David Slater recalled:

They roistered until the homemade liquor was exhausted. The farmhouse stood a few hundred yards from the edge of a demolished airstrip which was strewn with dismembered planes, scattered fuel drums, and the debris of disrupted war. One of Willie's pals, a self-proclaimed expert on alcohol (he had run some moonshine in Tennessee) led an expedition to replenish their supply.

The group went to the strip, where a treasury of torpedo fuel—almost pure alcohol—might be found, or perhaps a tin or two of medical stuff. They discovered an untouched drum of clear liquid and poured a sample. Then they lit it, and it burned with a pale blue flame. The "expert" pronounced the contents fit for consumption; it had passed the tests of appearance, odor, flame, and, finally, taste.

At first, they retched. It was more than a drunken emptying. A frightened Chamorro woman ran to the encampment and brought back ambulances. The heavier drinkers were already blind. The drum had contained coolant for Zero engines. Willie and four of his partying companions convulsed and died, Willie cursing off the Chaplain's comforts.[33]

The sweeps of northern Guam were conducted by the First Provisional Brigade up the western coast, the Third Marine Division through the island's center, and the Army's Seventy-Seventh Infantry Division along the east coast, while the Ninth continued to run patrols and improve its AA gun positions around Agana. On August 10, it was announced that "all organized Japanese resistance" on Guam had ceased and that the island was secured; Guam was officially American territory again.[34] Even before this announcement, in a ceremony fraught with symbolism on July 29, the US flag was raised at the Marine Barracks that had been captured by the Japanese in December 1941.[35] By this stage of the campaign, American casualties were 1,350 dead and 6,450 wounded—a relatively cheap victory, compared with bloody Saipan. Of these, the Ninth suffered one killed in action, five other deaths, and six severely wounded,[36] with several hundred others suffering with lesser injuries, malaria, and dengue.

In mid-August, the First Provisional Brigade had withdrawn to Guadalcanal for R&R and to form the nucleus of the new Sixth Marine Division. The Army's Seventy-Seventh Infantry Division withdrew in preparation for its redeployment to Leyte in the Philippines and, later in 1945, to Okinawa. The Third Marine Division remained in base camp on Guam until February 1945, as it readied for its bloody but triumphant campaign on Iwo

Jima. Of the other original units that participated in the W-Day landings, only the Ninth, the Fourteenth Defense Battalion, and a few other units were left to garrison Guam—but by no means did this mean that Japanese resistance was eradicated. Large pockets of Japanese forces had yet to be dealt with. By mid-August, the Americans controlled only 75 percent of the island, and as some 7,500 of the original 18,500-odd Japanese defenders had not yet been killed or captured, there was still much fighting and killing—and patrolling—to be done.[37]

Until this time, the battalion's big guns had not been brought ashore. On August 20, the third and final echelon of the Ninth, which had been left in reserve at Eniwetok, disembarked at the former Japanese Navy docks at Piti Point. The arrival of this last echelon included the heavy artillery, as well as the 90mm Group, which joined the Special Weapons' gunners in constructing gun positions around the Agana airfield.[38] For Pogiebait and the men of the 155mm Group, who had come ashore without their Long Toms some forty-five days earlier, there was no rest for the weary. With the possibility of Japanese naval raids being very remote and with no suitable field artillery missions existing for the Long Toms, the group remained the Ninth's own "infantry" component. For weeks its artillery pieces sat in a gun park at Piti while both Batteries A and B were "chopped" from the rest of the battalion to provide infantry, recon, and patrolling support to the Third Marine Division. The basic infantry skills learned years ago at Guantanamo would get more of a workout in the next four months than at any earlier time in the war.

Jack's Close Encounter with the Nisei

With almost eight thousand Japanese troops still on Guam in the late summer of 1944, because it was the largest US battalion left on the island, and with a negligible likelihood of Japanese air and naval counterstrikes, the Ninth's Marines were dispatched frequently on infantry patrols to flush out holdouts. In a few cases, there were success stories in which Japanese troops would surrender with token resistance. Sometimes the defenders would fight hard, and the Army and Marine teams would resort to grenades, demolition charges, and flamethrowers to seal them up in their caves and bunkers. In some cases, entire squads of Japanese occupied the bunkers, dying gruesomely but speedily via suicide by hand grenade. In the hopes of talking more Japanese into surrendering and learning from them useful intelligence, Guam's Island Command began sending out psychological warfare and intelligence teams alongsidee Army and Marine patrols. These groups were often equipped with propaganda leaflets, megaphones, and loudspeakers, and they included Japanese-speaking linguists as interpreters. These "psy-war" teams were tasked with talking the island's derelict defenders into giving up.[39]

On one of their patrols, Jack and other members of his Battery B platoon were combing the boondocks for Japanese holdouts. Guam's ravines and hills were not quite as heavily jungled as Guadalcanal, Rendova, or New Georgia, but the foliage was dense nevertheless. As he looked around on this patrol, Jack saw a figure moving in an area where he did not expect to see any Marines or Army troops. He crouched low, striving to identify the figure. As the man drew closer, Jack could see that he was wearing a GI helmet and fatigues and carried a rifle—but the face was certainly not Caucasian or Chamorro. In Jack's mind, the only explanation was that a Japanese soldier had found an American uniform and was trying to infiltrate or escape. Jack scuttled behind a tree and chambered a bullet. The sounds of the cartridge being loaded and the click of the bolt were loud enough that his buddies could hear it, which also meant that the Japanese soldier, who was only a few feet away, could probably hear it, too.

Jack was sweating profusely, and not just from the Guamanian heat and humidity: the Nalimbiu River shoot-out on Guadalcanal included, this was the closest he had ever gotten to a live, armed, hostile Japanese soldier. He had never killed anyone in combat, face to face, although he felt fairly certain that he'd helped kill people from a distance by serving part-time on the 155mm crews. The soldier was moving away; *good*, though Jack, *he hasn't heard me loading my gun*. Jack knew he needed to act quickly. He pulled the butt of his M-1 carbine tightly against his shoulder, drew a bead on the man through the carbine's sights, ensured the safety catch was off, and prepared to squeeze the trigger. A muffled command hissed from behind stopped him cold: "*Don't shoot! He's a 'Nissy!*'" Jack cocked his head slightly and softly croaked out: "What? What the hell you mean, 'don't shoot'? He's a Nip, ain't he? And what the hell's a 'Nissy?' "

A hand deftly grabbed the barrel of his carbine and pulled it downwards. "He's no Jap, goddammit! He's one of ours! O.K.?" Jack now learned, first-hand, one of the better-guarded American secrets of the Pacific War.

As part of American psy-war and intelligence operations, Marine and Army teams had begun in 1943, late in the Guadalcanal campaign, to use Japanese-speaking *Nisei* soldiers and officers in the field to help negotiate the surrender of Japanese troops and act as combat interpreters. Despite their internment (and the ongoing internment of their families and friends well into 1944), the *Nisei* wanted a chance to prove that they were as American as any boys from New York, Tennessee, Indiana, or California. Despite the incredibly shoddy treatment meted out to them and their families, the *Nisei* were truly the "Yankee samurai": their language skills were invaluable, and their courage was first-rate. Four teams of *Nisei* interpreters were deployed on Guam: two with the Third Marine Division, one with the First Provisional Brigade, and the last divided among the Army infantry regiments of the Seventy-Seventh Infantry Division. (One of the individuals assigned to the First Provisional Brigade's section had earlier suffered the ignominy of having been "captured" by Marines on Bougainville; despite his protests in fluent English, he had been displayed to the actor Gary Cooper, there with a USO show, as the first Japanese POW captured on that island![40]) Jack had unwittingly just drawn a bead on one of these highly dedicated interpreters and intelligence workers, but he had fortunately been stopped in the nick of time. "That was the closest I ever came to shooting a Japanese soldier. Good thing I learned he was a Japanese-*American* soldier, just in time!" Jack recalled.

All of this, however, apparently remained unknown to the interpreter who Jack had nearly shot and whose team had faced other adventures besides the one Pogiebait recalled: "When the [Guam] campaign was over the [*Nisei*] team reassembled in a rest area, drinking their first beer since leaving Hawaii. It made them slightly high, and some [of the men] broke into Japanese song. Years later, at a reunion of survivors, they wondered 'how we never got shot!'"[41] Oh, had the interpreters only known how close at least one of their number had come to that fate! "Friendly fire" casualties were prevalent enough among American forces in World War II—witness, for instance, the sinking of the *McCawley*, the shooting-down of the Corsair pilot off Rendova Harbor, and the deadly effects of the nighttime jitterbugging incidents on New Georgia—and it is an open question how many of these courageous US citizen-soldiers could have been injured or killed by their own side's guns. To Jack's and the *Nisei* soldier's mutual good fortune, however, each man emerged unscathed this day on Guam.

Battery B's Move to Pago Bay; Encounters with a Desperate Enemy

Morale of troops were consistently high and never any problem.
The troops were kept posted on the situation and progress of units in contact.
When this unit took over patrolling of the southern sector, gun crews were
in the patrol composition, which materially boosted morale.

—NINTH AAA BATTALION'S OPERATIONS REPORT
ON OPERATION TOENAILS, AUGUST 17, 1944[42]—

Finally, after weeks of pure infantry-type work, the order came to the 155mm Group to deploy its guns: Battery A to the Adelup Point area near one of the W-Day beachheads, and Battery B plus the 155mm Group's headquarters to the Pago Bay area on the eastern coast of Guam near the village of Yona. The batteries' missions were twofold: each was to mop up its assigned area and set up a clifftop fire base for its four long-idle Long Toms. The group's move was accomplished around August 31, 1944, though not without an incident typical of the fighting "after the fighting was over" on Guam. The battalion's history records Battery B's move to the secluded Pago Bay: "As fire control officer, Don Sandager set out to find a battery position which had been selected from air photographs. His recon with a rifle squad of the 3d Marines found there 'were still many snipers and the terrain was extremely rocky and wooded.'" When Sandager and Wells reported that it was "not feasible" to trundle Long Toms to this rugged position, "they were told to go anyway. After some negotiation a compromise position was reached near the point and a road built to reach it."[43]

For Chadwick, Landon, and Battery B's old salts who had survived the work on Hill 181 on Gavutu, the building of the Pago Bay trail and base camp was eerily reminiscent of those earlier labors. First, a trail had to be hacked by hand through the dense jungle to the cliffs where the Long Toms would be dug in. Battery B's leathernecks left their old camp near the airfield and marched to Pago Bay, their gear stowed in accompanying trucks and joined by a bulldozer. The Marines marveled at the large number of Japanese bunkers, OPs, and gun emplacements on the high ground around the bay and thanked their lucky stars that the defenses were now abandoned. As Frank Chadwick recalled: "It was very evident that whoever [had] planned the beach defenses was a real professional. The defenses [were] defenses-in-depth and [the] interlocking firing from all points on the beach was something that they could be very proud of."[44]

As they labored on the trail to Pago Bay, the "old-fashioned" artillerymen of Battery B got a first taste of a new mode of modern warfare: rocket bombardment. Navy rocket ships—likely converted LCI landing craft—sailed past the marching Marines and, upon reaching the northernmost point off Pago Bay's beach, began launching salvoes of ground bombardment rockets. The rockets' flash and roar were an awe-inspiring sight, but when patrolling the target area a few days later, these same Marines were disappointed to find that the practical results of these barrages were less impressive. The rocket bombardment had cleared away much of the underbrush (which undoubtedly aided patrolling), left several large craters, and knocked down some trees, but several dud rockets were also found. Chadwick remembered:

"We found that any enemy in caves, fortifications or below ground would be safe unless a direct hit had been achieved and if this had occurred on the fortification, they would have been shaken but still able to continue to fight. This was a great disappointment but, watching the firing that morning, we took this as a black omen to the upcoming operation."[45]

Under Major Wells's and Captain Teller's scrutiny, Battery B built its newest base camp. Telephone lines were laid back to the battalion's CP, and a barbed wire perimeter was strung. The bulldozer was used to widen the trail to the width of a truck; unfortunately, the trail itself remained little more than sand, coral, and soil, which would quickly turn into a glutinous mess with the addition of any rain. Most of the trees were left in place around the base camp to aid in camouflage and to afford some additional cover from the elements, but the vines, scrubby bushes, and tough grass covering the ground had to be hand-hacked by machete, the bulldozer failing to make a significant dent in such foliage. "Home" for Jack and his Battery B buddies was little more than foxholes covered with shelter halves or rubberized ponchos. These jury-rigged coverings did little to keep the rain out, and the foxholes filled rapidly whenever it rained, a frequent occurrence in the Guamanian summer. While Captain Teller put half of his battery's eighty-odd gunners to work in setting up camp and gun positions over the next few days, the other half ran patrols around the campsite. From their observations on earlier patrols, the Marines had learned the Japanese were starving and would take any opportunity to raid foodstuffs or garbage dumps for anything edible.

With the nearest American positions to the battery's Pago Bay location being some seven miles away, the unit was left to its own devices in matters of self-defense. The base camp was surrounded by double rows of barbed wire. The wire was intermittently festooned, as usual, with pebble-filled tin cans to provide early warning of movements against the wire barrier. Several tripod-mounted .30 caliber machine guns were emplaced at each side of the trail near the entrance into the camp. Interlocking fields of fire were cleared for the machine guns, and sandbagged strongpoints were placed at intervals along the wire. Still, knowing that only a few miles away Guam was being turned into a vast supply dump, with many of the creature comforts available in the rear areas, was an immensely frustrating fact to Jack and his buddies. Reduced to eating cold ten-in-one rations and with only a five hundred-gallon tanker of water delivered to provide three days of sustenance for eighty men, "it didn't seem fair," as Chadwick moaned.

Patrolling was very much a cat-and-mouse game, and when on patrol, Pogiebait, Chadwick, Bob Landon, Zombie Jones, Leo McDonald, and

Pogiebait (*far left*) and several of his buddies—
likely, two of Leo McDonald, "Zombie" Jones, or "Mabel"
Morgan—at Battery B's Pago Bay camp near Yona,
late summer 1944. Author's collection.

their brethren were ever fearful of stepping onto a hidden mine or booby trap, never mind the risk of being pegged by a sniper. "Half of the time," Chadwick later related, "you saw no enemy but only areas he used for bivouac, footprints on a trail, leftovers of a fire or broken branches to indicate [the enemy] were still in our area. Frustrating, scary and living like cavemen, dirty and stinking to high heavens in this hot, humid climate and no bathing, we were a pretty rancid, stinking bunch of Marines." With the average temperatures on Guam and the other Marianas that summer ranging between seventy-seven and eighty-eight degrees, with near eighty percent humidity and an average rainfall of six to nine inches,[46] Pogiebait and his buddies sweltered.

After about ten days in these conditions, more housekeeping gear was brought into the base camp. Eight-man pyramid tents were erected; patrols were cut by two-thirds, and the barbed wire fencing and gun positions were improved. A hole was scooped outside the camp perimeter to serve as a garbage dump, which, in time, would become a lure for more starving Japanese desperate for anything resembling food. A field kitchen and four showers made from converted fifty-five-gallon drums were also set up. "We were really living high on the hog, or so we thought," Chadwick recalled.

By mid to late August, intelligence reports determined that the roving bands of Japanese in the Pago Bay area had grown from mere two- or three-man clusters to platoon-sized elements of thirty or forty. The Marines sensed they were likely to face greater trouble when, while attempting to flush a squad of Japanese out of the brush surrounding the base camp, a patrol came upon a second trail. This one had been tramped out by the Japanese, tracing a rough circle around the base camp's entire perimeter and up to the cliffside heights overlooking the camp. Patrols were quickly resumed. Now beginning to suffer from dengue ("breakbone") fever, Jack was put on a work detail in the base camp during the daylight hours and was assigned to help man a machine gun position on the perimeter during the evening.

Several days after getting the first reports of the larger concentrations of Japanese soldiers in the area and finding the enemy-made trail, the base camp was attacked by about one hundred Japanese soldiers, which began a running firefight of about two hours.[47] The next morning, the Marines found eighteen dead Japanese and fresh shallow graves for perhaps twenty more nearby, with numerous blood trails leading back into the brushes. With fifty to sixty Marines manning the base camp at this time (the rest being on patrol, or ill with malaria and dengue fever, both of which were recurring with a vengeance), the odds would be against Battery B if more attacks like this continued. Several hours before dawn, particular care was given for all Marines not on patrol to "stand to" and man the perimeter until after sunrise.

One evening not long after this order was issued, although brittle-boned and feverish from the effects of dengue, Jack was on guard duty, helping man a .30 caliber machine gun in a perimeter foxhole. To his right was another team armed with a machine gun, rifles, and grenades. Toward dawn, he was shaken out of his torpor by the sound of rapid machine gun fire, followed by several rifle shots, then by the blast of a grenade. Pogiebait fingered the trigger of his machine gun and hunkered down in his foxhole, desperately looking around in his front to discover whether he was the next to be attacked. He was particularly edgy because he was less than familiar with how to operate his machine gun. After a few minutes, there was only the silence of the Guamanian jungle.

Later that morning, following the dawn stand-to before breakfast, Jack and a small patrol headed out of camp near the trail's entrance to see what had happened and to make sure that the survivors of the attack had not set up an ambush. One of the foxholes beside the trail's entrance had been in the direct line of march of a large patrol of Japanese stragglers who were apparently trying to infiltrate the base camp. When he heard the enemy patrol approach, Leo McDonald and several others on guard duty challenged the group with a hoarse yell of "*Halt!*" and a whisper for the password. When no response came, the Marines fired the machine gun, which jammed after several rounds; Leo then grabbed his rifle, which also jammed; and then he threw a hand grenade. It was all over in a matter of seconds, but now the bodies of the eighteen dead Japanese lay near the trail. While their uniforms were ragged, several had carried captured US field equipment as well as serviceable M-1 Garands, in place of their country's standard Arisaka rifles.

Jack looked at the dead Japanese: although many of the corpses were mangled and bloody, they seemed so young, and all looked half-starved. Then someone said, "Hey; look what this Jap has in his mess tin!" In the half-open mess tin, still clutched tightly in the soldier's hand, was a battered sliver of chocolate cake—apparently, some nearby American unit's dessert from the night before. Pieces of cake were in several other mess tins carried by the other dead Japanese. They had obviously already gotten inside somebody else's mess area or garbage pit undetected, had gotten their food and gotten out, but had encountered the perimeter defenses of the base camp where they were mowed down. Although their food situation was hardly great, Jack and the Marines of Battery B were faring exceedingly well in comparison to the starving Japanese.[48] Under such circumstances, it is little wonder that the members of a Japanese patrol would have risked their lives for anything edible or fight with desperation whenever trapped.

"They died for *cake*," Jack thought. He thought of their ages, and how small they looked, and how they were obviously starving to death. Then he thought to himself: "*The poor little bastards.*" Only later did Jack realize that it was the first time he had allowed himself a sympathetic thought toward the Japanese—*any* Japanese—in years.

Sometime after this incident, a patrol set out by jeep and was moving slowly down the trail when someone noticed a pile of freshly turned-up dirt. The obvious conclusion was that someone had recently planted a land mine. Swerving to avoid the patch of fresh earth, the driver pulled off the road and around it, halting the vehicle to examine the pile of dirt. Indeed, a Japanese patrol had recently planted a yardstick-type landmine in the trail. The clumsy placement of the mine seemed too obvious and smacked of a setup, so the patrol spread out cautiously, certain from the footprints and tracks that there was a large body of Japanese waiting in ambush nearby. As they returned to the vehicle, they found the driver had stopped inches away from another landmine just off the edge of the road, perfectly placed so that—had he not stopped the jeep as quickly as he did—he would have rolled over this second mine.[49]

Another Battery B patrol set up an ambush late one evening near a known watering hole. As dawn broke, the patrol spotted a solitary Japanese soldier with ten or twelve canteens hung onto a pole slung over his shoulder. The patrol bided its time as the soldier filled each canteen, debating whether they should try and capture him, wait to see if others would join him, or just let him have it after he completed his work. Chadwick recounted the Japanese water-bearer's insouciant response as he became aware that he was being watched: "When he filled all his canteens, the Jap looked directly at us, gave us the finger and fled. We got to laughing so much over his grin and fingering us, no one got off a shot."[50]

Most of the battalion's patrols did not end up in firefights, but when these did break out, such skirmishes usually only lasted five to ten minutes before the Japanese would fade back into the brush. Their uniforms were often tattered, but they were relatively well armed. Besides standard-issue Arisaka rifles, some of the dead found at the scene of such encounters had Garands and British-made Enfield rifles (the latter likely having been captured from British stocks in Burma, Hong Kong, or Malaya) and American field gear. Occasionally, dead Japanese would be found wearing US-issue fatigues, most likely looted from a supply depot. When one patrol of the Ninth shot two Japanese, they found that one had American gold coins and change apparently seized in the Philippines, along with English-script Japanese occupation currency, and the other had a Marine Corps ring, also apparently taken from a member of the star-crossed Fourth Marines in the Philippines. Nevertheless, despite the heterogeneous collection of uniforms, arms, and gear and their own sorry logistical situation, the Japanese evaders that the 155mm Group's patrols encountered remained resourceful, stealthy, and tenacious.

Battery B's last major firefight occurred on a patrol Chadwick accompanied as a BAR gunner. The group spotted and flushed a Japanese fugitive out of the brush not far from the base camp. As he jumped out of the brush, hands over his head, somebody in the patrol shot him. "It was then we discovered," Chadwick recalled, "that it was an ambush, and he was the bait. He had been shot before, and gangrene had set in. We pushed around the bushes and flushed out 10 more Japs who headed back into the jungle. The Jap we killed had gold U.S. coins plus other American coins he apparently picked up in the Philippines."

One thing seems readily apparent from Chadwick's account: little effort, if any, was made to take this wounded Japanese soldier prisoner. The ex post facto justification for this one killing, however, emerges after the dead man is searched and is found to have American coins on his person—therefore, it could be assumed that he must have been a veteran of the savage battle for the Philippines, could have been a veteran of the barbarous Bataan Death March, and had probably inflicted abuse on US prisoners in similar conditions. Hence, his death was arguably justifiable—an eye for an eye—to his potential captors.

Although this was the 155mm Group's last shoot-out with a Japanese patrol, it was hardly the last firefight for the rest of the battalion. Moving frequently, hoarding their food and equipment in caves and ransacking garbage dumps, camps, and Chamorro homes for food, small bands of Japanese soldiers roamed the northernmost reaches of Guam's jungles and mountains after the "end of hostilities" was declared in mid-August 1944. The last large groups of these stragglers were targeted in late October 1944 by the Third Marine Division. Accompanied by elements of the Ninth (now renamed the Ninth AAA Battalion), this drive to the north of Guam killed about one hundred Japanese. The Ninth's last combat casualty was killed in a firefight during this operation.[51]

These elements of the Ninth, however, pointedly did not include the 155mm Group. Major Wells had a run-in with Colonel O'Neil, who had ordered Batteries A and B to take part in this sweep. With the men of both batteries having seen ninety-odd unbroken days of patrolling in the boondocks, and with each of them soon due for rotation stateside, Walter Wells refused to comply with the order. Colonel O'Neil and Major Wells had already developed a strong mutual dislike for one another, and O'Neil apparently viewed Wells's refusal as rank insubordination. Waldo prevailed in the end, and his group did not go on this mission, much to his men's relief. "This order was particularly agitating to [Wells]," Chadwick recalled, "because all of the original members of the Ninth had already left and we were awaiting our turn. Wells was told he would be relieved of his command, but he stood his ground. Thank God, we didn't have to go, but the Marines from the 9th H&S Group replaced us."

Diehard Japanese defenders lingered in Guam's boondocks for years to come. Several MPs were killed by stragglers as late as December 1945, four months after the formal end of hostilities. The final holdouts would linger tenaciously for several decades: two were captured in 1960, and Sergeant Shoichi Yokoi, one of the last two Japanese soldiers to surrender, did so on Guam in early 1972 at the age of fifty-eight, twenty-seven years after the war had ended.[52]

A War without End

Of all the stories that my father told his family of his service in the Marines, the great majority concerned life on Guadalcanal, the Central Solomons, and Banika, or his service after his return stateside in early 1945. Very few of his tales concerned Guam—a realization that did not occur to me until many years later. Why might this have been the case? It might be because Jack's war on Guam was replete with terrors he never encountered on the other islands. From conversations with my father and his friends, it became apparent that while the Ninth had some good times on Guam later in the campaign, these good times were usually fewer and farther between, compared to the earlier campaigns. Although they were nominally reorganized as a AAA battalion, augmented by the 155mm Group for seacoast defense, the tales of many of the Ninth's men on Guam sound more like what one would expect of an infantry unit. Indeed, with all the emphasis on patrolling and mopping-up for its first four months on Guam, much of the Ninth—in particular, the 155mm Group—was largely functioning as a de facto "leg infantry" outfit.

All of this had an impact, including on morale. The Ninth Defense of fall 1944—or at least, the 155mm Group—was not the same unit as it had been in 1942 and 1943. One gets a sense that the morale of the group's men was not the same either, despite pronouncements by the Ninth's headquarters in its official reports that the "[m]orale of the troops was consistently high and never any problem."[53] While its overall morale may have been high, relatively speaking, the postwar descriptions of the Ninth's service on Guam—even a hint that can be discerned in the fairly anodyne tone of Jack's letters back home to his parents and brothers—indicate a form of war-weariness or burnout, or something like resignation.

Many of the veterans' reminiscences paint a picture of near-constant stress and exhaustion: a nagging suspicion that enemy stragglers lay in ambush behind every bush or trail, and a conviction that, if the mopping-up patrols did not end soon, a Japanese bullet, landmine, or malaria would eventually finish off the remainder of the Ninth Defense's war in the Pacific. When they actually succeeded on rare occasions to capture Japanese troops, exultation was about the last emotion the Ninth's leathernecks felt. Many of the more common feelings, particularly for the battalion's old-timers, seem to have been reflected in certain recurring questions: *"Hell, how many more of the bastards can be left? How much longer is this goddam war going to last?"* And, of course, like a marathon runner nearly out of energy: *"Am I going to make it to the end?"* Unsurprisingly, a bitter rhyme often made the rounds of the Ninth's men around this time: *"Golden Gate in '48; bread line in '49."*[54]

In light of more recent American history, even the terminology many veterans of the Ninth's Guam campaign used to describe their service on Guam has an eerily familiar ring to it. *Ambushes; base camps; patrols; infiltrators; mopping-up; psychological warfare teams; body counts.* Viewed from some eighty years later, the battalion's and other units' activities on that island might seem to prefigure so many of the terms, tactics, and concepts of a later kind of warfare, faced twenty years later in the jungles and highlands of Vietnam.

After months of hard campaigning with little respite, the stresses caused by three months of patrolling around Pago Bay also caused some of the Ninth's Marines to question whatever had become of their youth and idealism and prompted them to take on a more fatalistic attitude. As Frank Chadwick recalled, Battery B's struggles now truly felt like a war without end: "[W]e had no relief, or even hope of relief. You had no idea what day it was, even sometimes what month it was, and the time of day did not matter, as the sun rose and set and time went on. Talk about zombies or robots: we were in that classification. The old timers knew it and felt it." Despite the absence of heavy combat casualties in the fall of 1944, there were still several hundred victims of the Ninth's old nemesis—disease. Jack himself was incapacitated for a time by dengue fever on Guam. He now fully understood why dengue was called "breakbone fever": he felt as if he had aged several decades overnight, his joints and cartilage ached, and every movement resulted in massive onrushes of pain throughout his body. For many other old salts of the Ninth, it was the end of the road: many were surveyed out from malaria and dengue, including Dave Slater and John Dobkowski.

One of the Ninth's youngest Marines,
the teenaged Frank Chadwick. Courtesy
of Francis E. Chadwick.

As Biggie Slater lay on his stretcher in the Third Marine Division's hospital outside Agana awaiting treatment for a massive case of malaria, even in his feverish state, he felt something odd, like someone was stroking his arm. This time, he was not delirious: he looked up through feverish eyes to see his gunnery sergeant, Smith, himself awaiting evacuation but almost out of his own mind from fever and from the effects of chronic alcoholism. Not a word was spoken, but as Biggie looked up at old Gunny Smith, he could see that he was murmuring something unintelligibly to himself with tears in his eyes. "The Gunny took care of his own. I guess he felt like it was the only way he could say goodbye to one of his boys," Slater remembered.

For the older members of the battalion, perhaps the saddest thing was not that their buddies had left—after all, at least they now might have another chance at life—but that so frequently, many of those who were well and on patrol or off-site would return to camp to find their sick friends gone without a trace and without a chance to say goodbye, thanks, "Semper Fi," or good luck. One of these hasty departures was John Dobkowski, evacuated while his buddies since Cuba, Chadwick and Pogiebait, were out (Chadwick being on patrol and Jack himself being laid up in a medical tent with dengue fever) and unable to say farewell.[55]

All told, neither Jack nor his peers spoke very much about the Ninth's time on Guam. From what we have learned, it may be easy in retrospect to see why they felt that way. Of all the stories Jack told about it, however, the ones he recounted to his family most frequently were of his near drowning as he came ashore; of finding the dead members of the Japanese patrol at the Pago Bay base camp, their mess kits filled with American cake; and of how he almost shot the *Nisei* interpreter. The impressions these incidents made on him were indelible.

One of the more unusual series of pictures Jack kept in his postwar photo album and scrapbooks was a grouping of about a dozen snapshots taken in fall 1944 around Yona, Guam, with an old-fashioned Brownie camera

Playing "heroes and prisoners": Hero and prisoner (left), hero (middle), and prisoner (right). Yona, Guam, fall 1944. Author's collection.

someone had acquired. This sequence of photos depicts Jack and other leatherneck buddies playing what can best be described as a game of "Marines and Japanese." In some pictures, Jack is wearing his old campaign hat and is drawing a bead with his M-1 carbine on the back of a bare-chested Marine wearing Jack's Japanese sailor's cap. In other pictures, the roles are reversed. Someone else—Mabel Morgan, Leo McDonald, or Zombie Jones—is wearing the campaign hat and clutching the carbine, and Jack is the shirtless POW. In these pictures, Jack is either sitting unperturbedly while a crack Marine sharpshooter draws a bead on him, face flushed with triumph—*I got the rat!*—or, with hands held high, is cringing servilely, his face contorted with mock panic as he is taken prisoner. "Hey, Nick, did you ever see the picture of my Jap prisoner?" my father teased me when he first showed me some of the pictures in which he was shown "capturing" a fellow Marine. I once asked him, "What were you all doing here?" "Aw, son, we were just goofing off!" One of the ideas at the time was that, with these pictures, everyone in the battery could have a photo that he could send home to his family or girlfriend that would make him look like the conquering hero.

To me, now, it is a little amazing that after everything they had endured, these prematurely aged youngsters could still muster the humor and energy to reenact a favorite childhood game, playing "cowboys and Indians"—only, in this case, using real weapons and in a much grimmer situation. A psychologist might analyze this as being a form of role play that would help lessen their fears of the Japanese by casting the enemy in a ridiculous light and also by humanizing a still largely unseen foe. A simpler explanation, though, may be that despite everything they had endured, Jack and his buddies were still overgrown boys, not long out of their teens, with time on their hands for the first time in months, and they used this time to blow off steam in a juvenile, but creative, manner. That Jack and his pals could do this, even at this late stage of the war, may have been one sign of hope that they would survive and resume their old prewar lives and that the war would someday end.

The Culinary (and Other) Delights of Guam

Even with the rigors of base camp and patrolling, there were at least some opportunities for amusement on Guam. One patrol brought back the carcass of a cow they had killed, and a feast was planned for that evening's dinner. The meat was tough and chewy, but for Marines who were subsisting largely on ten-in-one, C and K rations and had not had fresh beef since the invasion began, it was a change of pace, and it tasted pretty good. While the beef was being prepared, Colonel O'Neil arrived on a surprise visit to the base camp and, since rank has its privileges, was promptly served the choicest piece of steak. He ate it with evident enjoyment but without comment. When dinner was over, Colonel O'Neil asked to see the group's officers in private. When they were all assembled, he tersely thanked them for the excellent meal before dropping a bomb—"Now, tell me, *why* aren't any of you familiar with our standing orders that we can't shoot domestic animals?"—and excoriated them for condoning the killing of such a domestic animal. Indeed, orders against the killing of Guamanian livestock had been posted since the early days of the invasion. The officers all listened attentively, but they also duly noted that the colonel had said nothing until after he had finished his meal. Standing orders and O'Neil's wrath aside, little deterred the Ninth's hardier field gourmets from trying to cook up other local farm animals or—when especially lucky—having a friendly Chamorro woman kill and roast a local pig for a hungry patrol.

The close proximity to civilians on Guam additionally brought a new set of concerns for the Ninth's leadership that the battalion had not experienced in the less civilized areas of the Pacific. As the campaign wound down, regrettably, several incidents of sexual misconduct cropped up among some members of the Ninth. In one instance, a senior officer was caught spying on a nurse's latrine area at a hospital located near Piti Point. For his punishment—although he was soon to be eligible for rotation stateside—in lieu of a court-martial, the officer was transferred to a Marine artillery battalion preparing for the Okinawa invasion.

In another instance, Lieutenant Sandager—who had received the Silver Star for his actions as Major Hiatt's airborne FO—was tasked to help supervise a prisoner-of-war compound. Some of the prisoners included Japanese women and Guamanian female collaborators and sympathizers. The camp assigned to a detail from the 155mm Group was split into two compounds: one for male Japanese POWs and another for female prisoners. Word reached Sandager of allegations that some of the women were having sexual relations with some of his Marine guards. Over the course of several evenings, Lieutenant Sandager observed as the Marine guards in question attempted to have sex with the women through the barbed wire. Accordingly, Lieutenant Sandager reported the guards for suitable punishment.[56]

While these incidents were extreme, many of the Ninth's men found more opportunities for sexual peccadilloes or romantic attachments on

Guam than elsewhere among the battalion's other Pacific outposts. Since many Guamanians harbored a longtime affection for "their" Marines that preceded December 1941, it is not surprising that once the shooting stopped, many of the Guamanian girls fell for the leathernecks and vice versa, although sometimes with heartbreaking results. Besides the obvious cultural difficulties and the fact that "there was a war on," the institutional attitudes of the Corps, combined with anti-fraternization rules, had a way of thwarting wartime love affairs. This was best summed up by a long-standing gripe of the old Marines: "If the Corps had wanted you to have a wife, it would have issued you one."

In the case of one of Biggie Slater's and Harry Jones's Commo Section acquaintances, a telephone man named Russell, the young Marine fell hard for a beautiful young Guamanian girl. He began surreptitiously dating her and was soon regarded as practically a member of her family. Russell, Jones, and their pals would often visit her family's small village of partly thatched huts, and Jones remembered her and her family as being "very poor but always neat and clean and very friendly" and as wearing the odd cleft-toed *tabi* rubberized sneakers of the Japanese soldiers. In time the Marine decided that his feelings for the young woman were deeper than a passing fancy, and despite his friends' entreaties not to do so, he decided to marry her. As Jones laconically noted: "[He] went to see the Chaplain about this and was immediately transferred to an unknown dimension and was seen no more."[57] Such harsh actions by the authorities may have deterred many serious romantic relationships from forming between the majority of the Ninth's men and other Guamanian girls, although little could stop them from forming friendships or other kinds of relationships.

Now the youngest man in the Ninth, beardless Bill Sorensen of its radar detachment befriended the Murray family, the father of whom had been the island's superintendent of schools before the war. The family allowed Sorensen and a group of his buddies to pitch camp on their property outside Agana, and they would occasionally prepare supper together and pool their own meager fare with "Chick" Sorensen's and his buddies' rations. In 1994, Sorensen and his wife flew to Guam for the fiftieth anniversary of its liberation; on landing, he was greeted by a pair of attractive women holding a sign that read *"Where's Bill Sorensen?"* Bill's wife Evelyn coolly eyed her husband and asked, "Is there something you hadn't told me yet, Bill?" The unexpected reception was provided by the granddaughters of old Mr. Murray, who had come to meet Bill at the airport at their grandfather's behest.

Not that the Ninth's officers were unbending in administering the anti-fraternization policy, however; Chris Donner recounted to his wife Madge one of Chaplain Janes's efforts to permit a little officially sanctioned socializing between the enlisted troops and some of Guam's young women once the occupation of the island became more stabilized in late 1944:

> The social season is picking up as we enter the winter months. Today's dance and buffet supper was delightful, absolutely delightful. The young ladies were so charming in their pretty afternoon dresses and far out show the men in the grace with which they whirled about the floor. Of course, I was there as something of an onlooker, because the real participants were the enlisted men, and I had been ordered by the Chaplain to attend as a chaperone (one who watches the door to prevent any couples from straying out and into the woods).
>
> When the Chaplain first conceived the idea, he asked the native Catholic Priest to help him. There was good reason for that for although our Chaplain is Protestant, on this island when a girl wants to attend a party—any of the thousands of girls—she asks her mother's permission, and the mother in turn asks the sanction of the only native priest, Father Calvo. The latter, who is a grand character, is therefore well acquainted with the younger set and its aspirations. So he was the logical person to round up the fifty or so girls. . . . Don't ask me why the Chaplain requested my services as chaperone. I don't know, darling. Twas a complete surprise but altogether an interesting evening.[58]

On the other, much less platonic and less sanctioned extreme—which may have partly justified the chaplain's desire and need for chaperones—Donner recalled a guitar-playing Battery A gunner from California who "obviously possessed a romantic soul" to match his romantic lyrics and musical nature:

> After we had established ourselves on Guam and were even granting "liberties" for visiting, [he] used to go forth quite frequently. But when he overstayed a couple of liberties, Townsend [who had received command of Battery A on Reichner's departure to become the 155mm Group's exec] gave him special duty and restriction. On the next liberty day, the Californian said he was sick, but our corpsman declared he could find nothing meriting removal of the man to the hospital. [He] thereupon gained access to Townsend and told the latter he was the cause of many nightmares. Townsend was astounded and ordered [him] out, [who] then claimed his right to see the Chaplain and was sent up to [headquarters]. The "Padre" called us up later and said he was

placing our man in sick bay, although he could not see anything wrong with him. That was at 5 p.m. At 8 p.m. the Chaplain again phoned. "Townsend," he said indignantly, "I am putting your man on report. No one is going to hide behind the cloak of the Lord and get away with it so far as I'm concerned." "Where was he found?" "In an enlisted man's head, having intercourse with a Guamanian girl!" (Rear echelon!)[59]

In partial defense of the lovelorn Californian, perhaps Chris Donner could only repeat what has so often been said: "All's fair in love and war."

An End and a Beginning

In September 1944, the Ninth Defense Battalion was officially redesignated the Ninth AAA Battalion, with the Seacoast & Field Artillery Group being administratively attached for the time being. A new CO, Lt. Colonel Frank Reinecke, who had served as the battalion's exec on Guam, assumed command from Colonel O'Neil. In November, the 155mm Group handed over its Long Toms and gun positions at Adelup Point and Pago Bay to a full-strength Army coast artillery battalion of some 250 men.[60] By this time, Battery B had dropped from about 120 men at its peak strength to about 45 able-bodied leathernecks. Malaria, dengue fever, other tropical diseases, and miscellaneous wounds had claimed the rest. "Turret Top" Hiatt became battalion exec, succeeding Colonel Reinecke, with Hiatt having been replaced as the 155mm Group's CO by Walter Wells. The entire battalion was now a reintegrated outfit for the first time since leaving Banika six months before, with its headquarters and billets near Agana.[61]

The unit was now officially an antiaircraft unit, and with most of its flak positions being clustered around Agana Field, Jack and his buddies could watch the gigantic B-29s of the Twenty-First Bomber Command as they left for their missions to Japan and returned from the already finished air bases on nearby Tinian. One would occasionally land on the soon-to-be fully constructed Guamanian airfields.[62] The enormous size and power of the Superfortresses impressed Jack immensely. How mightily powerful—and how technical and impersonal, as personified by the B-29—this kind of war seemed! "You really felt kind of small around them all," Jack recalled. By late 1944, Jack and his pals watched hundreds of B-29s and P-51 Mustang fighters en route to Japan from the Marianas. Their unpainted, bare-metal wings and bodies shimmered high above in the Central Pacific sun as the Guam-based fighter squadrons linked up with their sister bomber wings from nearby Tinian and Saipan. The sight of this air armada helped erase the last lingering doubts he had as to who would win the war. Yet, the ever-present question remained: "Will I be around to see it?" Apart from stragglers (still a serious enough matter), the war on Guam was basically over, and with the fighting nearing Japan, the worst was yet to come. Jack knew his rotation stateside was close at hand, but how long would any time at home last before the war began again for him? Would there ever be peace again?

The Ninth Defense Battalion received one Navy Unit Commendation for its actions on Guadalcanal, another Navy Unit Commendation for Rendova, and a third for Guam. The Ninth shared with the First Marine Division a Presidential Unit Citation for Guadalcanal and a fourth Navy Unit Commendation awarded to the First Marine Provisional Brigade for Guam, as well as an Army Unit Citation for New Georgia, plus numerous letters of commendation from the Army, Navy, and Fleet Marine Force. Despite its foibles and occasional disciplinary lapses, the battalion had amassed quite a reputation as a unit that trained good staff officers. Of its eight battalion commanders, five left the Corps at general rank, including Colonels Nimmer (who commanded III Amphib's corps artillery as a brigadier general during the savage fighting on Okinawa and retired a two-star) and Scheyer (also retiring as a major general), O'Neil and Reinecke (retiring as brigadier generals), and Major Wallace Thompson, the original CO of the Ninth Defense Training Detachment in February 1942 (also retiring as a one-star).[63]

Certain qualities had made the Fighting Ninth a unique unit within the American military of World War II. First, few other US ground units could claim that they had campaigned against both principal Axis enemies—the Germans (recall the *U-94's crew*) and the Japanese. Part of this uniqueness was undoubtedly attributable to its peculiar role as one of a limited number of defense battalions. Still, other aspects of its makeup and service provided the Ninth's men with a higher degree of camaraderie than may have existed in more conventional and better-known military formations. Years later, its veterans often spoke of the Ninth Defense Battalion as being more like a family than a military unit; moreover, many of their wartime letters and papers (which could hardly be chalked up to postwar nostalgia) seem to elicit the same feelings. What contributed to this sentiment?

Certainly, the battalion had taken relatively few serious casualties during its existence (apart from its numerous victims of tropical illnesses, there were only seventy-seven combat-related casualties—eight combat deaths, one missing in action, and sixty-eight wounded in action—during the entire war),[64] and while facing very difficult and dangerous conditions, it had not experienced the frontline rigors of Marine infantry units like those Marine regiments and battalions savaged at Tarawa, Saipan, Peleliu, Iwo Jima, and Okinawa.[65] Its casualty percentages and turnover of personnel scarcely compare with that of some Army combat units in Europe, like the Twenty-Eighth Infantry Division, which experienced a whopping 175 percent statistical turnover rate in a nine-month period, during which time that division saw 196 days of combat and had almost twice the number of battle casualties to non-battle casualties.[66] By comparison, in its hardest fought action, the Rendova/New Georgia campaign, the entire Ninth had a tiny number of casualties: thirteen deaths (including non-combat deaths), one MIA, and some fifty wounded in action.[67] Even with several hundred men having been surveyed out due to illness, the Ninth still had a relatively small turnover between February 1942 and March 1944, the time of its first rotations stateside. Consistently, the largest number of its casualties were non-battle casualties, most often from malaria and dengue fever.

Ironically, it may have been the battalion's long-term exposure to hazardous duty, without suffering the high casualties of many other combat units, that gave it this unique quality of feeling like a giant extended family. In combat units that have already experienced heavy losses, new troops were often shunned: hardly anyone wanted to get to know a green soldier fresh from a replacement depot who was only likely to be killed or seriously wounded in a short period of time anyway or who, through his inexperience, may well get someone else killed. In units like the Ninth, though, there was more time to assimilate and train the new men, and relatively more time to break them into the customs and routines, even in combat areas, than in a unit constantly engaged in direct frontline combat. Unlike many combat units, too, that saw extremely bloody and violent action but usually faced it within a compressed time frame before being pulled out of the line for R&R, the Ninth faced chronic dangers, maybe less direct than storming trenches or bunkers in hand-to-hand combat but every bit as deadly. The unit's experiences were as likely to kill one as if one had been shot in a direct assault. Naval and air bombardments, Pistol Pete's shellings, and Japanese patrols, stragglers, and infiltrators extending over a proportionately longer time period were hazardous. Few units had seen the kind of unbroken, lengthy service in the Pacific that the Ninth had, and this, too, contributed to the unique character of the unit.

With an exceptionally high proportion of its original members serving with the unit from its formation in February 1944 up until its conversion to a AAA battalion on Guam in late 1944—with over 40 percent of the personnel who formed the original battalion serving with it for the duration—there was a core of experienced, long-serving members of the original unit to help train and break in the new arrivals. The infusion of the more experienced enlisted men and NCOs of the Fifth Defense's Polar Bears on Cuba can only have helped to establish a sense of belonging. The Ninth's initial makeup may also have helped contribute to this feeling, with such a high proportion of its original enlisted men coming in as the Christmas Tree Marines straight out of Boot Camp. The leavening was provided by its cadre of senior NCOs and senior officers, who, in a unit as small as the prewar Corps had been, had either already served together or had an ample number of common experiences and connections to help tie them together. The shared hardships of the Ninth's campaigns and combat and the dearth of leaves or rotations stateside further forged the bonds made in Cuba. Finally, the "agony and the ecstasy" of July 2 and 4, 1943—from the horrors of the first raid to the triumph of the second—also helped bond all of the Ninth's original men together. "I don't think we ever would have been as close as we were if it wasn't for those two days," Joe Pratl reminisced.[68]

Jack and his fellow Pearl Harbor Avengers and Christmas Tree Marines may have signed up in 1941 out of patriotism, a desire for revenge, or simply to seek adventure and get away from home, but by war's end, something more tangible than ideals or military discipline held the men of the Ninth together. One combat infantryman explained that factor in this manner: "Ask any dogface on the line. You're fighting for your skin on the line. When I enlisted I was as patriotic as all hell. There's no patriotism on the line. A boy up here 60 days . . . is in danger every minute. He ain't fighting for patriotism."[69] On the other hand, it was not merely a question of saving one's own skin. As another former Marine (there are no "ex-Marines") of Jack's generation, William Manchester, put it: "Those men on the line were my family, my home. They were closer to me than [Manchester's civilian] friends had ever been or ever would be. They had never let me down, and I couldn't do it to them. . . . Men, I now know, do not fight for flag or country, for the Marine Corps or glory or any other abstraction. They fight for one another."[70]

"I love you like a brother!" Jack would frequently exclaim to his fellow veterans of the Ninth whenever he talked with them years after the war's end. In fact, he would also note to his family that he often felt closer to them than he did to his own brothers. Jack had experienced trials and hardships (good times, too) with the Marines of the Ninth Defense that he had never faced with his brothers: "You had to be able to trust them like brothers; it was the only way we'd ever get out of that war alive." The bonds and trust between the Marines had been the keys to their survival, both collectively and individually.

Going Home

I'm only a private
In the 155's;
To me 'tis a wonder
That I am alive—
So I'm singing the blues,
For the rest of my cruise,
As a private in the 155's.

—DITTY INSCRIBED IN JACK MCCALL'S
WARTIME PHOTO ALBUM—

To the joy of all concerned, by October 1944, it was clear that a large part of the battalion's old salts, particularly the 155mm Group, would finally be rotated home from Guam. As an additional Christmas present, the battalion issued promotion orders in early December, making Jack's promotion to corporal permanent. Had he been back at PI, he would now be a "little colonel," too, but Pogiebait's buddies took pains to ensure that the promotion did not go to his head. The Seacoast & Field Artillery Group's and Jack's departure from Guam was not, however, without some last harassments and petty indignities.

Shortly before the 155mm Group's departure, Major Wells provided one last gesture, which many of his Marines appreciated and for which he was remembered fondly. He unofficially spread the word that Island Command's MPs would conduct a shakedown inspection for contraband before the group's departure. The MPs had orders to confiscate all diaries, personal papers, and souvenirs. The major casually hinted that his men might, that evening, want to hide in the brush surrounding their billets any of these articles they might have, since the inspection would probably occur the next morning, December 6. As Wells had hinted, the MPs held an inspection early the next morning, but to their surprise, they netted little contraband. After the MPs left, the Marine artillerymen retrieved their carefully camouflaged goodies, broke camp, folded their tents, and—for the first time in years—turned in their weapons and ammunition, the latter activity being a sure sign they were going home for good. After stacking their arms and boarding trucks for departure, they took a last look back at their campsite. Frank Chadwick recalled: "We looked back and couldn't believe that we just abandoned all those arms, ammo and supplies. We now believed this was how the Japs had so much of our equipment found during the mop-up campaign."

Arriving at Apra, Guam's now bustling major port, the members of the 155mm Group were ordered to fall in, and a young Navy lieutenant attempted to take a roll call of the unit and complete a passengers' manifest for the troopship. It was a fruitless effort. Excited to finally be going home, Jack and his buddies laughed, joked and generally milled around in a throng, grabassing and congratulating each other on their good fortune. Totally frustrated with his inability to get them into order, the incensed Navy lieutenant broke into a torrent of profanity, which earned him the wrath of one of the 155mm Group's crustier platoon sergeants. The sarge told the Navy shavetail to watch his mouth, as he was dealing with a group of Marines who had been overseas for three years, had several campaigns under their belts, and were good and ready to go home. The irate platoon sergeant concluded with a warning: "And, *sir*, if you give these Marines any more shit, *sir*, they'll just throw your ass in the bay!" Muttering to himself that he'd had enough of this insubordination, the lieutenant stormed off, returning a few minutes later with a Marine captain and two squads of Marine MPs. The MP captain drew himself up and announced, with tongue firmly in cheek, that it was either going to be the brig for everyone standing there or a boat to the waiting troopship. Jack and his buddies took the hint, and soon they were all aboard the USAT *Sea Corporal* en route to Hawaii.[71]

This leg of Jack's trip homeward took twelve days and made all the Ninth's previous ocean voyages seem like only a bad dream.[72] The *Sea Corporal*, another Army transport much like the *Sea Fiddler*, arrived off Pearl City and Pearl Harbor on December 18, 1944. In Europe, the last Nazi offensive, the Battle of the Bulge, was underway through the worst winter weather in decades. In Hawaii, the weather was unusually miserable: it was cool and rained frequently. As the returnees were clad only in their frayed and faded dungarees without field jackets and with many still feverish from the aftereffects of malaria, the chill was even more noticeable. They moved into a temporary tent city that served as the FMF-Pacific Transient Center and ate Christmas dinner while they waited for the next ship to the mainland.

The fare mainly involved leftovers from a Navy mess hall—some turkey, potatoes, and stuffing washed down with coffee—but it was the first true semblance of a holiday dinner that any of them had eaten since December 1941. A Christmas Eve service was held at the Transient Center's chapel, and grateful that he had survived to see this day, Jack attended. Many of them also saw Pearl Harbor's Battleship Row and the shattered, sunken remains of the battleship USS *Arizona*. For Jack, the events of December 1941 were now turning full circle, as he witnessed the once far-off place where his war had begun, while he looked forward to his first trip home in three years.

On December 26, Jack and the 155mm Group (minus Jim Kruse, who somehow—possibly due to lingering malaria—caught a flying boat to San Francisco)[73] set sail for the American mainland on board the USS *Evangeline*. The ship arrived off San Francisco near midnight on New Year's Day, Jack having been heartbroken by listening to the 25-0 loss of his beloved Tennessee Volunteers to Southern California in the Rose Bowl, a game broadcast over the *Evangeline*'s intercom. Knowing his often-professed love for University of Tennessee football, Pogiebait's nearby buddies teased him mightily.

As the ship entered San Francisco Bay, it was almost like a dream: the troopship sailed under the Golden Gate Bridge, and as the undimmed lights of Frisco shone over the bay's waters, ships' bells, horns, and whistles ushered in the New Year, and a large illuminated sign near the harbor greeted the arriving ships: "*Welcome Home, Boys!*" The men of the Ninth thronged the *Evangeline*'s rails and feasted on a sight many once believed they might never see again. "I don't believe there was a dry eye on board," Chadwick recalled. Of all of his New Year's celebrations, that New Year's Day 1945 was the one that stayed in Jack's memory most fondly: he was home again, alive and in one piece. Since that was more than could be said for some of his friends, Jack was duly appreciative of this homecoming.

As the *Evangeline* docked at the San Francisco Navy Yard on January 2, a Navy band waited pierside. The Navy personnel were the first to disembark; as they stepped off the gangway, the band struck up "Anchors Aweigh." The Marines had at least expected the band to play the Marine Corps Hymn when it came their turn, but the band had already left before they stepped off the ship. Never mind: the happy and emotion-filled group marched proudly down the gangplank to a ferryboat that took them across the bay to the nearby Treasure Island naval base. The first treat there was the food: a real breakfast, fresh meat and eggs, fresh milk and juice, and ice cream for the first time in thirty-five months. It was a place where

Ration D bars, canned or powdered food, or Spam—or rice, mutton, and cans of orange marmalade—were nowhere to be seen. They gorged themselves until they felt sick. "We'd forgotten such food existed," Jack recalled. "So, this is how the rest of the services lived; what a change."

After two days of what seemed like paradise on Treasure Island—the name seemed very appropriate—Jack and the other men of the group boarded a train for the Marine Corps Recruiting Depot at San Diego. There, they received new uniforms—their own dress greens and field scarves, not ones they'd have to turn in again as after graduation from PI. With the new uniforms came campaign ribbons, and best of all, movement orders for the East Coast complete with leave papers—the first home leave that Jack and his buddies ever had. Finally, he'd be going back home to Franklin! And—for the moment, at least—they were "home alive in '45."

Despite the joy, there was still an air of sadness knowing that the Seacoast & Field Artillery Group, Ninth Defense and AAA Battalions, would soon no longer exist. Although many of the group's leathernecks knew they would be reunited in other units after their furloughs were completed, the atmosphere was still infused with a sense of loss. Frank Chadwick recounted the scene: "The [men] of the 155mm Group arrived [in San Diego] 36 to 37 months after their enlistment. This was a great and happy time to be back, but it was a sad day in many ways. It was like breaking up a family that had been together so long, fought many campaigns and suffered so many hardships and disease." Major Wells assembled the formation, and his last orders to the weary remnants of the 155mm Group rang out: "*Fall out!* Dismissed."

There was a lot of address-swapping going on before everyone boarded buses and trains for their furloughs, and several Marines bought souvenir booklets to record their chums' addresses. Although many of them suspected they might meet again, who knew for certain? While their war in the Pacific was at least temporarily over, nobody left the depot under any false illusions: there were many bloody months of fighting and killing left, and each of the Marines suspected that he might be drawn back into the war before too long, joining a unit possibly far different from the Fighting Ninth. It would be a different group of Marines from the ones he had lived, worked, drank, brawled, and commiserated with for three years.

The war went on; the killing went on. Only the faces, and the lives, had changed.

SEVEN

"Home Alive in '45"

Was I glad we dropped [the atomic bomb]? You're damn right I was glad!
It saved my life [and] it saved a lot of other peoples' lives. . . . Let me tell you:
it was the happiest day of my life because I knew I was going to make it.

—JACK H. MCCALL, SR.—

In January 1945, Jack made it back to Franklin on a month's furlough. His train pulled into Union Station in Nashville—the very place from which he had left three years and three weeks before for Parris Island, just south of the Customs House where he had enlisted. His mother and father were waiting for him at the platform behind the station. His mother cried as the train steamed slowly into the passenger shed area. She was beside herself with happiness, as was tough old A. G. McCall. It was a great family reunion for Jack, and it gave him his first chance to shed his uniform and be a Franklin boy again after three long years.

One of his mother's first questions was, "Son, what would you like to eat?" Jack had been mulling over his answer for this occasion for thirty-six months,[1] and he had had ample time to consider his choices. He didn't skip a beat in telling Ruth what he wanted: "Mama, you know those little cucumber and cream-cheese sandwiches you make for your church tea parties; the ones with the crusts cut off of 'em?" A. G. squinted suspiciously at his son, wondering if the tropical sun and malaria had baked his boy's brain. "Are you *sure* that's what you want, son?" Ruth asked hesitantly. There was absolutely no doubt in Jack's mind: her finger sandwiches were exactly what he wanted for his first civilian meal. They were fresh, crunchy and creamy at the same time, a little "frilly" and decadent, and therefore totally unmilitary. The sandwiches were like absolutely nothing he had eaten in years. And so, he spent his first day of leave at home with his folks, drinking glasses of cold milk as if he had never tasted it before, and munching contentedly on his mother's sandwiches. He thought he might have to pinch himself to make sure it wasn't just a dream.

It was so good to be back home in Williamson County.

Jack's furlough passed quickly, and he spent every minute seeing friends and people he had not seen in years. Everything seemed so clean, organized, and different from all he had faced at PI, on Cuba, and in the Pacific. He felt as though he was living in a different world, which indeed was the case. He saw his brother Bob and his beautiful new wife, Dorothy, whom Bob had met in Klamath Falls, Oregon while recovering at a clinic from tropical diseases he had incurred in the Ellice Islands, as well as his old-est brother Al and his wife Kitty. Jack learned that one of his old Franklin acquaintances had become an officer and an air hero. Claiborne Kinnard, whose family owned the Willow Plunge pool where Jack and his Franklin High friends had spent many a hot summer day (and who had dated Jack's cousin Lucy Robinson for a time), was an Army Air Force lieutenant colonel, ace, and fighter group commander in England. With fourteen confirmed German kills to his credit, three of which fell prey in one action, "Claib" Kinnard counted the Distinguished Flying Cross and several Air Medals among other decorations. Even more exotically, old class of '40 pal and fellow Marine Ambrose "Red" Caldwell was now a diplomatic courier, ac-companying various official US delegations to London, Paris, and Moscow. Jack eagerly read Red's occasional cards and letters from such destinations with fascination and maybe a little envy.

While it was a very joyful time for him, Jack also learned much sad news about other Franklin friends who had gone off to war and would not be coming back or who would eventually come home suffering from their battlefield injuries. During his absence in the Pacific, Jack's family had debated about whether to write Jack about the deaths of several of his closest friends while he himself was in such peril. After much agonizing, and despite Bob's and Al's objections, his parents decided it would be best not to tell him until he returned home. "Our mom made a bad mistake in not telling him about [all of] his friends who had died while [he was] over-seas," Al McCall noted years later. "She didn't tell him until he got home. Jack took it really hard."[2]

Soon after arriving in Franklin, Jack asked his mother if she had heard any more details about the death of his best friend David Gentry, who had been killed in Italy earlier in 1944. He learned the further roll call of his dead Franklin friends and schoolmates: *Roy Alley*, a lieutenant in the Thirteenth Air Force, killed in action in a B-25 Mitchell over Borneo; *Tommy Lyons*, missing in action after his B-24 disappeared over Italy; *Billy Lynch*, killed in action on June 6, 1944, on D-Day itself, somewhere in France; *Leroy Suggs*, after surviving a host of B-17 missions over Germany, killed in a midair collision while in training at Clovis Field, New Mexico; *Owen Sweeney*, killed on an airbase in China; *John Waldren*, another airman and a B-17 turret gunner, killed in action on a bombing mission in October 1944. The grim list went on and on: *Bobby Akin; Scoby Burchett; Vance Burke; Felix Hood; Reedy Sears; Cecil Sims*—in all, 103 citizens of Williamson County would not come home alive from the war.[3]

Another son of Franklin who would not survive the war was Bill Johnston.[4] Arrested by the Japanese not long after their invasion of Guam in 1941, he was deported to Japan along with many other American-born residents and Marine and Navy defenders of the island, dying in a prison camp in Kobe in October 1943. He left behind his Guamanian-born wife and seven children to fend for themselves in the ruins of Agana after its liberation.[5] In a county as small as Williamson County was in 1945, it was virtually impossible to be a resident of the area and not know at least one family who had lost someone in the war.

Although it was an immediate shock to him to learn who had died, it took Jack a longer time to absorb these facts: many of his best hometown friends were dead, and he was alive—at least, he was for now. While Jack's furlough was enjoyable, while he was able to have a few dates with several old girlfriends, and while he was very glad to be home, the knowledge that he was alive and reasonably well—plus the culture shock of being in a civilization far removed from the horrors of the Pacific War—was unsettling to him. With so many of the young men his age away in service—or dead—much of Franklin seemed unreal to Jack during his furlough. He found it difficult, if not impossible, to explain the vast gulf between his Pacific experiences and the relatively unchanged pace of life in Franklin to his family members, neighbors, and civilian friends. Like so many of his peers, he found his experiences to be best understood and appreciated only by someone who had faced similar experiences. Possibly as a result of these feelings, "he never talked much about the war to us," his oldest brother Al later recalled.

After a month's leave, Jack had to report to his next duty station, the Norfolk Navy Yard at Portsmouth, Virginia, from which he and the Ninth had departed three years earlier for Cuba. He bade a tearful goodbye to his parents at Union Station. He spent the next several months at the Navy Yard and at other nearby stations, mainly serving as an MP in the First Guard Company guarding naval and Marine supplies and facilities. To his delight, Jack learned that a large contingent of his Ninth Defense buddies, including Tojo Whalen, Ken ("Hargy") Gibbs, Zombie Jones, Bill Galloway, and Herc Hausen, were also posted to the Navy Yard.[6] He was at Norfolk when he heard the news of FDR's death on April 12, 1945; he felt it was a terrible tragedy to the nation and the world and, like many others, went to a memorial service on post. Jack also met a beautiful young female Marine, whom he dated for quite a while. Although, like many of the old salts, he once had his doubts and griped when women were admitted to the Corps, he now allowed that, on reflection, he may not have appreciated the female Marines and given them the credit they were due.

Despite serving as MPs in the Navy Yard's Guard Company, Pogiebait and his buddies were hardly prudes or the models of decorum, as was expected of those serving in military or naval law enforcement by the higher brass. Bill Galloway indulged his own need for speed by buying a motorcycle, which landed him in a local jail when caught speeding by a traffic cop. Low on cash and expecting to be there awhile, Galloway was amazed when the traffic court judge told him he was a free man: hearing the scuttlebutt about Galloway's plight, Jack and several other pals raised enough cash to pay off Galloway's fine in full. Jack and another old Ninth Defense pal, Tojo Whalen, "used to be the nemesis to the S.P.'s" of Portsmouth. Not that the SPs couldn't track down a pair of obnoxious Marines; as Jack recalled one face-off: "They caught us one night about midnight, strolling down the street with a case of beer on our shoulders." Dropping their case of beer, Pogiebait and Tojo took off running and eluded their pursuers.

It was spring 1945, and the war seemed far away again, yet it once more loomed ever closer. Despite Nazi Germany's surrender on May 7, the weapons, planes, and ships continued to pour from America's arsenals: later that month, Jack served as a member of an honor guard at the launching of a new aircraft carrier, USS *Tarawa*, dedicated by several of the heroes of Tarawa, including that fellow survivor of Black Friday at Suicide Point, Colonel David Shoup.[7] Not long after, Jack and some of his Ninth Defense buddies learned that many of them would be sent to Camp Lejeune, North Carolina, together for additional artillery training. Large numbers of Marines, some heavily decorated veterans of the Pacific War, were being gathered from

Pogiebait and buddies off duty at Norfolk. Left to right: Bob "Herc" Hausen, C. D. "Zombie" Jones, McCall, and Lloyd Whisnant. Author's collection.

dispersed postings into Norfolk and Camp Lejeune for advanced training in preparation for the invasion of Japan. One such combat veteran, barely seventeen years old, had been decorated several times with the Purple Heart and was billeted in Jack's barracks. Jack and his buddies frequently and good-naturedly tormented the "chick" with catcalls of: "Hey, kid, ain't you a little young to be a Marine?" "When you gonna see some action, kid?"[8]

With their artillery training and on-the-job experience, the Corps still had a need for Jack and his pals, even though the Ninth's 155mm Group no longer existed. The US military was experimenting with rocket artillery: rocket-launching landing craft had already seen service in the Pacific (as Jack and Battery B had, of course, already witnessed on Guam) and during D-Day on the Normandy beaches. By early 1945, the Marine Corps was creating field artillery units, sardonically dubbed the "Buck Rogers' Boys" for the extraterrestrial rocket man of the comic strips and movies, using truck-mounted multiple rocket launchers. Each launcher, mounted on a one-ton truck chassis, could fire a salvo of 36 4.5-inch rockets within seconds at a range of up to 4,600 yards. Better yet for its crew, the launcher could displace rapidly to a new firing location almost as quickly to avoid Japanese counter-battery fire.[9] After being transferred in July to Camp Lejeune,[10] Jack learned that his new mission would be to train with such a unit, one of five Marine provisional rocket artillery detachments, in preparation for the invasion of Japan. He and his peers were told that their new unit could expect to be in the front of the next landings, scheduled for Japan's home islands in autumn 1945.

The prospects filled him with enormous dread. On Guam, Jack and his buddies had heard of the suicides of hundreds of Japanese civilians and soldiers on nearby Saipan and of the *banzai* charges and last-ditch fights there; these ended only after some fourteen thousand American casualties and with about thirty thousand Japanese dead after twenty-four days of fighting. Of course, they had seen the desperation of many Japanese troops in their patrols on Guam. At Norfolk, Jack heard about the savage fighting on Iwo Jima in February 1945, and the scuttlebutt was already making the rounds as to the horrors of the fighting on Okinawa that had been ongoing since Easter Sunday. If the war was almost over, the Japanese did not seem to know it yet, and at the time it seemed obvious to every Marine that the Japanese would fight fanatically for every piece of their home real estate.[11]

By late July 1945, assigned again to III Amphib, Jack was scheduled to go from North Carolina to Camp Pendleton, outside San Diego,[12] to prepare for the formation of the new Marine rocket artillery units. These would lead the first waves of Operations CORONET and OLYMPIC, the planned invasions of the Japanese home islands of Kyushu and Honshu. Jack prayed that something would happen, that somehow the war would end before he found himself on a landing craft heading to another beachhead.

On August 6, 1945, Jack was aboard a troop train bound for Camp Pendleton from Camp Lejeune. He now knew that after his advanced training at Camp Pendleton, he would be heading once more to the Central Pacific, where III Amphib was being reconstituted for the Japanese invasion. He steeled himself for his mission and hoped that, with B-29s blasting Japan day and night and all those Allied troops freed from Europe preparing to come to the Pacific, the war would end soon. Still, that nagging question lingered, gnawing at his thoughts: *"When the end comes, will I be around to see it?"*

Then came August 6 and 9, 1945, and two events that removed all doubt in Jack's mind that he would be a survivor and see Franklin again.

Jack's Thoughts on the A-Bombs

If there was one aspect of the war about which Jack was unequivocal, it was his approval of President Truman's decision to use the atomic bomb. On several occasions, when asked what he thought of the use of the A-bombs,

Jack responded, "Was I glad we dropped it? You're *damn* right I was glad! It saved my life, it saved a lot of other peoples' lives, and, listen, if it hadn't been dropped, son, I wouldn't be here, and you and your sister probably wouldn't be here. Let me tell you: it was the happiest day of my life because I knew I was going to make it." Jack was absolutely convinced that, had an actual invasion of Japan taken place, he would have been killed. That the atomic bomb saved American lives, he was absolutely confident; that it may have also saved Japanese lives was nice. But, since he mainly viewed it as a question of his and his buddies' survival, the argument that the use of the A-bomb saved Japanese lives was, frankly, of less immediate consequence to him.

Jack's wartime buddy Robert "Hercules" Hausen was stationed on occupation duty in Japan not long after the end of the war, and he traveled to Nagasaki only a few months after the A-bomb strike of August 9, 1945. In 1975, Herc and his wife Maxine drove from Iowa to Franklin to visit Jack and his family; Herc brought along a scrapbook of wartime and postwar photos he had taken, including pictures of the devastation of Nagasaki. From his first-hand, Ground Zero view of what the place looked like only a matter of weeks after the A-bomb had been dropped, Herc was horrified at the devastation the bomb had wrought, even though it had helped hasten the war's end. For his part, Jack accepted that the atomic bomb had changed the world in some horrible and incalculable ways, but he never expressed feeling particularly sorry that it was used, and he thought that arguments that the United States should apologize for bombing Hiroshima and Nagasaki or that the *Enola Gay* (the B-29 that bombed Hiroshima and had flown on its mission from Guam's nearby sister island of Tinian) should be denied a place in the Smithsonian's National Air and Space Museum were patently ridiculous. To quote Jack: "They started it, at a place called Pearl Harbor. We ended it, and a lot of good American kids died in the process." Or, as bluntly: "Son, if it hadn't been for that bomb, you wouldn't be here today." As far as Jack was concerned, that was the end of the discussion.

With the hindsight of history, many of us can—and undoubtedly will—disagree on whether the decision to use the atomic bombs was morally, legally, spiritually, or militarily justifiable, or whether by creating and using it, the United States helped set the Cold War in motion and opened a Pandora's box that threatened the existence of humanity (and someday may still end it). For Jack, however, as for many veterans of the Pacific War, the rigors of fighting the Japanese, and the absolute conviction that any continued war with them would mean fewer and fewer Americans coming home intact or alive, outweighed the postwar niceties or arguments about the use of the A-bomb. This grim view appeared wholly justified to those who had taken part in the Pacific fighting.

To Jack, it was purely a question of survival, justified by experiences over almost four long, arduous years. The accounts of fanatical Japanese resistance on Saipan, Iwo Jima, and Okinawa and the horror stories of Bataan Death March survivors who escaped to Australia early in 1944 were daunting, combined with what Jack and his peers had already seen first-hand: the I-boat's foolhardy torpedo attack on the *Kenmore* off Koli Point; the near-suicidal strafing runs by the Zeroes over Rendova (prefiguring 1945's *kamikaze* attacks); the *banzai*-style charge faced by the overwhelmed Wantuck and Rothschild, where not even their machine guns could stop the attack; the human-bomb attacks on Captain Blake's tanks; diehard refusals to surrender and the suicides in Guam's caves. It made life seem cheap and the life of a first-wave Marine artilleryman in a prospective invasion of Japan's mainland "not worth a plugged nickel." When even some Manhattan Project scientists and military planners failed to conceive of their offspring as anything more than an enormous conventional bomb regardless of radiation's effects,[13] the Pacific War's veterans might be forgiven their failure to recognize at the time that the bomb's long-term consequences would haunt their lives and those of their children and grandchildren in the decades to come.

On Guam in summer 1945, now serving as a BAR gunner with the Third Marine Division, Frankie Yemma learned that his infantry battalion was scheduled to hit Kyushu in autumn 1945. After hearing that his unit, already bloodied on Iwo Jima, was to spearhead the invasion, Yemma recalled: "I said, 'Oh my God!' I thought I was dead, no kidding." When Frankie and his peers heard the news of the A-bomb attacks, their response was ecstatic: "God bless Truman, he dropped the bomb and ended the war . . . we were just tickled pink."[14]

There ought to be little wonder that the news of Hiroshima and Nagasaki, horrible as their consequences were, cheered Jack and many others like him as little else had for months: they now knew beyond a doubt that they would finally survive the war. On board his Camp Pendleton-bound troop train, the first news reports reaching Jack were little better than rumor—a bomb that could level an entire city? "We couldn't believe the damage the rumors had reported," Jack remembered. As the awesome truth dawned that one bomb had indeed wrought so much devastation, so did the realization that the end was now in sight.

War's end brought a burst of spontaneous exuberance not seen in America in years, but for Jack and many veterans, it brought something more sacred, special, and humbling: peace and quiet. When thinking about good friends lost, the silence was that of the grave. For some, the feeling was not unlike that of condemned prisoners who had now been granted not merely a stay of execution, but a pardon. One veteran remarked: "When word got around that the bombs had forced the Japanese surrender, we knelt in the sand and cried. For all our manhood, we cried. We were going to live. We were going to grow up to adulthood after all."[15]

In Jack McCall's words, "I was just so damn glad it was all over."

Following the war's end, the last few months of Jack's service was spent in camp in California, and the time passed quickly: more details, more MP duty, more of the usual police calls, drills, and inspections, more of the usual "chickenshit." Nothing, however, could alter the fact that he would be going home, for keeps, very soon. A Marine recruiting sergeant tried to convince Jack that a good, well-trained Marine Reserve corporal like him could make a decent career for himself in the peacetime Corps. Jack paid him no attention. Although he had enough memories of the good times with his buddies, he also had enough of the bad times to keep him from giving the proposal much thought. It was time to get out of the Corps and get on with his life. *To hell with it,* Jack thought. *It's time to get back to Franklin.*

Jack was honorably discharged at Camp Pendleton, Oceanside, California, on October 2, 1945, almost three months before the fourth anniversary of his oath of enlistment. In less than a week, he would be back home in Franklin—and this time, he was coming home for good.

One thing that struck him as peculiar soon after his arrival home, much like he had felt during his furlough in early 1945, was the enormous oddity of it all. His homecoming to his small town of Franklin, which had visibly changed little, was full of incongruous moments. Perhaps most jarring of all to Jack and so many of his fellow veterans was the apparent but usually unvoiced expectation for them to "put it all behind and just forget it ever happened," as if nothing overly significant had occurred over the last four years and with no time-outs for transitions or introspection. They were joyously welcomed home, but after all the cheering and American Legion rallies stopped, it was back to a business-as-usual ethos.

For many, including Jack, this made for a somewhat awkward initial return to civilian life. The absence of their wartime buddies, who themselves were going back to school under the GI Bill or were trying to make a living in the new postwar economy, was subtly affecting. Instead of the expected emotions—of happiness to be coming home, to be reunited with families and sweethearts, and just to have survived—other sentiments often manifested themselves. These reflected the loss of certain kinds of security: the loss of comradeship, of dead schoolmates, of being surrounded by people who had played, suffered, and fought together—the loss of the companionship of others, as Justice Oliver Wendell Holmes eulogized of the veterans of an earlier war, whose hearts, in their youth, were "touched with fire."[16]

It took some time, really, to get reaccustomed to life in peacetime America. Despite the GI Bill's and Veterans Administration's best efforts, some veterans, of course, never wholly bridged the gap, the yawning mental chasm, between the young men they had been before December 7, 1941, and the new, hardened men they had become. For even reasonably well-adjusted veterans like Jack McCall—Pogiebait no more—who made the transition back to civilian life fairly easily, the war never entirely left their psyches and memories.

But, then again, when the experience of war had changed so much, including men's souls, how could life ever be the same again?

The Laughter and the Tears

I came out of the Marines like a wildcat.

—JACK H. MCCALL, SR., 1987—

Years from now you can look in the mirror and say,
"I was there and I did my job—WELL."

—LT. COLONEL WILLIAM J. SCHEYER, 1943—

The young man who does not cry is a savage,
and the old man who does not laugh is a fool.

—GEORGE SANTAYANA, 1925—

Jack McCall would occasionally say to family and friends "Once a Marine, always a Marine." He was proud to have served as a Marine, but he knew from hard experience that a military career after the war was not for him. The terrors of combat, the tedium and repetitive tasks of his stateside garrison duty, and the countless petty indignities he put up with as an enlisted man convinced him that civilian life was just what he needed. In his own words, when he left the Marines, he came out "like a wildcat." So, apart from various business travels and his 1959 honeymoon with his "Georgia peach" bride Patricia Holmes, by choice, my father spent the rest of his life in Franklin. I think he truly "lived a lifetime in four years," another expression he sometimes used when talking about his wartime service.

He had seen enough of other parts of the country and the world to convince himself that home was where his heart was. Franklin was the kind of town where, as the Southern saying goes, its residents "know when you're sick and care about you when you die." To some degree, that would change:

there would come a time when Jack would go downtown and "not recognize a soul," but until the mid-1980s, Jack seldom walked Franklin's streets without seeing at least one person he knew and liked. To some veterans, surviving the war made them feel indestructible. For Jack, it had a mostly and markedly different effect: he realized how precious life is and how quickly it can vanish. By his and his friends' reckoning, there were at least six instances when Jack was consciously aware that he had almost been killed during the war, and probably many more times when he was unaware how close had come to being killed. Over time, Jack became a much more cautious man and, to use another pet expression, more of a "worrywart" regarding his family's and friends' safety.

As an old salesman himself, A. G. lectured Jack, "Don't you *ever* get in the dry goods business, son!" but to no avail. To make his pre-war dreams become reality, Jack took his GI Bill benefits and started as a freshman at the University of Tennessee in the fall of 1946, but the time he spent in Knoxville as a twenty-five-year-old "college kid" and Sigma Phi Epsilon fraternity boy did little for him, and he left college after a year. Jack decided to become a traveling salesman in the dry-goods business. As a salesman, business manager, and vice president for several clothing manufacturers—Rice-Stix, Inc., Hayes Garment Company, the Haywood division of Genesco and, finally, Washington Manufacturing, Inc.—his business had its exciting moments, but what he liked best was the opportunity it afforded him to interact with people, to tell jokes and swap stories while making the sale. The war had given him an ample stock of stories that he would share with family and friends but in which he never made himself out to be a hero. He generally downplayed the hardships and terror, although in later years, he would gradually admit to more of those. It was not until 1993, though, that he finally admitted that the greatest fear he had ever known were the times when he had almost drowned at Rendova and Guam.

Jack was fearful of thunderstorms and tornado warnings. When I was a child, during a power outage, as the whole family huddled in the blacked-out family den during a particularly fierce electrical storm, I recall him saying, "You know, that thunder reminds me a lot of a Jap bombardment." Distant heat lightning would also sometimes remind him of the long-distance naval shelling he had watched from afar on Rendova and New Georgia. Whether his reactions to storms predated or followed his time in the Pacific, I cannot say, but if he had always hated thunderstorms as a youth, the shellings he had experienced in the Solomons could only have amplified his feelings. Jack seldom seemed attracted to swimming pools or large bodies of water, and the family never made a trip to the beach. In retrospect, one wonders whether his life-or-death experiences on Rendova and Guam were so painfully seared into his psyche to afford Jack any real pleasure in postwar poolside, lakeside, or seashore amusements.

When I was in third grade, my parents gave me a Skilcraft geology lab for Christmas. This gift was a big hit until Jack realized that the kit included some fairly explosive chemicals for heating rocks and giving mineral samples an acid test. No more geology kit! Given how his own high-school chemistry experiences had landed him in some precarious situations, I now also wonder if he did not secretly breathe a sigh of relief when I decided, ultimately, to study history and political science and then practice law after leaving the Army, instead of going into science or the clothing business.

Occasionally, anger would bubble up in him. While it was sometimes ordinary parental irritation at my or my sister's childish foibles, one could sense, at times, a deeper source of frustration. This may have stemmed partly from the subconscious realization that, after being a small part of a major event in his nation's and the world's history, many aspects of Jack's daily life seemed trivial by comparison, and everything that followed seemed eclipsed by his own participation in the events of 1941-45. Few things in his subsequent life could either be the same, or as simple, as they were for Jack in the fall of 1941. The war had altered his and his family's life in incalculable ways, starting perhaps with his own outlook on daily experiences. It is also possible that, at times, Jack may have felt a dose of survivor's guilt for all those friends killed or crippled by the war.

When in eighth grade I told him that I had gotten into a fight with some boys over their claims that the "real war" was in Europe, that my dad was a "Jap," and that "nothing happened" in the Pacific, his eyes flashed fire. Although occasionally a profane man, his voice hardened even more noticeably. "Those little twerps and their dads weren't there," he growled to me, "so do you *really* think they know what the hell they're talking about?" His response to me needed no answer, but it helped set me on my own personal quest to learn more about his Pacific campaigns and what he had faced there. Without denying the perils of combat in Europe, my own research only confirmed for me what he had remarked often for years: some of the horrors of "his" war in the Pacific were unrivalled by some elements of the European campaign, and the outcome of that war was every bit as decisive to the fate of the nation and world as the battles that raged in the deserts of Tunisia and Morocco, in the hills of Italy, or on or above the fields of France and Germany.

Sometimes, Jack's job provided its own unexpected brushes with the past. One day in the early 1980s, as he pitched a dry-goods sale to a man roughly his own age named Vandegrift, he stopped in the midst of his deal-making: "Pardon me, but I have to ask if you're related to a Marine general named Vandegrift. You see, he was my old commanding general on Guadalcanal." "Why, yes; he was my uncle!" the man replied. Jack was as pleased that he had met and talked with A. A. Vandegrift's nephew as if he had met the "Old Man" himself.

In short, some aspects of Jack's postwar life seldom seemed as real, as tangible, and as immediate as what he had felt and seen during his four years of war. While he never went so far as to call his war years the "best years of his life," there was an immediacy and a sense of doing things that really mattered and made a difference in the here-and-now—being a part of a team, in the truest sense of the word—during the war that, I suspect, eluded Jack in many aspects of the remaining fifty years of his life. In the first ten-odd years after the war, he tried to recapture it—and, maybe, forget the bad memories of the war in the process—with fast cars and honky-tonk partying, both during and after his short-lived time at UT.

One favorite new postwar stunt, often played out with Hoyt Doak, an old high school buddy and Navy veteran of the Pacific, called for Jack to show up at a roadside tavern. On his arrival, he would grandly throw open the door and loudly announce: "I'm looking for my father!" Hoyt, his obliging partner in crime who was already comfortably ensconced, would chime back: "You better watch out for those swinging doors, son. Who's your father, kid?" Jack would respond, "Luke McLuke." "*Luke McLuke? I'm* Luke McLuke!" "*Father!*" "*Son!*" This goofily staged "family reunion" scene never failed to get an appreciative captive audience for Jack's pratfalls, plus occasionally a free drink or meal on the house. Several things, however, including a severe car wreck, curbed his appetite for late-night honky-tonking.

The deaths of his parents—Ruth in the fall of 1952, A. G. in the summer of 1959—further lessened his fondness for engaging in wild times. His father's death, just a few hours after he visited him in Williamson County Hospital, saddened Jack immensely, but his mother's death hit him especially hard. As her "baby," Ruth had often doted on Jack—after all, her cooking and sandwiches were among the fondest memories he had of coming home after his absence in the Pacific—and she had provided the three brothers with a sense of grounding, stability, and unconditional love that they sometimes found wanting in their father. Her loss, and Jack's efforts to help out his ailing father during A. G.'s last years, had required Jack to give up many of his own dreams of going west like Bob or of setting off on a course of his own. Jack stepped back further onto the straight-and-narrow path after he met a beautiful and gentle, but savvy, Georgia girl, Pat Holmes, whom he married in 1959.

In 1950, he was given an invitation to relive his Marine experiences by joining a Marine Reserve unit in Nashville and an offer at making lieutenant with better privileges than he had ever dreamed of as a corporal in the old-time Corps of 1941. Jack thought about it, but he declined. That decision may have saved his life: a large portion of the Nashville Marine Reserve unit (and several 9th Defense veterans, as well) fought and died with the 1st Marine Division in the frozen hell of North Korea's Chosin Reservoir later that year. Other Fightin' Ninth veterans, including now-colonels Bill Tracy, Hank Reichner, and Walter Wells (with the latter two commanding elements of the 11th Marines during some of the most bitter fighting in Korea), became two-war Marines in the process.

Jack's wartime experiences tended to give him an ability to grasp the wider essence of life and fostered a wholehearted aversion to those he called "pettifoggers," people obsessed with ridiculous or trivial details. His life-long love of history, cultivated as a kid playing in Fort Granger and finding Minie balls in Franklin, was passed on to his children. When I was three years old, Jack took me to see the centennial celebration of the Battle of Franklin, complete with re-enactors on the grounds of what had been the Willow Plunge pool, one of his old swimming holes. On fall and winter nights, he helped his old pal Fred "Brutus" Isaacs build a diorama of the battle, to be placed in the Carter House Museum. I watched, fascinated, sitting on the Isaacs' basement steps, as Fred and Jack painted and emplaced the miniature troops, horses, and guns, and built from scratch the tiny models of the Carter House itself and its cotton gin, the locus of some of the bloodiest fighting in the battle.

He would also, on occasion, take Holly and me with him to Franklin's Confederate Cemetery, where he would muse on life and death as he surveyed the 1,500 graves there. One tombstone, in particular, often made him stop and think: it was that of a young European-born Confederate named Hermann Bruner from Esslingen, Germany. The fact that this teenaged immigrant died at about the age Jack had been when he entered the Marines probably added to his curiosity as to the circumstances that had brought poor young Hermann Bruner to the United States, only to die in the Civil War, so far away from his homeland.

Jack became quite a model hobbyist, and soon his son's room was festooned—it still is—with the plastic planes, ships, and tanks he made. The Corsairs, Lightnings, and Zeroes, with Hellcats, Wildcats, and even a miniature Long Tom in Marine olive-green, all came to a landing on the shelves of my bookcase. (He also attempted to paint an oil self-portrait from a drawing made of him on Banika in 1944, but the result more resembled TV character Barney Fife of the *Andy Griffith Show* than it did Jack McCall.) This transplanted love of history led, in part, to my decision to try a military career, even if it was not in the Marine Corps but as an Army officer. "Everybody ought to spend some time in the service," Jack said as we drove to my pre-ROTC physical at Fort Campbell, Kentucky. during my senior year of high school. "It gives you a better appreciation of things. It'll give you an education, son, and I don't just mean getting a college degree."

I did *not* fully appreciate what he meant at the time, but I began to get an inkling the next day, as a harried Army nurse jabbed my arm three or four times, searching for a vein to draw a blood sample, much to my father's stifled mirth. My high school years had been a tough time for me and my father, just as I suspect that Al's, Bob's, and Jack's high-school years had tested their own relationships with A. G. McCall. Later, after I was commissioned as a lieutenant and as I gnashed my teeth in frustration over some bureaucratic hassle, he and I found that we could share a laugh together and swap stories of our own respective bouts with military snafus and "chickenshit." Given that the Marines were frequently dispatched to all the hot spots of the 1980s—Lebanon, Grenada, Panama, the Persian Gulf—I also suspect that my father was secretly relieved that I had received an Army, but not a Marine-option, ROTC scholarship, thus thwarting my desire to become a Marine officer. If he felt this way, however, he would never admit it openly, and he kidded me often about becoming a mere Army "shavetail." Since Jack tended to be a worrywart about his family members' safety under the best of circumstances, the knowledge that his son was out on a recon patrol somewhere or *en route* to Haiti or Beirut would not have helped him sleep any easier at night.

Jack was a heartfelt patriot, a father who delighted in serving as a Cub Scout and Webelos troop leader, and a man who flew the flag every Memorial Day and Fourth of July. He never glamorized war or its horrors, however, as he had seen the consequences of war first-hand. While the McCall clan emerged reasonably unscathed from World War II, he often recalled the hurt and pain the war had inflicted on many of his friends' families or, for instance, on the Solomons Islands natives or the poor Guamanian civilians who had lost all their worldly possessions in the ruins of Agana. He was disappointed that some Americans of later generations did not seem to understand and appreciate what freedom meant or what others of his generation had endured to protect freedom. When I would ask him whether he thought the American people could ever pull together behind a cause as as they had done during the Second World War, he would take a puff on his cigarette, blow the smoke out pensively, and say quietly, "Son, sometimes, I just don't know." He was no xenophobic nationalist, though, and he was as irked by right-wing reactionaries, ostensibly acting in defense of freedom and democracy but hiding behind the flag, a uniform, or a veneer of "patriotism," as he was by any left-wing agitators.

Jack tended to vote as a Democrat, just as his own father had. This provided a rich source for countless arguments with his brother Bob, who had been chief of staff to Republican Governor Robert Smiley of Idaho in the 1950s and early 1960s and who later served as an active participant on educational issues in many annual Republican Governors' Conferences. Still, Jack firmly believed it was far more important to vote for the man and not the party, and he proved it on several occasions by voting for Republican candidates, much to Bob's immense satisfaction. When brother Bob, a good

Jack McCall with his family in later years. *Left to right*:
Jack, cousin Lucy Robinson, the author, wife, Patricia,
and daughter, Holly. Author's collection.

party loyalist, once kidded Jack on his political views by saying, "Aw, come on, let's face it; you're just a 'mugwump:' your mug's on one side of the fence, and your wump's on the other!" his younger brother just responded: "Yep, and I'm damn proud of it!" Despite the hard knocks that he and others of his generation had taken in the Great Depression and the war—or, maybe, because he had survived those crises—Jack retained his sense of humor, even if he was not always possessed of the greatest equanimity in times of stress. He believed in the principle that character counts, long before any pundit had coined its use as a political catch phrase.

As he watched the decline of much of American industry, including his beloved clothing industry in the mid-1970s and 1980s, Jack sometimes felt very disappointed. He watched as each of his own old companies—first Genesco, then Haywood, then Washington "Dee Cee"—shut down their domestic plants and outsourced production overseas or closed down permanently. He was not so obsessed with the past, however, as not to own a practical car, even if it was Japanese-made. By 1983, he would be driving a Toyota Tercel. This led to some ribbing from several of his Marine pals, who nicknamed the car "Tojo's Revenge" and claimed Jack was "selling out" in his old age to the enemy of 1941. His pal Jim Kruse needled him in a 1985 letter: "Sorry to hear that you drive a Toyota, but I guess you are entitled to one mistake. Just WATCH IT! I go to a Marine Corps bash nearly every year, but I won't tell them."[1] With a sweet sense of irony, Jack proudly embellished his Japanese-made car with both a 1st Marine Division Association decal and a Marine Corps League sticker.

Still, while some other Asia-Pacific Theater veterans harbored lifelong grudges against the Japanese, Jack reserved his anger for the wartime Japanese leaders, whom he blamed for most of the atrocities. As for the Japanese soldiers, he philosophized: "They were just poor soldiers, just like the rest of us. We had to fight and kill 'em then, and they had to do the same to us. They didn't have any choice." While others in the Ninth had killed the enemy at close range, Jack was adamant that, so far as he knew, he had never killed a man directly. It was undoubtedly easier for his conscience to know that whatever killing he was involved with was only as a part of a team, as an occasional member of a 155mm gun crew, and not as one who had watched a man die at arm's length as the direct result of his own actions.

Jack remained similarly philosophical when he witnessed a videotaped chance reunion between his old wartime buddies Bill Box and Frank Chadwick and a retired Japanese businessman during their return to the Solomon Islands in 1988. His attitude was similar when Chadwick shared with Jack some of the off-camera details of this encounter between former enemies. This businessman, who had been stationed on Guadalcanal, New Georgia, and Bougainville and had been on the receiving end of the Ninth's bombardments, by coincidence was visiting his son who now resided on New Georgia:

> The old man [Chadwick recounted to Eric Bergerud] told us: "You chased me out of Guadalcanal, you chased me out of here, and then you chased me out of Bougainville." And he described their conditions. "You were sick and hungry and had one meal a day. But we would smell your food or see you eating. Sometimes we ate grass." He was bitter towards the fools running the Japanese Army. They would land troops with ammunition. But they only had three days' food supply each. The supporting stuff wasn't there. Medicine ran out. Our Marines had to put up with malaria, jungle rot, and dengue. The Japanese, he told us, faced the same thing, but their medics couldn't do anything to treat problems. It had to be horrible. . . . [After the Canal he] was evacuated to Munda. The old man told us, "We were given some good food. Then an officer gave us a big speech about our great victories to come. I thought to myself, the son of a bitch is crazy. Most of my crew were killed on Munda by American artillery. It was asinine."[2]

Toshihiro Oura, the malaria-plagued young officer near Munda Field whose unit was so battered by the Ninth's Long Toms, would likely have agreed with his compatriot's sentiments.

Other experiences and postwar accounts that he had read of the privations and suffering of the average Japanese soldiers and civilians had much reduced the level of animosity that Jack had felt towards the Japanese people as a whole during the war years. He would have undoubtedly agreed with the retired businessman's comment about the "fools running the Japanese Army." While he tended not to brood about such things, Jack would sometimes ruminate on the mysteries of life and death on such occasions. These were much like the sentiments he had expressed about Hermann Bruner, the dead German immigrant buried in the Confederate Cemetery in Franklin, on the ironies and tragedies of life and how the "little man"—whether American, German, or Japanese, whether white, black, or Asian, and whether in 1861, 1914, or 1941—seemed to have scant control over his own destiny. Unlike Chadwick, Bill Sorensen, or Bill Box, however, Jack never expressed any desire to revisit the scenes of his former "glory days"; his once-in-a-lifetime sojourn in the Pacific was quite enough for him.

While he never was actively involved with veterans' groups like the VFW and American Legion, except for a brief time during his first years as a civilian, Jack kept in close contact with many of his buddies from the

Ninth. Every July 4th, the telephone would ring: "Is this Pogiebait's boy?"
"Yessir." "I'm one of your dad's old Marine buddies. Can I talk to him?"
Talk on such occasions, as it did at the Fighting Ninth's reunions, usually
focused on the good times. "You have to talk about the good times, or else
you'd never want to talk about it again," as Frank Chadwick and Bill Box
recalled to me on separate occasions. In fact, the closeness he felt toward
men like Downs, Kruse, Chadwick, Galloway, Colonel Box, Herc Hausen,
and Tojo Whalen grew stronger in later years. Jack was saddened to hear
of Tojo's and Herc's deaths as if they had been members of his own family. He was unable to attend a 1987 reunion at Parris Island when many of
the surviving members dedicated a memorial in honor of the Battalion's
forty-fifth anniversary, but he placed a photo of the memorial on the wall
of his home next to his framed medals and campaign ribbons. Although
diagnosed with emphysema in 1990, Jack was able to muster the energy
to make it to one reunion of the Battalion in Nashville and to see some
old faces he had not glimpsed in years. The feelings of brotherhood he felt
toward his buddies of the Ninth were in large part, to borrow the words
of one historian, "the centerpiece of his soul."[3] When his children asked,
"Were you a hero, Dad?" Jack's inevitable response was, "No, I'm no hero.
I just did my job, like everyone else. We all had to pull together back then."

On Memorial Day weekend of 1997, Jack called as many of his surviving
pals from the Ninth Defense as he could find, as well as many of his old business colleagues, relatives, and friends. His disease was very pronounced by
this stage, confining him indoors for his last nine months of life; moreover,
possibly unknown to all around him except himself, by May he also had
contracted pneumonia and was very weak. Jack had a premonition that his
end was close, even telling his wife that Saturday that he felt death was
nearby—to be exact, that he perceived death as being closer than at any
time since the war—but his sense of duty was such that he wanted to close
the loop with each of his friends and loved ones, one last time, before he
left us for good.

Jack McCall died one week later, on the Saturday afternoon of May 31,
1997, seventy-five years and one month after he was born, surrounded by
his wife and children as they recited the Twenty-thirrd Psalm. For the
most part, it was as peaceful an end as he could have wished for. Despite
his frail condition, he rallied enough toward the end to tell jokes and make

wisecracks with his family and with the hospital staff. But, when it became apparent several days after he was admitted to the hospital that he would not be going home this time, he steeled himself with a remarkable fortitude and said his goodbyes to his wife and children with few tears but with a lot of love. "Take good care of your mom and sister," he told me, and then said, "Go on home, son; you've done all you can do for me here. I mean it, boy. *Go home.*" But, this time, I disobeyed him. I did not go, and I think my father knew that none of his family would leave him until the end came. In a coma before he died, however, the old fears reemerged: he began muttering, and while much of it was inarticulate, some of it came forth very loud and clear: *"Take cover! Get down! Tell the Old Man I need help down here!"* As my sister listened helplessly, it was quite clear that he believed he was back in action again, and he was replaying, one last time, all the terror of that day on Guadalcanal when he was surrounded by the Japanese patrol and thought he was to die. Then, later, there was a merciful silence, and peace. When he died, it was as if he had simply let himself go; it was as if he knew his time had come. All those years of life and struggle were gone, in an instant. He died less than a week after Veterans' Day 1997, a day of remembrance of wars and veterans gone by, and a day which none of his surviving family will ever regard again in a casual and unthinking way as "just another holiday."

It's strange what one remembers thinking at times like that. The evening that Dad died, his family—his wife, Pat, daughter Holly, daughter-in-law Jennifer, and I—took a long walk through downtown Franklin, several hours after he had passed away. It had rained for six or seven days, but that Saturday evening, as we crossed the Harpeth River bridge next to the riverbank and the ruins of old Fort Granger where Jack had played so often as a child, the clouds broke, and the sky was painted in bright pastel colors of blue and pink. Swallows and chimney swifts skimmed through the early evening air. I did not recall ever having seen a sky in those colors before. As we neared the square, the old granite statue stood, an eternal sentinel silently watching over Franklin as it had for almost one hundred years. The ebbing sun over the roofs of the town provided a fiery backdrop.

I thought to myself, *Dad, you know, you often had a tough life, but you also had a good life. You died the way everybody should: in your hometown, surrounded by your loved ones, with no pain. But, boy, am I ever going to miss you.* And, many years later, I still do.

I have often since wondered what it was that gave my father the bravery and humor that he mustered in his last months and hours to hold on against a treacherous disease for as long as did—he survived a full three years longer than his own doctor had predicted when his illness was diagnosed. How strongly it seemed to me that he faced that last lonely challenge, from which he knew there could be no no escape. I can only hope that I will be able to summon up a similarly rare fortitude within me when my own time comes, whenever that day may be.

A few weeks after Jack died, I looked among some of the artifacts he had kept and mentally tallied up something of what was left of him, as tokens of proof of his existence on earth: a lock of his hair; several scrapbooks of faded newspaper and magazine clippings; his dress-green uniform, slightly moth-eaten but in remarkably good shape for a fifty-year-old suit of cloth-ing; a battered Marine campaign hat with a large hole in its crown, nibbled away by a long-dead Cuban rat; a picture frame full of medals and cam-paign ribbons; a battered metal box for his water purification gear, with a brown, topless dancing girl painted on one side next to the words "Russell Islands"; photographs and drawings and a brass-sheathed Bible; and a black-and-white photograph of a young, toothy Marine, after long campaigning still looking much as he had when he graduated from high school, taken over fifty years before and a lifetime ago. Scrapbooks and photo albums full of faded clippings and pictures. A tombstone. Family and dear friends that miss him.

And memories of a fine man, a loving father, a good friend to have on one's side, and a proud Marine to the end.

"SEMPER FI, MAC"

"Once a Marine, always a Marine."

—INSCRIBED ON THE 9TH DEFENSE BATTALION MEMORIAL,
PARRIS ISLAND, SOUTH CAROLINA—

Among Marines of all ranks, one of the most common sayings—both for those in World War II and even for today's Marines—is the expression "Semper Fi." At its simplest, the phrase is a contraction of the Marines' official Latin motto, *Semper Fidelis*, "Always Faithful," and this motto is emblazoned on the Marine Corps' anchor-and-globe insignia, inscribed on a scroll clenched in the beak of an eagle sitting atop the world. In everyday Marine usage, though, "Semper Fi" was more than just a mere motto: like the Hawaiian word *"Aloha,"* it could mean either "hello" or "goodbye." Depending wholly on the context and the way it was uttered, the phrase was capable of having a wide range of sometimes contradictory meanings. As one wartime Marine officer noted, the meaning and usage of "Semper Fi" far surpassed its literal translation: "[I]t is commonly used by marines, as occasion demands, for 'Frig you, Mac—I got mine,' or 'Pull up the ladder, Mac—I'm aboard.'"[4] As one Marine veteran recounted: "But you know, what [Semper Fi] really meant was, 'Look, pal, you got to take care of yourself out here.' You might ask another Marine for a cigarette and he'd tell you, 'Semper Fi, Mac.' Then the chances are he'll give you one, but what he means is for you to try and get your own the next time. It was no picnic in the Pacific and you had to take care of yourself."[5]

At its essence, "Semper Fi" serves as a code instantly identifiable by any Marine. To a Marine in trouble, the yell meant that help was on the way. To a Marine griping about his lot in life, the retort meant, "Quit your bitching; you volunteered for this." To a Marine screwing up, it meant that he had better get himself squared-away. To a Marine leaving a unit or going home, it meant that his buddies were thinking about him. It can be used as a salutation; as "Taps" is played over a grave, Marines utter it as they bid farewell to one of their own, in a kind of martial Kaddish. Sometimes, when they say it, some of them will cry.

Most of the old veterans, however, remain stoical at these ceremonies of departure. This was a generation that grew up with incredible sadness, discipline, and privation, and tears still do not come easily to those who were trained that more respect is shown to the departed by retaining one's composure than by letting it all go. "Not showing our emotions doesn't mean we love them any less," Dave Slater once remarked to me. "After all, they were our buddies through thick and thin. It's just what they'd want us to do, and what we'd want them to do for us when we go."

At each annual reunion of the Ninth, fewer of Jack's buddies gathered due to the infirmities of age or the costs of travel, yet nobody wanted to end these reunions, and few wished to consolidate with other defense battalions' reunions. Such a move would imply more than the physical death of the unit's members; like cells in a living organism, it would imply a death of the Battalion, of the organism itself. "I guess we'll continue to hold a reunion until the last two of us meet in our wheelchairs in a phone booth somewhere," David Slater, secretary of the Ninth's "alumni" association, wistfully remarked to those gathered at one of the later reunions. Sadly, that day may not be far off.

Of the twelve million who served in all the various branches of the American armed forces during World War II, by 1998—one year after Jack McCall's death—only approximately half were still surviving, and according to Department of Veterans Affairs estimates, those were dying at a rate of about 32,000 a month.[6] As the old veterans of the Ninth and their brethren faced the future, so many years after the end of their war, they found that they were saying "Semper Fi" more and more frequently as a last goodbye to their buddies. Will somebody be there to say it over their own graves? I, for one, fervently hope so.

It is also one of the last things I ever said to my father, as he lay on his deathbed. By the time I uttered them, he was unconscious, but as I whispered them to him, I could swear I saw his dark eyebrows flutter ever so briefly. I would like to think that those words gave him a last, pleasant memory of times and friends long gone. I whispered it again to myself, some two and a half months later, as a squad of young Marines fired a rifle salute over his and his brother Bob's grave and as the mournful sound of "Taps" rolled forth, as their family laid them to rest, side by side, just as brothers should be, on a cool September morning, in the soft, dark, Tennessee earth outside Franklin. Two of A. G. and Ruth McCall's boys were finally back home again.

Semper Fi, Mac. Semper Fi, Dad. Goodbye, old timer. I love you.

> They shall not grow old as we that are left grow old.
> Age shall not weary them, nor the years condemn.
> At the going down of the sun and in the morning
> We shall remember them.
>
> —ROBERT LAURENCE BINYON—

Postscript to the Second Edition

> The geste says this, and the man who was on the field . . .
> and wrote the book. . . . The man who does not know this
> has not understood anything.[1]
>
> -*THE SONG OF ROLAND*-

Since the ancient days of warfare, at least as far back as *The Song of Roland*, people have placed a high premium on the experiences of those who "were there." In recounting Pogiebait McCall's experiences, I had many of his own stories to my family and me on which to draw and rely, and he was certainly a critical and formative firsthand witness to this son and author. After his death in 1997, as the early drafts of the manuscript that later became this book morphed from the original intent of simply being a manuscript to provide to local historical archives into something more full-fledged, I had the honor and privilege of receiving the testimony of a host of additional witnesses and fellow veterans of the Ninth Defense Battalion.

Over time, especially after the 2000 first edition was published, I came to know many of them, not just as men who knew my dad or as potential sources, but also much as one might regard one's uncles or as long-lost (albeit much older) big brothers whom I never knew I had. At the time of the publication of this second edition, all of them are now departed from the scene. The James Michener quotation that I selected in 2000 to open this book is now absolutely true. These men of the South Pacific lived a long time, and seemingly fewer Americans can identify the significance of the word *Guadalcanal*, much less locate it on a map.

At least one of the Ninth's veterans, with whom I became close, warned me that there would be an emotional wallop that would hit me hard one day. David Slater sensed my attachment, not just as a writer and historian, but as a young friend to him and so many of the elderly veterans of the Ninth, to the point that he felt it necessary to send me a kind of *memento mori* reminder of what his and his buddies' future would hold. In summer 2006, Biggie Slater wrote to me: "Our roster becomes smaller as each month goes by, and my own energies seem to be spiraling inward so that the tasks of maintaining the threads among the 9th are a little daunting."[2] During one of our regular phone discussions around the same time, he gently added: "Are you sure you want to do this—to keep up with all of us old men—Nick? You know, one day, it's going to be very sad for you." I replied that, yes, I felt certain that one day I would have to face a grim reality. However, when one has undertaken an honor and a duty, one does not shrink from things just because the end result will be difficult or sad.

Coincidentally, 2006 marked the final reunion of the 9th Defense and AAA Battalion Association. In its last years, the number of healthy (or at least, relatively mobile) members willing to travel to a reunion had dwindled to the point that Dave Slater found himself organizing joint reunions with several sister defense battalions. It was not exactly the "reunion in a telephone booth" that Biggie had once predicted, but the attendance from the Ninth was a fraction of what it had been in the glory days of the unit's reunions. While it was still good to gather together, a near-universal sentiment was expressed by the Ninth's attendees at the joint gatherings: "It's okay, but it's just not the same." So, even these joint reunions came to an end.

Around this time, I was forced to reckon with the stark reality that the days of the Ninth, as a living, breathing, if aged entity, were quickly dwindling, as the lives of its remaining Marines were fading away rapidly. Each death brought home that sense of sadness and loss of which Biggie Slater had tried to warn me.

By early 2017, with the death of Colonel Hank Reichner, those eternal master snipers, time, health, and age, had taken away all of the men with whom I spoke and corresponded for some eighteen years after my father's own death. As each one died, I annotated my copy of the 9th Defense and AAA Battalion Association's reunion roster with the date of his death. There are an awful lot of death annotations on that roster now.

Over time, I have come to realize that by writing and completing *Pogie-bait's War* when I did, I honored not only my father's wish and his memory, but those of his buddies as well. Now that these men are all dead, and precious few veterans of the Ninth Defense now remain, this book is one of the very few ways that the Fighting Ninth and its men—men who I had come to know not merely as sources of information or names on a page, but as individual, living, breathing souls, often very personally—shall live on. My posthumous thanks and undying respects must be acknowledged to each of these particular contributors and veterans of the Ninth Defense Battalion:

Colonel (Retired) William T. (Bill) Box, 1918-2009, aged 91
Francis E. (Frank) Chadwick, 1925-2001, aged 76
Major (Retired) Christopher S. (Chris) Donner, 1912-2012, aged 99
Alfred R. (Al) Downs, 1919-2011, aged 92
William E. (Bill) Galloway, 1920-2002, aged 81
James V. (Jim) Kruse, 1919-2005, aged 85
Colonel (Retired) Robert M. (Bob) Landon, 1924-2009, aged 85
Joseph J. (Joe) Pratl, 1921-2014, aged 93
Colonel (Retired) Henry H. (Hank) Reichner Jr., 1918-2016, aged 98
David (Biggie) Slater, 1921-2012, aged 91
Jack (Brother Andrew) Sorensen, 1921-2007, aged 86
Samuel E. Stavisky (Marine combat correspondent with the Ninth),
    1915-2008, aged 93
Frank F. (Frankie) Yemma, 1923-2004, aged 81
Colonel (Retired) Walter C. (Waldo) Wells, 1917-2006, aged 88

My eternal thanks are acknowledged, as well, to these vital contributors from the McCall family, to each of whom I owe so very much—in one case, my life itself:

Albert G. McCall Jr. (Jack's oldest brother), 1914-2002, aged 87
Dorothy K. McCall (Bob McCall's wife), 1924-2017, aged 93
Patricia H. McCall (Jack's wife and my mother), 1932-2014, aged 81
Lucy Robinson (Jack's first cousin), 1922-2006, aged 84
Colonel (Retired) Joseph G. Wheeler (Jack's cousin), 1918-2011, aged 92

Last, I express my gratitude to Lt. Colonel (Retired) Dye Ogata (1916-2015; aged 99 at his death), one of the two Japanese American (*Nisei*) interpreters who translated Japanese junior officer Toshihiro Oura's diary in 1943 and who verified its provenance to me. Not only did Dye survive New Georgia, he also survived wounds from a Japanese bomb on Bougainville. Dye Ogata was truly, in the words of author Joseph Harrington, an American samurai.

·

Acknowledgments
(From the 2000 Edition)

This could never have been prepared without the help, advice, and incredible assistance (and patience) of various persons, all of which contributed to make this project a true team effort.

First and foremost, I would like to thank several of Jack's personal friends, Frank Chadwick, Al Downs, Bill Galloway, Jim Kruse, and Frank Yemma, who have graciously spent much of their personal time and energy in helping provide me with their memories and details of their experiences that augmented what my father had told me or what he had recounted in his own letters, notes, and papers. In a real sense, this story is their story as well, since it recounts many experiences they all shared together during four grueling years. In particular, Frank Chadwick has spent a considerable amount of time talking with me, providing me with correspondence and notes derived from his own considerable research and recollections of the 9th Defense Battalion; in commenting on several drafts; and in sharing with me and my father several years ago a copy of a remarkable videotape, prepared by him and Colonel Bill Box, on a visit to Guadalcanal and Rendova-New Georgia in 1988, in which the two veterans revisited what must have been almost every piece of real estate on which the 155mm Group had been stationed from late 1942 to early 1944. Frank is a veritable living history museum of the Marine Corps, and in particular one small part of it, the 9th Defense Battalion. I owe an immense debt of gratitude to Frank, as without his "labor of love," I sincerely doubt if this book could have advanced as quickly and as completely as it has.

I am equally indebted to David ("Biggie") Slater, who graciously spent the better part of a month reviewing and commenting on several early drafts of this book as well as sharing his own personal reminiscences of the Pacific war, *Jungle Vignettes*, portions of which are published here for the first time, and to Colonel Hank Reichner, Colonel Bill Box, Professor Chris Donner, and Joe Pratl, each of whom also spent a considerable amount of time reviewing and commenting on early drafts of this book and who also generously shared their own accounts of the fighting with me.

I am deeply indebted to other members of the "Fighting Ninth," in particular, to Paul Berry; Horace ("Smiley") Burnette; Ray Carman; Cliff Cribbe; Milt Davis; Herb Dougherty; John Dobkowski; Willie Dufour; John Hall; Ted Hitchcock; John Henry Johnson; Colonel (Ret'd) Bob Landon; Jerry Morris; Brother Andrew Sorensen (who also provided copies of his sketches drawn overseas); Bill Sorensen; Dr. George W. ("Doc") Teller; Colonel Walter C. Wells; Nick Zingarelli; the late Amsa Bodine; and to the numerous other members at large of the 9th Defense and AAA Battalions Association for their contributions to the unit's alumni newsletters, *Poop!* and *Son of Poop!*, which provided me with scores of tidbits and insights I have been able to work into this narrative.

Acknowledgments are due to the following, as well: for his critiques of an early draft of this book and for sharing with me his own accounts of life as a 1st Marine Division leatherneck in World War II and Korea, former Chief Historian of the Marine Corps Benis M. Frank; Professor Charles Johnson, Director Emeritus of the University of Tennessee Center for the Study of War and Society, for encouraging me to take this from a mere one-hundred-page manuscript to a full-fledged book; Louise Lynch, Chief Archivist of the Williamson County Archives, Franklin, Tennessee (where Jack's uniform and some of his other personal effects from the war are on display); Major (Retired) Charles Melson, the current Chief Historian, US Marine Corps, himself a noted expert on the Ninth and its sister defense battalions (and son of 155mm Group vet Bill Melson) and for graciously providing his time and the fruits of his own research on the Marine Defense Battalions; and, for his own comments and encouragement, Professor Eric Bergerud, author of *Touched with Fire: the Land War in the South Pacific*, and a sequel dealing with air and anti-aircraft operations in that theater.

Others to whom my thanks are fully due include my law colleagues John A. Lucas and Martin B. Bailey of Hunton & Williams (the latter of whom was instrumental in helping me track down the fate of *U-94*, the German sub whose crew was guarded by the Ninth); Donald F. Paine and Robert W. Ritchie, who reviewed several early drafts with me and provided me with their insightful criticisms; Jeffrey Bucheit of the Historical Electronics Museum in Baltimore, Maryland, for sharing with me his museum's extensive archives on the early development and usage of radar by the US military; military historians and writers Mark F. Cancian, Jon T. Hoffman and Dr. Frank N. Schubert; and for their general comments, observations, and encouragement, former Marine combat correspondent Samuel E. Stavisky; Damon Gause; Captain (Retired) Wilbur Jones, US Navy; Dr. Toni E. Lesowitz; Lisa R. Lee; Major General (Retired) William B. McGrath, US Army; Edward T. Brading; Bennett Cox; Lyn Sullivan Pewitt; the late Wilson Herbert; Colonel (Retired) Joe G. Wheeler; John Doak; Hoyt Doak; Billy Inman; Major Joseph A. Sharbel, Headquarters, US Marine Corps; Ernie Tracy of Tracy Photography, Knoxville, Tennessee; and Mr. Wade Davies.

My late debt of gratitude is overdue to several professors and teachers who cultivated my own love of history and literature over the years, namely Ron Pritchard; Dr. Tom Phelps; my father's old high school friends and veterans of the war in Europe, Coach Jimmy Gentry and Fred and Julia Isaacs; and several Professors of History and Political Science at Vanderbilt University, Charles Delzell, my faculty mentor Robert H. Birkby, William C. Havard, and the late Professors Howard Boorman, Forrestt Miller, and Captain Sidney Banks.

I also have to thank my mother, Patricia H. McCall, my sister Holly McCall, and my uncle and aunt, Albert G. McCall, Jr. and Dorothy McCall (Mrs. Robert McCall), for their recollections and remembrances of my father, my uncle Bob McCall and other family members, which have been integrated in this account as well. I also thank my wife, Jennifer Ashley-McCall, and my daughter, Margaret, for their patience and love in allowing me to take considerable amounts of time and energy away from them in preparing this. I dedicate this account to Margaret, in the hopes that she and her generation never have to contend with anything as deadly and savage as the war in which my father participated, and that, if she must—God willing—she may survive it with the same sense of humor and high spirits that helped her "Tete" to survive.

Last, I wish to thank my father, Jack H. McCall Sr., for making this account—and me—possible in the first place, and for providing me with friendship, love, support, discipline, and a hero through thirty-six years of my life. My only regret is that he was not able to tell this story himself, in his own words. I hope that he would be proud, nevertheless, of this accounting of his life during four momentous years, and I hope I have done credit to the memory of a fine man, a great father, a good friend to have, and a true Marine.

I respectfully dedicate this account to his memory, and to the memory of another fine Marine and former Franklin boy, his brother Robert B. McCall (1916-1994), and Jack's friends and buddies of the 9th Defense Battalion, Fleet Marine Force, US Marine Corps, 1942-44, and of Franklin High School's Classes of 1940 and 1941.

Grateful acknowledgement is made for permission to reprint excerpts from the following copyrighted, published works:

Eric Bergerud, *Touched with Fire: The Land War in the South Pacific*. Copyright © 1996 by Viking, an imprint of Penguin Random House. Used by permission of the publisher.

Toshihiro Oura, *I Will Fight to the Last*. Translated by Dye Ogata & Frank Sanwo and edited by Jack H. McCall. Copyright © 2005 by *MHQ: The Quarterly Journal of Military History*. Used by permission of the publisher.

Henry H. Reichner Jr., *But One Life to Give*. Bloomington, Indiana, Xlibris Corp., 2009. Copyright © 2009 Henry H. Reichner Jr. Used by permission of the author.

After the Colors Faded:
What Happened to Them After the War
(From the 2000 Edition)

Lt. Colonel "Baker" (155mm Group CO): Colonel "Baker" remained in the Corps for several more years. He was last seen by Hank Reichner—also a career Marine—running the Second Division Officers' Mess in Sasebo, Japan, during the occupation of Japan and married to a very attractive young woman. As many a man of the 155mm Group might have said of their temperamental and eccentric former group commander: "Go figure."

William T. Box (CO, Battery B; 155mm Group Staff): In a 1985 letter, Bill Box shared his life after the war with Jack McCall: "Certainly, for us, WWII was the 'Good War' and a period of time we fondly remember. You and I and the 9th were part of that. I lost a son in the 'Bad War,' Vietnam. He was in the Army. I had six children. My first wife died in 1956. I married a widow with three boys; we've been married 26 years [in 1985]. We got all our children through college. They're all good people and making their way in life. . . . At the moment, we have four grandchildren, so we're not doing too good in that department." Now retired from the oil business (and a retired Marine Corps Reserve colonel), Bill Box lives in the San Francisco Bay area. He and Frank Chadwick revisited the scene of their "glory days" in the autumn of 1988, traveling throughout the Guadalcanal and the Central Solomons areas. He remains to this day one of the most respected and best-loved officers of the Fighting Ninth.

Horace "Smiley" Burnette (Battery A): Platoon Sergeant "Smiley" Burnette returned to the East Tennessee hills and became a dental technician in Sevierville, Tennessee. Only retired since 1997, he now lives with his family outside Charlotte, North Carolina. Undoubtedly one of the best-loved NCOs in the 155mm Group, Smiley never forgot his "boys." He and Colonel Hank Reichner were instrumental in pressing the Department of the Navy to award, some fifty years after the fact, a long-delayed Purple Heart to their battery mate, Bill Galloway, for the wounds Bill received in September 1943 when the defective 155mm shell destroyed Galloway's Long Tom at Piru Plantation, an incident that nearly killed or maimed Jack McCall in the process.

Francis Chadwick (Battery B): After the breakup of the 155mm Group and a tour of duty stateside, Frank Chadwick reenlisted in the Corps for another two years on the promise of thirty days leave, promotion to platoon sergeant, and a choice of duty station on the Eastern Seaboard. After being stationed at Brooklyn Navy Yard for only two weeks after getting married, Frank was transferred to Bermuda for two years. He left the Corps in December 1947. Chadwick writes: "Upon my discharge from the Corps I decided I needed an education to support my wife and daughter. When I joined the Corps, I had an *eighth-grade* education." He went back to prep school for a year, attended Tri-State University on the GI Bill, and graduated in three years with a BS in chemical engineering. After several jobs, Chadwick began a lengthy career with IBM that led to an MS in engineering management and later a PhD in engineering economics. Chadwick retired as a senior engineer—project engineering (chemical) from IBM at the age of fifty-nine. He now splits his time between his home in Florida and visiting with his family in his old hometown of Binghamton, New York.

John J. Dobkowski (Battery B): After his discharge from the Corps, John Dobkowski became involved in the plastics and manufacturing industries and ultimately started a business in his hometown of Erie, Pennsylvania, that specialized in the manufacture of various types of prototype products for various companies. This was quite a booming enterprise, and it stood John in good stead for many years. Now semi-retired and a widower of several years, he delights in traveling throughout the US in his RV and enjoys the leisure time he seldom had for much of his life.

Christopher S. Donner (Battery A): Due to his lack of sufficient points for rotation stateside with the rest of the 155mm Group, Chris Donner was not among those who were present in San Francisco at the group's formal disbanding. Instead, after Christmas liberty in Hawaii, Captain Donner was ordered to join the First Marine Division's artillery regiment, the Eleventh Marines, in time for service in the invasion of Okinawa on April 1, 1945. He was assigned as a forward observer (FO) and artillery coordinator to the Seventh Marines, an infantry outfit. As an FO, Chris participated in some of the most hellish fighting of that campaign alongside the Seventh's infantrymen in the assaults on the village of Kakazu and Wana (Dragon Tooth) Ridge, for which he was awarded the Silver Star. Finally up for rotation home, Donner was en route to Pearl Harbor aboard the carrier *Card* when word of the A-bombings reached him. A retired Marine major who (like several other veterans of the Ninth) was reactivated for the Korean War, former Penn State sociology professor and high school teacher and counselor, Donner returned to visit the Solomons in 1967, and he wrote of his experiences for the *Marine Corps Gazette*. An avid scuba diver and snorkeler, Chris Donner now lives in Florida.[1]

Al E. Downs (Ninth Platoon, Parris Island; Battery B): After leaving the Ninth on Banika in 1944, Al Downs returned home to marry his beloved Rosie at Camp Lejeune, North Carolina, a marriage that has lasted over fifty years. He was stationed at Camp Lejeune and Jacksonville, Florida, and like so many other Marines was awaiting orders for the invasion of Japan at war's end. He returned home to his native Pittsburgh and was a municipal bus driver for twenty-five years before retiring to his family's home of over seventy years just outside Pittsburgh, where he still lives, a proud father and grandpa.

William Galloway (Battery A; Norfolk Navy Yard and Camp Lejeune): Bill Galloway became a tugboat and barge boat skipper and operator after the war and lives with his wife Maril in Titusville, Florida. Some forty-five years after the war, Bill finally received the Purple Heart he justly deserved for his wounds from the exploding Long Tom, thanks to the efforts of Colonel Reichner and Sergeant Smiley Burnette.

Robert "Hercules" Hausen (Battery B; Norfolk Navy Yard and Camp Lejeune): An Iowa farm boy, "Herc" Hausen left the Marines in 1946 and moved back to Iowa to follow his longtime plans of working a family farm. Like many Midwestern farmers, however, he fell on hard times in the mid-1980s and finally sold it. He died shortly thereafter in the late 1980s. Jack and Herc's friends chalked the cause of Herc's death up to heartbreak.

Otto Ites (Oberleutnant zur See, U-94, Kriegsmarine): Previously the destroyer of fourteen Allied ships and holder of the *Ritterkreuz* ("Knight's Cross," roughly the Nazi equivalent of the US Medal of Honor), Otto Ites—one of the first of many POWs taken by the Ninth—survived his wounds and life in a US POW "cage" to become a dentist after the war. With the creation of the West German government and *Bundeswehr*, though, he next joined the Federal German Navy in 1956. Ironically enough, given his own experiences off Cuba in 1942, Ites served as the skipper of the anti-submarine destroyer Z-2. He retired as a *Bundesmarine* rear admiral in 1977. A wartime enemy turned postwar ally, Ites died three days before his sixty-fourth birthday in February 1982 in Norden-Ostfriesland, West Germany.

James V. Kruse (Ninth Platoon, Parris Island; H&S Battery, 155mm Group): Jim Kruse returned to his hometown of Elkhart, Indiana, where he served as a member of the Elkhart Police Department and for many years was a member of its scuba and rescue squad. He now lives in Florida.

Robert Landon (Battery B): After returning from the Pacific with the 155mm Group, Bob Landon did not leave the military for many years. After completing his active-duty Marine service, he transferred to the Air Force, just in time to be sent to the Korean War. He became an Air Force commissioned officer and was responsible for the security of several Air Force nuclear missile units. These responsibilities were later shifted to the Army's Military Police Corps, so Bob then found himself becoming an Army officer, retiring as a full colonel in the MPs in 1973 after several command tours. After his retirement, Bob was the warden of the North Dakota State Penitentiary and served in various capacities in Virginia's Department of Corrections, including as the department director. He retired in 1987 after spending several more years with the Corrections Corporation of America., Bob now lives outside Chattanooga, Tennessee, with his wife, Yvonne.

Albert G. McCall, Jr.: Jack's oldest brother spent the war years as a draftsman and aircraft designer for the Glenn Martin Aircraft Company (later to become Martin Marietta and now, Lockheed Martin) in Baltimore. At Martin he was a member of the design teams for the B-26 Marauder medium bomber, the PBM Mariner and Mars flying boats, and other aircraft. He remained with Martin after the war and was actively involved in the design of other Martin aviation products, including the Air Force's MATADOR and MACE cruise missiles in the 1950s; the Project ORION anti-satellite missile program of the early 1960s (one of the precursors of the SDI/"Star Wars" missile defense programs); and the Air Force's DYNA-SOAR and lifting body projects in the mid-1960s, which were predecessors of today's Space Shuttle. After leaving Martin in 1969, Al began a second career with Teledyne Isotopes and was instrumental in designing components of the SNAP series of nuclear generators used to power various NASA satellites and interplanetary space probes, including NASA's 1976 VIKING Mars probe. Now retired and eighty-six years old, Al is the proud father of two children and the grandfather of two. He resides in a Baltimore suburb.

Robert B. McCall (Second Defense Battalion): After leaving the Corps in

1945, like his older brother Al, Bob McCall never moved back to Franklin. He and his wife Dorothy moved from California back to Idaho, not far from his duty station at the naval depot in Pocatello, where he joined the Idaho State Police. Bob became locally famous as a radio celebrity with his own weekly public-service show, *An Idaho Tragedy*, sponsored by the Idaho State Police. The popularity of this radio show and his own statewide contacts provided Bob with a springboard into state and national Republican politics. He served as the chief of staff to Idaho's governor Bob Smiley. Afterwards, Bob moved to Denver and became the executive director of the Education Commission of the States, a non-governmental education agency; a consultant on state-level education and funding for education; and a frequent participant in the annual National Republican Governors' Conferences for many years. He and Dot later sold their small ranch in Idaho and condominium in Denver and moved to Fargo, North Dakota, the home of his daughter and only child and her family. Bob McCall preceded his little brother Jack in death on February 15, 1994, after waging his own brave and lengthy battle with cancer. He was seventy-seven.

Archie E. O'Neil (155mm Group; Battalion Commander): A Naval Academy graduate, Colonel O'Neil had served in Nicaragua and was at Midway when World War II broke out. He joined the Ninth during the central Solomons operations, succeeding Colonel "Baker" as CO of the 155mm Group and, for Guam, succeeded Colonel Scheyer as the Ninth Defense's battalion commander. After relinquishing his command of the Ninth on Guam, O'Neil would remain in the Corps and be promoted to brigadier general, retiring in 1957. He died in Columbia, South Carolina, at the age of eighty-one in January 1986.

Joseph Pratl (Tenth Defense Battalion; Battery A): After the 155mm Group's breakup, Joe and his longtime sweetheart Barb were married in their hometown of Chicago on his thirty-day furlough, but their wartime honeymoon was short. After serving at Camp Peary, Virginia, and Camp Lejeune, Joe was preparing for reassignment to Camp Pendleton for advanced infantry training in August 1945 and, after that, the invasion of Japan. With war's end, Pratl was transferred to Washington to guard the Navy Department's headquarters and was discharged at Quantico in October 1945. Joe became a machinist, which had long been a dream of his. After working a series of machinist jobs, he ultimately worked for the Chicago Transit Authority for twenty years, retiring in 1986. Joe and Barb Pratl raised seven children, one of whom died as an infant. Still, Joe reports, "Life has been good to me here in Chicago."

Henry H. Reichner Jr. (CO, Battery A): Following the breakup of the 155mm Group, then-Captain Reichner served as operations officer of the Third Battalion, Tenth Marines on Saipan and served in the occupation forces in Japan until late 1946. Lieutenant Colonel Reichner served in Korea from 1952 to 1953 as a staff officer and later as commander of the Fourth Battalion, Eleventh Marines, where he was fondly remembered for the gesture of making a personal farewell to as many of his troops as possible in their frontline positions. Later he taught at the Naval War College and served as chief of staff to the US Naval Mission to Haiti; CO of the Tenth Marines; deputy chief, Far East Plans, to the joint chiefs of staff; and assistant G-3 (plans), Military Assistance Command-Vietnam. Retiring from the Marines in 1968 as a full colonel, he then embarked on a varied second career in the business and civic affairs of his hometown, Philadelphia. Among other roles, he has served as an officer and director of the Greater Philadelphia Chamber of Commerce, was involved in various public works projects, and was a founding director of the New Jersey State Aquarium. Colonel Reichner still serves as a securities arbitrator for the New York Stock Exchange, the National Association of Securities Dealers, and the Municipal Bond Securities Board, as well as being vice president and a director of the Philadelphia Belt Line Railroad and a director of Independence Blue Cross. As Hank Reichner says: "In short, my civilian career of 30-plus years has three years on my service with my beloved Marines."[2]

Maier Rothschild (Battery I): Severely wounded in the Zanana Beach fight by a sword-wielding Japanese officer, Maier Rothschild also faced the ordeal of watching his buddy John Wantuck die gruesomely in the savage nighttime attack. Awarded the Navy Cross in lieu of the Medal of Honor, Rothschild soon distanced himself from his peers after his recuperation. Unlike some other Marine Corps heroes, though, he seemed reluctant to take advantage of his potential celebrity as a Navy Cross winner, when he could have done so to return honorably stateside for War Bond, recruiting, or USO tours. Rothschild broke off contact with his fellow Ninth Defense veterans after returning to his native New York City and has not been heard from again. Like his buddy Wantuck, Rothschild was another casualty of the hellish New Georgia campaign.

William J. Scheyer (Battalion Executive Officer and Commander): Like Archie O'Neil, an Annapolis graduate, Scheyer's pre-Ninth career had already been impressive. His duties included service in Haiti, Nicaragua, and Cuba; time aboard several warships; service with the Fourth Marines in Shanghai; and service as a senior officer instructor. After leaving the Ninth in late 1943, Scheyer served as the personnel officer for III Amphibious

Corps during the Marshall Islands campaign, and he was twice decorated with the Legion of Merit—once for his service with the Ninth Defense, and once for his III Amphib staff service. He served as chief of staff of the Fleet Marine Force-Western Pacific during the Chinese Civil War; as director of instruction for the Marine Corps Schools at Quantico; and after his promotion to brigadier general, as the Corps' assistant director of personnel and—in his final role—as the deputy and acting camp commander of Camp Pendleton. Forced to retire early due to health reasons, Scheyer was promoted to major general, and he died in May 1956—just two years after his retirement—at the young age of fifty-six.

David "Biggie" Slater (H&S Battery, Ninth Defense; Battery E): Discharged in 1946, David Slater used his GI Bill benefits to obtain a master's degree in electrical engineering from New York University. He was employed by NYU's Engineering Research Division from 1951 to 1970, reaching the rank of senior research scientist and project director. An offshoot of his last project became the Palisades Institute for Research Services, Inc., of which Biggie Slater served as president and chairman. From 1954 to 1973, he was an NYU adjunct professor, teaching laboratory courses at night. From 1961 to 1994, he was also a director, treasurer, and consultant of Tensor Corporation, which ultimately became SoftNet, Inc. By the year 2000, after twenty-five years as its secretary, Dave became the secretary emeritus of the Advisory Group on Electron Devices, an activity of the Undersecretary of Defense for Research and Engineering. He is still an active NYU alumnus, having served as a member of its Board of Trust, and he has received several awards in recognition of his labors on behalf of his alma mater. One of Biggie Slater's proudest accomplishments and participations has been his role as a director and former president of the Ninth Defense & AAA Battalion Association.

Jack (Brother Andrew) Sorensen (Tenth Defense Battalion; Battery A): After returning to civilian life, Jack Sorensen, the battalion's prize illustrator and a beloved member of Battery A, took orders at the age of thirty-nine and became a Catholic brother. He now resides at a monastery in Nebraska and makes a pilgrimage of sorts to attend the Ninth's annual reunion every fall. Writing to Jack McCall from Mount Michael Abbey in 1987, Brother Andy fondly recalled of his buddies: "I once knew a lot of pretty wonderful guys who were just kids as far as age was concerned, but they were probably as staunch a group of men that anyone could be privileged to know—honed into good Marines by a D.I., a war, and any other hardships that one must endure in the islands."[3]

William Sorensen (Battery E): Bill "Chick" Sorensen now lives in

Connecticut after working in the aviation business. He maintains quite a collection of Marine Corps memorabilia and remains active, despite having suffered a stroke. He is the current president of the Ninth Defense & AAA Battalion Association.

Samuel E. Stavisky (Attached Marine Combat Correspondent, Ninth Defense): After his time with the Ninth on New Georgia, Staff Sergeant Sam Stavisky reported on the fighting on Bougainville later in 1943, ultimately spending a total of thirty-four months as a Marine combat correspondent. At war's end, he resumed his prewar employment with the *Washington Post* as a reporter, staff writer, and editor until 1954. He also wrote for various magazines, including *The Saturday Evening Post, Look, Life*, and *Collier's*. In 1954 Sam started his own public relations and lobbying firm, with offices in Washington, DC, New York, and several other cities internationally. He and his wife Bernice divide their time between Washington, DC, and Singer Island, Florida; the couple has two daughters and a grandson. Sam's autobiography of his days as a Marine combat correspondent was published in 1999.

George W. "Doc" Teller (Batteries A and B): After the war, "Doc" Teller returned to his first love: medicine. After many years of practice, he is now a retired physician in Eugene, Oregon. One wonders if he still recalls his recipe for the "noodle soups" so prized as a tonic by Hank Reichner and Battery A's officers.

William Tracy (CO, Battery E): Following his retirement as a "bird colonel" from the Corps, Bill Tracy became an active participant in the civic life of his hometown, Meriden, Connecticut, serving in various local political roles, including as mayor for several years. The former Battery E commander and one of the heroes of the "Glorious Fourth" of July in 1943, Colonel Tracy now divides his time between Meriden and a home in rural New Hampshire.

Frank Yemma (Battery B): After being evacuated with malaria from the Russell Islands, Frankie Yemma was posted to Camp Lejeune in mid-1944 for advanced artillery training. There he experienced a surprise: "They're putting us through all this schooling, how to fire a 155mm rifle. They're showing combat films, and they're pictures of us! I told the instructor, 'For God's sakes, that's us on Rendova!' And he laughed and said, 'Yeah, that's the way it goes.'" By early 1945, Yemma was transferred to Camp Pendleton for infantry training and in April 1945 was shipped to Guam to join the First Battalion, Twenty-First Marines, Third Marine Division, in preparation for the invasion of Kyushu. After briefly working for the Carrier Corporation after war's end, he served for twenty years as a professional firefighter for the City of Syracuse, New York. After retiring from that career at age forty-nine, Frankie went back to work for the US Postal Service as a mail carrier in Vero Beach, Florida, for another eight and a half years. Following his retirement from the USPS, Frank now lives in Florida, where he is active with the local chapter of the Marine Corps League and the Italian American War Veterans, volunteering frequently at the local VA clinic.

Walter "Waldo" Wells (CO, Battery B; Exec, 155mm Group): Like his friend and erstwhile rival Hank Reichner, Columbia-educated Walter Wells made the Marine Corps his career, retiring as a full colonel after some thirty years of service, including duty in Korea and during the Vietnam War. Although in his eighties, he is still living an active life in California, maintaining a physical training regimen that would tax many men much younger than himself. Colonel Wells has stated to the author that although he met many Marines during his lengthy career, "the men of the Ninth Defense [Battalion], on average, were superior when compared to those I knew later in my career." Quite a tribute, indeed, from the long-serving, tough, and fearless Waldo.

John "Tojo" Whalen (Battery A): Already known among his wartime Marine buddies as being pugnacious and scrappy (perhaps partly because of the nickname he was saddled with), the short but wiry "Tojo" Whalen became a semi-professional boxer for several years after war's end but hung up his gloves to resume his main prewar occupation as a barber in the Catskills' resort of Ballston Spa, New York. He died in the early 1990s.

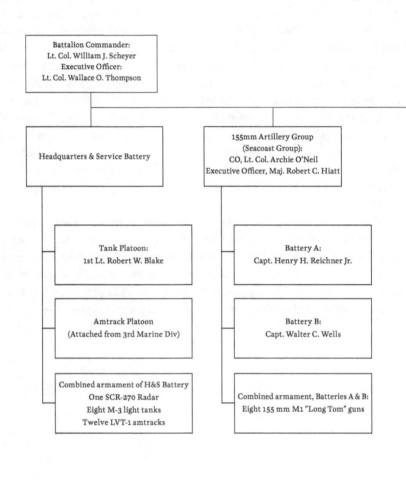

Battalion Commander:
Lt. Col. William J. Scheyer
Executive Officer:
Lt. Col. Wallace O. Thompson

Headquarters & Service Battery

155mm Artillery Group
(Seacoast Group):
CO, Lt. Col. Archie O'Neil
Executive Officer, Maj. Robert C. Hiatt

Tank Platoon:
1st Lt. Robert W. Blake

Battery A:
Capt. Henry H. Reichner Jr.

Amtrack Platoon
(Attached from 3rd Marine Div)

Battery B:
Capt. Walter C. Wells

Combined armament of H&S Battery
One SCR-270 Radar
Eight M-3 light tanks
Twelve LVT-1 amtracks

Combined armament, Batteries A & B:
Eight 155 mm M1 "Long Tom" guns

Abbreviated Organizational Chart, Ninth Defense Battalion, Mid-1943

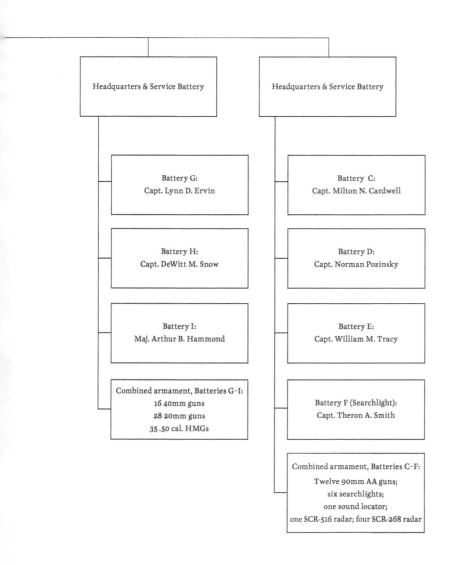

Headquarters & Service Battery

Headquarters & Service Battery

Battery G:
Capt. Lynn D. Ervin

Battery C:
Capt. Milton N. Cardwell

Battery H:
Capt. DeWitt M. Snow

Battery D:
Capt. Norman Pozinsky

Battery I:
Maj. Arthur B. Hammond

Battery E:
Capt. William M. Tracy

Combined armament, Batteries G–I:
16 40mm guns
28 20mm guns
35 .50 cal. HMGs

Battery F (Searchlight):
Capt. Theron A. Smith

Combined armament, Batteries C–F:
Twelve 90mm AA guns;
six searchlights;
one sound locator;
one SCR-516 radar; four SCR-268 radar

Navy Unit Commendation Citation, Ninth Defense Battalion

The Secretary of the Navy takes pleasure in commending the

NINTH MARINE DEFENSE BATTALION

for service as follows:

"For outstanding heroism in action against enemy Japanese forces in Guadalcanal, November 30, 1942 to May 20, 1943; Rendova-New Georgia Area, June 30 to November 7, 1943; and at Guam, Marianas, July 21 to August 20, 1944. One of the first units of its kind to operate in the South Pacific Area, the NINTH Defense Battalion established strong seacoast and beach positions which destroyed 12 hostile planes attempting to bomb Guadalcanal and further engaged in extensive patrolling activities. In a 21-day-and-night training period prior to the Rendova-New Georgia assault, this group calibrated and learned to handle new weapons and readily effected the conversion from a seacoast unit to a unit capable of executing field artillery missions. Joining Army Artillery units, special groups of this battalion aided in launching an attack which drove the enemy from the beaches, downed 13 of a 16-bomber plane formation during the first night ashore and denied the use of the Munda airfield to the Japanese. The NINTH Defense Battalion aided in spearheading the attack of the Army Corps operating on New Georgia and, despite heavy losses, remained in action until the enemy was routed from the island. Elements of the Battalion landed at Guam under intense fire, established beach defenses, installed antiaircraft guns and later, contributed to the rescue of civilians and to the capture or the destruction of thousands of Japanese. By their skill, courage and aggressive fighting spirit, the officers and men of the NINTH Defense Battalion upheld the highest traditions of the United States Naval Service."

All personnel attached to and serving with the NINTH Defense Battalion during the above-mentioned periods are authorized to wear the NAVY UNIT COMMENDATION Ribbon.

/s/ JOHN L. SULLIVAN,
Secretary of the Navy

"Then We Can Die Laughing": Annotated Translation of Captured Japanese War Diary from New Georgia

Author's Introduction: American forces in the Second World War were strictly prohibited from keeping personal diaries and journals, and enlisted men like Jack McCall faced rigorous censorship of their letters home. Those who did keep diaries risked punishment, so they often kept their notes hidden in their pocket Bibles or secreted in similar personal documents (like the Marines' Eugene B. Sledge[1] and the Navy's James Fahey[2]). In contrast, apparently no such prohibitions were imposed on the Japanese military. In their capture of Japanese-held islands throughout the Pacific, Marines and Army troops often seized Japanese personal diaries. These were often found to be rich sources of intelligence information, as was undoubtedly the document that follows.

This diary is that of probationary officer (roughly equivalent to an officer candidate or cadet) Toshihiro Oura, a Japanese platoon leader stationed near the Munda Point airfield. The diary's entries run from June 28 to July 23, 1943. The diary was translated by T/3 Dye Ogata and T/3 Frank Sanwo, two Nisei interpreters serving with the Army's Thirty-Seventh Infantry Division, under the authority of Captain Gilbert B. Ayres and Lt. Colonel D. W. Johnston of that division's G-2 (i.e., intelligence) staff. The only changes to the original Thirty-Seventh Infantry Division translation are some condensations for brevity's sake, grammatical and typographical corrections, and spelling-out of certain military abbreviations.

The inclusion of this diary in no way detracts from the sacrifices and heroism of the officers and men of the Marine Corps' Ninth Defense Battalion. Rather, it helps confirm, from a unique perspective—that of the enemy—many of the observations reported to the author by Jack "Pogie-bait" McCall and his fellow Ninth Defense veterans. The diary chronologically tracks much of the Ninth's activity on Rendova and the surrounding islands, although, of course, from the perspective of those on the "receiving end" of the Ninth Defense's bombardments during July and August 1943.

Oura was the leader of a "3rd Platoon"; this was apparently part of one of the subordinate companies of the Fifteenth AA Field Defense Unit, Imperial Japanese Army, under Colonel Shunichi Shiroto. This unit provided antiaircraft and antitank, light automatic cannon defenses for Munda Field. From the descriptions in the diary—Oura's platoon was serving primarily as antitank gunners—his platoon was likely a part of the Twenty-Seventh Machine Cannon Company. His unit was equipped with "pom-pom" guns, automatic cannon similar to the Ninth Defense's own 20mm and 40mm light AA guns. At one point, the diary indicates that Oura's detachment acquired responsibility for a larger, 100mm dual-purpose gun, with which he is ordered to shell Rendova. The diary is incredibly detailed; besides Oura being a keen observer, it is clear that Oura's Third Platoon was extremely well situated to see the Ninth's set-up and identify its specific kinds of equipment on Rendova quite accurately.

The diary is also a very poignant document in its own right. Besides occasionally indulging in self-exhortations to keep up his own spirits, Oura also writes of his family in Japan, his soldiers, and in several cases, his subordinates' tragic fates. His increasing doubts, despair, and bitterness toward the Imperial General Staff are manifestly apparent toward the end of the diary, when he also acknowledges to himself that he is suffering from malaria.

Although brief excerpts and an annotated abbreviation of this diary have appeared elsewhere,[3] to my knowledge, this is the first time that the bulk of Toshihiro Oura's diary has been published. I am greatly indebted to Joe Pratl and the family of the late Frank Bellis, another Ninth Defense veteran, for providing me with the Thirty-Seventh Division's translation of this unique document, and to Dye Ogata, one of the two Nisei translator-interpreters of the Thirty-Seventh Division's G-2 staff, who interpreted the diary in 1943 and corroborated the diary's provenance.

Introduction

Since the 25th, enemy planes have come over every night and early morning to bomb our unit. After going without sleep and rest, I have finally come to feel that the beginning of the enemy attack on New Georgia is near. On the other hand, our planes have never come over, leading me to wonder as to whether our air force actually exists. Officers and men have no alternative other than to wait to be destroyed while doing their best to the very last. This morning I finished breakfast early and while wondering what the time was, the roar of planes attracted my attention. At 0630 the roar of a large formation came from the east. All the officers and men went to their posts as the fourth day of battle started. The aircraft watcher identified them to be friendly planes. Our tenseness suddenly left us, and we shed tears of joy to think that our air force was still active. After receiving fierce bombing on Munda, New Georgia, since the middle of June, present conditions would indicate that the landing of the enemy is near.

Written by Oura, Toshihiro
June 28, 1943

June 29: I wonder if they will come today. Early yesterday morning there was no bombing as friendly planes appeared on the scene. It seems as if we had planned for a continuous bombing, and at 1500 we suddenly were bombed from the north. The enemy achieved his objective again on the fourth day and today is the fifth day. Last night it drizzled and there was a breeze making me feel rather uncomfortable. Although this is a continuous attack, we did not receive any last night. When I awoke at 0400 this morning, rain clouds filled the sky but there was still a breeze. The swell of the sea was higher than usual. However, the clouds seem to be breaking. I wonder if they will come. I have become used to combat now, and I have no fear. The continual bombing has made me determined to die. I will fight under all circumstances, whether they come or otherwise. In yesterday's raid our air force suffered no losses, while nine enemy planes were confirmed as having been shot down and three others doubtful. Battle gains are positively in favor of our victory. Large formations pass, and our belief in our invincibility is at last high. . . .

With rain clouds covering everything, we received our first warning at 0800. When the rain clouds began to break up to the southeast, the approaching roar of a Lockheed plane[4] came in from the west. I could not see it because it was at an altitude of about 5000 meters and still above the clouds. I wonder what this plane will report as to the weather over Munda when it returns to Guadalcanal. Whether we are bombed or not will depend on it.

Some doughnuts were brought to the officers' room from the Field Defense HQ, which were made by the *Nanto* [Southeast] Detachment. They were awfully small ones, but I think each one [of us] had 20 or so. They were really swell! Whether they were actually tasty or not didn't make much difference because of our craving for sweets. Each one was a treasure in itself. While eating the doughnuts, I lay down in the sand, and I pulled out the handbook my father had bought for me and which was now all in pieces from a bomb fragment. As I looked at the map of my homeland, which was dear to me, I thought I would like to go to a hot spring with my parents when I get back home.

I thought of going there, and here. This map of the homeland, when back home, would be of no use other than for traveling. Right now, it has spiritual meaning rather than a material value: a meaning which is ten times its value back home by making me happy and consoling me. At 1400 one plane flew over Rendova, and then came the alert, but the all-clear soon followed. Sometimes in carrying out liaison, I go to the Field Defense HQ. Because of mist, Rendova could not be seen. I gossiped with the Adjutant (a 1st Lieutenant) for about an hour. It seems that the COs and Captain Kobayashi are planning to use the positions of the 31st Company.[5]

I keenly felt the differences between the command post officers and the officers taking over the command for training. If I were the officer assuming command, I would say that coral positions are unsafe and are unfit for use, as they are being destroyed. The superior officers neither come out to observe the positions, nor do they experience actual bombing. Consequently, we are at a loss. . . .

No rations ever come. Today we did not have any bombing. This was probably due to the good fortune of bad weather, but we didn't relax.

June 30: At last, the final decisive battle has come. I will relate briefly the progress since last night. Last night, at 1910 Kolombangara received naval gunfire. At 2000, the blue signal flare from Rendova Point went up. I saw 4 enemy warships. At 0410 this morning rain clouds hovered over us. At Rendova four cruisers, two destroyers, two transports and countless numbers of boats appeared. The enemy fired lightly and the shore batteries replied fiercely. Our guns and air power seemed weak. The enemy used countless numbers of boats and landed on Rendova. The air force of the enemy was only fourteen planes (Grumman). . . .[6] At 0800 our (Zero) planes finally came. There were several planes which took part in aerial combat in four or five different places. (Grumman)—six planes were shot down. Two or three (Douglas) planes[7] flew north from the east.

At 0830 the warships withdrew. . . . There were no friendly planes above. The enemy kept (Vought Sikorsky,[8] Grumman, Curtiss[9] and Lockheed[10]) planes circling overhead. At 0930, 50 more shells were received. All sections received 150 rounds. Early in the morning we fired 30 rounds at enemy ships at a distance of 8500 meters. At 0940, the enemy again appeared with two cruisers and four destroyers and proceeded towards Rendova. They shelled near the piers on Bakieta Point and Munda. At daylight there was naval gun fire and a daylight enemy landing. The shore batteries had very little effect, and again there was no air force. When we are bombed, we had only to wait till death comes our way. The enemy must be operating against Shortland. What has happened to Rabaul?

During the daytime, there are only a few fighter planes. Furthermore, we are having trouble in unloading as it is. Even I have to do debarkation work. It annoys me even more when they ask for help at the *Nanto* Detachment. I have had hardtack for breakfast and even for supper. I cannot have rice. From where we cook rice, we can see warships, consequently we cannot cook. Above us there always are about 30 fighter planes, which keep roaring over in every direction. At 1400, some planes came from the west (Rabaul), I believe, because about 30 medium attack planes are sure a sight. We are moved to tears and waved our hands, saying "We're counting on you; we're counting on you." It must have been the fellows from the Wickham area[11]: a report soon came in that transports and warships had been sunk. At 1430 a large formation of 70 planes composed of Douglas[12] and fighter planes raided our positions with immense bombs, bigger than I had ever heard, but no direct hits were scored.

After that, they carried out horizontal bombing to the north. During the evening there were aerial combats in various places between our planes and the enemy. I could see the dogfights that I had been hoping to see for some time. The enemy also landed on the island, which is in front of the Searchlight Battalion.[13] I wouldn't be a bit surprised if we were to be shelled by naval gunfire again. During the afternoon the 2nd Platoon, as an anti-tank unit, with three pom-poms,[14] was ordered to advance to [new] positions. After having hardtack for breakfast, I worked on shelters. Officers and men alike exhausted themselves in work. . . .

July 1: We received heavy shelling from naval vessels. There was a new attack on Rendova by [American] forces. The day passed on after the report of the destroyers shelling Rendova was received and conjectures of all sorts were exchanged. It was 1830 when I was able to depart from the emplacements.... After making preparations, filled with determination, I separated from the Company staff. Only a few enemy night fighters appeared, and they only circled the coast to the south from time to time. Rain clouds fell about us and at times when we were doing shelter work, we couldn't see. We transported all of the ammunition, and when we completed the work, it was 0230. All through the night the enemy's boats moved about. There were no landings, but at dawn (0400) there were already four enemy warships in the nearby waters. It seems that the point of landing is going to be the east area of Munda, New Georgia. At 0440 enemy fighter planes appeared. After that 20-30 enemy fighter planes constantly flew overhead. About every hour the type of planes changed. At 0930 a friendly carrier-based fighter plane appeared. Two destroyers were bombed, and one destroyer gave forth bellows of smoke, just in front of our positions. There were aerial combats in all directions. Enemy planes gave forth smoke, which changed to fire as they dived earthward. At times, the proportion was four Curtisses to one Zero.... Gun reports could be heard from all directions, and there was a roar of friendly light bombers. I filled my stomach with hardtack and at 0700 we finally finished our fatigue work....

At 1000 I ate my first rice in three days. There has not been any bombing of Munda as yet. We expect friendly bombers during the afternoon. Sleepless days being on duty, ready to fire while the 4th air raid continued....

At 1400 the platoon leader came running and asked us to assemble at the Company's position. The enemy is preparing for heavy artillery fire at Rendova and is about ready to fire.... Enemy planes are constantly overhead. No bombing by our air force. The [men of the] 2nd Platoon are to do their utmost, and there is to be no evacuation.... The shells from large ships and the artillery are now falling before our eyes. The positions that are left are all destroyed.

July 2: [We] heard the reports of guns at times during the night. The sound of boats was heard last night. Because of rain, I got into an air raid shelter and took a nap, getting soaking wet. In the early morning enemy planes (20-30) came to patrol. At 1000, there is supposed to be a raid on enemy positions by our fighter planes and heavy bombers. Up until now there has not been any telephone liaison because an order came from the Field Defense HQ for the 2nd Platoon to evacuate after the 1st Platoon had completed preparations for firing from the hillside. Since early morning all individual field equipment was moved in groups of three in the direction of the new positions. This afternoon we are to evacuate. Still, only one gun has been taken (0600). Furthermore, the slope of the mountain is 35 degrees, and there aren't enough personnel to pull. I heard that not even one gun was pulled up. Above us, enemy planes kept watch. . . .

[I made] liaison with the Field Defense HQ: it seems we are to go to the 5th Squad's location (a searchlight), which is back of the Field Defense HQ. . . . At 0800 we received naval gunfire from one enemy cruiser. Two guns were fired, and the first shell fell in front of the 2nd Platoon. After that, I saw two shells hit the ground 150 meters southeast from me. I was scared to death. We made an advance path, which has already been reconnoitered by Lance Corporal Hara. I stooped over to take a smoke when the shells came. After that, the shelling continued for about two hours. . . . I suppose there will be another naval shelling tonight. If there were only some of our air forces there, the warships would soon be put out of action. When 1000 rolled around, friendly planes did not appear, as was expected.

After 1000, the shelling was from three ships. . . . We are supposed to withdraw to the 1st Platoon's position and take cover in completed shelters tonight. The shelling is directed towards the Field Defense HQ, the airfield and the area near the piers. According to what Probationary Officer Takagi told me, a report has been received by the *Nanto* Detachment that the enemy was affecting simultaneous landings at Lae, New Guinea and Arundel. The telegraph on the 30th was interfered with, and we could not reach the 8th Area Army.[15] And, because the 8th Area Army had mustered its entire force and there were enemy warships at Arundel, Zero planes could only be sent periodically for scouting over New Georgia. . . . On the 2nd, we heard that the 8th Area Army has reinforced the nearby Army and Navy units to full strength and has already turned the offensive. Don't the super-dreadnoughts, *Yamato* and *Musashi*, ever move?[16] New Guinea and New Georgia are both strategic fronts; New Georgia is the southernmost front. I wonder what sort of operations will be carried out. . . .

The heavy naval shelling continues. At 1320, I thought an order would come when I heard what I thought was the shelling of several naval ships: it turned out to be friendly bombers. The roar was terrific. After 60-70 loud reports they appeared from out of calm clouds. They came from the north, but I am sure they were friendly because the reports came from those who watch from the shore. To those who are in position without binoculars, these were identified as Boeing. I wonder how they felt about these supposedly "thirty Boeings with fighter planes" until they were informed they were friendly. What they thought to be an enemy formation were new model heavy bombers. Those were similar to Boeings and were really large.[17] The bombing from the planes came twice and though I couldn't see them, there must have been two formations. . . .

July 3: Last night, the 1st Platoon moved. The positions are near the airfield. About 2000 there was some artillery fire, but as a whole it was a quiet night. We dispersed to various shelters and I got quite a bit of sleep. That was the size of the situation and there was no watch during the night. I figure on a withdrawal tomorrow.

Friendly fleet units are assembling at Shortland. At North Munda, 2,000 infantrymen are opposing the enemy. These are Kolombangara infantrymen. On the 27th, 1,300 new men landed on Kolombangara. I guess we will not get any aid from our own naval shelling because last night they were ordered to land in the vicinity of Arundel. Ever since 0400 this morning, enemy fighter planes have been overhead. Twenty bombers that I have never seen before came in from the east and went to the west. . . . The present strength of the 2nd Platoon is 38 men. They are under their own command, and they are suicide troops. Their mission is anti-tank fire. . . . [18]

After about 1000, four naval ships' turret guns opened fire twice, making it eight rounds fired. Even from the turrets it must have been eight guns. . . . The enemy planes have doubled in number. About 20–30 planes flew everywhere in a straight-line formation, like potatoes in a row. The planes are in the air from Rendova Island to Munda, flying about as though it was their own base. . . . What kind of an operation could our troops be planning? Everything is as the enemy wishes it. Today, again no friendly planes appeared. Not even a boat came. Since the enemy landed, four days have passed, and it must be about time they have completed their positions and general preparations.

If we are going to fight, now is the time—come and get us. I pray that our movements begin an hour sooner or even a day sooner. If it were now, we could beat them. However, if they have already landed, it would be useless because we are outnumbered 10-to-1, and our material and provisions are limited. If they would only sacrifice a little and pound them on Rendova with the air force and naval shelling, it would be all right. If we were then to lose, then it could not be helped. But the way things are going right now, we aren't doing what we could do. We're just waiting to be struck by the enemy. . . .

I heard the enemy has landed on the east side of North Munda. An infantryman swam back from Rendova and reported that the enemy were Australians and natives. He also said that when we attack, they cry and run away. The enemy artillery barrage gradually increased. The sergeant said that the 4th is Independence Day for America; consequently, they were more than likely to do something. Friendly planes again never appeared.

July 4: At 1800 last evening, we received a report that the enemy is on the nearest island about 1,000 meters south of our positions, so we fired with our 25mm naval guns[19] with instantaneous fuzes [*sic*]. The guns were located 300 meters north of our positions. The shells passed over the positions. We cautioned everyone because they were instantaneous fuzes. The enemy did not return the fire. We couldn't tell whether they were there or not. The enemy artillery fire from Rendova ceased about 1700. At 2000, they fired several rounds, but it didn't amount to much.

Last night it rained heavily, and it was miserable in the shelters. Covering my head and crouching, I slept in the corner of the shelter. It was a big storm, and there was terrific thunder from the direction of Rendova, but it was better than being shelled. Everyone got soaking wet, but nobody said a word. Sleeping on the ground at night and cooling the stomach caused everyone to get diarrhea. We kind of sized up the healthy men, but there were some like Corporal Nishimura, who had developed a fever of 42 degrees Celsius [106 degrees Fahrenheit]. Last night, we got wet, too, and I believe it is because of this that our bodies are filthy and our buttocks seem like they were affected by poison oak. It affects our arms and legs. . . .

Early this morning, the artillery ammunition train was evacuated. The 1st Platoon's vehicles could not move one way or the other. The 2nd Platoon was left in the front lines for the first time, but the second movement of the 1st Platoon was greatly rejoiced over. It makes it bad for the subordinates because the Field Defense HQ takes to flight easily. Just look at the naval AA pom-pom unit: they haven't moved from their former positions yet. Consolidated seaplanes,[20] about 20-30 in number, are flying low at an altitude of 200 meters. They must be keeping a perfect liaison with the artillery. The Field Defense HQ must have been ordered back to their former positions, to defend to the last, because friendly movements have been reported. That movement must be the shipment of 3,000 Navy[21] men to Munda today or tomorrow. There is a rumor that a large fleet unit is going to surround Rendova. They also say that the entire Naval Air Force is going to be sent in this direction. Unless they actually do this, things are hopeless. . . .

1200: Last night, we did not sleep a bit. The sergeant and I ate in the shelter, and we were talking of landing of 3,000 infantrymen tomorrow night, when suddenly the descent of a shell interrupted us. Just like yesterday, they dropped 40-50 giant bombs on the lines 100 meters north of us. I asked the lookout about the bombing, and he said that because of the low-hanging clouds they couldn't see us. I could see the Zeroes chasing the

Curtisses. Suddenly, a bomber formation of about eighteen planes appeared from the south.

I thought we were going to get it again, but they turned out to be friendly. After a short time, I heard 40–50 explosions from the direction of Rendova. Fighter planes still patrol the skies. During the noon bombing, an anti-personnel bomb fell on the middle section of the former 3rd and 4th positions and one fell seven meters to the rear of my emplacement. The canvas shelters of the 4th and all the platoon leaders were destroyed. All the equipment of the 5th Squad (the sick squad), which had already returned, was scattered. The company commander, Probational Officer Takagi, and all his subordinates were, as before, the last platoon which has been under the command of the 41st Battalion. With the guns out of action, it is really bitter. Out of our 16 medium attack planes,[22] six were shot down by Curtiss planes.

July 5: Last night's report [indicated] that an enemy force of 500 had landed at North Munda, just east of Aidawa [the Japanese name for the Barike River, the mouth of which emptied into Roviana Lagoon some two miles east of Munda Point], and was being engaged by one company of our troops. We counter-attacked against the small island midway between here and Rendova last night. Our Marines [*rikusentai*][23] have completed occupation of it.

Our Army, Navy and Air Force operations in this area are progressing well. The CO placed the 1st Platoon under the command of the 41st Battalion. The 2nd Platoon were brought to their present positions for anti-tank firing. The main force was mustered at the former positions. When worst comes to worst, the 3rd Platoon is to withdraw with the main force to the Yoshiba Unit, which is the artillery AA pom-pom unit and is located to the rear of the Field Defense HQ. This is to be the very last line of resistance for the Company.

Sometime last night Kolombangara was shelled by naval fire. It is directly north of here. They shelled for perhaps thirteen minutes. For awhile, I thought they were coming this direction, but because of the presence of enemy and friendly submarines or something, they never came. Last night, because of the poor visibility, both sides ceased firing. They don't fire howitzers after dark because the flame gives away their position. Last night, a friendly seaplane scooted around for about ten minutes and dropped one bomb on Rendova as it went away. Aside from the rain and the naval shelling on Kolombangara, everything was normal.

We couldn't go out in the open all day because of the heavy barrage. I'm lying in the air raid shelter with a wet blanket wrapped around me, after having the rain beat down on me day after day. About 1400, they were saying that a formation had come, so I got out of the shelter. I was in my own little shelter and after waiting a little while, it didn't seem like they were coming. I got out of the shelter for the second time to telephone the airfield when there was a terrific explosion. I thought it was beyond the airfield but found out that it was fifty meters away from my position. I neither boil water nor cook my meals. I didn't even go to receive my provisions. I would like our planes to get control of the skies. Right now, they are shelling to the rear of the airfield near the piers, our former positions located south of the jungle and, at the front, the Field Defense HQ, the infantry lines the positions, the islands to the south and the east line. That is about the size of the shelling. It must be because of the good camouflage, I guess, that our positions have not been determined yet.

July 6: I felt like crying last night, in the midst of all the rain and the condition I was in. There is a little mountain artillery fire[24] from our side. We could hear the sound of the enemy's boats but aside from that, everything was normal. . . . At 0500, there was the sound of bombs bursting around North Munda. This more than likely is the landing of friendly troops and of our transports being attacked. There was the sound of several bomb explosions in one or two different places. After about 0630, the shelling from the enemy started. The giant shells whistled over our heads and passed on. I prayed that their range wouldn't shorten.

Because of the rain, day after day, and the lack of time for things to dry out, the moldy, sharp odor is terrific. Everything is soaking wet. The artillery shelling becomes more and more violent. The shells burst 4-5 meters away from the air defense unit. Fortunately, they did not receive a direct hit, but some burst on the former positions. Arima, who was sleeping in the message center tent because of illness, had fallen on his side but was not hurt. They say that he couldn't see for awhile, and he lost his senses momentarily. It is really frightening because they fire 6-9 rounds at a time, as if it were an all-out attack. All of the men at the former positions withdrew to the Field Defense HQ because of this.

1st Class Private Tagawa relieved 1st Class Private Yasue (6th Squad) because of illness (malaria). Private Ota is an orderly for the platoon leader at our present position because Iwasato is sick. He used to live with his mother, who is his only living relative. He had supported her by working at a factory. Because he was called up, his 64-year-old mother had to go to work. If they only knew back there that he had come to the front, possibly some help would come from the factory, but he never knew where he would land, and he finally came here. When they talk of conditions back home, they say he turns to tears. I feel sorry for him.

July 7: The shelling stopped last night. There were no enemy planes either. I came out and, for the first time in some time, I felt like a human being. After it got dark, the quarter moon was to my west at the height of 20 degrees. First it dropped and then it appeared overhead. If this moon gets round, I bet that the battle will also get more violent. Last night, reinforcements landed from Kolombangara. In order to cover this, the flat-trajectory guns, mountain artillery and searchlights also cooperated. The enemy landed on a small island, which covers Munda, so we had to fire still more.

The enemy has brought searchlights, AA guns and pom-poms[25] with him. ... Yesterday, according to the Field Defense HQ's orders, we brought up artillery ammunition and we were supposed to shell the enemy artillery positions, but it was called off. If we were to do this kind of thing at night, one can never tell what sort of a shelling we would receive because they can see everything from the hills of Rendova. I prayed that the shells wouldn't fit well, but they did. I'm almost positive now that they'll come to order us to fire.

Several enemy fighters were circling around early this morning. We certainly must not have control of the skies. Our forces must still be mustering warships and transports. They must be using our air force for that purpose. This morning's shelling commenced at 0800. I went about unconcerned, lying down when some shells burst 30-40 meters away from me, which caused me to jump out of my breeches. One landed to my right, and then six or seven more came. They must be firing like the dickens. Sometimes, they all come at once. I don't exactly appreciate this shelling. ...

Sergeant Major Ishirane, who had gone to Shortland, returned to this unit last night. He brought some stationery and cigarettes, which he had received from the Army CO. 2nd Platoon Lieutenant Obazaki (35), who was supposed to take up duties here, also arrived. ...

During the afternoon, a transport laden with AA guns and pom-poms entered Rendova. During the evening, our seaplanes bombed the enemy submarine[26] base and Rendova. I could see the firing of the enemy AA guns and their searchlights well. From that action, I judge that there must be six or eight guns.[27]

Three thousand men have already landed on Kolombangara. Only 800 men landed at Munda last night because of the shortage of boats. We should have been reinforced as time goes by. The enemy also landed south of North Munda at two different points, and right now, our forces are attacking and pursuing the enemy.

July 8: About 0800, artillery fire started. They dropped several rounds at different points. Some were close to our positions. Our company HQ right now is located at the foot of the mountain where the former Field Defense HQ was situated. No one wants to go there because of the shelling. Superior Private Ito from the 4th and Superior Private Sakai from the 5th are really bold. They don't hesitate about going, and I think this is worth writing about. Last evening, I received my first and possibly last mail from home. The letter from the folks was almost 20 pages long, and the address on the newspapers was written with large letters by my father. . . . It appeared that they haven't received my letters yet and are somewhat doubtful as to whether I'm still alive or not. They used the address that I used when I sent the money order from Rabaul. They learned from Lance Corporal Mori that I was on New Georgia. They will really worry if the news of the enemy landing on New Georgia is announced in the newspapers.

Father repeated in his letter that I must fight to the last as an honorable warrior. I will fight to the last, always for the Emperor. I will show them that we will fight to the last. March 6: "There is nothing quite so doubtful as to whether life or death be with one, yet we write at random like searching and traversing a battlefield." March 31: "Pray for cherished glory," even though it be for my aged father, as if revived, again wrote on April 12: "Even though your soul should remain in the South Sea Islands, follow the will of Heaven."

Hardly any correspondence of the entire company was more than my own. The men came up and said, "Sir, it really turned out to be a great mistake to send the Sergeant Major to Shortland, since it turned out to be all for your good." Everyone laughed. It's all because of my father's thoughtfulness. . . .

July 9: The enemy's attack has started. The artillery barrage started at 0200. They increased their tracer shells quite a bit. As time went on, they began firing with great many flat trajectory guns similar to pom-poms[28] from the nearby islands to the south and from their base at Rendova. . . . There were great numbers of incendiary shells, which made it like daytime. However, the tracer shells went overhead, and the small shells did not hit within the positions. At 0500, the firing ceased. There are places where the Army has medium artillery positions. There are two positions at the extreme northeast and west sections on Rendova and the small islands lying between. They have done lots of shelling, but the positions are normal. In this shelling, 2nd Lieutenant Imura, a graduate of Naseda University who was with us at Kolombangara and attached to the searchlight headquarters battalion, and one other soldier were killed by a direct hit. Many officers of my immediate acquaintance were dying right along. When the shelling ceased, three Zero planes came over to reconnoiter and then returned. At 0730, about fifty Grummans, which were carrier-based, came over and dropped large bombs in various areas. Since our positions could be clearly seen from Rendova, we could not fire against the tanks. I was really fed up when the order came from the Field Defense HQ to fire. A demolition shell landed thirty meters from our positions, but there were no casualties.

The 2nd Platoon is only at the first line of defense. The 1st Platoon is [now] under our command. The CO began to feel sympathy towards the men. [He] couldn't figure out any way to fire that wasn't to our disadvantage. After he laughingly said, "I would like to die now after seeing the action of our troops," he continued by saying that he would leave all the decisions up to the platoon leaders. He showed a sense of sympathy and never came out with an order to fire.

If our operations would only start, I would fire again and again, even though our last positions would be exposed and we in turn would be fired upon. As it is now, we are being fired upon, and we have not returned fire. Enemy planes are constantly overhead, so I can't even take a step outside of our shelters. If we were to fire now, they would concentrate their fire on us, and our emplacements would be leveled. And then all of us would be annihilated together as our belief in our invincibility would go. We shall fight. Sure, we will fight. Right now, living is more important. In the last stages of this battle, if we can stop the tanks from coming in from the south, then we can die laughing.

The life in caves goes on and on. The relentless evening shells fall around me, and sometimes they whistle over us to fly somewhere distant. I had blankets spread in the hole and lay there with my shorts on, as there was no time to take them off. . . .

July 10: Last evening, two friendly seaplanes with marker lights on either side came over for reconnaissance, and they dropped a bomb apiece. They were caught in three searchlights and were fired at with great ferocity. . . . There was naval shelling going on towards Kolombangara. I heard that the attack on Munda last night was also the cause of heavy naval shelling.[29] Artillery shelling started at 0300. The shelling was almost twice as furious as the previous one. At 0630, one Curtiss flew over at the altitude of 200 meters to reconnoiter in various areas. It must be attempting to expose our positions because the firing is terrific. Several bombs were dropped. One fell at the entrance of the communications trench, but fortunately, it did not explode. Our shelter is considerably shaken, but only because that bomb did not explode can we say that we are still alive. Superior Privates Ito and Yagi, who were in the shelter, hit the ground as their breath was taken away. The 4th Squad leader worked to save two men in the midst of shelling. The position already has received over one hundred or more close hits. Those land artillery men are firing 7-8 rounds at a time.

At 0710, from out of the white clouds, about one hundred carrier-based Grummans suddenly appeared. They dropped large bombs in various areas. Two of them hit close by. Because of the action from the northwest and to the south, we couldn't hear ourselves talk. As yet, our units are intact. According to reports, the results of this bombing were nil. Our lines of communications were disrupted. Two maintenance men, who spent until 1030 repairing lines that were out in ten different places, returned. I admire these maintenance men who go out to do this suicidal work. My, but the shelling is fierce. I would think that the explosives would have some effect, but aside from a little scare, the results have been nil.

But still, if one of them were to hit our shelter, we're goners. All of the personnel, wearing steel helmets within the shelters, waited quietly for action on our part. The heat in the shelter was like that of a cellar, and an unpleasant odor drifted about. . . . It is suicidal to go to the latrine. I put on my helmet and after I had made complete preparations, I took off for the bomb crater, which was in front of me. While I was defecating, six or seven shells fell, so I took off and came back. Direct hits are bursting in the communications unit's and the 4th Mess's trenches. All of our positions are being aimed at. Several shells are being dropped on our positions today.

At 1530, the shelling ceased. Our forces have not attained a thing, while the enemy has finally become active. The artillery shelling's accuracy has become a real thing. We never can tell when we are to die. Oh, God! I would like to die after seeing the action of our invincible Imperial forces. After looking at a dud, I can see that the enemy's artillery is 150mm.[30] Today's shelling is continuous. The enemy's firepower is becoming more and more violent. . . .

July 11—Report: The 13th Infantry Regiment, which was scheduled to land last night, did so safely. Right now, they are assembling at Bairoko Harbor. The battle situation is that we are about to take the initiative. At 0740, 45 carrier-based Grummans appeared. Aside from a close hit, all of the rest of the bombs were dropped elsewhere. Everywhere, things are normal. During the afternoon for about 2 1/2 hours, concentrated fire rained on us. About 70-80 rounds of land shells were fired at us with great violence. The enemy has fired at least 2,000 rounds today. Some hit within five meters of my shelter. At this rate, day after tomorrow, I'll be a goner. The enemy is firing about twenty rounds at a time. Regardless of what shelter I may be in, at the present rate, it will be of no avail. Our last important mission is that of [serving as] tank destroyers. One of our precious guns was lost in today's bombing. . . .

July 12: [During the last] evening, I was watching the shelling, and there were some that fell within three meters of the positions. It is really a mystery why there have not been any personnel losses up until now. Right now, I am lying on my side, facing in the direction of Rendova, with the acting operator, 1st Class Private Tomioka, but today or sometime tomorrow I guess we'll be hit. If our last gun were to be destroyed, then our company would become a labor outfit.

From about 1030, we received naval shelling for approximately an hour. Incendiary and tracer shells struck the jungle beyond the airfield heavily. Fortunately, very few hit our positions. I imagine they fired forty to fifty rounds at us. The screeching noise continued as the shells hit. The evening heavens rumbled.

Since our mission is that of a tank destroyer unit, we couldn't very well stay hidden and not go out of the seacoast area. We went out to take a peep at the frontal waters to the south several times. Fortunately, there were no tanks. They must be concealing the entering of ships, which are to the front and the rear of the naval shelling because they are firing quite heavily from their artillery positions. When the shelling completely ceased, we were on the verge of collapse from fatigue and lack of sleep.

Planes have been flying around since early morning. From about 0300, the artillery shelling began with a barrage of 50 rounds at a time. They are firing in all directions from their positions. I suppose there will be another concentration of fire around noontime. Last evening, medium attack planes and a scout seaplane bombed Rendova. My, the great number of AA guns and pom-poms; they've got five searchlights already![31]

At 0700, about 40 Douglas bombers appeared and effected a general bombing. After about 0850, we had a concentration of fire on our positions. The 4th Squad's gun was knocked out. One burst south and to one side of our shelter, and this made several marks on the aiming apparatus and the barrel. The ammunition was set afire. Demolition shells must be good only for things above the level of the ground because, queer as it may seem, the personnel are still intact. This winds up things for this 3rd Platoon leader, with the loss of three guns. Losing the guns puts a sense of guilt on my part, yet the personnel is intact. There is nothing for us to do but to feel fortunate in the midst of all the bad luck. . . . Our company is without a single gun now. From now on, we are a labor company.

July 13: All the personnel assembled at the foot of the mountain where the Field Defense HQ was located, in the midst of the shelling. We assembled in the vicinity of the 41st Battalion after having come through the dark jungle and over muddy paths, while we were harassed by the shelling. The 1st Platoon and the 6th Platoon were attached to the 41st Battalion. We dug dugouts in the empty area. After getting wet from the evening dew, we lay down. The distance we traveled really was hard going, so much that it hardly can be expressed in so many words.

Sergeant Takagi died last night in the naval shelling. The dead already amounted to six or seven men. Lance Corporal Ito and four men, who were handling rations, are missing. At 0330, about 50 carrier-based Grummans effected a bombing, concentrating on the jungle lying between the hills. There were several close hits. There was a terrific sound of explosions in the jungle and the mountains. . . .

I must say that there is close cooperation between their air, land and naval forces. Our forces have not carried out a large-scale bombing; they haven't shelled Rendova with a single battleship, nor have they given the infantry or the Army any heavy artillery pieces.

What do you call this? How could such action be called modern war? I keenly feel the poor liaison of the Japanese forces and the weakness of our military strength. My! This is really disheartening. We haven't been fighting, merely dying in the midst of bombs and shelling.

However, the Japanese forces couldn't let the enemy have his own way; we must look forward with rich expectations that something will be done. Probationary Officer Oura has been ordered to be the rifle platoon leader. Probationary Officer Takagi has been ordered to be the CO of the 41st Battalion. Now we are to provide defense and security against the enemy, who is penetrating into the area of North Munda. The organization is now 27 men and a company of three squads. The platoon leader is at the fixed position of the 1st Squad, and 2nd and 3rd Squads are to be reserves. We are to make it impossible for an advance and attack to be made from any direction. We are to stop the enemy, hitting his front and flank.

July 14: . . . The explosion of the shells during the night was terrific. Several enemy planes came over early this morning and circled at a low altitude to our rear. After every reconnoitering, the shelling from the artillery positions would follow. We are doing our best camouflaging right

now. Evidently, we haven't been exposed because the shells are landing 300 meters to our left and right. . . . The sick, with 2nd Lieutenant
Hattori, are to return from the 41st Battalion sometime today. I am supposed to be in charge of them, and they are to be the 2nd Platoon. I am also
to be in command of the Rifle Platoon. . . .

On our way, we rested at Battalion Headquarters for a little while when
the order came for us to wait at the former position, so we returned. Shells
were falling, and there were patients being carried in on stretchers while
fighter planes hovered over us in plain daylight. It was so bad, I can't go on
talking about it. . . .

At 1100, the order came for Probationary Officer Oura and 6 men to go
to the east lookout post, another new position for the Field Defense HQ;
2nd Lieutenant Imura was killed and a total of four wounded today. I immediately departed in the rain, and I stumbled time and time again while
going through the jungle. On my way, I stopped at the Field Defense HQ
and received orders from the CO. I arrived safely at 1400. I took command
of 12 men, including the medical unit. As usual, the shelling was concentrated on the pom-pom gun positions. The sounds of the explosions and
the concussion was terrific. I lay down in the canvas shelter unconcerned.

July 15: I picked Lance Corporal Sugiyama, Wakita, Shimura, Muramatsu,
and Ota, the best six men. Tomorrow, Corporal Takahashi and his five men
will come and then we will have a personnel strength of 12 men. None of
last night's continuous shelling hit near our canvas shelters, but several
were directed at the base of the Field Defense HQ, the anti-tank positions,
our future positions, and the pom-pom positions. From today, we are going
to start installing a 10cm gun. This east lookout post is the eye of all the
forces in Munda and consequently the main object to be fired upon.

I set down some strict regulations and made security command. I set up
the AA binoculars and observed the enemy positions. The U.S. flag could be
seen fluttering on the PT boats. A destroyer, which had been camouflaged,
was at anchor. You could call it a war movie or perhaps a Newsweek movie
[the Japanese equivalent of Movietone News or Paramount newsreels]. At
any rate, it is interesting to an outsider. The movement of the large boats
and the bursting of shells looked as if you could almost grab them in your
hands. . . .

This morning's shelling was a shelling of all shellings. By 0700, they had
already fired 1,000 rounds into the vicinity of the Kawai Detachment's
positions. At 1000, as six or seven of us were sitting outside the dugout,
which was built for protection from naval shelling, two shells struck the

top of a tree. All of us hit the ground, but Lance Corporal Sugiyama was struck. I believe it will take him about a month and a half to recover. . . .

We received a report at 1200 that the entire enemy air force had departed from Guadalcanal to bomb Munda. Today, ten destroyers entered port. The LSTs and large boats are very active. The small island to our front is bare now from this morning's bombing. The shells are hitting close by right now, so we can't go outside. This is disgusting when we have no tent. The offending odor of perspiration in the dugout is unbearable. The place where we stand guard has already become the death ground of two men. No one back home would ever think that we are [living in a] crater and looking round. . . . It is really smelly. They said that they hadn't found the two legs of the men yet. Four-motored Consolidated bombers[32] are flying around at low altitude. I can see plainly through my AA binoculars two men looking this way from the window, which is to the rear of the insignia. There is no intermission in the firing of the artillery. . . .

July 17: I had to lie down inside the narrow dugout because the close hits were bursting in great numbers. It sure is hot. Last night, Private First Class Yama Ora of the medical unit was dispatched to the east lookout post. On account of a lance corporal being evacuated to the medical unit, the present strength is CO and 13 men.

Report: The control of the sky and sea belongs to the enemy. Boats are moving in great numbers. . . . The enemy is becoming stronger and stronger, and they are landing on almost every island that surrounds Munda. From the east lookout post, we can hear the shooting and orders coming from a spring that is to our left front. It seems that our force is concentrating its entire strength to capture the enemy artillery post at Aidawa. The area south of the east lookout post will become the front line. If that is the case, the enemy on the island to the south would probably attempt a landing. This artillery position is decisively holding back movements of our infantry. The east lookout post is also being shelled fiercely on account of the artillery at Aidawa, and the communications lines are being blown to pieces. We have no help from the air or sea. . . .

From 1500, the 41st Battalion fired (ranging fire) their AA guns against the artillery positions at Roviana for about one hour. I was appointed as the observer. One shell made a direct hit, but only after many unsuccessful efforts. . . .

July 18: It rained heavily last night. The sound of explosions of the enemy shells is terrific. The movements of the boats are tremendous. Anticipating a forced landing by the enemy between tonight and dawn, we guarded more closely. I held the AA binoculars from 0300 to 0630, when it was pretty certain that it was safe. I could not sleep on account of the rain and telephone calls that came from Field Defense HQ and the 41st Battalion, and my fatigue mounted. I inquired about the shell that burst nearby this morning. . . .

I hear that the enemy is increasingly concentrating his troops on Guadalcanal for a new offensive. It is most distressing. However, we must not complain because our navy and our air force might be striking at Guadalcanal. If we can only crush Guadalcanal, the enemy at Rendova will be automatically annihilated.

General Imamura[33] is at Rabaul. It is impossible for him to operate at the front lines. It is probable, as the [enemy's] troops are distributed between Guadalcanal and New Georgia, that we are going to attack simultaneously. They say that Port Moresby[34] might fall at the end of this month. I also heard that the [enemy's] airport at Guadalcanal was severely damaged. I am sure that the enemy planes flying overhead have decreased. . . . The shelling is really dangerous; however, we will fight until the end.

July 19: Last night's shelling was terrific. The road that runs to the rear of the east side of the Field Defense HQ is the infantry's route of advance. The enemy appears to have observed this by air and are concentrating their fire in this sector. This concentration of fire is just over our dugout. Since it has only one entrance, the air is stuffy, and the sounds of the explosions cause ringing in our ears. There were explosions of several shells 15cm in diameter and 70cm long.[35] It is really more than I can bear. The men were really scared, and they all ran into my dugout. I had to take them out mercilessly and assign them to other dugouts. There were nine men in the dugout, and if it were to receive a direct hit, the entire personnel would be buried alive, so I had to take them out. It was really hot inside the dugout. . . .

July 20: At 1800, there were two reports of rifle fire 60-70 meters away in the direction of the Field Defense HQ. When I inquired, they said they would investigate it. About an hour later, a report came in that a soldier was shot and wounded by an enemy patrol when he had gone to a pom-pom position 60-70 meters away to get some water. They must have come in from the vicinity of the east lookout post. Strict guard was thereafter posted. I woke everyone up and had them keep their rifles handy at their bedside. One hour later, two rifle shots were heard again below the Field Defense HQ. Figuring that the enemy had drawn all the men from below, we came up and planned to rain more bullets on them as they crept up. After an hour had elapsed, a report came in that the enemy had attacked the spring position of the *Nanto* Detachment. The entire unit took up positions to fight when the report came in that the shot was only an explosion from a fire ignited by the wireless set. . . . During the early morning, the entrance to the Field Defense HQ (present east lookout post) was camouflaged. It was a miserable night. The violence of the artillery fire continued. 150mm shells exploded near the summit of our east lookout post without cessation.

According to a report, our infantry has completely encircled the enemy at Aidawa and have cut off his ammo supplies. Between ten and twenty trucks were reported to have been destroyed. A general offensive is to start within a few days. I was thinking that the enemy might withdraw to Rendova, but instead, they are reinforcing here. They are transporting guns and equipment to Aidawa on large boats. The artillery position at Aidawa is still intact.

At 1400, some twenty carrier-based bombers came over and dropped a string of huge bombs from the vicinity of the east lookout post into the jungle. Compared to artillery shelling, it is much louder. The concussion is terrific. The Navy AA gun below the east lookout post has already been fired upon with about 1,000 artillery shells, but it is still firing at the bombers. It's a wonder they are still living. It is so hard to believe that they can endure so long. They are showing us vividly the spirit of the Imperial Navy. . . .

July 21: All night long, there were the reports of small arms and artillery firing. I heard two wild dogs barking in the distance; I wonder what they could be eating. Huge shells are bursting at the base of the east lookout post with great violence. Isn't there any other place for them to fire at? In the midst of all the noise, I still slept well. All of this must be because of my former experiences. I have come to a point where I have developed a belief that I will not be struck by a shell. The first thing I'm grateful for is my well-being and three meals a day, each consisting of a bowl and a half of rice. All three meals are very appetizing. My health seems to give me a continuous source of vigor. To be able to eat a heavy meal during the rain of continuous shells is one thing I have looked forward to.

It must have been because a Consolidated[36] made a low-level reconnaissance this morning when we were eating and our shadows must have been detected. Nevertheless, as a result, at 0800 we received concentrated shellings of several hundred rounds from Aidawa. The second tent was thrown helter-skelter, and the first tent received a large hole. The siren shed and the tent where the CO had been staying were destroyed. The lower dugout received a direct hit, but there were no casualties. The huge trees, which had stood for so many years, and others were knocked down. Consequently, there was hardly any vegetation to be seen in the direction of the east lookout post. I could hear the whistling of three near hits, which landed about three to four meters from my own dugout. I laid flat along the edge of the dugout for about 20 minutes, thinking that this was our end. But there were no casualties among the men. . . .

July 22: [It] appears that the constant increase of AA guns over Rendova has already made it difficult for planes. The number of shells that their AA guns and ours shoot is quite different. It really is a barrage, and they make it so you can't get in. The difference between the enemy's firing and ours is that their searchlight units and guns work separately. Even if our planes do not get in the rays of the searchlights, several thousands [of shells] set up a barrage around the area.

At 0800, carrier-based bombers flew over and bombed several places. More of the bombing was on the troops in the rear, and they strafed them heavily. I imagine the rear-area troops are laying low. To the south of the east lookout post, our Navy pom-poms are firing away, so it is a little dangerous, but aside from that, everything is fine. If I am to die, there is nothing I can do about it, so I just lay in my dugout, smoking a cigarette and listening to the wild American-made music of "rat-tat-tat" and "boom-boom-boom."

Just think: I haven't washed my body or my face nor have I brushed my teeth for a month already. One of my upper front teeth has been broken off. My body smells like that of a wild dog from not washing.

At 1400, I received such a fierce shelling that I finally had to dispatch Corporal Takahashi to ask Captain Kobayashi as to our future dispositions. They must have gone crazy in the Aidawa area because they really are shelling there for all they are worth. From the way it sounds, it seems like a wild man beating a drum. Since last night, Superior Private Makita has been with me in my dugout. They must have fired several hundred rounds while we both lay flat on the edge of the dugout. We were prepared for our last, while we kept thinking which shell would get us. I used a life preserver for a pillow and a blanket to cover myself. My ears rang as a shell burst one meter to the left and in front of the guard post, and at the same time, I was covered with coral. The wood in my dugout gave way about 30 centimeters away from me. I thought that I was really a goner this time, but I was saved. It's just one barrage after another, and I cannot move. Huge trees come tumbling down with a crash. The guard posts on Rendova and Roviana, which could just be seen previously, were now openly exposed.

We are receiving concentrated fire over the summit, so there is no doubt that we are being aimed at. Above us, a float observation plane flew about at a low altitude. We're not taking any camouflage measures against enemy land or aerial observation right now. Regardless of whether we are to complete our mission in this way and await death, or move into the hills, in either case it would result in a trap for us.

Only by staying in the dugout can I say that I'm still alive. The drum in front of the dugout is full of holes. My dugout is two meters south of the front and left side of the guard post. A piece of shrapnel hit my back, and for awhile, I thought I was finished. Mysteriously, there were no deaths. From 1330, concentrated fire was again directed at the east lookout post pom-poms and at the roads on the lower left of the post. Since the guard post was exposed, we had to do away with a standing guard. We're just staying out and leaving everything open to the enemy. Oh, friendly forces! Please come to our aid! Show them the might of the Japanese Army.

July 23—Battle Situation: Nothing aside from annihilation. No cooperation from the Navy. If I were to compare the complete cooperation of the enemy, it would be like the war of a child and an adult. Our mountain artillery positions were knocked to pieces by enemy tanks. We are encircled, so they say, and about to be overrun. Consequently, all we can do is to guard our present positions. . . .

As things are now, even if our air and naval forces start a battle, we could not regain the lost ground. Great numbers of enemy planes are constantly up in the sky. In front of the island, camouflaged destroyers and PT boats swarm in and out. What in the world could our forces at Rabaul or the staff of the grand Imperial Headquarters be doing? Where have our air forces and battleships gone? Are there any, or aren't there any? Are we to lose? Why don't they start some operations? We are positively fighting to win, but we have no weapons. We stand with rifles and bayonets to meet the enemy's aircraft, battleships and medium artillery. To be told we must win is absolutely beyond reason.

The Japanese Army is still depending on the hand-to-hand fighting of the Meiji era, while the enemy is using highly developed scientific weapons. Thinking it over, however, this poorly armed force of ours has not been overcome, and we are still guarding this island, so it is something worthy of comment. But this is no time for praise. More than likely, they have something in the rear. If the air and naval forces don't move, this island will soon be taken. If we, as well as the enemy, were to fight to the end with all available weapons that each possess, then I would be willing to give up, whether we win, lose, be injured or be killed.

But in a war like this, where we are like a baby's neck in the hands of an adult, even if I die, it will be a hateful death. How regretful! My most regretful thought is my grudge towards the forces in the rear and my increasing hatred towards the Operational Staff.

In the rear, they think that it is all for the benefit of our country. In short, as present conditions are, it is a defeat. However, a Japanese officer will always believe, until the very last, that there will be movements of our air and naval forces....

There are signs that I am contracting malaria again.

The July 23 entry was Toshihiro Oura's last diary entry. His fate is unknown; given the tiny number of prisoners taken during the entire New Georgia campaign and the sparse number of Japanese at this stage of the battle who escaped to Kolombangara and thence to safety, it appears unlikely that he survived.

Notes

PREFACE

1. Jack H. (Nick) McCall, Jr., *Pogiebait's War: A Son's Quest for His Father's Wartime Life* (Bloomington, IN: Xlibris Corp., 2000).

2. This particular outlook was not limited to the men of the Marines Corps' Ninth Defense Battalion. In various examples of the available literature, diaries, and letters from the Pacific War, one gets the sense that other American troops, marines, airmen, and sailors shared a similar measure of grudging respect for their Japanese adversaries—or at least their professionalism and formidable and fatalistic dedication—even if that was not expressed in so many words. For example, see Hale Bradt, *Wilber's War: An American Family's Journey through World War II*, 3 vols. (Salem, MA: Van Dorn Books, 2017), for an Army officer's viewpoint; James J. Fahey, *Pacific War Diary, 1942-1945* (New York: Houghton Mifflin, 1992), for a sailor's perspective; Abraham Felber (with Franklin S. Felber & William H. Bartsch), *The Old Breed of Marine: A World War II Diary* (Jefferson, NC: McFarland & Co., Inc., 2003), for a Marine senior NCO's viewpoints; and Eugene B. Sledge, *With the Old Breed at Peleliu and Okinawa* (New York: Oxford Univ. Press, 1990), for the views of an enlisted Marine.

INTRODUCTION

1. Henry Berry, *Semper Fi, Mac: Living Memories of the U.S. Marines in World War II* (New York: Quill/William Morrow, 1996), 36.

2. See, e.g., James LaPorta, "Honoring the Heroic Montford Pointers, The African American Marines the Corps Didn't Want," *Washington Post*, Aug. 1, 2016, online edition, https://www.washingtonpost.com/news/morning-mix/wp/2016/08/01/honoring-the-heroic-montford-pointers-the-african-american-marines-the-corps-didnt-want/?hpid=hp_hp-morning-mix_mm-story-c%3Ahomepage%2Fstory&utm_term=.96d4b048cfea.

3. See pages 208-9.

PROLOGUE

1. Personal reminiscences, Major Christopher S. Donner (January 1946), at p. 20 (author's collection), reprinted in Christopher S. Donner, *Pacific Time on Target: Memoirs of a Marine Artillery Officer, 1943-1945*, ed. Jack H. McCall, Jr. (Kent, OH: Kent State Univ. Press, 2012), 32.

2. D. C. Horton, *New Georgia: Pattern for Victory* (New York: Ballantine Books, 1971), 61.

3. Wiley Sword, *Embrace an Angry Wind: The Confederacy's Last Hurrah: Spring Hill, Franklin and Nashville* (New York: HarperCollins Publishers, 1992), 156-271; James Lee McDonough and Thomas L. Connelly, *Five Tragic Hours: The Battle of Franklin* (Knoxville: Univ. of Tennessee Press, 1983), 156-68.

4. Sam R. Watkins, *Co. Aytch: A Side Show of the Big Show* (New York: Collier Books, 1962), 232-33.

5. Sword, *Embrace an Angry Wind*, 268, 396-97; McDonough and Connelly, *Five Tragic Hours*, 172-77.

6. McDonough and Connelly, 158.

7. Lyn Sullivan, *Back Home in Williamson County* (Nashville, Tennessee: Williams Printing Co., 1986), 89.

8. James A. Crutchfield, "World War Heroes Were Williamson Countians," *The Tennessean* (Nashville), Nov. 7, 1996; Luke Lea, "The Attempt to Capture the Kaiser," ed. William T. Alderson, *Tenn. Hist. Quarterly* 20, no. 3 (Sept. 1961): 232-60; Jack H. McCall, Jr., "'Amazingly Indiscreet': The Plot to Capture Wilhelm II," *Journal of Military History* 73, no. 2 (April 2009): 449-69; Mary Louise Lea Tidwell, *Luke Lea of Tennessee* (Bowling Green, OH: Bowling Green State Univ. Popular Press, 1993), 105-24.

9. Taken from the names of citizens listed on a memorial plaque dedicated to the dead of World War I, Williamson County Courthouse, Franklin, Tennessee.

10. Ambrose W. "Red" Caldwell, *Secrets of a Diplomatic Courier-World War II* (Nashville, Tennessee: privately published, 1992), 4-6.

11. Personal papers, Jack H. McCall, Sr. See also Charles J. V. Murphy and David E. Scherman, "The Sinking of the Zamzam," *Life Magazine* 10, no. 25 (June 23, 1941): 21-27, 70-79, https://books.google.com/books?id=bU0E AAAAMBAJ&pg=PA21&source=gbs_toc_r&cad=2#v=onepage&q&f=false.

CHAPTER 1

1. *Nashville Banner* (Nashville, TN), Dec. 8, 1941.
2. Joseph Frank Marshall, *The "Fighting Ninth"—9th Defense Battalion*, ed. Christopher S. Donner (unpublished and undated manuscript, author's collection), 6-7.
3. After each training cycle's graduation parade (approximately 640 boots), the dress greens were returned to the Recruiting Depot's quartermaster for reissue to the next batch of graduates.
4. Maj. Charles D. Melson and Francis E. Chadwick, *The Ninth Marine Defense and AAA Battalions* (Paducah, Kentucky: Turner Publishing, 1990), 10.
5. Military time is expressed in terms of a twenty-four-hour clock: one minute after midnight begins the day at 0001, and the clock continues sequentially up to midnight (2400 hours).
6. David Slater, later of H&S Battery, Ninth Defense Battalion, recalled to the author one boot in his platoon who received a package from home containing, to his mortification, pajamas. This earned him the "shitbird from Yemassee" treatment, with the boot tearing his new pajamas to shreds while he sang and ran up and down the recruit company's street.
7. Leon Uris's semi-autobiographical novel *Battle Cry* featured a ditty sung by the men of Uris's fictionalized battalion, the 2/6 Marines or "Huxley's Whores", which paid tribute to the power of pogey bait over young Marines' minds: *"I'm a pogey bait Sixth Marine,/I can't keep my rifle clean,/I don't want a BAR,/I just want a candy bar."* Leon Uris, *Battle Cry* (New York: G. P. Putnam's Sons, 1953), 291.
8. See the glossary for a more complete listing of various terms and geographic names used throughout this book. True connoisseurs of Marine jargon should also note the glossaries provided in Henry Berry, *Semper Fi, Mac: Living Memories of the U.S. Marines in World War II* (New York: Quill/William Morrow, 1996), 35-37; Captain (Ret'd) Wilbur D. Jones, Jr., *Gyrene: The World War II United States Marine* (Shippensburg, PA: White Mane Books, 1998), 284-92; and William Manchester, *Goodbye, Darkness: A Memoir of the Pacific War* (Boston: Little, Brown, 1979), 121 for other terms frequently used by many Marines.
9. Frank Chadwick, who was one of the youngest members of the Ninth Defense Battalion, recalled another pet expression of his platoon's DI that "put the fear of God" in him:

I had just turned 16 when I joined the Corps and did not receive any mail from home. [*Author's note*: Chadwick had joined up without his family's permission or knowledge, as he had run away from home to enlist. To get proof that he was old enough to volunteer, Chadwick visited a bookie, who forged the necessary documents for $5.00.] The D.I. called me to his tent and questioned my age. I kept stating, "17, with parents' consent." He put his face into mine and informed me, in no uncertain terms, that if I received no mail by the next week, I had better give my soul to God as my ass belonged to him. He chewed me out in such a manner I could feel my body shaking. You can bet I very shortly had mail! After Boot Camp, I met him in the slop [chute]. He bought me a beer, called me a liar and kicked my ass out of the slop shop.

10. While vividly recalled by Jack and others in generalized terms, this particular dialogue is largely adapted from a sketch by Marine combat correspondent and Pulitzer Prize winner Jim Lucas of his Boot Camp experiences at Parris Island. Jim Lucas, "Boot Camp Days," in *The United States Marine Corps in World War II*, ed. S. E. Smith (New York: Random House, 1969), 78.

11. The failure to hit any part of a target was called "pulling a Maggie's Drawers" because a bright red flag (vaguely suggestive of women's panties and with the racy, if implicit, meaning that "Maggie's" suitor had "fired blanks" in making love to her—hence, the red color) was raised by the crew manning the targets in the butts to identify any boot who had failed so miserably.

12. Another former boot recalled that "strict control of ammunition, weapons handling and general movement of personnel was mandatory. The rules of safety were harshly enforced. If a man was caught behind the firing line with his bolt closed, he was required to remove the bolt from the piece, throw it on the ground and grind it into the dirt with his foot, repeat the performance with the rifle, then present them to the D.I. cleaned for inspection. All this to the tune of imaginative dissertations on his future as a Marine, his heritage and family background, and all facets of a fancied lineage." Marshall, *The "Fighting Ninth,"* 9.

13. Maj. Charles D. Melson, *Condition Red: Marine Defense Battalions in World War II: Marines in World War II Commemorative Series* (Washington, DC: History & Museums Division, Headquarters, US Marine Corps, 1996), 1-5; Melson and Chadwick, *The Ninth Marine Defense*, 9-10.

14. Eric Bergerud, *Touched With Fire: The Land War in the South Pacific* (New York: Viking, 1996), 152.

15. Melson, *Condition Red*, 5; Melson and Chadwick, *The Ninth Marine Defense*, 10-11; Headquarters, Ninth Defense Battalion, Fleet Marine Force, c/o Fleet Post Office San Francisco, "Report of Operations, Ninth Defense Battalion," May 2, 1944, 4 (hereafter cited as 9th Defense Operations Report).

16. Gordon Rottman and Mike Chappell, *Fighting Elite—US Marine Corps 1941-45*, ed. Lee Johnson (London: Osprey Military/Reed International, 1998), 11-12.

17. Melson, *Condition Red*, 4; Melson and Chadwick, *The Ninth Marine Defense*, 10.

18. Melson and Chadwick, 11; 9th Defense Operations Report, 4.

19. The fast-paced training regimen of these new lieutenants was summarized by one of their number, Henry H. Reichner Jr., later the CO of Battery A, Ninth Defense Battalion. Correspondence, Col. (Ret'd) Henry H. Reichner Jr. (June 10, 1998):

    > We all enlisted in the Corps with the expectation that we would be sent to "Officers' Candidate Class" at the conclusion of which we would become Second Lieutenants or, if flunked out, would be released to the civilian life and the draft or we could stay on as Enlisted Marines. We all arrived at Quantico around 20 February 1941 [and] went through a "ninety day" period of rigorous training.... I would say that the physical aspects were about the same without the type of treatment handed out by Parris Island DIs, although our enlisted overseers were pretty tough on us. Our barracks were more comfortable (if that is the word) than those at PI. At the end of May [1941], most of us were commissioned although quite a few fell by the wayside. Many of this latter group became Army or Navy officers. After being commissioned, all of us went through another three-month period of intensive infantry training. After this the great majority were assigned to infantry units. A smaller group went on the Base Defense Weapons and Artillery Classes, graduating in February 1942. Hence, we were [really] 365-day wonders when the Ninth was formed. [Ten members of Hank Reichner's Base Defense Weapons Class were assigned to join the Ninth Defense.] Even so, we often felt that we were only a chapter ahead of the [enlisted] Marines we were privileged to serve with. Also, we were quite close after our experience with the Ninth as we had been together for a year before that. Bill Box [one of Jack's future Battery B COs], Tracy [Battery E's CO] and Lynn Ervin (Special Weapons) and I are still very close friends....

20. Personal account, Col. (Ret'd) Henry H. Reichner Jr.

21. Melson and Chadwick, *The Ninth Marine Defense*, 11.

22. These Marines were so-called not only because of their service in

Iceland's freezing climate but because, as a gesture of solidarity, this battalion and other Marine units in Iceland wore the shoulder patch of the principal British unit stationed there, the Forty-Ninth (West Riding) Division, depicting a polar bear standing on an ice floe.

23. Marshall, *The "Fighting Ninth,"* 12–13; Melson and Chadwick, *The Ninth Marine Defense*, 11; *9th Defense Battalion*, Historical Section, Division of Public Information, Headquarters, US Marine Corps, File No. AG-1265/ HPH, Dec. 17, 1947, 1.

CHAPTER 2

1. While he did not recall it exactly as it was written, it seems probable that this rhyme that Jack McCall often recited to his family was derived from "The Ballad of the Leatherneck Corps," by fellow Marine (and later novelist) Herman Wouk, several stanzas of which appear to refer to the role in Iceland of the same "Polar Bear Marines" who joined the Ninth Defense Battalion in Cuba. Herman Wouk, "Ballad of the Leatherneck Corps," *Marine Corps Chevron* III, no. 14 (US Marine Corps official newspaper, San Diego, CA), April 8, 1944, 6, http://historicperiodicals .princeton.edu/historic/cgi-bin/historic?a=d&d=MarineCorpsChevron 19440408-01.2.49&e=——-en-20—1—txt-IN——#.

2. In the words of the battalion's own official report of operations: "Three submarine alerts were sounded enroute [*sic*] and escorting destroyers claimed destruction of two U-boats in three attacks on the hidden enemy. An estimated 70% of the Ninth aboard the *Biddle* experienced their first sea-sickness during the voyage and all hands were glad to go ashore at Guantanamo. . . ." 9th Defense Operations Report, 5.

3. Joseph Frank Marshall, *The "Fighting Ninth"—9th Defense Battalion*, ed. Christopher S. Donner (unpublished and undated manuscript, author's collection), 17-18.

4. Interview, Herb Doughtery and John Hall with author, Ninth Defense & AAA Battalions Reunion, Oct. 3, 1998.

5. Interview, Colonel (Ret'd) William T. Box with author, May 4, 1998.

6. The *U-94* was a Type VIIC U-boat, commanded by *Oberleutnant* (First Lieutenant) and Knight's Cross winner Otto Ites, on Caribbean patrol out of St. Nazaire, France. She sank off Cuba after depth-charging by a US Navy PBY seaplane of VP-92 and ramming by HMCS *Oakville*, with 19 dead and 26 survivors. In her ten combat patrols, *U-94* claimed 26 victims sunk, for a total of 138,467 tons, and two more ships damaged at a

total of 12,480 tons. This information is provided courtesy of *U-Boat Net*, available at http://uboat.net/boats/u94.htm (last accessed Nov. 2, 1998).

7. Correspondence, David Slater, Feb. 11, 1998; Marshall, *The "Fighting Ninth,"* 20-21.

8. Melson and Chadwick, *The Ninth Marine Defense*, 12.

9. Note that this group was officially called the Seacoast Group, Seacoast Artillery Group, or Seacoast Defense Group in recognition of its primary intended mission; on Cuba, this portion of the Ninth was first armed with elderly 5-inch ex-naval guns. After mid-1943, this element was renamed the Seacoast & Field Artillery Group in recognition of additional field artillery missions assigned to it during the Central Solomons campaign. These names are used interchangeably throughout the text.

10. The first 155s issued to the Ninth in Cuba were of a French-made World War I vintage. This was the M1918 or "GPF," its original French designation. Jack was told that the GPF stood for "Great Power, French." In fact, it was actually a French abbreviation—one roughly similar in translation—for *Grand Puissance Filloux*, Filloux being the designer. The Ninth used this older type of weapon on Guadalcanal. See Headquarters, US Department of the Army, Technical Manual TM 9-3305, *Principles of Artillery Weapons*, May 1981, 2-6; William G. Dooly, Jr., *Great Weapons of World War I* (New York: Bonanza Books, 1969); D. C. Horton, *New Georgia: Pattern for Victory* (New York: Ballantine Books, 1971), 28.

    A newer model, the M1, was issued to the Ninth in 1943 in time to serve on Rendova and New Georgia. This model weighed 30,600 pounds, required a full crew of twelve (the usual crew size used by the Ninth) to fifteen men, could fire up to forty shells per hour, and had improved accuracy and a modern gun carriage. See Melson, *Condition Red*, 23; John Kirk and Robert Young, *Great Weapons of World War II* (New York: Bonanza Books, 1961), 248-51. Even after these new guns were issued, defective ammunition plagued the troops and proved almost as hazardous to the Ninth Defense's gunners (and to Jack) as to the Japanese. One battery alone of these guns, known universally in the US military as "Long Toms," "could deliver a ton of steel and explosives in two minutes, a dozen 95-pound shells a minute onto enemy positions or ships as far as 15 miles away." Melson and Chadwick, *The Ninth Marine Defense*, 10.

11. Melson and Chadwick, *The Ninth Marine Defense*, 12. This thirteen-ton tank was armed with .30 caliber machine guns and a 37mm gun that could fire both explosive and antitank shells, as well as "canister," similar to a shotgun shell in its effect. It "could move across terrain that

could stop any other vehicle [and] could run through jungle underbrush and knock down small trees"; however, it was poorly ventilated, loud, and vulnerable (especially with all hatches closed) to Japanese magnetic mines and tank traps. Bergerud, *Touched With Fire*, 332–35. Frank Chadwick described this tank as being a "steam bath in the hot, humid tropics," and as "a coffin" due to the tanks' hatches and the inability of the tankers and their accompanying infantry to communicate effectively. While the Marines could have used the more powerful but heavier M-4 Sherman tank, the size and abilities of the then-available landing craft "limited the choice of Marine tanks . . . 'to the Tinker Toy level.'" Joseph H. Alexander, *Storm Landings: Epic Amphibious Battles in the Central Pacific* (Annapolis, MD: Naval Institute Press, 1997), 31.

12. Ronald H. Spector, *Eagle Against the Sun: The American War with Japan* (New York: Vintage Books, 1985), 24–25.

13. Spector, *Eagle Against the Sun*, 24.

14. I am indebted to Professor B. Franklin Cooling III for this observation.

15. The Ninth's communications and radar personnel were, in the main, the bane of every first sergeant's and platoon sergeant's existence: specialists, hence prima donnas, in the eyes of the old salt NCOs. Jack, his fellow water purification specialists, the Ninth's radiomen and signalers, and other types of technicians were often sardonically called the "Gizmos" due to the various types of equipment each needed for his job. As David Slater, one of the battalion's "commo" men, noted: "Our various radar 'chiefs' had been wisely enlisted from the ranks of radio hams at the beginning of the war by inducing (or seducing) them with the *immediate* rank of Staff (Technical) Sergeant and a reduction of the rigors of P.I. These men were mainly introduced and trained at Quantico on secret equipment (at that time), the SCR-270, SCR-268, etc." Correspondence, David Slater, Feb. 17, 1998.

16. In the absence of official manuals on the 40mm AA guns, one Special Weapons Group officer, Lieutenant Lynn Irvin, had to rely on an issue of *Popular Mechanics,* featuring a reader's interest article on the British version of the weapon, to provide his men with at least an introduction as to the Bofors gun and its capabilities. Marshall, *The "Fighting Ninth,"* 19.

17. Base Order No. 46, Commandant, US Naval Operating Base, Guantanamo Bay, Cuba, Sept. 6, 1942 (Personal papers, Jack H. McCall, Sr.).

18. Melson and Chadwick, *The Ninth Marine Defense*, 12; Marshall, *The "Fighting Ninth,"* 14–15.

19. Interview, John Dobkowski with author, Ninth Defense & AAA Battalion Association Reunion, Sept. 25, 1999.

20. Interview, Colonel (Ret'd) William T. Box, May 4, 1998; letter, Jack H. McCall to William T. Box, Feb. 10, 1985.

21. Interview, Frank Chadwick.

22. 9th Defense Operations Report, 10.

23. Melson and Chadwick, *The Ninth Marine Defense*, 12-13; Marshall, *The "Fighting Ninth,"* 22-23; *History of the First Antiaircraft Artillery Battalion, Redesignated Second 90-mm Antiaircraft Artillery Gun Battalion*, Battalion Bulletin No. 5-47, File No. 1990-50-20, Mar. 17, 1947, 1 (hereafter cited as *First AAA History*); 9th Defense Operations Report, 10.

24. 9th Defense Operations Report, 11, noting: "Five enlisted men who took unauthorized leave at [the] Panama Canal Zone were necessarily left behind." This is also corroborated by the Ninth's muster rolls for October 1942: the muster roll for the Special Weapons Group has six entries for men who went AWOL in the Canal Zone and were caught and held by the commandant of the Fifteenth Naval District in Balboa, Panama. Roll of Officers and Enlisted Men, US Marine Corps, Special Weapons Group, Ninth Defense Battalion, Fleet Marine Force for Oct. 1-31, 1942.

25. Jim Kruse similarly recalled: "[The *Kenmore*] wasn't exactly the Love Boat, but it did keep us off the bottom of the Pacific. To this day, I can still smell the hot, steamy galley and feel slightly nauseous." Looking at a photo of the ship while writing, he added: "By the looks of the bow wave, it must have been up to full speed when this picture was taken. Maybe 10 or 12 knots." Letter, James V. Kruse to Jack McCall, Mar. 26, 1985, personal papers, Jack H. McCall, Sr.

A word on the *Kenmore* and many of her sisters is provided by the Marine historian Colonel Joseph Alexander, which explains in part the relatively decrepit condition of many of these early-war transports:

> The United States had paid the price for not starting earlier to provide [for transports] in the prewar years. Only with the "Two-Ocean Navy Act" of 1940 did Congress provide funds for such unglamorous and undersponsored auxiliaries as troop transports. The first transports appeared almost overnight, reflecting the hasty conversion of a dozen passenger-cargo liners from commercial trade. . . . Most of these steamers were already long in the tooth. Their freshwater, ventilation, and sewer systems could not accommodate a thousand or more "passengers" on any sustained basis. The Navy Department thoughtfully renamed the conversions after legendary Marine Corps general

officers—*Doyen, Harris, Zeilin, Heywood, Biddle, Harry Lee* [the last of which would, in due time, be a Ninth Defense transport]—but the troops developed their own uncomplimentary nicknames, the least of which was "the Listing Harry Lee." Maligned and cussed, these old ships developed a can-do spirit and became valuable workhorses.

Joseph H. Alexander, *Storm Landings: Epic Amphibious Battles in the Central Pacific* (Annapolis, MD: Naval Institute Press, 1997), 34–35.

26. Marshall, *The "Fighting Ninth,"* 27.

27. Marshall, 28.

28. 9th Defense Operations Report, 12; Melson and Chadwick, *The Ninth Marine Defense*, 13.

29. Marshall, *The "Fighting Ninth,"* 28.

30. Marshall, 29; transcript of taped reminiscences, Frank Yemma, Oct. 12, 1998. Additional confirmation of these remembrances are validated by a photograph, taken off Noumea, of the captain of the *South Dakota* conducting a memorial service on the ship's deck not long after Admiral Lee's epic sea battle; in the distance, a transport, whose silhouette closely resembles the *Kenmore*'s, can be seen.

31. John J. Miller Jr., *Guadalcanal: The First Offensive* (Washington, DC: Department of the Army, Office of Chief of Military History, 1949), 215.

32. Personal reminiscences, Christopher S. Donner, January 1946, 5–6, reprinted in Donner, *Pacific Time on Target*, 20.

33. Interview, Colonel (Ret'd) Henry H. Reichner Jr., June 21, 1998.

34. This same officer was encountered by an only slightly more senior Hank Reichner, who recalled: "Tempers ran short. There was one particularly obnoxious officer running things in the #1 hold. I was on deck when one of the winch operators looked at me and said, 'Say the word, Lieutenant, and I'll drop this next pallet on the son-of-a-bitch.' Fortunately, cool heads prevailed." Correspondence, Col. (Retired) Henry H. Reichner Jr. with author, June 10, 1998.

35. Personal reminiscences, Col. (Ret'd) Henry H. Reichner Jr., 10.

36. *First AAA History*, 1; Melson and Chadwick, *The Ninth Marine Defense*, 14.

37. The latter nickname partly originated from a grim wordplay in Japanese: *Gadarukanaru*, roughly approximating the pronunciation of Guadalcanal in Japanese, literally translates as "island of death."

38. Interview, Willie Dufour, Ninth Defense & AAA Battalions Reunion, Oct. 4, 1998.

CHAPTER 3

1.   Richard B. Frank, *Guadalcanal: The Definitive Account of the Landmark Battle* (New York: Random House, 1990), 618.

2.   Capt. Henry H. Adams, *1942: The Year that Doomed the Axis* (New York: Warner Paperback Library, 1973), 255.

3.   Frank, *Guadalcanal*, 462–92; Robert D. Ballard (with Rick Archbold), *The Lost Ships of Guadalcanal* (New York: Warner/Madison Press Books, 1993), 163–79; Paul Dull, *A Battle History of the Imperial Japanese Navy* (Annapolis, MD: Naval Institute Press, 1978), 254.

4.   Ballard, *Lost Ships*, 180–82; Dull, *Battle History*, 263–69; Frank, *Guadalcanal*, 462–92; Maj. John L. Zimmerman, *The Guadalcanal Campaign* (Washington, DC: Headquarters, US Marine Corps/Govt. Printing Office, 1949), 155.

5.   Personal account, Col. (Ret'd) Henry H. Reichner Jr., 22. See also Task Force Sixty-Two, USS *Argonne*, Operation Plan No. A24-42 (File No. FE25/A16-3(1)), Nov. 27, 1942, 1–5 (hereafter cited as Task Force 62 Operation Plan); 9th Defense Operations Report, 12.

6.   Miller, *The First Offensive*, 196–200; Zimmerman, *The Guadalcanal Campaign*, 133–41.

7.   9th Defense Operations Report, 19. Frank Chadwick thought this incident had occurred earlier, during the effort to free the *Kenmore* from the sandbar; as he recalled, "a Jap sub surfaced and fired one or two torpedoes (depending on who you talk to), passing the bow of the ship and ending up on the beach. The sub submerged before the destroyers could get on station and slipped away."

8.   Radarman Ted Hitchcock of the Ninth, who was aboard the *Hunter Liggett*, also recalled the crash of the SBD. Interview, Ted Hitchcock, Ninth Defense Battalion Reunion, Sept. 25, 1999. Japanese submarine activity, including the use of two-man midget submarines and cargo-carrying subs, was particularly intensive off Guadalcanal. See Zenji Orita (with Joseph D. Harrington), *I-Boat Captain* (Canoga Park, CA: Major Books, 1976), 119–31. See also Melson and Chadwick, *The Ninth Marine Defense*, 15.

      The *Kenmore* was not alone, however, in running aground in the treacherous shoals off Guadalcanal. A few days before the "Killmore" suffered this embarrassment, the *Neville*, Battery A's transport, met a similar fate. See correspondence, Colonel (Ret'd) Henry H. Reichner Jr. (June 19, 1998); interview, William Galloway, July 13, 1998.

9.   Melson and Chadwick, *The Ninth Marine Defense*, 14.

10.   Melson and Chadwick, 15-16; correspondence, David Slater to author, Feb. 11, 1998.

11.   Marshall, *The "Fighting Ninth,"* 32.

12.   Personal account, Col. (Ret'd) Henry H. Reichner Jr.

13.   See chapter 2, note 10. The US Army adopted this artillery piece in 1917 as its standard heavy, long-range field gun.

14.   Dull, *Battle History*, 254-56; Melson and Chadwick, *The Ninth Marine Defense*, 16-18.

15.   Henry H. Reichner, *A Battery* (manuscript, privately printed, 1999), 19.

16.   Melson and Chadwick, *The Ninth Marine Defense*, 14, 18.

17.   See Alexander, *Storm Landings*, 2-4; Task Force 62 Operation Plan, 4-5.

18.   In an ironic twist, one of the members of the cruiser *Pensacola*'s shipboard Marine detachment, Ray Carman, would later be transferred late in the war to join the Ninth, whose men had gaped at his battered ship as they arrived at Tulagi and Gavutu. Interview, Ray Carman, Ninth Defense & AAA Battalions Fall 1998 Reunion, Oct. 3, 1998.

19.   Taped reminiscences, Frank Yemma, Oct. 12, 1998.

20.   Melson and Chadwick, *The Ninth Marine Defense*, 15-18.

21.   In any event, the 155mm Group's supply of ammunition was also sorely lacking: Batteries A and B were instructed to conserve ammunition and not fire unless Japanese ships were directly in front of the battalion's position or attempting a landing at Koli Point. "Many nights, you sat at the guns and watched the Jap destroyers sailing through the channel. It was very frustrating," Frank Chadwick recalled.

22.   Frank, *Guadalcanal*, 577-97; Melson and Chadwick, *The Ninth Marine Defense*, 18-19.

23.   Unless a malaria victim had a fever greater than 101 degrees, he would try to perform his regular duties and thus avoid being sent to the Ninth's sick bay. The onset of malaria usually brought about a high fever and collapse, so a severe case of malaria could hardly be concealed from one's buddies, NCOs, and officers. A Ninth Defense malaria victim was first sent to the battalion's medical station on the Metapona River, about one and a half miles from the Koli Point beach, which consisted of several tents and was supplied with a highly visible stack of coffins—a sight likely to deter most but the truly sick from visiting. Anyone who failed to recover quickly at the battalion level was sent to the main hospital (inherited by XIV Corps when the First Marine Division withdrew from the Canal) near Henderson Field. If his situation then deteriorated or

failed to improve, he was evacuated to Australia, Espiritu Santo, New Zealand, or Hawaii.

24. Miller, *The First Offensive*, 175. The choice of Koli Point was favored by General Vandegrift, who had strenuously opposed a location at Aola Bay chosen by Rear Admiral Richmond Kelly Turner, the Navy task force commander for Guadalcanal. When the terrain and dense vegetation at Aola Bay proved to slow down the Seabees' construction efforts earlier in November, Vandegrift recommended its abandonment, and Admirals Aubrey Fitch (the air chief for the South Pacific area) and William Halsey ("ComSoPac," the South Pacific area commander) concurred. The units sited at Aola Bay were moved to the more level and grassy plains around Koli Point, a move completed by December 3, just in time for the arrival of the Ninth's main body. Ibid.

25. Correspondence, David Slater with the author.

26. Frank, *Guadalcanal*, 103, 294, 516, 603; Ballard, *Lost Ships*, 116, 127-29, 172.

27. Interview, Theodore T. Hitchcock with author, Ninth Defense & AAA Battalion Reunion, September 25, 1999. Hitchcock also noted that a modified version of the SCR-270, the SCR-271, became famous for being the set used in Army Signal Corps experiments that in the 1940s succeeded in bouncing radar waves off the moon's surface.

While the 268 sets could have been directly connected to the 90mm guns of Batteries C, D, and E, Hitchcock noted his doubts as to whether the correct flow of "juice" from the Ninth's generators could be guaranteed to enable the electrical connections and automatic gun layers to function properly at the correct electrical cycles. This was were necessary to ensure proper synchronization between the radars, the automatic AA gun director, and the guns themselves. Another Ninth veteran, John Henry Johnson of Battery E, recalled his battery commander, Captain Bill Tracy, expressing concerns that the use of automatic connections directly into his 90mm guns might result in injuries among the gun crews (if, say, a gunner was ramming a shell into the breech at the very time that the radar commanded the gun to swing vertically) and using this as his reason for refusing to interconnect the guns and radars. Interview, John H. Johnson with author, Ninth Defense & AAA Battalion Reunion, September 25, 1999. In any event, due to these and related concerns, the direct gun-laying feature was not used between the Ninth's 90mms and its SCR-268s, and the 268 sets were only directly connected to Captain Theron Smith's six searchlights of Battery F, with radar-guided gunnery being conveyed to Batteries C, D, and E by voice command.

28. Melson and Chadwick, *The Ninth Marine Defense*, 18; letter, David Slater
    to the author. The legend on a photograph made by Harry C. Jones,
    one of the battalion's communications staff, and lent to the author
    by David Slater refers to this as being the sole instance in which the
    Ninth's semaphore lights (on which Jones was an operator) were used in
    action. The official rap on the SCR-268 was not very good: "The long-
    range radar used on Guadalcanal, the SCR 270, functioned fairly well,
    although the antiaircraft batteries' fire control radar, the SCR 268, was
    too primitive for accurate fire control." Miller, *The First Offensive*, 222.
    Still, on December 28, 1942, the Ninth's radar sets enabled Battery E of
    the 90mm Group to shoot down a Japanese bomber obscured by clouds
    purely by radar target-finding. This success compensated for the earlier
    glitches of December 4. Lt. Col. H. B. Meek, "Marines Had Radar Too,"
    Marine Corps Gazette, Oct. 1945, 17.

29. Miller, *The First Offensive*, 222.

30. An Army Twenty-Fifth Infantry Division infantryman on Guadalcanal,
    Robert Ballantine, shared the following memory of Washing Machine
    Charlie's nighttime depredations: "You'd sit there and watch him. The
    searchlight beams from the antiaircraft units would catch the plane. He
    was not very high, and he would fly in and out of the beam. Of course,
    they couldn't hit him, but it was quite a sight. . . . You sure could hear
    the bombs coming down. If it makes a kind of swooshing, whirling noise,
    the bomb is by and will miss. If it's hissing, it's going to be close, and you
    might have to change your underwear." Bergerud, *Touched With Fire*, 401.

31. Marshall, *The "Fighting Ninth,"* 37.

32. Melson and Chadwick, *The Ninth Marine Defense*, 19; personal papers,
    Jack H. McCall, Sr.; correspondence, David Slater with the author, Feb.
    11, 1998. At one point during the 1943 spring monsoons, some of the
    Ninth's personnel around Koli Point beach were transfixed by the sight
    of a waterspout, which only broke up when hitting a nearby coral reef.
    When one of their sergeants asked why they did not take shelter from
    this seaborne tornado, they responded: "Well, Sarge, none of us had ever
    seen one of those things before." More seriously, a large group barely
    escaped major injuries when another gawkish Marine pointed toward
    the waters of The Slot and yelled: "Hey, look at that big wave!" The "big
    wave" in question—which wreaked havoc on the battalion's beachside
    positions and supply areas at Koli Point when it hit—was a storm surge
    from an offshore typhoon, estimated as being approximately twenty feet
    high at its crest. Interview, Frank Chadwick, Mar. 9, 1998.

33. Correspondence, James V. Kruse to Jack H. McCall, Jan. 3, 1985, personal papers, Jack H. McCall, Sr.

34. Letter, James V. Kruse to Jack McCall, Jan. 3, 1985, personal papers, Jack H. McCall, Sr.

35. Notes of interview with William Galloway, Ninth Defense & AAA Battalions Reunion, Oct. 4, 1998.

36. Miller, *The First Offensive*, 210.

37. "Grant to Help Solomon Islands Battle Malaria," *San Diego Union-Tribune*, July 4, 1997.

38. Melson and Chadwick, *The Ninth Marine Defense*, 20. These authors noted that the Ninth's average sick call rate from December 1942 to June 1943 was 27.86 per month. See also 9th Defense Operations Report, 21 (noting the following average daily sick rates: December 1942, 19.83; January 1943, 35.19; February, 41.21; and March, 31.71). Later in spring 1943, these numbers would more than double to an average of 65 men per month. *First AAA History*, 2.

39. Melson and Chadwick, *The Ninth Marine Defense*, 20. Following his departure, Colonel Nimmer—later retiring as a general—would continue to provide valuable service to the Corps. Assigned to the Joint War Plans Committee in April 1943 following his return stateside from Guadalcanal, through a series of studies and experimental tests in New Caledonia, he and the father of a future commandant of the USMC, Lt. Col. Victor H. ("Brute") Krulak, were instrumental in encouraging the widespread use of LVT (Landing Vehicle, Tracked) "amphtracs" in future Marine amphibious landings in the Central Pacific. Joseph H. Alexander, *Storm Landings: Epic Amphibious Battles in the Central Pacific* (Annapolis, MD: Naval Institute Press, 1997), 46-47.

40. Melson and Chadwick, *The Ninth Marine Defense*, 20; personal reminiscences, Col. (Ret'd) Henry H. Reichner Jr., 14.

41. Interview, Col. (Ret'd) William T. Box, May 27, 1998.

42. Marshall, *The "Fighting Ninth,"* 36.

43. Letter, Col. (Ret'd) Henry H. Reichner Jr. to author, June 10, 1998.

44. David Slater, *Jungle Vignettes* (unpublished, undated manuscript, author's collection), 4. On Guadalcanal, two of the Ninth's men died from malaria, and one had died at Noumea from drowning; 9th Defense Operations Report, 22.

45. Taped reminiscences, Frank Yemma, Oct. 12, 1998.

46. Spector, *Eagle Against the Sun*, 356.

47. Correspondence, Frank Chadwick to the author; transcript of taped reminiscences by Frank Yemma, Oct. 12, 1998.

48. For more on malaria, quinine, and Atabrine, see Bergerud, *Touched With Fire*, 92-96; Manchester, *Goodbye, Darkness*, 182; Melson, *Condition Red*, 18-19.

49. Personal reminiscences, Col. (Ret'd) Henry H. Reichner Jr., 15.

50. Taped reminiscences, Frank Yemma, Oct. 12, 1998.

51. The Marine Corps' Chief Historian, Charles Melson, whose father served in the Ninth as an armorer, vividly recalled to the author his father's criticisms of the Reising gun as being especially prone to rusting. Interview, Charles Melson, Oct. 30, 1998. See also Henry I. Shaw, Jr., *First Offensive: The Marine Campaign for Guadalcanal: Marines in World War II Commemorative Series* (Washington, DC: History & Museums Division, Headquarters, US Marine Corps, 1992), 37.

52. See, for example, a photograph in Melson and Chadwick, *The Ninth Marine Defense*, 52, depicting Major Hiatt armed with a drum-fed Tommy gun as he accompanied Bill Box and a reconnaissance team.

53. For details as to the small arms of the Marines, see Bergerud, *Touched With Fire*, 283-309; Ian V. Hogg, *The Encyclopedia of Infantry Weapons of World War II* (London: Bison Books, 1977), 36-40, 55-58, 79-80; John C. McManus, *The Deadly Brotherhood: The American Combat Soldier in World War II* (Novato, CA: Presidio Press, 1998), 42-47; and Rottman and Chappell, *Fighting Elite*, 12-16.

54. Frank, *Guadalcanal*, 596-97.

55. Melson and Chadwick, *The Ninth Marine Defense*, 19.

56. Edward Jablonski, *Airwar* (Garden City, NY: Doubleday & Company, Inc., 1971), 2:90-93.

57. Jablonski, *Airwar*, 2:20.

58. B-24 Liberators were also prized by some characters for more than just their heavy armament: they were full of copper tubing, which was pilfered from deadlined or wrecked B-24s by a few enterprising and thirsty souls to make stills. "We may have grounded more B-24s than the Japs," one Ninth Defense veteran wisecracked. Correspondence, David Slater, Feb. 11, 1998.

59. This was almost an understatement: this letter was written during one period of monsoon-like rains, which swamped the Ninth's entire area and completely flooded out all of the radar and 90mm gun positions. The Ninth's official report stated: "On May 9-10, 1943, torrential rains put all rivers on the [n]orthern watershed on the [i]sland to flood stage, immediately inundating many of the Battalion's positions. All radars and the 90mm batteries were temporarily out of action, due to the high

water. All bridges [in the Koli Point area] were washed out." 9th Defense Operations Report, 22.

60. He is referring here to his high school friend Reams Osborne, the son of his family's next-door neighbors Nathan and Elona Osborne, who had enlisted in the Navy and would end up in the Seabees. In a few months, Jack would meet up with Reams under some fairly improbable circumstances. See chapter 4.

61. Jack is probably referring here to the draft rating "4-B," which meant that his father had an extremely low chance of ever being drafted. The lowest rating was 4-F; Jack, at the other end of the spectrum, had been picked as 1-A.

62. To reduce shipping space during the war years, Marines and GIs would write letters home from overseas on specially provided and lined paper; the letter would then be put on a microfilm-like paper and would be printed out and mailed, so that parents, friends, and loved ones would receive a miniaturized copy of the original letter as the final product. This final product was known as "V-mail." Most surviving pieces of V-mail also bear another hallmark of the war years: a military censor's stamp. Each unit had one officer with a designated additional duty of reviewing all mail before it was sent, both to prevent disclosures of military secrets ("Loose lips sink ships") and to gauge the unit's overall morale.

While quite a few of Jack's letters home still exist, due to the rigid censorship imposed on enlisted troops, they are all essentially as ano-dyne as the one cited in its entirety here, and he was very circumscribed in his letters to his loved ones. Hence, sadly, few of his letters offer any particularly detailed glimpse of his activities, thoughts, or surroundings, nor did they disclose—even as late as 1944—where he actually was in the Pacific. (There is one letter in which, having thought that he now had permission from his Battery B officers to tell his parents his exact location, Jack does so—and that location is blotted out in a block of solid black ink.)

63. See, e.g., Miller, *The First Offensive*, 316.

64. Bergerud, *Touched With Fire*, 479-82; McManus, *The Deadly Brotherhood*, 15-28; Miller, *The First Offensive*, 316.

65. Taped reminiscences, Frank Yemma, Oct. 12, 1998; see also Bergerud, *Touched With Fire*, 482, citing another Battery B member, Frank Chadwick, as to the same incident. "It was about ten feet along and maybe 500 pounds. The meat was excellent. It didn't last long in that

climate. The next day the boat came in and we had Spam and rice again," Chadwick ruefully remembered.

66. Frank, *Guadalcanal*, 527.

67. John Hersey, *Into the Valley: A Skirmish of the Marines* (New York: Schocken Books, 1989), 59.

68. Correspondence, David Slater, Feb. 17, 1998. It may have been this same Army unit that was the butt of another one of Jack's practical jokes that could have easily backfired on him. As his brother Albert recalled, Jack told him that a freshly landed Army outfit was being given a class on mosquito control and malaria-avoidance techniques near his Nalimbiu River water station. This training included a Medical Corps lecturer who advised the dogfaces to wear full long-sleeved fatigues at all times and to use mosquito netting at nighttime. The lecturer's safety points were quickly eroded by the sight of a Marine—none other than Jack, who had been listening unnoticed to the lecturer—swimming about languidly in the nearby river. When challenged by the soldiers on whether he was jeopardizing his health, Jack called back: "Hell, no! *We* don't have any trouble with mosquitoes. They wouldn't dare bite a Marine!" Interview, Albert G. McCall, Jr., Feb. 22, 1998.

69. Correspondence, Frank Chadwick with the author, Dec. 1, 1997.

70. Miller, *The First Offensive*, 348.

71. Personal reminiscences, Col. (Retd) Henry H. Reichner Jr.

72. Other Marines elsewhere penned a similarly bitter verse: "And while possibly a rumor now,/Some day it will be fact/That the Lord will hear a deep voice say,/'Move over, God, it's Mac.'" Stephen E. Ambrose, *Americans at War* (New York: Berkley Books, 1998), 148.

73. Frank, *Guadalcanal*, 526, 548-49 (on earlier US strikes against Munda Field); Eric Hammel, *Munda Trail* (New York: Orion Books, 1989), 3-21; Horton, *New Georgia*, 14-16, 19-21; Jablonski, *Airwar*, 2:87; Maj. Charles D. Melson, *Up the Slot: Marines in the Central Solomons: Marines in World War II Commemorative Series* (Washington, DC: History & Museums Division, Headquarters, US Marine Corps, 1993), 1; John N. Rentz, *Marines in the Central Solomons* (Washington, DC: Headquarters, US Marine Corps/Govt. Printing Office, 1952), 9-13.

74. By this time, I MAC was made up of three Marine divisions (logically enough, the First, Second and Third); six defense battalions; four Marine Raider battalions (the Marines' equivalent of the British commandos or Army Rangers); three parachute battalions ("Paramarines"); two Marine air wings; and various headquarters, administration, and logistics support units.

75. Correspondence, Col. (Ret'd) Henry H. Reichner Jr., Jan. 22, 1999, 2; interview, Joseph J. Pratl, Mar. 26, 1999.

76. Donner, 11, reprinted in Donner, *Pacific Time on Target*, 24; Melson and Chadwick, *The Ninth Marine Defense*, 21.

77. Melson and Chadwick, *The Ninth Marine Defense*, 21; Rentz, *Marines*, 52–53.

78. Staff Sgt. Samuel Stavisky, "Alligator Crews Undaunted by Rendova Mud," newspaper clipping, newspaper unidentified, July 13, 1943 (personal papers of Jack H. McCall); 9th Defense Operations Report, 47. For more on the LVT, see Shaw, *First Offensive*, 11.

79. Melson and Chadwick, *The Ninth Marine Defense*, 21; Henry I. Shaw, Jr. & Douglas T. Kane, *The Isolation of Rabaul* (Washington, DC: Historical Branch, G-3 Division, Headquarters, US Marine Corps/Govt. Printing Office, 1963), 56–57.

80. Shaw and Kane, *The Isolation of Rabaul*, 56–57.

81. Melson and Chadwick, *The Ninth Marine Defense*, 21.

82. The arrival of the draftee Marines into the Ninth was accompanied by the expected doses of grousing of both the old salts and the all-volunteer Christmas Tree Marines, Jack included. As Jack wrote in response to a letter of his brother Al, in which Al had both noted that some Marines were now coming from draftees and questioned whether he might himself be drafted as a Marine: "A drafted Marine ain't no Marine at all!" Interview, Albert G. McCall, Jr., Mar. 15, 1998.

83. Personal reminiscences, Joseph J. Pratl, Feb. 25, 1991, 3 (author's collection).

84. Donner, 12, reprinted in Donner, *Pacific Time on Target*, 24–25.

85. Marshall, *The "Fighting Ninth,"* 39 (extract from the War Diary of the 9th Defense Battalion, June 27, 1943).

CHAPTER 4

1. Samuel E. Stavisky, *Marine Combat Correspondent: World War II in the Pacific* (New York: Ivy Books, 1999), 148.

2. Bergerud, *Touched With Fire*, 226–27 (noting, however, that Vice Admiral William Halsey's staff estimate of four thousand defenders "was correct when originally made" because, at the time the original intelligence reports were drafted, the Japanese had not brought reinforcements to the Central Solomons from Bougainville. This, they subsequently did. This movement was part of a decision taken by the Japanese leadership

and their Central Solomons area commander, Maj. Gen. Noburo Sasaki, to "defend every possible position" in the island chain so as to delay the US advance northward into the Central Pacific for as long as possible). Hammel, *Munda Trail*, 24, however, states that the original estimates of three thousand defenders at Munda were "extremely accurate" at the time they were made.

3. Japanese "special naval landing forces" were naval infantry units, often used in a garrison capacity on occupied islands or in roles roughly similar to that of US Marine defense battalions. While sometimes described as the "Japanese Marine Corps," this is not entirely correct, as it implies a separate organization and higher level of training than was often the case for SNLF units. Still, in many cases (Tarawa, for instance), *rikusentai* troops proved to be ingenious and fanatical fighters. See Alexander, *Storm Landings*, 16-19, 206; Bergerud, *Touched With Fire*, 215, 255; Hammel, *Munda Trail*, 8; and US War Dept., *Handbook on Japanese Military Forces* (London: Greenhill Books, 1991), 76–79 (reprint of US War Dept. Technical Manual TM-E 30-480, Oct. 1, 1944; hereafter cited as *Japanese Forces Handbook*).

4. Horton, *New Georgia*, 24.

5. Horton, *New Georgia*, 24-26; Melson and Chadwick, *The Ninth Marine Defense*, 21-22; Rentz, *Marines*, 28, 35-36.

6. Melson and Chadwick, 22.

7. Melson and Chadwick, 21-22; Rentz, *Marines*, 35-36.

8. Memorandum Order No. 29-43, Headquarters, Ninth Defense Battalion, June 28, 1943, reprinted in Melson and Chadwick, *The Ninth Marine Defense*, 78.

9. Personal reminiscences, Pratl, 4.

10. Interview, James V. Kruse, March 13, 1998. This incident was also vividly recalled by Joe Pratl in his reminiscences, 4.

11. Melson, *Up the Slot*, 12; Melson and Chadwick, *The Ninth Marine Defense*, 22, 25; 9th Defense Operations Report, 48.

12. Alexander, *Storm Landings*, 37; Melson, *Up the Slot*, 12; Rentz, *Marines*, 157.

13. Melson, *Condition Red*, 15, with a photo depicting various Special Weapons AA guns in defensive arrangements on the deck of an LST; Melson and Chadwick, *The Ninth Marine Defense*, 24-25.

14. Samuel E. Stavisky, *Marine Combat Correspondent*, 139.

15. Melson and Chadwick, *The Ninth Marine Defense*, 21.

16. Taped reminiscences, Frank Yemma, Oct. 12, 1998.

17. Bergerud, *Touched With Fire*, 451.

18. Donner, 16, reprinted in Donner, *Pacific Time on Target*, 29.

19. Later the commander of the Third Defense Battalion during the Bougainville operations; Melson, *Condition Red*, 30.

20. Alexander, *Storm Landings*, 39, 54, 210.

21. Melson and Chadwick, *The Ninth Marine Defense*, 22, 24.

22. Stavisky, *Marine Combat Correspondent*, 141.

23. Access to Tokyo Rose's broadcasts was more readily available to radiomen like David Slater than to the average radio-less Marine. He recalled: "As a radioman, I had access to receivers, although my CO, Major 'Sparky' Adams, at one time reamed me for wearing down the batteries. On the 'Canal, her broadcasts began with the *Stars and Stripes Forever* and her greeting [was] to 'the soldiers, sailors and Marines beyond the horizon.' By New Georgia, [her morning greeting] had become '*on* the horizon.'" Correspondence, David Slater, April 16, 1998.

24. Contrary to many depictions, coconut trees were not all that common in many South and Central Pacific islands, although they were indeed plentiful in many parts of the Solomons. Between the wars, Lever Brothers had built numerous plantations on New Georgia and the surrounding islands for the cultivation of coconut palms. The Japanese used their tough, fibrous trunks to reinforce many of their bunkers and defensive positions on New Georgia, Rendova, and Kolombangara.

25. Alexander, *Storm Landings*, 38. Richmond Kelly Turner was hardly a favorite admiral of the Marines, unlike the bulldog-like William "Bull" Halsey. Turner's behavior during the New Georgia campaign was illustrative of a charge first made against him during the Guadalcanal campaign—that he was a man who "studied everything, remembered everything, interfered with everything": "Turner simply could not resist exercising active command over troops ashore, just as he did aboard ship. . . . 'It wasn't the Navy that was wrong and caused trouble; it was Turner,' declared one marine officer who served with him. 'Turner was a martinet; very, very gifted, but he was stubborn, opinionated, conceited, thought that he could do anything better than anybody in the world. . . . I challenge anyone to name a naval officer other than Turner with whom the Marines had command difficulties. . . . By and large naval officers, they were wary of trying to run land operations, but Turner, no; because Turner knew everything!'" Spector, *Eagle Against the Sun*, 238 (citing Marine Corps Maj. General Omar Pfeiffer). Turner's meddling with Army and Marine affairs during the drive for Munda Field would

have serious repercussions, as he bypassed normal Army command channels, placing a division commander—Maj. General John H. Hester, of the relatively untested Forty-Third Infantry Division—in charge of land operations instead of Hester's XIV Corps commander and nominal superior officer, Maj. General Oscar Griswold. Ibid.

26. Horton, *New Georgia*, 55.

27. Melson and Chadwick, *The Ninth Marine Defense*, 24; 9th Defense Operations Report, 50.

28. These men, comprised of the Second Company of the Kure Sixth SNLF *rikusentai* and the Seventh Company, 229th Infantry, made good their getaway. Both Rendova and its environs were cleared of Japanese defenders relatively quickly. Such would not be the case on New Georgia itself. The New Georgia area commander who was then based at Munda, General Sasaki, believed that the Americans would first land in earnest elsewhere on New Georgia and failed to appreciate the significance of the Rendova landings, believing them to be merely a diversion. When he finally appreciated what had happened, it was too late for him to act in strength.

29. The Army engineer battalion would not land on Rendova until the next day, at which point it moved inland and began to set up a base camp for elements of the Forty-Third Infantry Division.

30. 9th Defense Operations Report, 50-51, 104.

31. David Slater, *Annotations to 9th DB History, Rendova-New Georgia Campaign* (undated, on file with author), 3.

32. Eric Hammel, *Munda Trail*, 53.

33. Bill Box having been "surveyed out" from Guadalcanal due to malaria, Wells replaced him as Battery B's CO during much of the New Georgia campaign. Box performed yeoman services for the 155mm Group during this campaign, helping to coordinate the group's movements on Rendova and New Georgia and overseeing ammunition resupply.

34. Hammel, *Munda Trail*, 71-72; Marshall, *The "Fighting Ninth,"* 40-41; Melson and Chadwick, *The Ninth Marine Defense*, 24.

35. Correspondence with David Slater, Feb. 13, 1997. Slater was one of the members of the H&S Battery's recon party that encountered the Barracudas on Kokorana.

36. One raiding party involved twenty-six twin-engined medium bombers, eight single-engined Val dive bombers, and seventy-two Zero fighters which were intercepted over Rendova by US aircraft, with a loss of eighteen medium bombers and thirty-one Zeroes; a later afternoon raid involved twenty-four medium bombers and twenty-five Zeroes, with a

loss of seventeen of the bombers. By comparison, seventeen American fighters were lost on all of June 30. Published figures differ widely as to the exact number of Japanese aircraft involved or shot down during the July 1 raids. Hammel, *Munda Trail*, 55–59; Horton, *New Georgia*, 60; Rentz, *Marines*, 62 n.24; 9th Defense Operations Report, 50.

37. Melson and Chadwick, *The Ninth Marine Defense*, 24; 9th Defense Operations Report, 50, 97.

38. Rentz, *Marines*, 57; 9th Defense Operations Report, 51. Besides the climate and mosquitoes, Rendova and New Georgia provided two new pests with which to contend: ferocious red ants and land crabs. Inch-long red ants were found in profusion on Rendova, the product of a pest control effort that had backfired dramatically: David Slater understood that they had been "imported by Lever Brothers from Africa as a countermeasure to the coconut crabs that attacked the crop. However, the ants loved coconuts and "would consume the valuable meat that the natives harvested for copra, the product that Lever so valued. Those ants would attack anything and, if asked, I'm sure almost every member of the 9th would remember being bitten." Correspondence, David Slater to author, Feb. 17, 1998.

39. 9th Defense Operations Report, 51, 97. Lt. Colonel Archie O'Neil was an artillery expert who was also a veteran of the first Japanese attack on Midway Island shortly after Pearl Harbor, which was repulsed by the Sixth Defense Battalion (in which he served as CO of that battalion's 5-Inch Artillery Group) and for which he won a gold star to the Bronze Star. Citation, Secretary of the Navy, Gold Star in lieu of a second Bronze Star Medal, awarded to Maj. Archie E. O'Neil (personal papers, David Slater).

40. Melson and Chadwick, *The Ninth Marine Defense*, 24–25; Rentz, *Marines*, 62.

41. Personal reminiscences, Pratl, 5.

42. Personal reminiscences, Pratl, 5; notes of interview with Col. (Ret'd) Henry H. Reichner Jr., Dec. 21, 1998; Donner, 19, reprinted in Donner, *Pacific Time on Target*, 31.

43. Melson and Chadwick, *The Ninth Marine Defense*, 25.

44. Letter, James V. Kruse to Jack H. McCall, Sr., Feb. 16, 1985, personal papers, Jack H. McCall, Sr.

45. 9th Defense Operations Report, 97.

46. Staff Sgt. S. E. Stavisky, "Long Wait Pays Off for Pair," newspaper clipping, newspaper unidentified, July 1, 1943 (personal papers of Jack H. McCall).

47. Melson and Chadwick, *The Ninth Marine Defense*, 25.

48. Stavisky, *Marine Combat Correspondent*, 155.

49. Donner, 19, reprinted in Donner, *Pacific Time on Target*, 31. See also 9th Defense Operations Report, 51.

50. Horton, *New Georgia*, 61; Rentz, *Marines*, 62-63; 9th Defense Operations Report, 52, 90, 97-98.

51. Slater, *Annotations to 9th DB History, Rendova-New Georgia Campaign*, 5. Slater added: "They failed to take cover and were decimated. He [the Seabee officer] was said to have shot himself that night."

52. Horton, *New Georgia*, 61; Stavisky, *Marine Combat Correspondent*, 149-50.

53. Donner, 20, reprinted in Donner, *Pacific Time on Target*, 32.

54. Staff Sgt. Samuel Stavisky, "Alligator Crews Undaunted by Rendova Mud," newspaper clipping, newspaper unidentified, July 13, 1943 (personal papers of Jack H. McCall, Sr.); see also Stavisky, *Marine Combat Correspondent*, 161-63, for a lengthier recounting derived from his wartime news report and notes. Melson and Chadwick, *The Ninth Marine Defense*, 25, identified the attackers as being eighteen Betty medium bombers accompanied by Zero fighter escorts; see below for indications that in fact these may not have been the Japanese Navy's Betty bombers, but Japanese Army Ki-21 Sally bombers instead.

55. Taped reminiscences, Frank Yemma, Oct. 12, 1998.

56. Donner, 23, reprinted in Donner, *Pacific Time on Target*, 34.

57. Horton, *New Georgia*, 61.

58. See Hammel, *Munda Trail*, 72-74; Marshall, *The "Fighting Ninth,"* 42-43; Rentz, *Marines*, 63.

59. Three factors contributed to the lapse in US air cover on July 2: the fact that the Ninth's radars were out of commission; aircraft recognition difficulties (at a distance, certain types of Japanese medium bomber generally resembled the American B-25 Mitchell medium bomber, with Hank Reichner himself later recalling that, at first glance, that was what he had thought the incoming Japanese bombers were); and deteriorating local weather conditions between Guadalcanal and the Russell Islands, where the Allied fighters supporting TOENAILS were based, and Rendova. Hammel, *Munda Trail*, 73. None of the Japanese raiders were downed in this raid, with only minor damage being inflicted. John N. Rentz, *Marines*, 63.

60. See Melson and Chadwick, *The Ninth Marine Defense*, 25-26; Rentz, *Marines*, 63; 9th Defense Operations Report, 52.

61. Horton, *New Georgia*, 61. Coastwatcher Horton recalled the two

uninjured scouts paddling the wounded man to the islet where the Coastwatching Service had established its campsite, saying "We're frightened, Master!" Horton replied, "So am I—but if we don't get this brother of yours to the hospital, he will die!"

62. Alexander, *Storm Landings*, 23, 38.

63. Notes accompanying photograph of Battery A's incapacitated gun, provided to the author by William Galloway; Stavisky, *Marine Combat Correspondent*, 158, 160-61; Seacoast Artillery Officers of a Marine Defense Battalion (various authors), "We Had to Do It," *Coast Artillery Journal* (July-Aug. 1944): 8-9 (hereafter cited as "We Had to Do It"); 9th Defense Operations Report, 52.

64. Donner, 21, reprinted in Donner, *Pacific Time on Target*, 32-33; correspondence, Bill Galloway; Melson and Chadwick, *The Ninth Marine Defense*, 25-26; Rentz, *Marines*, 63; Staff Sgt. Samuel E. Stavisky, "Corpsmen High in Regard of Leathernecks," *Nashville Tennessean*, undated newspaper clipping (personal papers of Jack H. McCall, Sr.); personal reminiscences, Col. (Ret'd) Henry H. Reichner Jr.

   "Doc" Krepela was widely regarded as being something of a miracle-worker among his charges. On one occasion on New Georgia, he gingerly removed a Japanese high-explosive shell with a hair-trigger fuse that was imbedded in one Marine's thigh. In another incident, Battery B's Ned Williams was brained by the recoil of a 155mm gun, which as Frank Chadwick described, would "make you feel like you had been hit by a ten-ton truck at 60 miles an hour." The impact shattered Williams's cranium and threw a fragment of skull loose, exposing his brain. Retrieving and cleaning the fragment with alcohol and using a paste made out of flour, Doc Krepela repaired Williams's skull in his field aid station and had him evacuated stateside for treatment. The Ninth Defense Marines whom I interviewed unanimously believed that Krepela truly deserved the Legion of Merit, the nation's highest non-combat award, which he received for his services to the Ninth.

65. Slater, *Jungle Vignettes*, 5.

66. Melson and Chadwick, *The Ninth Marine Defense*, 39.

67. Rentz, *Marines*, 64.

68. Stavisky, *Marine Combat Correspondent*, 160.

69. Donner, 22, reprinted in Donner, *Pacific Time on Target*, 33.

70. Personal reminiscences, Col. (Ret'd) Henry H. Reichner Jr., 24.

71. Melson and Chadwick, *The Ninth Marine Defense*, 25; Rentz, *Marines*, 64.

72. Bergerud, *Touched With Fire*, 331.

73. Taped reminiscences, Frank Yemma, Oct. 12, 1998.

74. Melson, *Condition Red*, 15.

75. Marshall, *The "Fighting Ninth,"* 43.

76. Rentz, *Marines*, 62 (but identifying the erroneously fueled radar set as the Ninth's SCR-602 set); Melson and Chadwick, *The Ninth Marine Defense*, 26; John J. Miller Jr., *Cartwheel: The Reduction of Rabaul* (Washington, DC: Department of the Army, Office of Chief of Military History, 1959), 91; 9th Defense Operations Report, 52.

77. 9th Defense Operations Report, 53.

78. Donner, 23, reprinted in Donner, *Pacific Time on Target*, 34-35; Horton, *New Georgia*, 67; Marshall, *The "Fighting Ninth,"* 43; Melson and Chadwick, *The Ninth Marine Defense*, 26; Rentz, *Marines*, 65-67; 9th Defense Operations Report, 53.

79. Hammel, *Munda Trail*, 77.

80. Sgt. Bill Miller, "Ack Ack Etc.," *The Leatherneck*, Pacific Edition, Sept. 15, 1944, 5; Colonel W. O. Thompson, "News and Comment-Comment on Antiaircraft Firing," *Antiaircraft Journal* (Jan.-Feb. 1949): 74-75.

81. Rentz, *Marines*, 67. David Slater of H & S Battery recalled observing "some guy pegging away with an air-cooled .50 mounted on a truck cab. There was plenty of .50, 20mm and 40mm going but, naturally, without effect." Correspondence, David Slater, Feb. 13, 1998.

82. Melson and Chadwick, *The Ninth Marine Defense*, 26.

83. Slater, *Annotations to 9th DB History, Rendova-New Georgia Campaign*, 6.

84. Interview, Clifford Cribbe, Battery C, 90mm Group, Nov. 24, 1999.

85. *First AAA History*, 2; 9th Defense Operations Report, 53; Hammel, *Munda Trail*, 77-78 (but stating there were only two bombers to survive the AA bursts); Marshall, *The "Fighting Ninth,"* 43-44; Meek, *Marines Had Radar Too*, 17-18; Melson and Chadwick, *The Ninth Marine Defense*, 26; Rentz, *Marines*, 65-67.

86. Not to be confused with the 155mm guns of either the GPF or M1 models of the Ninth or the smaller, standard 105mm Army howitzer, Colonel Shafer's FA battalion was armed with M1918A3 howitzers. These howitzers were the same caliber as the Long Toms but had a much shorter range. Like the Ninth's old GPFs, this model was French-made, World War I-vintage equipment and was being replaced in the European Theater by a more modern version of 155mm howitzer. It was nevertheless extensively used by Army forces in the Pacific. See Bergerud, *Touched With Fire*, 323; George Forty, *U.S. Army Handbook 1939-1945* (London, England: Ian Allan, 1979), 146, 149.

87. Hammel, *Munda Trail*, 77-78.

88. Melson and Chadwick, *The Ninth Marine Defense*, 26.

89. Slater, *Annotations to 9th DB History, Rendova-New Georgia Campaign*, 6.

90. See Frank, *Guadalcanal*, 524-25, 611-12.

91. A similar debacle involving Britain's Royal Air Force occurred near Sedan, France, in 1940. After the Sedan disaster and after inflicting heavy losses on German *Luftwaffe* bombers using similar tactics early in the Battle of Britain, the Allies generally abandoned such prewar formation flying in favor of looser, box-type formations for their bombing missions that allowed more leeway for evasive actions.

92. Melson and Chadwick, *The Ninth Marine Defense*, 18, 26.

93. Although it could have been done this way to a large degree, even as early as 1943; see note 27 on page 105 discussing the decision not to electronically integrate the Ninth's SCR-268 radars with the 90mm batteries.

94. Headquarters, US Marine Corps, *Standing Operating Procedure for Radar Air and Surface Warning and Radar Fire Control in the Marine Corps*, May 15, 1943; Kirk and Young, *Great Weapons*, 260-63; Melson, *Condition Red*, 14, 26; Rentz, *Marines*, 95; correspondence with David Slater, Feb. 13, 1998.

95. *First AAA History*, 2; Rentz, *Marines*, 84.

96. 9th Defense Operations Report, 97. Frank Yemma even recalled the Japanese raiders looking like civilian-style transports at first glance due to their uncamouflaged, bare aluminum bodies. Transcript of taped reminiscences, Frank Yemma.

97. Rentz, *Marines*, 63. See also Melson, *Up the Slot*, 14, citing Battery A's Joe Pratl.

98. To add to the confusion, the Imperial Japanese Navy's air service fielded another model of medium bomber, the Mitsubishi G3M2 "Nell," which was instrumental in the sinking of the British battleships HMS *Prince of Wales* and *Repulse* off Singapore in December 1941. Like the B-25, the Nell had a highly distinctive twin-rudder tail assembly. Enzo Angelucci and Paolo Matricardi, *World War II Airplanes* (Chicago: Rand McNally & Company, 1977), 2:122-23 (for the G3M-series "Nell"), 2:152-53 (for the G4M-series "Betty") and 2:154-55 (for the Ki-21-series "Sally"); *Japanese Forces Handbook*, 65-66; and US War Department and US Navy Department, Training Division, Bureau of Aeronautics, Field Manual FM 30-30/BuAer 3, Military Intelligence: Aircraft Recognition Pictorial Manual, April 1, 1943 (unpaginated, but with several photographic

arrays of the B-25 and each of the Betty, Sally, and Nell model Japanese bombers). Frank, *Guadalcanal*, 65, 84-85, 206-8 briefly describes Nells and Bettys and also describes the Japanese bombers' typical "vee-of-vee" attack formations. Still, at least one veteran of the Ninth was adamant that the bombers were Nells, neither Bettys nor Sallys. According to David Slater, an eyewitness to both raids: "The planes that attacked us on July 2 and 4, 1943 were definitely NELLs. I watched the entire affair on the 4th from start to finish, and I was good at aircraft identification (plus eagle eyes). An aside is the memory that it was reported at the time that a Lt. (j.g.) in command of a Sea Bee work detail on the 2nd had seen the planes and kept his crew working because he remarked about them being B-25s. His bunch was heavily hit and constituted the major number of casualties that day." Correspondence, David Slater, Feb. 6, 1998.

99.   The author is greatly indebted to Mike Driskill for helping solve the seventy-nine-year-old riddle of the identity of the Japanese raiders on July 2 and 4, 1943 that had vexed the author and a host of Ninth Defense veterans. As Mr. Driskill explained, the Japanese put up a heterogenous collection of aircraft in the effort to knock the American forces off Rendova. E-mail, Mike Driskill to author, June 7, 2016. See also Japanese Monograph No. 99, "Southeast Area Naval Operations Part II (February-October 1943)," 29-30:

> On the morning of the [2nd] July, 24 heavy bombers and 24 fighter planes of the army, combined with 20 navy fighter planes to storm RENDOVA and to bomb the landing point. They reported great explosions at two places and the sinking of two small transports. However, [considerable] damage was sustained by the army heavy bombers. On the morning of the 4th, 17 heavy bombers and 17 fighter planes of the army joined with 49 navy fighter planes for a second attack on the enemy convoy at RENDOVA. Enemy losses reported included the sinking of five transports and many small craft, setting fire to one point in the dump area, and the shooting down of 23 enemy planes. However, 11 of our planes failed to return or made forced landings. The army decided to discontinue air assault operations as a result of mounting casualties suffered in the two air results.

Cited in "Rendova raids, July 2 and 4, 1943," j-aircraft.org, http://www .j-aircraft.org/smf/index.php?topic=16472.0. See also Ikuhiko Hata, Yasuho Izawa, and Christopher Shores, *Japanese Naval Air Force Fighter Units and their Aces, 1932-1945* (London: Grub Street Publishing Ltd., 2011), 58.

100.   Hammel, *Munda Trail*, 73 (as to Reichner), 77 (as to Shafer).

101. Interview, Jerry Morris, Ninth Defense & AAA Battalions Reunion, Oct. 4, 1998.

102. Alexander, *Storm Landings*, 35, 38; Adams, *The Year that Doomed the Axis*, 261 (noting the nickname "The Wacky Mac"); Henry Berry, *Semper Fi, Mac: Living Memories of the U.S. Marines in World War II* (New York: Quill/William Morrow, 1996), 53–57 (citing account of Col. (Ret'd) William Hawkins, a passenger on the *McCawley* up to the day of her loss); Rentz, *Marines*, 60; Marshall, *The "Fighting Ninth,"* 41–42; Spector, *Eagle Against the Sun*, 234 (but solely crediting Japanese air attack as being the cause of the *McCawley*'s loss); Stavisky, *Marine Combat Correspondent*, 168–69.

103. Horton, *New Georgia*, 77–81; Stavisky, *Marine Combat Correspondent*, 178–82. Jack McCall recalled that his friend Doug Ayres served in the Tank Platoon and was the driver in a tank that took a hit in the nose, almost directly underneath his seat, either from a shell or a magnetic mine. The force of the explosion drove splinters deeply into Doug's buttocks and left him shaken but more or less intact. For many months afterward, the unfortunate Ayres periodically had to go to the aid station to have the splinters removed as they became infected. The tankers' weirdest casualty was sustained by a crewman whose leg was crushed by a tree limb that hurtled through his open hatch. See also letter, James V. Kruse to Jack McCall (Jan. 3, 1985), personal papers, Jack H. McCall, Sr.

The Tank Platoon likely saw more sustained, direct combat than any other portion of the Ninth. On New Georgia, Blake himself and his crew were nearly roasted alive by a Japanese flamethrower that doused their tank with gasoline but, fortunately, failed to ignite, and several tanks— including Blake's own—were crippled by magnetic mines. Blake received the Silver Star for his heroism. In the words of his citation: "By his great courage and indomitable fighting spirit he contributed materially to the success of this campaign and undoubtedly saved the lives of many infantrymen." As one Ninth veteran remembered: "Blake was the epitome of true heroism." Correspondence, David Slater, April 16, 1998.

104. Melson, *Up the Slot*, 17–18; 9th Defense Operations Report, 53–54.

105. Melson and Chadwick, *The Ninth Marine Defense*, 28.

106. Horton, *New Georgia*, 74.

107. Miller, *Cartwheel: The Reduction of Rabaul*, 110; Shaw and Kane, *The Isolation of Rabaul*, 94; Stavisky, *Marine Combat Correspondent*, 177.

108. Melson, *Up the Slot*, 20; Melson and Chadwick, *The Ninth Marine Defense*, 28; Language Section, G-2 (Intelligence Section), Thirty-Seventh Infantry Division, translation of captured Japanese war diary of Probationary

Officer Toshihiro Oura, *Record of the Decisive Battle Against Aircraft* (T/3 Dye Ogata and T/3 Frank Sanwo, translators; undated), 15. In 2002, one of the original translators, Lt. Colonel (Ret'd) Dye Ogata, was able to verify the provenance of the Oura diary, an annotated excerpt of which was later published in *MHQ: Military History Quarterly*. Toshihiro Oura, "I Will Fight to the Last," ed. Jack H. McCall, trans. Dye Ogata and Frank Sanwo, *MHQ: The Quarterly Journal of Military History* (Spring 2005): 70–79. I gratefully acknowledge my thanks to the late Colonel Ogata for his assistance, friendship, and support. The bulk of this diary is reprinted as Appendix 4.

109. Stavisky, *Marine Combat Correspondent*, 177.
110. Dull, *Battle History*, 285–88; Horton, *New Georgia*, 81; Rentz, *Marines*, 71, 271; Spector, *Eagle Against the Sun*, 234–35.
111. Donner, 24, reprinted in Donner, *Pacific Time on Target*, 35.
112. Dull, *Battle History*, 288; Melson, *Up the Slot*, 17–18; Melson and Chadwick, *The Ninth Marine Defense*, 28; Rentz, *Marines*, 74; Spector, *Eagle Against the Sun*, 235.
113. Donner, 24, reprinted in Donner, *Pacific Time on Target*, 35.
114. Donner, 25, reprinted in Donner, *Pacific Time on Target*, 36.
115. Melson and Chadwick, *The Ninth Marine Defense*, 31.
116. See Hammel, *Munda Trail*, 134–35; Horton, *New Georgia*, 82–84; Miller, *Cartwheel: The Reduction of Rabaul*, 135; Shaw and Kane, *The Isolation of Rabaul*, 98–100, 104.
117. Horton, *New Georgia*, 87–88; Marshall, *The "Fighting Ninth,"* 48; Rentz, *Marines*, 84; letter, Frank Chadwick to author.
118. Horton, *New Georgia*, 88; Rentz, *Marines*, 84; Shaw and Kane, *The Isolation of Rabaul*, 104–5.
119. Rentz, *Marines*, 84.
120. While some described them as "*banzai* charges," technically speaking, the Japanese attacks on July 12 and 13 did not fit the pattern of a true *banzai* charge. Derived from the Japanese saying "*Tenno heiko banzai!*" ("May the Emperor live ten thousand lives!"), a *banzai* charge was a last-ditch attack, often with bayonets and swords and frequently preceded by a Shinto religious ritual, made by a surrounded unit or one that deemed itself to be beyond hope. While commonly applied to many kinds of Japanese bayonet charges, strictly speaking, only a semi-suicidal attack devoted to the memory of the Emperor, such as occurred later on Saipan and in several instances on Iwo Jima and Okinawa, was actually a *banzai* charge.

121. Hammel, *Munda Trail*, 143-45; Marshall, *The "Fighting Ninth,"* 48; Melson and Chadwick, *The Ninth Marine Defense*, 31, 82; Rentz, *Marines*, 83; Stavisky, *Marine Combat Correspondent*, 183; interview, Frank Chadwick, Nov. 4, 1997; 9th Defense Operations Report, 54.

122. Horton, *New Georgia*, 88; Melson and Chadwick, *The Ninth Marine Defense*, 31, 82; letter, Frank Chadwick to author, Jan. 14, 1998; personal papers of Jack H. McCall, Sr., containing various newspaper clippings on the memorial services held for Wantuck in his hometown of Elmira, New York and the dedication of the Navy destroyer in his memory.

123. Stavisky, *Marine Combat Correspondent*, 183.

124. See Hammel, *Munda Trail*, 140-42; Horton, *New Georgia*, 84-87; Shaw and Kane, *The Isolation of Rabaul*, 104-5.

125. Miller, *Cartwheel: The Reduction of Rabaul*, 136.

126. Miller, 142-43; Rentz, *Marines*, 83.

127. Miller, *Cartwheel: The Reduction of Rabaul*, 136; Spector, *Eagle Against the Sun*, 237; Harold R. Barker, *History of the 43rd Division Artillery, World War II, 1941-1945*, (Providence, RI; John F. Greene Co., Inc., 1960), 53-55.

128. Barker, *History*, 53-54; Shaw and Kane, *The Isolation of Rabaul*, 104-5.

129. Oura Diary, 22.

130. Memorandum to All Hands, HQ, First Marine Amphibious Corps "In the Field," Oct. 15, 1943 (personal papers, Jack H. McCall).

131. "Japs Admit Big Offensive," *Nashville Tennessean*, Aug. 6, 1943, newspaper clipping in personal papers, Jack H. McCall, Sr.

132. Spector, *Eagle Against the Sun*, 236.

133. Melson, *Up the Slot*, 23; Melson and Chadwick, *The Ninth Marine Defense*, 33. A total of twenty-six Japanese aircraft would be claimed by the Ninth during its time on Rendova; 9th Defense Operations Report, 55.

134. The consensus among Jack and the Ninth Defense's Marines appeared to be that PT boats were enjoyable to watch, but it was sometimes tough for the Marines to gauge their true contributions to the Guadalcanal and New Georgia campaigns. Lightly armed (.30 and .50 caliber machine guns and 20mm and sometimes 40mm guns) and lightly armored, the PT boats found several types of Japanese craft to be quite a match for them, particularly the steel-plated, shallow-draft barges often used by the Japanese for coastal resupply. As a nautical sidelight of the Central Solomons campaign, the Japanese destroyer that rammed *PT-109*, the *Amagiri*, was one of the Tokyo Express ships involved in the naval battles and shore bombardments witnessed from afar by Jack on Rendova in early July. Dull, *Battle History*, 286-87.

135. Oura Diary, 25–27.

136. Melson and Chadwick, *The Ninth Marine Defense*, 28.

137. Joseph H. Alexander, *A Fellowship of Valor: The Battle History of the United States Marines* (New York: HarperCollins, 1996), 120; Spector, *Eagle Against the Sun*, 237; Bruce Gamble, *The Black Sheep: The Definitive Account of Marine Fighting Squadron 214 in World War II* (Novato, CA: Presidio Press, 1998), 148.

138. Melson and Chadwick, *The Ninth Marine Defense*, 36.

139. Melson, *Up the Slot*, 23; Rentz, *Marines*, 87–93. The fight for New Georgia had marked the US's first significant combat employment of flamethrowers, which were extensively used in the last stages of fighting around Munda Field's and Bibilo Hill's bunkers and hillside caves.

140. Bergerud, *Touched With Fire*, 373. Chadwick noted in an interview with the author that the TNT blocks used for Battery B's bunker-busting missions around Kindu Point were in fact quarter-pound sticks, not forty-pound sticks as originally indicated in the quotation appearing in Professor Bergerud's book. Interview, Frank Chadwick with author, July 16, 1998.

141. Melson and Chadwick, *The Ninth Marine Defense*, 36; Rentz, *Marines*, 146–47. Unlike Jack and his fellow leathernecks of the Ninth, who had waded for over a month in the muck and rot of Rendova and its environs before moving to Munda, the Marine pilots were in for a rude awakening: "[The pilots] found the conditions on the ground appalling. In some ways, the push through the New Georgia jungle had been even more vicious than that on Guadalcanal. . . . Munda offered only ugly devastation—ground-up earth, denuded trees, unburied enemy bodies. And the island was not secure." Gamble, *The Black Sheep*, 148.

142. Hogg, *Encyclopedia of Infantry Weapons*, 178–79; *Japanese Forces Handbook*, 209–10; Bergerud, *Touched With Fire*, 299–300.

143. Deactivated grenades were also the source of devious pranks that still raised the ire of some victims years later: "Some practical jokers liked to remove the powder from our grenades (from the bottom) and scare the hell out of their pals. One time, standing watch at 90 H&S (about 1,000 yards off the end of Munda runway), I heard this cap-pistol pop and the hiss of a grenade at my feet. I dived into my hole FAST, and then heard the sound of heavy laughter. That was the closest I'd ever come to plain murder. Fortunately, I don't remember who it was because if he's still alive, I'd send him a letter bomb." Correspondence, David Slater, Apr. 16, 1998.

144. 9th Defense Operations Report, 56. An alternative nickname,

"Millimeter Mike," was used by Munda's fighter pilots; Gamble, *The Black Sheep*, 149.

145. Other nearby Marine units were not so lucky: several men of MAG-21 were killed while standing in a chow line. Gamble, *The Black Sheep*, 153.

146. Melson and Chadwick, *The Ninth Marine Defense*, 36.

147. "We Had to Do It," 13.

148. Frank Yemma was one of the witnesses to Pistol Pete's shellings, the Army's ill-fated raid on Baanga, and the Fijians' subsequent rescue effort:

> Well, the Army wasn't doing its job with the 105s. We were madder than hell. We knew we could blow the hell out of them, but for some reason or another, they just wouldn't give us permission. However, this went on for a couple of days and then [the] Higgins boats came in with some Army troops, and they piled into 'em, and over they started. It was—honest to God—it was like watching a John Wayne movie. I sat there and the next thing I know, these Nambu machine guns opened up on it. And holy macaroni, they turned it, and guys dove over the side of the [Higgins boats] and swam to these little islands in front of Baanga Island. The Higgins boat came back into shore. I ran down there and the sailor, this coxswain, he was shot up bad.... Well, needless to say, they didn't try that again.
>
> The next thing I saw were these big black Fiji Islanders, [and] they all carried these British Bren guns. [The Fijians] got into canoes—two—one in the front and one in the back of the canoe, and over they went right where all these soldiers got shot up.... The Fiji Islanders went over, and they picked up one or two guys off the islands. You could see the bullets going around the canoes. Well, that didn't stop these Fiji Islanders! They'd pick up one or two soldiers and bring them back. [T]hey got them all back, believe it or not.

149. Miller, *Cartwheel: The Reduction of Rabaul*, 167, 172; 9th Defense Operations Report, 56.

150. Some forty-five years after the war, Bill Box and Frank Chadwick found the wreckage of the Pistol Petes still in place on Baanga in the fall of 1988.

151. Rentz, *Marines*, 125.

152. Horton, *New Georgia*, 122.

153. Melson and Chadwick, *The Ninth Marine Defense*, 36; Rentz, *Marines*, 125.

154. Melson and Chadwick, *The Ninth Marine Defense*, 36.

155. *9th Defense Battalion*. Historical Section, Division of Public Information, Headquarters, US Marine Corps, File No. AG-1265/HPH, Dec. 17, 1947, 6 (hereafter cited as 9th Defense History).

156. Taped reminiscences, Frank Yemma, Oct. 12, 1998.

157. Bergerud, *Touched With Fire*, 444.

158. "Vet's Medal Arrives 46 Years Late," Ninth Defense & AAA Battalion Association Newsletter, Oct. 1989, reprinted in *Poop! A Newsletter*, 3 (author's collection).

159. 9th Defense Operations Report, 83.

160. Rentz, *Marines*, 95. The Ninth's after-action report noted that the M-51 fuse "was declared unsafe by Army Ordnance"; 9th Defense Operations Report, 84.

161. Interviews and correspondence, William Galloway with author.

162. Slater, *Jungle Vignettes*, 8.

163. Slater, 8; 9th Defense Operations Report, 84

164. Melson and Chadwick, *The Ninth Marine Defense*, 33; see also Rentz, *Marines*, 95 and 9th Defense Operations Report, 55. Nor were the Ninth's Marines the only victims of ammo problems. In mid-July, an Army 105mm howitzer exploded on Kokorana Island, pelting the nearby dogfaces and Marines with large chunks of metal. The apparent cause was the oversized charge needed to place the shells at the 105mm's extreme range. Correspondence, David Slater with author, Feb. 13, 1998.

    Besides ammunition problems, mechanical defects also plagued the overworked guns. For several months until finally repaired, Battery B's Gun #2 had a leaky hydraulic recoil system. This meant that following the recoil from firing, instead of snapping back quickly into place, the gun would creep back slowly, and in desperation, its gunners would have to push the heavy gun barrel back into position for the next shot. These recoil system, or "equilibrator," issues were noted as a defect of the new-model M-1 Long Toms, along with defective axles; 9th Defense Operations Report, 83.

165. Marshall, *The "Fighting Ninth,"* 43.

166. Interviews and correspondence with Frank Chadwick, David Slater, and Frank Yemma.

167. It took forty-six years for Bill Galloway to be awarded a long-overdue Purple Heart for this wartime injury, finally receiving it on June 29, 1989, after heavy lobbying by Colonel (former Captain) Hank Reichner and Sergeant Horace "Smiley" Burnette of Battery A on Galloway's behalf. "Vet's Medal Arrives 46 Years Late," 3.

168. Rentz, *Marines*, 56–57.

169. Stavisky, *Marine Combat Correspondent*, 140.

170. Melson and Chadwick, *The Ninth Marine Defense*, 36; correspondence, Frank Chadwick to the author (as to Sandager's interchange with the pilot of the TBF). For more on Sandager's aerial observation missions, see "We Had to Do It," 11–13.

171. Rentz, *Marines*, 62; Stavisky, *Marine Combat Correspondent*, 155-56; 9th Defense Operations Report, 82.

172. Interviews and correspondence with Frank Chadwick and Frank Yemma.

173. Ibid.

174. This fact suggests that the Army patrol was likely a detachment of the 161st Infantry Regiment, 25th Infantry Division, detached from General Collins' command to augment the 37th and 43rd Divisions in the bitter fighting for Munda. Originally a Washington National Guard outfit, the 161st had seen combat in the latter stages of Guadalcanal and came to be an Army unit that was fairly well respected by the Marines.

175. Rentz, *Marines*, 125; "We Had to Do It," 4, 11 (which also contains a photograph of the mahogany tree and its makeshift ladder on page 4).

176. Notes of interview with Amsa Bodine, Battery A, Oct. 3, 1998.

177. See Horton, *New Georgia*, 122.

178. Rentz, *Marines*, 125.

179. Rentz, 126-27; Horton, *New Georgia*, 122; "We Had to Do It," 10-12.

180. Rentz, *Marines*, 95.

181. Horton, *New Georgia*, 122-24; Melson and Chadwick, *The Ninth Marine Defense*, 36-38; Rentz, *Marines*, 127.

182. Alexander, *A Fellowship of Valor*, 120; Bergerud, *Touched With Fire*, 229; Melson, *Up the Slot*, 24-25; Rentz, *Marines*, 131; Spector, *Eagle Against the Sun*, 239-40.

183. Melson and Chadwick, *The Ninth Marine Defense*, 79.

184. Melson and Chadwick, *The Ninth Marine Defense*, 38; correspondence and interviews, Frank Chadwick, Col. (Ret'd) Robert Landon, Col. (Ret'd) Henry H. Reichner Jr., and Frank Yemma. Donner took a dim view of Hiatt's targeting of this one defender and similar stunts: "[T]he stories came back of targets such as a single Jap on a motorcycle, a group swimming, or of 'creeping' by full volleys for four adjustments— all of which landed in the water. Such stories are passed around when confidence is lacking." Donner, 33, reprinted in Donner, *Pacific Time on Target*, 42.

185. Alexander, *A Fellowship of Valor*, 120; Melson and Chadwick, *The Ninth Marine Defense*, 38.

186. Melson and Chadwick, 38.

187. Ibid., 80.

188. 9th Defense Operations Report, 61.

189. Ibid., 81.

190. Ibid., 80.

191. Ibid., 80.

192. Bergerud, *Touched With Fire*, 230.
193. Office of the Surgeon General, US Army, *Neuropsychiatry in World War II: Overseas Theaters* (Washington, DC: Gov't Printing Office, 1973), II:463–64.
194. Bergerud, *Touched With Fire*, 230.
195. D. C. Horton, *New Georgia: Pattern for Victory* (New York: Ballantine Books, 1971).
196. Hammel, *Munda Trail*, xiii.
197. Slater, *Jungle Vignettes*, 11.

CHAPTER 5

1. These were also found in profusion on New Georgia. One Ninth H&S veteran, David ("Biggie") Slater, recalled sitting on midnight radio duty in the half-underground, corrugated iron-roofed pit near Munda Field that served as the battalion HQ's radio shack while the New Georgia land crabs' mating season began. The relentless mating march of thousands of land crabs and their intrusion into Biggie Slater's iron-sided radio shed makes for a scene worthy of Alfred Hitchcock: "Behind the iron walls, Biggie heard iron sounds. He could not escape until the next watch relieved him. The ordeal went on, and his duties were forgotten when he saw the first brown claw push its way in from beneath the edge of the wall. Then one intruder showed itself from under the transmitter rack. Biggie declared war and attacked the intruder with entrenching shovel and hammer. It was only the first." Slater's relief at midnight, in a radio shack now filled with pulverized land crabs, was "perhaps just in time to save Biggie from an overwhelming disgust and primeval fear." His attempt at sleep later that evening was frustrated by a similar invasion of his tent: "He awakened to the thumpings against the legs of his cot. Shining the beam of his flashlight to the ground, he watched the hours-long ebb of the clanking tide, until dawn itself, too, came from the sea." Slater, *Jungle Vignettes*, 10.
2. 9th Defense History, 9. The voyage to the Russells provided its own share of adventures for some. Jim Kruse, for instance, found himself aboard the USS APC-50, which was "a small craft that took a couple of us from Roviana Island to the Russell Islands. We had to travel slowly as we were leading an LST that had its compass shot out. Why was I on this craft? Mine is not to reason why, mine is but to do or—hell, we made it." Letter from James V. Kruse to Jack H. McCall, Sr., Feb. 16, 1985.

3. 9th Defense Operations Report, 119. ("Any visions held by battalion personnel of luxuriating in a rest camp after their two arduous campaigns were soon dispelled by (1) the necessity of first establishing camp in a locale with mud reminiscent of Rendova [and] (2) the movement a few days later to a more suitable camp. . . .")

4. "Unofficial" beer supplies were, on the other hand, a different matter and provided some good trading opportunities. As Biggie Slater recalled his section's escapades:

> There was a ration policy and each subordinate unit (battery and platoon) could send out transportation [to the PX] and a chit covering the unit allotment. Perhaps some groups were less enterprising than others; for example, 90 H&S . . . was off by itself on a spit of land [and] artfully forged chits for much more than our legitimate allotment and wound up with a large pile of beer. I counted 400 bottles stacked around our tent pole one day—"Red" Lenihan, "Bummy" Seifried, Pat Malloy, "Ruddy Ray" Sommer and myself. A few hundred yards offshore lay various supply vessels, including a refrigerator ship. We had salvaged a sort of clunky scow-like "boat" capable of holding five guys in a pinch. . . . A couple of guys took several cases of beer out to the 'reefer' and traded them for a case of cured hams and a barrel of ice. . . . For several days after that, we rarely left our tent area, having ham sandwiches, beer and coffee for chow.

Correspondence, David Slater with author, Feb. 17, 1998.

5. See, e.g., 9th Defense Operations Report, 120–21, summarizing the Ninth's recreational opportunities on Banika.

6. Melson and Chadwick, *The Ninth Marine Defense*, 59. Frank Chadwick's experiences of the drill instructors' views toward church services during Boot Camp seem to be fairly typical. Boot Camp started every morning at 4:00 a.m. and generally ended at 9:00 p.m., except on Sundays. On the first Sunday of Boot Camp, church call for Chadwick's platoon was scheduled for 9:00 a.m.:

> The DI always said, "For God, country and Corps," but then said he could not make us go to church or believe in God. About forty of us went to church [out of a platoon of 64 men]. Upon returning about 10:30, the DI gave us permission to sit on the tent floor boards with our feet on the ground (no sand was allowed in the tents), but the other twenty or so Marines were nowhere to be found. They returned to the tent area just before noon chow. They were dirty and disheveled and all had toothbrushes, which they had used to clean the heads and garbage cans. From that day on, we were the most God-fearing, religious Marines you ever met.

7. 9th Defense Operations Report, 120-21.

8. Clifford Merrill Drury, *The History of the Chaplain Corps, United States Navy*, vol. 2 (Philadelphia: Naval Publications & Forms Center, undated, NAVPERS doc. no. 15808), 323, http://www.navybmr.com/study%20 material/14282.pdf; Muster Roll of Officers and Enlisted Men, US Marine Corps, Headquarters & Service Battery, Ninth Defense Battalion, Fleet Marine Force for Apr. 1-30, 1944, found at Ancestry.com, *U.S. Marine Corps Muster Rolls, 1893-1958* [online database] (Provo, UT: Ancestry.com Operations Inc., 2007), original data: *U.S. Marine Corps Muster Rolls, 1893-1958*, Microfilm Publication T1118, 123 rolls, ARC ID: 922159, Records of the US Marine Corps, Record Group 127, NARA, Washington, DC; "United States Navy Chaplains and Denomination, December 1941-February 1943," https://bluejacket.com/usn_chaplains_1941-1943.html. Before he was assigned to the Ninth, Chaplain Janes was on the staff of I MAC.

9. Letters, Christopher S. Donner to Madge H. Donner, May 9, 1943, and March 22, 1944 (in author's collection). I was unable to ascertain whether Chaplain Janes's novel ever made it into print. After the war, Janes become the pastor of a Presbyterian church in the Pacific Palisades neighborhood of Van Nuys, California.

10. Letter, James V. Kruse to Jack H. McCall, Sr., Mar. 28, 1985 (personal papers, Jack H. McCall, Sr.).

11. Personal reminiscences, Col. (Ret'd) Henry H. Reichner Jr. Similarly, in *Goodbye, Darkness*, William Manchester recalled a tamer version of this song, which made the rounds of his own Marine outfit. Manchester, *Goodbye, Darkness*, 44.

12. Melson and Chadwick, *The Ninth Marine Defense*, 159-60. Several magazine clippings in Jack's scrapbook also depicted Ninth Defense Marines shooting fish from the top of an LVT Alligator off New Georgia's coast (personal papers, Jack H. McCall, Sr.).

13. Slater, *Annotations to 9th DB History, Rendova-New Georgia Campaign*, 9.

14. Correspondence, David Slater, Feb. 17, 1998. In the same letter, Slater vividly recalled boarding an offshore Australian subchaser to buy three bottles of grog, only to find upon returning to Banika that the watered rum was nothing but pure water. "Off we went, seeking redress (armed) to where the boat had been anchored. Gone! A pitched battle between allies narrowly averted!"

15. Marshall, *The "Fighting Ninth,"* 36.

16. "All along," Hall recalled, "I didn't want Captain Tracy to find out what I was up to because he could have court-martialed me." Years later, Hall

learned that despite his best efforts at secrecy, the Old Man knew what Hall was doing but let him continue his Raisin Jack distillery as a morale booster for Battery E's men. Interview, John Hall with author, Ninth Defense & AAA Battalion Reunion, Sept. 25, 1999.

17. A former college wrestler and an expert on judo, hand-to-hand combat, and bayonet fighting, Waldo Wells—unlike many Marine officers, but not unlike many of the old-salt NCOs—was not averse to administering personally what could euphemistically be called "corporal punishment" when so motivated. His pugnaciousness was not limited to his treatment of the enlisted men. His peer and predecessor as Battery B's skipper, Bill Box, remembered, "He was not somebody you could get very close to." Interview, Col. (Ret'd) William T. Box, May 27, 1998. Even a close acquaintance of Wells, Hank Reichner, noted the difference he observed in Battery B between Box's and Wells's styles of leadership when Wells was selected over Box to lead Battery B: "It was a source of disappointment to me that Bill Box did not have the same experience [as Reichner did in Battery A] with 'B' Battery. They deserved him." Correspondence, Col. (Ret'd) Henry H. Reichner Jr. to author, June 10, 1998. More bluntly, Bob Landon, one of Battery B's leathernecks, reported: "Waldo was kind of like Bluto in the Popeye cartoons." Listening in to Landon's recollections, another Battery B veteran, Frank Yemma, interjected: "We were always kinda terrified of Wells, since he was so much bigger than the rest of us." Interviews, Bob Landon and Frank Yemma, Ninth Defense & AAA Battalions Reunion, Oct. 2, 1998.

18. Bergerud, *Touched With Fire*, 160.

19. By most descriptions an eccentric, unusual individual ("a real weirdo," to quote Chadwick), this colonel's proclivities were starkly at odds with most of the other senior officers of the Ninth. As a result, his name cropped up with great frequency in my interviews and correspondence with the Ninth's veterans. While some stories seemed like exaggerations, the volume and range from all ranks—officers as well as enlisted Marines—indicate that there had to be a high range of truth to many of them. Several men vividly recounted this officer's apparent fascination with sex, pin-up photos, and women's bodies. David Slater remembered serving as a communications man in the 90mm Group's CP on New Georgia when an air raid alert was called. "Upon Condition Red, here comes [Lt. Colonel Baker], cussing all the while, yelling, 'I just finished with Lana Turner and was starting upon [some other actress' pictures] when these yellow bastards got me up!'" One of his junior officers,

Captain Reichner, recalled the Colonel as once taking a small boat and a case of grenades out to sea ostensibly to drop them, much like mini-depth charges, on submerged Japanese submarines! Correspondence and various interviews, Frank Chadwick and David Slater; interview, William Galloway, Oct. 4, 1998, and Joseph Pratl, Mar. 26, 1999; Melson and Chadwick, *The Ninth Marine Defense*, 20; personal account, Col. (Ret'd) Henry H. Reichner Jr.

20. Correspondence with Frank Chadwick, undated.

21. Stavisky, *Marine Combat Correspondent*, 153–54.

22. See page 164 and footnote 64.

23. Correspondence with Frank Chadwick, undated.

24. Ibid., 154.

25. See Bergerud, *Touched With Fire*, 483–84.

26. Shaw and Kane, *The Isolation of Rabaul*, 56–57.

27. Although the comedian Joe E. Brown had staged a USO show at Henderson Field in a driving rainstorm around Christmas 1942, it was primarily put on for the benefit of the First Marine Division's weary troops before their withdrawal from the Canal, and only a few Ninth Defense leathernecks attended. A later USO show held on Guam, attended by more of the Ninth's personnel, featured the vivacious singer Betty Hutton (described by comedian Bob Hope as "a vitamin pill with legs"). Correspondence, David Slater, Feb. 17, 1998.

28. Both female Marines and war dogs, however, joined the Corps in 1943, and Black Marine units were also in the process of being formed. Correspondence, Benis M. Frank, Former Chief Historian, US Marine Corps, with author, May 7, 1999.

29. Rottman & Chappell, *Fighting Elite*, 62. Notably, these attitudes were not limited to the male Marines: similar hostility greeted the employment of Army WAACs in General MacArthur's Southwest Pacific theater of operations. Some of these attitudes were ostensibly the result of greatly unfounded rumors that Army WAACs were "taken into the service to take care of the sex problems of soldiers" or that female military personnel were "simply officers' concubines." Spector, *Eagle Against the Sun*, 394–95.

30. Reichner, *A Battery*, 22.

31. Muster Roll of Officers and Enlisted Men, US Marine Corps, 155mm Artillery Group, Ninth Defense Battalion, Fleet Marine Force for Jan. 1-31, 1943, found at Ancestry.com, *U.S. Marine Corps Muster Rolls, 1893-1958* [online database] (Provo, UT: Ancestry.com Operations Inc., 2007), original data: *U.S. Marine Corps Muster Rolls, 1893-1958*, Microfilm

Publication T977, 460 rolls, ARC ID: 921599, Records of the US Marine Corps, Record Group 127, NARA, Washington, DC.

32. See, e.g., George Feifer, *Tennozan: The Battle of Okinawa and the Atomic Bomb* (New York: Ticknor & Fields, 1992), 113.

33. See Feifer, *Tennozan*, 121-23. The latter perception was, of course, not shared by all Japanese and notably not by at least two senior officials, both of whom had high respect and appreciation for Americans and had spent a considerable amount of time in the United States. As historical ironies, one of these men, Admiral Isoruku Yamamoto, the chief of the Combined Fleet, planned and led the Pearl Harbor and Midway operations; the other, Ambassador Kichisaburo Nomura, was forced to provide notification of Japan's declaration of war to US Secretary of State Cordell Hull hours after Pearl Harbor had already been attacked. Neither Yamamoto nor Nomura harbored any false illusions as to the bitterness of the war that followed Pearl Harbor or any doubts as to America's capacity to fight back.

34. These were words that many Marines and Army troops apparently lived by. It made for some grim situations: "On New Georgia, a sentry fired at a movement at night. Investigating at first light, they found a Jap (evidently looking for food) wounded in several places. One of the party gave him a *coup de grace*, asserting that 'he was going to die anyway.'" Correspondence, David Slater with author, Feb. 17, 1998. Similar incidents occurred in the Ninth's campaign on Guam.

35. James G. Stahlman, "From the Shoulder," *Nashville Banner* (Nashville, TN), Dec. 8, 1941.

36. Bergerud, *Touched With Fire*, 408-10; Frank, *Guadalcanal*, 130-31; Zimmerman, *The Guadalcanal Campaign*, 58-60.

37. In a raid on Chichi Jima in the Bonins in September 1944, Lt. (JG) and future US president George Bush's TBM Avenger torpedo bomber of Navy squadron VT-51 was shot down. The sole survivor of his three-man crew, he would be rescued by the submarine USS *Finback*. Postwar reports would confirm that Lt. (JG) Bush was doubly lucky in being rescued by the *Finback*: in several contemporaneous instances, the garrison commander of Chichi Jima had ordered the cannibalization of several captured pilots as part of a ritual intended to strengthen his officers' will.

38. Robert W. Blake, "Death on the Munda Trail," in *The United States Marine Corps in World War II*, ed. S. E. Smith (New York: Random House, 1969), 427, emphasis added.

39. Contrary to many American perceptions, however, the Japanese were not all that much more prepared for jungle warfare than were the Americans. Most of the Japanese home islands were more closely aligned, in a climatic and geographic sense, with portions of the United States than they were with the Solomons.

40. Robert B. Edgerton, *Warriors of the Rising Sun: A History of the Japanese Military* (New York; W.W. Norton & Company, 1997), 309. See also Feifer, *Tennozan*, 113-19.

41. Alexander, *Storm Landings*, 97. Flamethrowers were ordinarily considered specialized equipment issued only to combat engineers and sappers in other nations' armies, but they became widely issued to Marine and Army infantry battalions in the Pacific after New Georgia, being touted as the only effective way to clear Japanese caves and bunkers with minimal loss of American lives. See Bergerud, *Touched With Fire*, 372-73. Although they were not a part of the Fighting Ninth's arsenal (making it just about the only kind of conventional weapon the unit lacked), the Ninth *did* face Japanese flamethrowers, which were issued to Japanese combat engineering units: in the fighting on New Georgia, Captain Blake's command tank was doused with flamethrower fuel, which failed to ignite. His crew machine-gunned the operator, and the captured flamethrower became a grim trophy for the Tank Platoon.

42. See, e.g., Edgerton, *Warriors of the Rising Sun*, 316-17.

43. This author had his own personal encounter with this kind of conduct at a Ninth Defense and AAA Battalion reunion in 2001. For reasons which will soon become clear, I will not identify this veteran. He reminded me that the sixtieth anniversary of the liberation of Guam was coming up. The veteran then asked me if I wanted to join him on a trip to Guam in 2004. That this was not merely a sentimental journey became clear when the veteran said that he needed help digging up the heads of several Japanese soldiers he had decapitated circa 1944-45. "They had a lot of gold in their teeth," he said, adding he knew that he had buried the heads in a safe place and knew that he could still find them. His request was delivered with a weird smile on his face; the veteran—a man then in his early to mid-seventies—gave me absolutely no sense that he was joking. I was horrified to hear this, but based on my earlier research and the accounts (and photograph) of one other Ninth member's wartime skull "trophy," I was not entirely shocked. I declined the offer rapidly and left him with no doubt where I stood on this horror. For more on this grisly subject, see Simon Harrison, *Dark Trophies: Hunting and the Enemy Body in Modern War* (New York: Berghahn Books, 2012), 129-40.

44. Notably, by mid-1943, the Marine Corps itself was forced to accept draftees because of wartime expansion and shortage of volunteers. As noted earlier, several of these draftees joined the Ninth Defense, to the disgust of the old salts, just in time for Rendova and New Georgia. "At first, a lot of them had lousy attitudes, but we broke them in, and they became pretty good Marines," Jack once recalled, winking; "But not as good as us volunteers."

45. See generally Ambrose, *Americans at War*, 147. Incidentally, by only the closest of margins, the Ninth Defense missed the opportunity to directly serve under MacArthur. Following the First Marine Division's action at Cape Gloucester, with all available Army units in the Southwest Pacific fully engaged, MacArthur requested that the joint chiefs of staff provide additional Marine Corps support for his upcoming operations against Emirau in the Admiralty Islands. The Ninth's Marines were "saved" by Admiral Halsey: "The pace of preparations for Emirau was so swift that it put a crimp in the [joint chiefs'] plans for employment of Marines released by the cancellation of the Kavieng operation [and on March 14, 1944] MacArthur received and passed on to Halsey for compliance, a JCS directive that the 3rd Marine Division, the 4th Marines, and the 9th and 14th Defense Battalions were to be released to [MacArthur's control] immediately. By the time the Admiral received this order, it was too late to replace the 4th Marines and still meet the Emirau D-Day of March 20. . . ." Shaw and Kane, *The Isolation of Rabaul*, 521. One veteran noted years later in the Ninth's postwar newsletter: "Well, guys, it looks like we missed another great opportunity to live it up in one more tropical para-dise and maybe have become Dugout Doug's personal Defense Battalion. Instead, we have the incredible good fortune to see Banika and Ray Mil-land with his USO beauties. What the H___, ya can't winnem all." *Son of Poop!* (Ninth Defense/AAA Battalion Newsletter), Fall-Winter 1997, 2.

46. Reminiscences, Col. (Ret'd) Henry H. Reichner Jr.; Miller, *The First Offensive*, 352-54.

47. There was also an element of snobbishness involved, shown in the demeanor of the cocky all-volunteer Marines toward the "civilians-in-peace, soldiers-in-war," "part-time" men of the National Guard.

48. Bergerud, *Touched With Fire*, 230, emphasis added. Elements of the Forty-Third had also been severely hindered in their preparations for combat by the loss of much of their equipment in the December 1942 sinking of one of its transports, the *President Coolidge*, off Espiritu Santo while the division was en route to Guadalcanal. Miller, *The First Offensive*, 212; Richard Goldstein, "Col. Robert S. Scott Dies at 85; Won

Medal of Honor in 1944," *New York Times*, Feb. 12, 1998. Colonel Scott, a captain in the Forty-Third's 172nd Infantry (from which the ill-fated Barracudas of the Rendova landings were selected), won the Medal of Honor for his bravery near Munda Field on July 29, 1943 and was one of only two Medal of Honor recipients during the New Georgia campaign. The other, Sgt. Rodger Young of the Thirty-Seventh Infantry Division, received the medal posthumously for his elimination of a Japanese machine gun position on the Munda Trail, in memory of which a once popular folk song, "The Ballad of Rodger Young," was written.

49. Bergerud, *Touched With Fire*, 230.

50. Alexander, *Storm Landings*, 78; Harry A. Gailey, *The Liberation of Guam* (San Francisco: Presidio Press, 1988), 67; Cyril J. O'Brien, *Liberation: Marines in the Recapture of Guam: Marines in World War II Commemorative Series* (Washington, DC: History & Museums Division, Headquarters, US Marine Corps, 1994), 44.

51. Interview, Patricia H. McCall, July 3, 1999.

52. Rentz, *Marines*, 65-66 n.33.

53. Bergerud, *Touched With Fire*, 356.

54. Memorandum Order No. 29-43, Headquarters, Ninth Defense Battalion, June 28, 1943, reprinted in Melson and Chadwick, *The Ninth Marine Defense*, 78.

55. Miller, *Cartwheel: The Reduction of Rabaul*, 113.

56. Donner, 25, reprinted in Donner, *Pacific Time on Target*, 36.

57. Hammel, *Munda Trail*, xiv, 98-100, 154-57, and Bergerud, *Touched With Fire*, 379-80, 446-52. See also Spector, *Eagle Against the Sun*, 236. Compare this with a comment in the Ninth's after-action report to the effect that "[t]here were few cases of psychoneurosis or combat fatigue," although the report adds that physical ailments and disease were another matter entirely: "Besides malaria, there was a considerable amount of dysentery, diarrhea and minor fevers. Fungus infections, ring worm and boils were not uncommon. . . . Much of the recurrent malaria was undoubtedly brought out by the hard work under combat conditions, lack of sleep, and often inadequate diet." 9th Defense Operations Report, 61.

58. This opinion was not confined to the Marines: it was also a verdict reached by Army Medical Corps experts, who stated that a "[s]tudy of the records of neuropsychiatric evacuees and of other evidence [indicated] that incompetent or questionable leadership in small units was operating as a major precipitating factor" in the Forty-Third's incidents of jitterbugging and similar war neurosis cases on New Georgia. *Neuropsychiatry in World War II: Overseas Theaters*, II:464.

59. Bergerud, *Touched With Fire*, 443.

60. Ibid., 444.

61. Slater, *Annotations to 9th DB History, Rendova-New Georgia Campaign*, 3. Interestingly, this perspective was also shared by some of the Japanese, as Toshihiro Oura, the New Georgia diarist, wrote: "I set up the AA binoculars and observed the enemy positions. The U.S. flag could be seen fluttering on the PT boats. A destroyer, which had been camouflaged, was at anchor. You could call it a war movie or perhaps a Newsweek [the Japanese equivalent of Movietone News, Pathe, or Paramount newsreels] movie." Oura Diary, 20.

62. Marshall, *The "Fighting Ninth,"* 43.

63. Melson and Chadwick, *The Ninth Marine Defense*, 26.

64. Slater, *Jungle Vignettes*, 1-4.

65. Robert W. Blake, "Battle Without a Name," in *The United States Marine Corps in World War II*, ed. S. E. Smith (New York: Random House, 1969), 405.

66. A sartorial note: Marines could be readily distinguished from the Japanese by their choice of legwear and footwear. Marines often wore light khaki-colored leggings, which were side-lacing spats that reached over the ankles. Japanese troops were frequently issued puttees, wrap-around woolen strips resembling an Ace bandage, which reached to mid-calf and were worn either with short boots or *tabi*, an odd-looking rubber sneaker with a cleft big toe separated from the rest of the other toes.

67. Slater, *Jungle Vignettes*, 5-6.

68. Interview, Albert G. McCall, Jr., Mar. 15, 1998.

69. Bergerud, *Touched With Fire*, 400-401.

70. Correspondence, David Slater with author, Feb. 17, 1998.

71. Donner, 24, reprinted in Donner, *Pacific Time on Target*, 35. The nearby Marine pilots based at Munda Field also experienced the effects of these nightly nuisance raids, to their detriment. "Many a night [they] were rousted from their cots and into sweltering dugouts only to learn after an hour or so that the alarm had been false. There was no way to tell for certain if the alarms were real until the bombs fell, which was often enough to make the men heed every warning." Gamble, *The Black Sheep*, 161.

72. Slater, *Jungle Vignettes*, 1.

73. Bergerud, *Touched With Fire*, 457-58.

74. Several veterans of the Ninth also recalled, with a certain bitterness, postwar rumors that Navy Lt. (j.g.) John F. Kennedy's father, Ambassador Joseph Kennedy, had requested—and had come close to seeing—that his son receive the Medal of Honor for *PT-109*'s loss. The future president instead received a lesser medal for what many leatherneck veterans

regarded as being a court-martial offense, had Kennedy been a Marine under similar circumstances instead of a Navy Reserve officer.

75. Correspondence, David Slater, Feb. 17, 1998.

76. Bergerud, *Touched With Fire*, 160.

77. Alexander, *Storm Landings*, 64–65.

78. Carl Berger, *B-29: The Superfortress* (New York: Ballantine Books, 1970), 102; Gailey, *The Liberation of Guam*, 49–52; Maj. O. R. Lodge, *The Recapture of Guam* (Washington, DC: Historical Branch, G-3 Division, Headquarters, US Marine Corps/Govt. Printing Office, 1954), 16–17, 169.

79. Spector, *Eagle Against the Sun*, 279.

80. Lodge, *The Recapture of Guam*, 18, n.11; 25.

81. Alexander, *Storm Landings*, 74; Lodge, *The Recapture of Guam*, 23, n.29.

82. Gailey, *The Liberation of Guam*, 30–31, 34–35, 38–40; Lodge, *The Recapture of Guam*, 8–9; Manchester, *Goodbye, Darkness*, 280–83. By some estimates, perhaps as much as ten percent of Guam's population died under the Japanese occupation. See also James Brooke, "Decades After Abuses by the Japanese, Guam Hopes the U.S. Will Make Amends," *New York Times*, Aug. 14, 2005, https://mobile.nytimes.com/2005/08/14/us/decades-after-abuses-by-the-japanese-guam-hopes-the-us-will-make-amends.html.

83. "War-Hit Johnstons Foresee New, Brighter Era," *Nashville Tennessean*, Aug. 25, 1946 (newspaper clipping in personal papers, Jack H. McCall, Sr.).

84. Manchester, *Goodbye, Darkness*, 283. One Guamanian citizen recalled: "Both children and adults learned and sang the song throughout the occupation period though forbidden by Japanese authorities. It was a ditty urging the return of the Americans." Joseph Santo Tomas, "Song of Hope, Song of Faith," in *LIBERATION-Guam Remembers: A Golden Salute for the 50th anniversary of the Liberation of Guam*, Nat'l. Park Service online publication, https://www.nps.gov/parkhistory/online_books/npswapa/extContent/Lib/liberation8.htm.

85. Melson and Chadwick, *The Ninth Marine Defense*, 59.

86. 9th Defense Operations Report, 121.

87. Ibid.

88. *First AAA History*, 2.

89. Ibid.

90. *Son of Poop!* (Ninth Defense/AAA Battalion Newsletter), Fall–Winter 1997, 2.

91. Ibid.

92. Correspondence, Harry C. Jones, accompanying a photograph of USAT

Sea Fiddler (personal collection of David Slater). Interestingly, several transports that were largely crewed by Dutchmen and Dutch East Indies natives plied the waters of the Solomons and Central Pacific, one being commanded by a pro-Allies cousin of Germany's Field Marshal Rommel. Berry, *Semper Fi, Mac*, 175–76.

93. Melson and Chadwick, *The Ninth Marine Defense*, 61.
94. Located 2,420 miles west of Hawaii and four hundred miles past the next largest American-held island group at Kwajalein, this atoll, with its nearby sister Bikini, later achieved infamy as the location for postwar A-bomb and H-bomb tests.
95. For Operation FORAGER, twenty-four aircraft carriers of all types, plus eleven battleships, twenty-four cruisers and 152 destroyers, comprised the US Navy's mightiest battle group assembled to this point in the Pacific theater campaign. See Lodge, *The Recapture of Guam*, 190–92. The total ships allocated to the Guam portion of Operation FORAGER was 274 ships to land and support fifty-four thousand soldiers and Marines. Alexander, *A Fellowship of Valor*, 187.

CHAPTER 6

1. Manchester, *Goodbye, Darkness*, 28.
2. Smith, *United States Marine Corps*, 576–77.
3. Smith, *United States Marine Corps*, 576–77; Spector, *Eagle Against the Sun*, 302–3.
4. See, e.g., Alexander, *Storm Landings*, 72–73.
5. Lodge, *The Recapture of Guam*, 30; Melson and Chadwick, *The Ninth Marine Defense*, 61–62.
6. Gailey, *The Liberation of Guam*, 77.
7. Melson and Chadwick, *The Ninth Marine Defense*, 66.
8. Ibid., 62.
9. Thomas Heggen, *Mister Roberts* (New York: Houghton Mifflin Co., 1946), xi.
10. Melson and Chadwick, *The Ninth Marine Defense*, 62–64.
11. Ibid., 61.
12. Alexander, *A Fellowship of Valor*, 187; Manchester, *Goodbye, Darkness*, 283; Smith, *United States Marine Corps*, 609.
13. Alexander, *Storm Landings*, 75, 77; O'Brien, *Liberation*, 12. In stark contrast, the Ninth's campaign report stated that "all hands had a complete knowledge of the mission, terrain and *difficulties to be encountered in*

crossing the reef and getting guns in position. . . ."; Headquarters, Ninth AAA Battalion, Reinforced, In the Field, "Operation Report on Marianas," Aug. 17, 1944, 2 (hereafter cited as Ninth AAA Marianas Report), emphasis added. The Ninth's official report's statement stands in variance to the memories of its men, including my father. The testimonies that I received from the Ninth's veterans were generally more in keeping with Alexander's summation of the lack of awareness of the reef and the risks it posed, and less so that of their own battalion's operations report.

14. Alexander, *Storm Landings*, 75, 77; Lodge, *The Recapture of Guam*, 53–54.

15. Melson and Chadwick, *The Ninth Marine Defense*, 63.

16. Ibid., 63–64.

17. Berry, *Semper Fi, Mac*, 173–74 (citing account of Capt. John L'Estrange, CO of a DUKW motor transport unit supporting Operation FORAGER on Guam).

18. Alexander, *A Fellowship of Valor*, 174; Dull, *Battle History*, 315–23; O'Brien, *Liberation*, 5; Spector, *Eagle Against the Sun*, 310; Smith, *United States Marine Corps*, 598. The variance in losses depends in part on whether one counts solely carrier-based planes or both sea- and land-based Japanese planes destroyed in the two-day fray; Jablonski, *Airwar*, 2:135.

19. Melson and Chadwick, *The Ninth Marine Defense*, 64; Lodge, *The Recapture of Guam*, 54–56.

20. Melson and Chadwick, 65, citing Marine combat correspondent Sgt. William Allen.

21. Ibid.

22. Ninth AAA Marianas Report, 3.

23. Lodge, *The Recapture of Guam*, 67, 74.

24. Manchester, *Goodbye, Darkness*, 285–86. See also Gailey, *The Liberation of Guam*, 106; Lodge, *The Recapture of Guam*, 144.

25. Melson and Chadwick, *The Ninth Marine Defense*, 66, citing Ninth veteran Richard H. Cade. This kind of sabotage was not unlike the results of Nazi slave labor efforts: some Army GIs in Europe recalled the frequent late-war ineffectiveness of many German artillery shells and shell fuses, a sizeable number of which had been sabotaged by slave laborers and concentration camp inmates forced to work in war production plants, much as described by the novelist Thomas Keneally in *Schindler's List*. See Stephen E. Ambrose, *Citizen Soldiers* (New York: Simon & Schuster, 1997), 65–66.

26. Melson and Chadwick, *The Ninth Marine Defense*, 67.

27. Gailey, *The Liberation of Guam*, 159.

28. Gailey, 68.

29. Slater, *Jungle Vignettes*, 6.

30. See Alexander, *Storm Landings*, 73; Smith, *United States Marine Corps*, 604-7.

31. See Gailey, *The Liberation of Guam*, 204, as to the necessary size of runways for the B-29s.

32. Others of the battalion had similarly bizarre experiences. One evening, while the battalion HQ staff were watching movies outdoors with some neighboring Seabees and Guamanian civilians, the projectionist and his assistant captured several Japanese infiltrators among the spectators, an incident that Jack McCall also vividly recalled to his family. In another instance, a mess cook investigated someone rustling among the mess hall's crates and supplies, and he took a stick to drive away what he thought would be a scavenging dog or a scrounging Marine. Instead, he was faced with a starving, knife-wielding Japanese soldier, who he bludgeoned to death. Correspondence, David Slater, Feb. 18, 1998.

33. Another Marine remarked as to the extremes to which some would go to get alcohol: "The real drunks would drain Aqua Velva through bread. They learned a trick from the natives. You could take a coconut, punch three holes in it, pour in sugar, and plug it up again until it fermented. There was some Jap medical alcohol around too: you could dilute it with water in your canteen, and put in powdered lemonade. If you were lucky, you could find little vials of ether, crack them against the canteen, and cool it off. It was like drinking a Tom Collins. [Y]ou could inject it into [an] orange." Bergerud, *Touched With Fire*, 486. David Slater recalled several Ninth Defense characters who tried a similar distilling technique with Bay Rum aftershave. Correspondence, David Slater, Feb. 17, 1998. Another truly desperate wartime method of distilling alcohol involved pasting shoe polish onto a piece of bread, setting the bread in the sunlight, and letting the alcohol in the shoe polish leach through into a cup underneath the bread. I have yet to meet a veteran of the Ninth who would own up to having tried this distilling tactic.

34. Gailey, *The Liberation of Guam*, 187; Lodge, *The Recapture of Guam*, 158; Melson and Chadwick, *The Ninth Marine Defense*, 68.

35. O'Brien, *Liberation*, 30; Lodge, *The Recapture of Guam*, 95.

36. Melson and Chadwick, *The Ninth Marine Defense*, 68.

37. Gailey, *The Liberation of Guam*, 190-93, 205; Lodge, *The Recapture of Guam*, 158. Ultimately, 11,000 Japanese died in defense of Guam; Alexander, *Storm Landings*, 77.

38. Melson and Chadwick, *The Ninth Marine Defense*, 69.

39. See, for instance, Gailey, *The Liberation of Guam*, 195-97.

40. Joseph D. Harrington, *Yankee Samurai* (Detroit, MI: Pettigrew Enterprises, Inc., 1979), 133–34, 149.

41. Harrington, *Yankee Samurai*, 149.

42. Ninth AAA Marianas Report, 1.

43. Melson and Chadwick, *The Ninth Marine Defense*, 69.

44. Correspondence, Frank Chadwick, undated.

45. Correspondence, Frank Chadwick, undated.

46. McManus, *The Deadly Brotherhood*, 81.

47. For his part, as one of the team assigned to daytime patrolling missions, Frank Chadwick was not on duty during the evening and was asleep in one of the eight-man tents when the shooting broke out: "All I remember is that I was on my cot sleeping when an estimated column of over 100 Japs came down the road and the attack was on. It had rained hard that evening. A pool of water covered the area inside the tent. I rolled off my cot on the wrong side into the water and could not find my rifle. It took me a few seconds to realize my predicament and take corrective action."

    Wartime memories have a weird way of resurfacing in the present-day lives of veterans. Over fifty years after the Pago Bay firefight, a hot water heater burst and flooded the floor of Chadwick's home with about a half inch of water. In the middle of the night, Chadwick rolled out of bed and into the water. Immediately, "I was frantically looking for my rifle and was scared to death when I couldn't find it. . . . This apparently triggered something in the back of my mind and it took over 3 months or more to forget it again. Believe it or not, it took me about 5 minutes to realize I was on my bedroom floor laying in the water, now about an inch deep, and finally pulled myself together and got the water turned off." "Sounds foolish," Chadwick noted ruefully. Many veterans, however, have recounted similar flashbacks.

48. The journal entries of a Japanese medic, who was killed in November 1944 by a Marine patrol, reveal:

    12 August—Fled into a palm grove feeling very hungry and thirsty. Drank milk from five coconuts and ate the meat of three.

    15 August—Tried eating palm tree tips but suffered from severe vomiting in the evening.

    23 August—Along my way I found some taro plants and ate them. All around me are enemies only. It takes a brave man, indeed, to go in search of food.

    10 September—This morning I went out hunting. Found a dog and killed it. Compared with pork or beef it is not very good.

    19 September—Our taro is running short and we can't afford to eat today.

> 2 October—These days I am eating only bread fruit. Went out in search of some
>   food today but it is very dangerous.
> 15 October—No food.

Lodge, *The Recapture of Guam*, 162.

49. Melson and Chadwick, *The Ninth Marine Defense*, 69-70;
    correspondence, Frank Chadwick to the author.

50. A similar incident was related by Bill Melson of the 155mm Group's H&S
    Battery. Melson and Chadwick, 69-70.

51. Melson and Chadwick, 72-74. Japanese casualty reports from the Ninth
    during its occupation and mopping-up duties varied widely, but what
    can be found paints a grim picture. During one period in late summer
    1944, nearly forty Japanese a day were killed. By comparison, earlier in
    October, the Ninth had reported twenty-one Japanese KIA or wounded
    as a result of its patrols by the end of the prior month versus the one
    hundred reported as a result of the late October sweep. Melson and
    Chadwick, 69-74.

52. Gailey, *The Liberation of Guam*, 197-98.

53. Ninth AAA Marianas Report, 1.

54. The origins for this saying appear to be traceable to a directional sign
    that appeared on Tarawa around mid-1944, with one arrow reading, "To
    Tokyo, 3130 miles"; another reading, "To Frisco—what the hell do YOU
    care? You're not going there"; and a third, the one cited here in the text,
    predicting, "The Golden Gate in '48; the Bread Line in '49." Alexander,
    Storm Landings, 103; see also Berry, *Semper Fi, Mac*, 252. Several Ninth
    Defense veterans remembered the latter saying becoming quite popular
    on Guam, especially among the more jaded members of the battalion's
    old breed.

55. Only almost fifty years later, at a Ninth Defense reunion, would
    Chadwick see Dobkowski again and finally learn what had happened
    to him in autumn 1944. Interview, John Dobkowski with author, Ninth
    Defense & AAA Reunion, Oct. 3, 1998.

56. Correspondence, Frank Chadwick, undated.

57. Notes accompanying photographs, Harry C. Jones, kindly lent to the
    author by David Slater.

58. Letter, Christopher S. Donner to Madge H. Donner, Nov. 19, 1944 (in
    author's collection). Earlier on Guam, Chaplain Janes had scored a note
    of publicity throughout the Corps, being credited in a Marine Corps
    newspaper as having given one of the first religious services after the

landings while the beaches were still under sniper fire and officiating over the first burials on Guam. Sgt. Bill Allen, "Divine Services held for Marines Fighting on Guam," *Marine Corps Chevron*, Sept. 2, 1944, 5, http://historicperiodicals.princeton.edu/historic/cgi-bin/imageserver .pl?oid=MarineCorpsChevron19440902-01&getpdf=true.

59. Donner, 36, reprinted in Donner, *Pacific Time on Target*, 44–45.

60. *First AAA History*, 3; Melson and Chadwick, *The Ninth Marine Defense*, 72, 74.

61. Melson and Chadwick, *The Ninth Marine Defense*, 74.

62. The progress on the B-29 air bases on Guam was slow: the first B-29 airfield would not fully open for business until late February 1945. Gailey, *The Liberation of Guam*, 202–4.

63. Melson and Chadwick, *The Ninth Marine Defense*, 95.

64. 9th Defense History, 11.

65. By comparison, one rifle company alone of the Third Battalion, Twenty-Fourth Marines, began Iwo Jima with 133 Marines and had only nine riflemen left twenty-six days later. Another similarly sized infantry company, Company F, Second Battalion, Twenty-Sixth Marines, emerged from Iwo after thirty-six days with all of its platoon leaders and 221 men dead, wounded, or missing. Alexander, *Storm Landings*, 188.

66. Ambrose, *Citizen Soldiers*, 280. Because of these differences and the unique "all-arms" nature of the Ninth, it is difficult to compare directly the combat effectiveness of this heterogeneous battalion with more traditional (all-infantry or all-armored, for instance) US combat units, as found in the research—most often in the context of the European Theater—of historians such as Professor Ambrose, Craig Cameron, Peter Mansoor (e.g., *The GI Offensive in Europe: The Triumph of American Infantry Divisions, 1941–1945*), Martin van Creveld (*Fighting Power: German and US Army Performance, 1939–1945*), Peter Schrijvers (*The Crash of Ruin: American Combat Soldiers in Europe During World War II*), and Gerald Linderman (*The World Within War: America's Combat Experience in World War II*).

67. Melson, *Up the Slot*, 29.

68. Interview, Joseph J. Pratl, Mar. 25, 1999.

69. James M. McPherson, *For Cause and Comrades* (New York: Oxford Univ. Press, 1997), 90.

70. Manchester, *Goodbye, Darkness*, 391.

71. Correspondence, Frank Chadwick, undated.

72. While aboard the *Sea Corporal*, the spiritually minded Catholic officer

Chris Donner was pressed into religious duties, as he wrote home to his wife, Madge:

> The only thing out of the ordinary at the moment has to do with religion. Inasmuch as I am the only Catholic officer onboard, the Protestant Chaplain asked me to conduct services for men of my faith. There is a Catholic organist who helps out by playing the small portable organ—we used [Christmas carols] today-and I have led the men in the Rosary and read the selections from the Gospels. Friday, a holy day, there were fifty in attendance and 63 this morning. I was as nervous as if I had been facing a new class of college students. At my request the Presbyterian Chaplain gave a short sermon on a point of Catholic catechism and we all got something worthwhile from his talk. Held service on the open deck.

Letter, Christopher S. Donner to Madge H. Donner, Dec. 10, 1944 (in author's collection).

73. Letter, James V. Kruse to Jack H. McCall, Sr., Feb. 16, 1985.

CHAPTER 7

1. See page 127.
2. Interview, Albert G. McCall, Jr., April 6, 1998.
3. Derived from the "Roll of Honor—World War II-1941-1945" bronze memorial plaque at the Williamson County War Memorial Public Library, Franklin, Tennessee.
4. See pages 304-05.
5. "War-Hit Johnstons Foresee New, Brighter Era," *Nashville Tennessean*, Aug. 25, 1946 (newspaper clipping in personal papers, Jack H. McCall, Sr.).
6. Muster Roll of Officers and Enlisted Men, US Marine Corps, Second Guard Co., Marine Base, Portsmouth, VA, April 1-30, 1945, found at Ancestry.com, *U.S. Marine Corps Muster Rolls, 1893-1958* [online database] (Provo, UT: Ancestry.com Operations Inc., 2007), original data: *U.S. Marine Corps Muster Rolls, 1893-1958*, Microfilm Publication T977, 460 rolls, ARC ID: 921599, Records of the US Marine Corps, Record Group 127, NARA, Washington, DC.
7. Dedication Program, USS *Tarawa*, Norfolk Navy Yard, May 12, 1945 (personal papers, Jack H. McCall, Sr.).
8. Interview, Albert G. McCall, Jr., Mar. 15, 1998.
9. Alexander, *A Fellowship of Valor*, 222; Rottman and Chappell, *Fighting Elite*, 28, 30.
10. Muster Roll of Officers and Enlisted Men, US Marine Corps, First Casual

Company, Headquarters Battalion, Camp Lejeune, NC, July 1-31, 1945, found at Ancestry.com, *U.S. Marine Corps Muster Rolls, 1893-1958* [online database] (Provo, UT: Ancestry.com Operations Inc., 2007), original data: *U.S. Marine Corps Muster Rolls, 1893-1958*, Microfilm Publication T977, 460 rolls, ARC ID: 921599, Records of the US Marine Corps, Record Group 127, NARA, Washington, DC.

11. The bloody fighting on Okinawa (resulting in 49,151 US casualties, including over 7,450 dead, versus 100,000 dead Japanese) was widely seen as a precursor of what would happen when the Japanese mainland was invaded. Edgerton, *Warriors of the Rising Sun*, 299. As the Japanese mobilized all ages of their population and prepared a host of new *tokko* ("special attack", i.e., suicide) weapons—including suicide motorboats and frogmen, *Ohka* (i.e., "cherry blossom," called by US sailors and troops *"baka,"* or "stupid") rocket bombs, and spear-wielding civilians, the US joint chiefs of staff actively contemplated the use of poison gas and tactical use of the atomic bomb on Kyushu's invasion beaches for the landings scheduled for November 1945. Alexander, *Storm Landings*, 172-92; Williamson Murray, "Armageddon Revisited," *Military History Quarterly* (Spring 1995): 6-11; Stanley L. Falk, "A Nation Reduced to Ashes," ibid., 54-63; Rod Paschall, "Tactical Exercises: Olympic Miscalculations," ibid., 62, 63; Edward J. Drea, "Previews of Hell," ibid., 74-81; Peter Maslowski, "Truman, The Bomb, and The Numbers Game", ibid., 103-7; and Thomas B. Allen and Norman Polmar, "Gassing Japan," *Military History Quarterly* (Autumn 1997): 38-43. For a description of the sinister *Ohka* flying bomb, see Angelucci and Matricardi, *World War II Airplanes*, 202; Kirk and Young, *Great Weapons*, 84-87.

12. On arriving at Camp Pendleton, Jack reported to the post's main guard shack to have his leave and travel orders signed. To his immense surprise, the sergeant of the guard on duty that day was none other than his brother Bob, recently transferred to Camp Pendleton from his prior duty guarding a Navy arsenal in Pocatello, Idaho. Interview, Albert G. McCall, Jr., Mar. 15, 1998.

13. See, for instance, Peter Wyden, *Day One: Before Hiroshima and After* (New York: Warner Books, Inc., 1985), 16-19, 161-62, 292-93, 324-26.

14. Notes of taped interview, Frank Yemma, Dec. 28, 1998, 8-9.

15. Alexander, *Storm Landings*, 192.

16. Benis Frank, a First Marine Division vet and contemporary of Jack (and later USMC chief historian), captures the unexpected feelings of alienation and loss that so many felt as they returned home: "I was discharged at Bainbridge Naval Base on 14 February 1946 and caught a

B&O train for Newark, from which I had to take a ferry to New York to go to Grand Central Station to catch a train to Stamford, Connecticut. It was only a 48-minute trip from New York to Stamford, but it seemed longer than that. As I got closer to home and to my parents who were waiting at the train station, I wished that I could have turned around and returned to my old outfit and my buddies where and with whom I felt secure and comfortable. Of course, life had to go on, and so it did." Correspondence, Benis M. Frank to the author, May 7, 1999.

EPILOGUE

1. Letter, James V. Kruse to Jack McCall, Jan. 3, 1985, personal papers, Jack H. McCall, Sr.
2. Bergerud, *Touched With Fire*, 415. This aged Japanese veteran was captured briefly on film in a videotape made by Colonel (Ret'd) William T. Box and Francis E. Chadwick, *Return to the Solomon Islands*, autumn 1988 (author's collection).
3. John C. McManus, *The Deadly Brotherhood: The American Combat Soldier in World War II* (Novato, CA: Presidio Press, 1998), 290.
4. John Monks, Jr., "Bougainville: Beachhead and Swamp," in *The United States Marine Corps in World War II*, ed. S. E. Smith (New York: Random House, 1969), 447.
5. Berry, *Semper Fi, Mac*, 13.
6. Tom Brokaw, *The Greatest Generation* (New York: Random House, 1998), xxx, 11.

POSTSCRIPT TO THE SECOND EDITION

1. Samuel Hynes, *The Soldiers' Tale: Bearing Witness to Modern War* (New York: Penguin Books, 1997), 1 (quoting this line from the *Chanson de Roland*, as cited by First World War poet David Jones in *In Parenthesis*).
2. E-mail, David Slater to the author, Aug. 23, 2006.

APPENDIX 1

1. Chris Donner's memoirs, written immediately after war's end—excerpts from which were used with Donner's permission in this work—were published in 2012, just days before his death at the age of ninety-nine. Christopher S. Donner, *Pacific Time on Target: Memoirs of a Marine Artillery Officer, 1943-1945*, ed. Jack H. McCall, Jr. (Kent, OH: Kent State Univ. Press, 2012).

2. Hank Reichner's memoirs—excerpts from an early draft of which were used with Colonel Reichner's permission in this work—were published in 2009. Henry H. Reichner Jr., *But One Life to Give* (Bloomington, IN: Xlibris Corp., 2009).

3. Letter, Brother Andrew (formerly John) Sorensen to Frank Chadwick, July 12, 1987, personal papers, Jack H. McCall, Sr.

APPENDIX 4

1. Eugene B. Sledge, *With the Old Breed at Peleliu and Okinawa* (New York: Oxford Univ. Press, 1990).

2. James J. Fahey, *Pacific War Diary, 1942–1945* (New York: Houghton Mifflin, 1992).

3. Toshihiro Oura, "I Will Fight to the Last," ed. Jack H. McCall, trans. Dye Ogata and Frank Sanwo, *MHQ: The Quarterly Journal of Military History* (Spring 2005): 70–79.

4. Likely an Army Air Forces' P-38 Lightning.

5. In the Japanese order of battle, the Thirty-First Independent Field AA Battalion (as opposed to a Thirty-First Company) was identified as defending the Munda Field sector on New Georgia. John N. Rentz, *Marines in the Central Solomons* (Washington, DC: Headquarters, US Marine Corps/Govt. Printing Office, 1952), 177.

6. Likely Grumman-designed TBF or TBM Avenger bombers.

7. He is probably referring to Douglas SBD Dauntless dive bombers.

8. Likely Vought F4U-1 Corsairs.

9. Probably Curtiss P-40 Warhawk or Kittyhawk model fighters, used both by the Army Air Forces and the Royal New Zealand Air Force, which were based on forward airfields in the Russells as well as on Guadalcanal.

10. P-38 Lightnings.

11. The Wickham anchorage was located far toward New Georgia's southeastern tip, some forty miles (straight-line distance) from Munda Field.

12. Likely Douglas SDB Dauntless dive bombers.

13. This unit would most likely be the Third Field Searchlight Battalion.

14. A kind of light automatic cannon, also used for AA work, some models of which resembled an oversized Maxim-type machine gun.

15. This was the Japanese Army's higher headquarters for the Solomons, the Bismarck Islands and the eastern half of New Guinea (i.e., Papua) and was commanded from Rabaul by Lt. General Hitoshi Imamura.

16. He is referring here to the pride of the Imperial Japanese Navy, the sister super-battleships *Yamato* and *Musashi*, armed with 18.1-inch guns.

17. As there were no Japanese four-engined land-based bombers (like the US Boeing B-17 "Flying Fortress") generally in service at this time, Oura's description suggests that these "new model heavy bombers" were likely Japanese Navy G4M1 Betty bombers or the Japanese Army's comparable Ki-21 Sally bombers.

18. Assuming this antitank mission continued through the campaign, the Second Platoon may have been among the stubborn defenders of the Munda Trail who engaged Capt. Robert Blake's tanks of the Ninth Defense, sometimes with grenades and magnetic mines at ultra-close range, making them very much into the suicide troops that Oura described.

19. Often used in triple mounts as an AA weapon, this was a type of automatic cannon employed both on ships and land by the Japanese Navy.

20. Likely PBY Catalinas.

21. SNLF *rikusentai* troops.

22. A reference to the bombers that were shot down by the Ninth on July 4, 1943.

23. The *rikusentai* (SNLF) detachments deployed to New Georgia were the Kure Sixth SNLF and the Yokosuka Seventh SNLF—both of which were noted for their exceptionally good organization and training—directed by the Eighth Combined SNLF Headquarters.

24. The Japanese Tenth Mountain Artillery Battalion had troops stationed on New Georgia, and it was likely this unit's guns to which Oura referred.

25. Obviously describing the AA components of the Ninth Defense: by "pom-poms," Oura must mean the Ninth's 40mm Bofors guns, which were roughly comparable to Japanese "pom-pom" (so-called for the sound they made) light AA guns.

26. In lieu of "submarine base," perhaps "torpedo boat base"—meaning the Navy's PT boat base on Tombusolo Island, near Rendova—would be more accurate.

27. Eight, in fact (four 155mm Long Toms apiece in each in A and B Batteries of the Ninth Defense Battalion); the Army's shorter-ranged and older model 155mm howitzers were based on islands besides Rendova.

28. Quite likely, 40mm or 20mm automatic cannon.

29. On July 8–9, a US destroyer group commanded by Capt. Thomas J. Ryan, Jr. extensively shelled the Munda Point area in support of the Army's Forty-Third Infantry Division.

30. Close enough: it was, in fact, 155mm caliber.

31. Again, a fairly accurate estimate: the 90mm Group of the Ninth Defense had six searchlights assigned to it.

32. These are B-24 Liberator heavy bombers.

33. Lt. General Hitoshi Imamura was the commander of the Japanese Eighth Area Army, headquartered at Rabaul and with forces deployed throughout the Solomons, Bismarck Islands, and New Guinea.

34. The capital of Papua New Guinea, Port Moresby was the linchpin of the American and Australian efforts to retake Japanese-occupied New Guinea. It held.

35. These were US 155mm shells.

36. This reference could be to either a B-24 Liberator or a PBY flying boat, both made by Consolidated Aviation.

Glossary

.30   Caliber of bullet used for the BAR, Springfield, and Garand rifles and also for the M1917 and M1919 light machine guns.

        A smaller .30 caliber round was used by the M1 carbine.

.45   Colt .45 caliber M1911A1 automatic pistol.

.50   Browning M2 heavy machine gun. Often fitted on a portable tripod for ground usage (in the M2-HB—"heavy-barrel"—model) or on an M2 pedestal with water-cooled jacket for AA use or on vehicular mounts, the .50 caliber machine gun was often used for AA defense but was originally designed in 1919 as an antitank weapon.

1-A   Highest qualification rating for draft eligibility by the US Selective Service Board. (The polar opposite rating was "4-F.")

III Amphib

    Third Amphibious Corps (sometimes also identified as "III AC"), the successor to I MAC.

4-F   Lowest Selective Service Board draft rating; unqualified or physically unfit to serve in the military.

90mm   Principal US medium antiaircraft gun of World War II, the M1A1 was originally issued to Army AA units and was first issued to Marine defense battalions in the summer of 1942. The Ninth had twelve of these guns. It had a horizontal range of 18,890 yards and a vertical range of 11,273 yards. The 90mm fired a 23.4-pound shell and required a full crew of ten men, who, if well trained, could fire twenty-eight rounds per minute. The gun had a distinctive, honeycomb-patterned firing stand, and the bogey wheels were dismounted for firing. Ninth Defense 90mms of Battery E destroyed twelve Japanese high-altitude bombers and one fighter with eighty-eight shells on Rendova on July 4, 1943, setting a world record.

AA   Antiaircraft (also sometimes called "ack-ack").

AAA   Antiaircraft artillery (also sometimes called "triple-A").

AAF   US Army Air Forces (the predecessor of today's US Air Force).

agi   A homemade Guamanian alcoholic beverage distilled from fermented heart of coconut palm sap. See also entry for "tuba or tupa."

Alligator

LVT-1 amphibious, fully tracked tractor and cargo carrying vehicle. Also called "amphtracks" or "amtracs," LVT stood for "Landing Vehicle, Tracked." The LVT-1s issued to the Ninth Defense for the New Georgia campaign were unarmored, light-steel vehicles, with no landing ramps or built-in armament. Later models of LVT were armed with. .50 caliber machine guns (several models of which were equipped with tank turrets), were partly armor-plated, and had rear-mounted landing ramps to improve safety in disembarking troops and supplies from the LVT when under fire.

APC   Aspirin with caffeine tablets (widely used as both an analgesic and a stimulant).

Arisaka Japanese 6.5mm and 7.7mm bolt-action rifles.

Arundel Island located off the westernmost tip of New Georgia, due south of Kolombangara.

Atabrine

Anti-malarial drug issued to US forces in the South Pacific as a substitute for quinine.

Avenger See entry for "TBF."

AWOL   Absence without leave. The Marines' terminology for this offense was "unauthorized absence."

B-24   See entry for "Liberator."

B-25   Douglas twin-engined medium bomber, known as the "Mitchell," which, besides being one of the most common US Army Air Force and RAAF bombers used in the Pacific, was also the plane used by General James Doolittle's raiders in their bombing raid on Japan in spring 1942. Roughly the shape of the Nell (both had a twin-rudder tail configuration), the two bombers were occasionally mistaken for one another by AA gunners. Several Marine medium bomber squadrons also used the Mitchell, called "PBJ" by the Marines and Navy.

B-29   Large, four-engined Boeing heavy bomber, officially nicknamed the "Superfortress," used by US Army Air Forces for long-range bombing of Japan in 1944 and 1945. The B-29s *Enola Gay* and *Bock's Car*, stationed on the island of Tinian, not far from Guam, dropped the atomic bombs on Hiroshima and Nagasaki on August 6 and August 9, 1945, respectively.

Baanga Small island off the tip of Munda Point, New Georgia, on which the Japanese stationed the New Georgia versions of Pistol Pete.

Baka   Japanese word for "stupid" or "foolish" and name applied by US troops and sailors to a rocket-powered model of kamikaze plane (the Yokosuka *Ohka*) in 1945.

Banika Island in the Russell Islands where the Ninth Defense was posted in early 1944.

Banzai Derived from the Japanese expression *"Tenno heiko banzai!"* (may the Emperor live ten thousand lives), technically, a banzai charge was a last-ditch attack, often with bayonets and frequently preceded by a Shinto religious ritual, entered into by a surrounded unit or one that deemed itself to be beyond hope. While commonly applied to many kinds of bayonet charges or other Japanese attacks, strictly speaking, only the semi-suicidal attack devoted in honor of the Emperor was actually a banzai charge.

BAR   .30 caliber Browning Automatic Rifle. Really a light machine gun, the 19.5-pound, forty-eight-inch-long BAR resembled a large rifle mounted on a folding bipod, which was attached to the front of the barrel, and fired a twenty-round clip.

Barracuda

A member of an ad hoc task force drawn from the Army's 172nd Infantry Regiment, Forty-Third Infantry Division, which was used as an advance party and beach assault force during the initial landings on Rendova and New Georgia.

battery Artillery unit equivalent of a company; usually commanded by a captain.

Betty   Allied codename for Mitsubishi G4M2 (Type 1) two-engined Japanese medium bomber.

Black Sheep

Nickname for Marine Fighter Squadron VMF-214, commanded by the famous Maj. Gregory ("Pappy") Boyington and based at Munda Field on New Georgia in mid-1943.

Bofors The name of the Swedish designer and manufacturer of the 40mm M1 light, automatic antiaircraft gun often used by US and Allied forces. Capable of firing a nearly two-pound shell at the rate of 120 rounds per minute to a range for four miles, the clip-fed Bofors gun could be used against ground targets and tanks as well as aircraft and was credited with 50 percent of the enemy aircraft downed by US AA fire between 1944 and 1945.

boondockers

Marine Corps-issue field boots.

boondocks
> Marine slang for rough terrain, particularly if woody or jungled, and derived from a Filipino word for mountain or hill.

boot   Marine nickname for a new recruit undergoing basic training at Boot Camp. See also entry for "PI."

breakbone fever
> Dengue fever.

brig   Navy and Marine term for a jail.

bucket issue
> Initial issue of various sundry items to boots at Parris Island, known as a "bucket issue" because they were placed in a metal wash bucket.

butts   Pits at the Parris Island rifle range from which the paper targets were raised and lowered.

C3   Command, control, and communications.

Caimanera
> Village on the outskirts of the naval base at Guantanamo Bay, Cuba, noted for its bars, black markets, and brothels; nicknamed "Caimanooch" by the Ninth's Marines.

caliber   See entry for "mm (or MM)."

campaign hat
> Old-style Marine hat with wide, round brim and a pointed conical top, worn today by Marine DIs; resembles the "Smokey Bear" hat.

Canal, the
> Nickname for Guadalcanal.

Carney Field
> American airfield built in the Koli Point area of Guadalcanal and used mainly by B-24 bombers of the Thirteenth Air Force.

CARTWHEEL
> Allied codename for a series of operations (including mid-1943's Operation TOENAILS and later landings on Bougainville in November 1943) intended to outflank the major Japanese air and naval bases on New Britain, including Rabaul.

Catalina
> Consolidated PBY twin-engined seaplane used by the US Navy. A version called the "Black Cat" was used for night operations.

cat fever
> Catarrhal fever.

CB   Official abbreviation for a Naval construction battalion. See "Seabee."

Central Solomons

> The portion of the Solomon Islands encompassing New Georgia, Rendova, Kolombangara, Vella Lavella, and their environs.

cerveza Spanish word for beer.

Chamorro

> A native of Guam; "Guamanian" is now the preferred term for citizens of Guam.

Chick Marine nickname for any especially young or beardless Marine (derived from "spring chicken").

chop Detachment and reattachment of a military unit from its normal controlling headquarters (short for "*ch*ange of *op*erational control").

chow Marine slang for food.

Christmas Trees

> Nickname given to Marine recruits who volunteered between Pearl Harbor and New Year's Day in 1942. Also sometimes called the "Pearl Harbor Avengers."

CO Commanding officer (the "old man"; an endearment never expressed to his face, however).

Cobber Nickname for a New Zealander, derived from New Zealand slang for a buddy or friend (and adopted as such especially by the men of the First Marine Division, who were sent to New Zealand for R&R after Guadalcanal).

commo Communications.

ComSoPac

> Commander, South Pacific Area; from late 1942, this position was held by Navy Vice Admiral William ("Bill" or "Bull") Halsey.

Condition Black

> Highest stage of non-AA alert: enemy landing imminent.

Condition Green

> "All clear."

Condition Red

> Highest degree of air alert: air raid imminent or ongoing.

Condition Yellow

> Air raid expected. In practice, once unidentified aircraft ("bogies") were picked up by radar and were on a bearing for the unit, "Condition Yellow" was announced. Once the bogies passed a certain point and remained on the same bearing, the alert status was upgraded to "Condition Red" (see above).

corpsman
Navy medical technician assigned to serve as a medic in a Marine unit; most often called simply "doc."

Corsair Vought F4U single-engined fighter; readily identified by its gull-shaped wings and long nose, the Corsair was a mainstay of US Marine and Navy fighter units beginning in February 1943. Called "Whispering Death" by the Japanese due to the (relative) quietness of its engine.

CP Command post.

C ration "Ration C" featured a cardboard box containing two cans: one filled with crackers, powdered coffee or tea, candy, toilet paper, various condiments, and four cigarettes, and the other filled with food to be warmed—among other menu items, hash, stew, chicken and noodles, and (more frequently than not) the ubiquitous Spam. Less often encountered in the Pacific theater.

Dauntless
Douglas SBD single-engined dive bomber, with a two-man crew, used by US Marine and Navy bomber squadrons.

DI Marine drill instructor.

Diamond Narrows
Channel of water between the Munda and Kindu Point areas of New Georgia and Kolombangara.

digger Nickname for an Australian soldier (ostensibly originating from the Australian troops' expertise at trench-digging during their Gallipoli campaign in Turkey during World War I).

Doc Nickname for any Navy surgeon, doctor, or corpsman. Also the personal nickname for Battery A's exec, who later served as Battery B's CO, George Teller.

dogface Nickname usually applied to Army infantrymen, but also applied to other troops in other combat services; thought to derive from the stubbly bearded and haggard appearance of soldiers after several days or weeks in combat.

D ration
A hard, vitamin-reinforced chocolate bar.

Dugout Doug
Sarcastic Marine nickname for general of the Army Douglas MacArthur, the Allies' Southwest Pacific Area commander.

Duke Radio call sign for the Ninth Defense Battalion's headquarters element.

EM Enlisted man.

exec   A unit's executive officer, or second in command. (See also entry for "XO.") This term was more commonly used than "XO" during the Second World War.

F4U   See entry for "Corsair."

FA   Field artillery.

FCO   Fire control officer.

feather merchant
    Marine slang for a short or lightweight person.

field music
    Marine term for a unit's bugler or other musician.

field scarf
    Marine Corps-issue khaki necktie.

Fleet Marine Force
    The administrative and command designation used for the Marine Corps "in the field"; that portion of the Corps made up of all deployed field units, from Corps and division level downwards to the ship detachments on board US Navy vessels. The Fleet Marine Force ("FMF," for short) was further subdivided into theater-level components (e.g., Fleet Marine Force-Pacific), which might loosely be viewed as being the USMC's equivalent of an Army/Army group command.

FMF   See the preceding entry for "Fleet Marine Force."

FMF-PAC
    Fleet Marine Force-Pacific; the FMP's Pacific theater component.

FO   Forward observer.

FORAGER
    US codename for the operation involving the recapture of the southern Mariana Islands group, including Saipan, Tinian, Rota, and Guam.

Garand .30 caliber M1 semiautomatic rifle.

Gavutu Small island just to the north of Guadalcanal, due south of Florida Island.

GI   Nickname for Army troops (derived from the Army abbreviation for "government issue").

Gitmo   Marine nickname for Guantanamo Bay, Cuba.

gizmos Nickname applied to Jack and his fellow water purification experts in the Ninth and more generically applied to any technicians whose jobs required working with anything mechanical, electrical, or hydraulic in nature.

God Box
    Marine nickname for a chapel or church.

Goettge Massacre

Incident involving the isolation and shooting of members of a small Marine reconnaissance patrol on Guadalcanal led by Lt. Colonel Frank Goettge, the First Marine Division's G-2 (chief intelligence officer).

goldbrick

A slacker or lazy person.

GPF Official designation for the old model (M1918) 155mm gun, originally used by the Ninth Defense's Seacoast Group. Commonly thought to stand for "Great Power French," GPF was a French abbreviation for "Grande puissance Filloux," (Filloux being the French designer's name).

grabass Marine slang for horseplay or a bull session.

Green Dragon

See entry for "LST."

gung ho Chinese expression meaning "work together," popularized by Marine Raider Battalion Colonel Evans Carlson and later coming to describe anyone exhibiting a can-do, aggressive, or positive attitude.

gunner Marine Corps rank equivalent to that of an Army warrant officer.

gunny Marine nickname for a Gunnery Sergeant (Marine NCO rank comparable to an Army Sergeant First Class or E-7).

gyrene Term of abuse used by Army and Navy against Marines (possibly originating as a contraction of "GI Marine").

H&S Headquarters and Service (also said by some to stand for "Ham and Shitheads"); typically, an abbreviation for a battalion's headquarters battery or headquarters company.

head Marine and Navy slang for a toilet or latrine (these facilities were usually located at the "head" of a sailing ship).

Henderson Field

Major US airfield on Guadalcanal, originally constructed by the Japanese in summer 1942.

Hester's Happy Hustling Housewives

Insult used by members of the Ninth Defense for the Army's Forty-Third Division, originally commanded on New Georgia by Maj. General John H. Hester.

HMCS His Majesty's Canadian Ship (the Canadian equivalent of HMS).

HMG Heavy machine gun (meaning either the .50 caliber or the water-cooled and tripod-mounted .30 M1917 machine gun).

hooch Slang for alcohol.

I-boat   Japanese submarine.

I MAC   First Marine Amphibious Corps.

Ironbottom Sound
> That part of The Slot between Guadalcanal, Savo, Florida, and Gavutu Islands.

jellybean
> Slang expression, popular in the 1920s and 1930s, for a dandy or a nattily dressed man.

jitterbugging
> Also called the "jungle jitters," this was the nickname given to outbreaks of combat neurosis and panicky nighttime shootings that occurred in several American units during the New Georgia campaign; named after the popular dance craze of the late 1930s and early 1940s.

jungle juice
> Alcoholic drink made by mixing whatever kind of fruit juice was handy with any kind of drinkable alcohol or "torpedo juice."

Ka-Bar   Marine Corps-issue combat knife used for various field chores and self-defense.

kamikaze
> Japanese suicide plane or its pilot. Means "divine wind," in honor of a medieval typhoon that destroyed an invading Chinese fleet and saved Japan from foreign occupation.

Kempetai
> Japanese military secret police.

knee mortar
> Japanese 50mm grenade launcher with a curved base plate that led Allied troops to think it was supposed to be braced on the fire's leg. It definitely was *not* intended for such purpose, as attested to by the broken legs of numerous Allied soldiers who tried firing the mortar off their legs and knees.

Kokorana
> Small island off the northernmost tip of Rendova.

Koli Point
> Small cape located on the central northern coast of Guadalcanal, where most of the Ninth Defense Battalion was stationed from late 1942 to June 1943.

Kolombangara
> Island in the Central Solomons adjacent to (northwest of) New Georgia and southeast of Vella Lavella.

KP   Kitchen police (kitchen or mess-hall preparation and cleanup duty, generally regarded as one of the grubbiest duties and epitomized by wartime cartoons of troops peeling piles of potatoes). More usually called "mess duty" by the Marines and Navy.

K ration

More frequently encountered in the Pacific theater than the C ration, this was provided in three forms, "B," "L," and "D" (the initials should be self-explanatory). Ration K's boxes contained ham and eggs (the usual breakfast entree), canned cheese (the usual lunch selection) or Spam, corned beef hash or other meat selections, crackers, instant coffee, candy, cigarettes, toilet paper, and gum.

kunai   A type of tropical grass commonly found in the Solomons and New Guinea, noted for its very sharply edged leaves and often growing four to five feet tall.

LCI   Landing Craft, Infantry. Dubbed the "Elsie-Eye," by 1944, some LCIs were converted to light gunboats ((LCI(G)s) or rocket-launching platforms for 3.5-inch bombardment rockets, several of which were used to support the landings on Guam.

LCM   Landing Craft, Medium (also called a Higgins boat, after its inventor).

LCP   Landing Craft, Personnel (early-model Navy landing craft, without a bow ramp for unloading troops).

LCT   Landing Craft, Tank.

leatherneck

Nickname for US Marines; derived from a heavy leather collar or stock often worn by early US Marines in the late 1700s and early 1800s to help ward off saber blows to the neck.

leggings Marines' term for their distinctive, khaki-colored canvas field spats or gaiters.

Liberator

Consolidated B-24 four-engined heavy bomber used by both the Army Air Forces and the Navy (called the PB4Y in Navy service).

Lightning

Lockheed P-38 twin-engined fighter-bomber used by US Army Air Forces.

Lister bag

A sanitized, rubberized canvas bag, similar in size to a duffel bag and fitted with small faucets, used for storing and dispensing potable water.

Long Tom

> Common nickname for 155mm guns of both models (GPFs and M1s).

Louie the Louse

> See entry for "Washing Machine Charlie."

LST   Landing Ship, Tank. Because these vessels were often heavily camouflaged in green paint during the 1943 Solomons campaigns, they were nicknamed "Green Dragons." Due to their bulkiness, the abbreviation for these vessels was also said to stand for "Long, Slow Target."

Lt.   Lieutenant.

Lt. Col. Lieutenant colonel.

LVT   Landing Vehicle, Tracked. See entry for "Alligator."

M1   Depending on the context, this refers to either the .30 caliber Garand rifle (see entry for "Garand") or the smaller, .30 semiautomatic carbine. Also the official model number for the newer model 155mm heavy gun issued to the Ninth Defense after Guadalcanal (see entry for "Long Tom").

M-3   US light tank armed mainly with a 37mm gun and several .30 caliber machine guns. Officially nicknamed the "Stuart" tank for Civil War Confederate cavalry general Jeb Stuart.

Maggie's Drawers

> Nickname for a red flag used to identify the score of a boot who completely failed to hit a target during rifle range training at Boot Camp. (The risqué implication behind the nickname was that "Maggie's drawers," or her panties, were stained red from menstrual blood, as her lover had "fired a blank" in making love to her.)

magnetic mine

> Japanese oval, grenade-type explosive with several large industrial-strength magnets attached, frequently used as an antitank bomb. Because the "mine" was not intended to be buried but had to be hand-placed on the hull of an enemy tank, it was virtually a suicide weapon.

Marianas

> Chain of volcanic islands in the western Central Pacific, the largest islands in the group being Guam, Tinian, Rota, and Saipan.

marmite can

> A kind of insulated container used for storing and serving food.

Marshalls

> Chain of coral atolls in the Central Pacific approximately one thousand miles south of the Marianas, comprised of Kwajalein, Bikini, and Eniwetok among other islands and located approximately twenty-five hundred miles west of the Hawaiian Islands.

masthead

> Marine and Navy term for a non-court-martial disciplinary proceeding.

meatball

> Red "Rising Sun" insignia painted on Japanese aircraft and many ground vehicles.

MIA   Missing in action.

Mitchell

> See entry for "B-25."

mm (or MM)

> Millimeters. "Millimeter" and "caliber" refer to the diameter of a gun's bore, measured at the mouth of the barrel, caliber being this measurement in inches or fractions of inches (e.g., .30 caliber is equal to three-tenths of an inch in diameter). US weapons were gauged in millimeters, calibers, and inches (the latter mainly for naval ordnance), with caliber usually being used for small arms (i.e., machine guns, rifles, and pistols) and millimeters being used for larger guns (20mm and up). Note, by way of example, that .50 caliber is equal to 12.7mm.

MP   Military police.

Munda Point

> Prominent spit of land located at the southwestern tip of New Georgia and the location of the Munda Field airbase, the prime US objective of the Rendova-New Georgia campaign.

Nalimbiu

> Central river on the northern coast of Guadalcanal, located near the Koli Point area.

Nambu   6.5mm automatic pistol often carried by Japanese officers and externally resembling the German Luger pistol. Also applied to several models of 6.5mm or 7.7mm Japanese light machine guns, both pistol and machine guns having been designed by a Colonel Nambu of the Japanese army.

NCO   Noncommissioned officer (i.e., corporals and all grades of sergeant).

Nell   Allied codename for Mitsubishi G3M2, or Type 96, two-engined Japanese medium bomber.

New Georgia

Island located in the Central Solomon Islands.

Nisei   Japanese American citizens. (Technically, the term is applicable only to second-generation Japanese Americans, the first generation being known as *Issei*.)

Nissen hut

Prefabricated, corrugated-metal building.

noodle soup

Personal codename used by Battery A's Captain Hank Reichner and his exec, Lieutenant George ("Doc") Teller, for Doc's favorite cocktail, a lethal mix of 190-proof medical alcohol and lemon extract.

Nusalavata

Small island off the northern tip of Rendova.

OD   Officer of the day (staff duty officer) or officer of the deck (watch officer on board ship).

Oerlikon

Swiss-designed 20mm light, automatic AA gun often used by US and Allied forces. Capable of firing 450 rounds a minute with a 4,800-yard range, the 20mm Oerlikon was roughly similar to a large machine gun and, by mid-1943, was often issued to Marine defense battalions on four-wheeled, automatically operating gun carriages in pairs as "Twin Twenties."

Old Man, the

Generic nickname for a commanding officer (although never used to his face).

old salt A veteran sailor or Marine.

OP   Observation post.

P-38   See entry for "Lightning."

Panama mounts

Semi-permanent concrete pedestal mounts with turntables often used for 155mm guns in a seacoast-defense role; the name was derived from similar mounts first emplaced for coast defense guns stationed around the Panama Canal.

Pappy Marine nickname for any older Marine; also the personal nickname of Major Gregory Boyington, CO of VMF-214 (the Black Sheep squadron).

Paramarines

Marine parachute troops (not their preferred nickname) of the First Parachute Battalion and similar units.

PBY   See entry for "Catalina."

Pearl Harbor Avengers

Another nickname for the Christmas Tree Marines.

PFC (or Pfc.)

Private, first class.

PI   Parris Island, South Carolina, home of the Marines' recruiting depot and Boot Camp.

Pistol Pete

Nickname for Japanese gun or guns that sporadically shelled New Georgia, particularly Munda Point, from Kolombangara; derived from a gunfighter character in a Walt Disney cartoon of the time. (Another Pistol Pete was active on Guadalcanal in 1942 in shelling Henderson Field.)

pogey bait

Marine and Navy slang for candy, snacks, or sweets. While also more commonly spelled as "pogy bait," Jack McCall chronically spelled it as "pogiebait" when using it as his nickname.

Polar Bears

Nickname given to Marines from the Fifth Defense Battalion, so called because of their assignment to Iceland in late 1941/early 1942. While stationed there, these Marines wore, as a gesture of solidarity, the shoulder patch of the British division that was the principal British garrison of Iceland, the Forty-Ninth (West Riding) Division, which was a design of a polar bear standing on an ice floe.

pollywog

Anyone who has not been initiated during a crossing of the Equator.

poop   Navy and Marine slang for information or news (probably derived from the maritime term "poopdeck," from which a ship's master would often issue orders to the crew). See also entry for "scuttlebutt."

poop sheet

Marine slang for a newsletter, newspaper or orders.

POW   Prisoner of war. Also, sometimes, "PW."

psy-war

Psychological warfare.

PT   Physical training.

PT boat Lightly armored, 78-foot plywood-hulled motor boat used by the US Navy as a fast torpedo and attack boat ("PT"="Patrol Torpedo"). Usually equipped with torpedo tubes, an assortment of .50 caliber machine guns and 20mm Oerlikon guns, and occasionally a 40mm Bofors gun. The most famous example may be John F. Kennedy's

PT-109, which was part of a PT squadron based on Rendova and Tombusolo.

PX Post exchange.

Q-ship Term used for a surface raider or "auxiliary cruiser" disguised to resemble a civilian steamship, often by use of neutral flags.

Rabaul Large village and anchorage on the island of New Britain, off the northeast coast of New Guinea, which was the headquarters for large Japanese air and naval units in the South Pacific.

R&R Variously either "refitting and recuperation" or "rest and recreation."

recon Reconnaissance.

Reising .45 caliber submachine gun only issued to Marines (usually to personnel of Marine Raider and parachute units) but supplied to several hundred of the Ninth Defense's personnel on Guadalcanal. The Reising Model 51 was supplied in two models: one with a fixed wooden stock and one with a folding metal stock.

Rendova

Island in the Central Solomons adjacent to (due south of) New Georgia.

rikusentai

See entry for "SNLF."

Roviana

Small island adjacent to Rendova and New Georgia.

Russells

Island group in the south-central Solomon Islands, roughly midway between Guadalcanal and New Georgia. Its principal islands were Banika and Pavuvu.

Sally Mitsubishi K-21 twin-engined heavy bomber used by the Japanese Army Air Force.

SBD See entry for "Dauntless."

SCR-268

Early-model US fire control radar used for direction of AA search-lights and guns. The Ninth Defense Battalion had five of these beginning in mid-1942. ("SCR" was an Army abbreviation standing for "Signal Corps Radio.")

SCR-270

Early-model US long-range surveillance radar with a range of two hundred miles. The Ninth Defense Battalion had one of these beginning in mid-1942.

SCR-516

Early-model US height/elevation-determination radar with a range of fifty miles.

scuttlebutt

    Navy and Marine slang for gossip or rumors (derived from an old maritime word for the ship's drinking water bucket, which is where rumors were often naturally circulated onboard ship). Related to "poop."

seabag Marine and Navy term for a duffel bag.

Seabees Members of a US Navy construction battalion ("CB").

seagoing heads

    Open-air latrines built on a ramp or pier extended out over the waterline of a beach.

secure the butts

    Marine expression originally meaning to close down a rifle range ("butts" being the rifle-range pits from which the bullseye targets were raised and lowered), but extended through common usage to mean the cessation of any kind of activity.

Semper Fi

    Marine abbreviation and popular saying derived from the Marines' motto, *Semper Fidelis* ("Always Faithful"), whose all-purpose meaning at any given time—whether as a greeting, a farewell, a jeer, a threat, or a grouse—depended entirely upon the context.

Sgt. Sergeant.

shavetail

    Sardonic nickname, popular among enlisted Marines, for any second lieutenant.

shellback

    Anyone who has been initiated during a crossing of the Equator.

skipper Another popular Marine and Navy nickname for a CO.

skivvies

    Marine slang for underwear.

skylarking

    Marine slang for horseplay or goofing off.

slop chute

    Marine slang for a bar or tap room that served mainly beer and snacks, but often widely used for any bar or watering hole.

Slot, The

    Officially named Sealark Channel, the channel of water running between the Central Solomons and Guadalcanal.

snafu Acronym for "Situation normal: all f—cked up."

snapping-in

    A form of exercise or firing drill done with rifles and involving moving quickly into various rifle-shooting positions. The "snap" is the click of the hammer as the rifle's trigger is squeezed.

SNLF "Special Naval Landing Force" (in Japanese, *rikusentai*) or Japanese naval infantry; a rough Japanese equivalent of the US Marine Corps, comprised of sailors and naval officers given light infantry training and usually intended for beach landings or garrison duty. Frequently encountered by US forces in the Solomons area.

Solomons

Chain of South Pacific islands generally to the east of New Guinea and to the north and northeast of Australia; location of Guadalcanal, New Georgia, Rendova, Kolombangara, Bougainville, and the Russell Islands.

Southern Cross

Constellation of stars only visible from the Southern Hemisphere.

SP Shore Patrol, the Navy equivalent of military police.

Springfield

M1903 .30 caliber bolt-action rifle. Also called the "03" for short.

Stuart See entry for "M-3."

Superfortress

See entry for "B-29."

surveyed-out

Marine term for being medically evacuated.

swab (also swabby or swab jockey)

Term of abuse used by Army and Marines toward sailors (from their regular daily chores of mopping and scrubbing their ships' decks).

tabi Split-toed rubber shoes frequently worn by Japanese soldiers.

Tanambogo

Small island connected to Gavutu by a three hundred-foot causeway.

TBF Grumman Avenger single-engined Navy torpedo and attack bomber. Also extensively made by Eastern Aircraft, a subsidiary of General Motors, whose variant was called the TBM. Navy Avengers were used by Ninth Defense FOs for scouting and reconnaissance missions on New Georgia and Kolombangara.

TD-9 Caterpillar-made tractor, similar to a bulldozer but without the shovel blade, used as a prime mover for the Ninth's 155mm and 90mm guns. A larger model was known as the TD-18.

ten-in-one rations

Rations intended to feed ether one man for ten days or ten men for one day, usually featuring a much wider selection of entrees than were found in C rations and K rations.

TOENAILS
>   US codename for the Rendova/New Georgia campaign.

Tokyo Express
>   American nickname for Japanese naval convoys to and from Guadal-
>   canal, often commanded by Rear Admiral Raizo ("Torpedo") Tanaka.

Tokyo Rose
>   Japanese radio personality who often directed her broadcasts to
>   American forces in the Pacific. Over twenty women broadcast radio
>   commentary and music programs as Tokyo Rose from Radio Tokyo
>   in a generally fruitless effort to lower US troops' morale.

Tombusolo
>   Small island adjacent to Rendova and New Georgia;
>   sometimes also spelled as Tambusolo.

torpedo juice
>   A highly potent alcoholic drink devised by Marines and sailors in the
>   Pacific, usually mixed with lemonade or fruit juice. (The name was
>   said to derive from the alcohol being drained from Navy torpedoes.)

TORSO Abbreviation for "The Original Revolving Son of a Bitch": the
>   sobriquet applied to Lt. Colonel "Baker," one of the Ninth's senior
>   field grade officers, by his junior officers.

Trashcan Charlie
>   See entry for "Washing Machine Charlie."

trench knife
>   A particularly vicious looking US military
>   knife designed during World War I whose hilt (handle) included a
>   set of brass knuckle-dusters and which was once popular with many
>   Marines.

Tropic Lightning
>   Nickname for the US Army's Twenty-Fifth Infantry Division, partly
>   derived from its shoulder patch, which featured a lightning bolt
>   on a taro leaf. Commanded by Maj. General J. Lawton ("Lightning
>   Joe") Collins, the Twenty-Fifth served alongside Marine units on
>   Guadalcanal and New Georgia.

tubâ or tupa
>   A homemade alcoholic drink made on Guam from hearts of palm sap,
>   fermented for several days into a form of wine.

Tulagi Small island and anchorage just to the north of Guadalcanal, due
>   south of Florida Island and due west of Gavutu.

Twin Twenties
>   See entry for "Oerlikon."

ubermenschen
> German word meaning "supermen," characteristically used by the Nazis to describe the ideal Germanic or "Aryan" human.

U-boat German submarine (from *unterseeboot*, or "undersea boat").

USAT United States Army Transport.

USMC United States Marine Corps.

USS United States Ship, the designation for all official Navy (as opposed to Army or Merchant Marine) vessels, both combat and non-combat.

Val Allied codename for Aichi D3A1 (Type 99) single-engined Japanese dive bomber.

Vella Lavella
> Island in the Central Solomons northwest of Kolombangara and the New Georgia group.

V-mail "Victory mail": miniaturized US military forces mail delivered from the combat areas to the United States. To reduce shipping sizes and bulk quantities, Marines and GIs would write a letter home on specially prepared paper; the letter would then be put on microfilm, reconstituted and printed out in the United States, and mailed, so that parents, friends, and loved ones would receive a miniature letter as the final product.

WAAC Women's Auxiliary Army Corps (later shortened to Women's Army Corps, or "WAC.")

Washing Machine Charlie
> One of the Marine nicknames for Japanese reconnaissance bombers that made solo nighttime raids over Guadalcanal and New Georgia and dropped bombs and flares (and sometimes empty bottles) for nuisance value. Also called "Louie the Louse" or "Trashcan Charlie," among other variations.

W-Day "D-day," or first day of the invasion, on Guam, July 21, 1944.

Wildcat Grumman F4F single-engined fighter. The Navy's principal fighter aircraft in the early stages of World War II, the Wildcat was largely superseded by the F6F Hellcat in 1943.

XO Executive officer (second-in-command). Also often called the "exec."

Zero Allied codename for Mitsubishi A6M-series single-engined Japanese fighter.

zoot suits
> Marine nickname for camouflaged uniforms issued in the Pacific, derived from a popular style of baggily cut men's civilian suits of the 1941-42 period.

Bibliography

I. INTERVIEWS AND CORRESPONDENCE

Bodine, Amsa (Notes of interview)

Box, Colonel (Ret'd) William T. (Notes of interviews, photographs, and correspondence)

Burnette, Horace (Notes of interviews)

Carman, Ray (Notes of interview)

Chadwick, Francis E. (Notes of interviews and correspondence)

Cribbe, Clifford (Notes of interviews and correspondence)

David, Milton (Notes of interview)

Dobkowski, John (Notes of interview)

Donner, Dr. (Maj., Ret'd) Christopher S. (Correspondence and personal reminiscences)

Dougherty, Herb (Notes of interviews)

Downs, Alfred R. (Notes of interviews)

Dufour, Willie (Notes of interview)

Galloway, William (Notes of interviews, photographs, and correspondence)

Hall, John (Notes of interviews)

Hitchcock, Theodore T. (Notes of interview)

Johnson, John Henry (Notes of interview)

Kruse, James V. (Notes of interviews and correspondence)

Landon, Colonel (Ret'd) Robert (Notes of interviews)

McCall, Albert G., Jr. (Notes of interviews, photographs, tape-recorded personal reminiscences, and correspondence)

McCall, Jack H., Sr. (Various letters, personal records, and correspondence; author's collection)

McCall, Patricia H. (Notes of interviews, photographs, and correspondence)

Melson, Major (Ret'd) Charles (Notes of interviews and correspondence)

Morris, Jerry (Notes of interview)

Ogata, Lieutenant Colonel (Ret'd) Dye (Notes of interviews, reminiscences, correspondence, and e-mails as to his and Frank Sanwo's translation of captured Japanese diary from Munda Field area)

Pratl, Joseph J. (Notes of interviews, reminiscences, correspondence, and translation of captured Japanese diary from Munda Field area)

Reichner, Colonel (Ret'd) Henry H., Jr. (Notes of interviews, personal reminis-
    cences, manuscripts, draft of autobiography, and correspondence)
Slater, David (Notes of interviews, photographs, personal reminiscences, and
    correspondence)
Sorensen, Brother Andrew (Copies of wartime sketches and correspondence)
Sorensen, William (Notes of interviews)
Tracy, Colonel (Ret'd) William E. (Notes of interviews)
Yemma, Frank (Notes of interviews, tape-recorded personal reminiscences,
    and correspondence)

                        II. OFFICIAL DOCUMENTS

9th Defense Battalion. Historical Section, Division of Public Information,
    Headquarters, US Marine Corps. File No. AG-1265/HPH. Dec. 17,
    1947.
Extracts, Ship's Log. United States Ship *William P. Biddle*, for period February
    12, 1942 to February 20, 1942. Pages 99-115.
Headquarters, US Department of the Army. Technical Manual TM 9-3305.
    Principles of Artillery Weapons. May 1981.
Headquarters, U.S. Marine Corps. *Standing Operating Procedure for Radar
    Air and Surface Warning and Radar Fire Control in the Marine Corps*.
    May 15, 1943.
Headquarters, Ninth AAA Battalion, Reinforced, In the Field. "Operation
    Report on Marianas." Aug. 17, 1944.
Headquarters, Ninth Defense Battalion, Fleet Marine Force. C/o Fleet Post
    Office San Francisco. "Quarterly Report, Antiaircraft Operations."
    June 17, 1943.
Headquarters, Ninth Defense Battalion, Fleet Marine Force. C/o Fleet Post
    Office San Francisco. "Report of Operations, Ninth Defense Battal-
    ion." May 2, 1944.
Headquarters, Ninth Defense Battalion, Fleet Marine Force, In the Field.
    "Chronological Record of Operations of Ninth Defense Battalion for
    period 29 June to 31 July, 1943, inclusive."
*History of the First Antiaircraft Artillery Battalion, Redesignated Second 90-mm
    Antiaircraft Artillery Gun Battalion*. Battalion Bulletin No. 5-47. File
    No. 1990-50-20. Mar. 17, 1947.
The Initial Use of Radar by the U.S. Marine Corps. Maj. John A. Kelly for Maj.
    D.F. Bittner, Independent Studies in Military History, Marine Corps
    Command & Staff College, Quantico, Virginia. May 1977.

Language Section, G-2 (Intelligence Section), 37th Infantry Division. Translation of captured Japanese war diary of Probationary Officer Toshihiro Oura, *Record of the Decisive Battle Against Aircraft* (T/3 Dye Ogata and T/3 Frank Sanwo, translators; undated).

Military Personnel Records Files of Corporal Jack H. McCall. US Marine Corps Reserve, National Personnel Records Center, St. Louis, Missouri.

Task Force Sixty-Two, U.S.S. *Argonne*, Operation Plan No. A24-42. File No. FE25/A16-3(1). Nov. 27, 1942.

US War Department and US Navy Department, Training Division, Bureau of Aeronautics. Field Manual FM 30-30/BuAer 3, *Military Intelligence: Aircraft Recognition Pictorial Manual*. April 1, 1943.

III. PUBLISHED BOOKS AND MONOGRAPHS ON THE NINTH DEFENSE AND ITS BATTLES AND CAMPAIGNS

Alexander, Joseph H. *Storm Landings: Epic Amphibious Battles in the Central Pacific*. Annapolis, MD: Naval Institute Press, 1997.

Bergerud, Eric. *Touched With Fire: The Land War in the South Pacific*. New York: Viking, 1996.

Donner, Christopher S. *Pacific Time on Target: Memoirs of a Marine Artillery Officer, 1943-1945*. Edited by Jack H. McCall. Kent, OH: Kent State Univ. Press, 2012.

Frank, Richard B. *Guadalcanal: The Definitive Account of the Landmark Battle*. New York: Random House, 1990.

Gailey, Harry A. *The Liberation of Guam*. San Francisco: Presidio Press, 1988.

Hammel, Eric. *Munda Trail*. New York: Orion Books, 1989.

Horton, D. C. *New Georgia: Pattern for Victory*. New York: Ballantine Books, 1971.

Hoyt, Edwin P. *The Glory of the Solomons*. New York: Stein & Day, 1983.

Kent, Graeme. *Guadalcanal: Island Ordeal*. New York: Ballantine Books, 1971.

Lodge, Maj. O. R. *The Recapture of Guam*. Washington, DC: Historical Branch, G-3 Division, Headquarters, US Marine Corps/Govt. Printing Office, 1954.

Melson, Maj. Charles D. *Condition Red: Marine Defense Battalions in World War II: Marines in World War II Commemorative Series*. Washington, DC: History & Museums Division, Headquarters, US Marine Corps, 1996.

———. *Up the Slot: Marines in the Central Solomons: Marines in World War II*

Commemorative Series. Washington, DC: History & Museums Division, Headquarters, US Marine Corps, 1993.

Melson, Maj. Charles D., and Francis E. Chadwick. *The Ninth Marine Defense and AAA Battalions*. Paducah, KY: Turner Publishing, 1990.

Miller, John J., Jr. *Cartwheel: The Reduction of Rabaul*. Washington, DC: Department of the Army, Office of Chief of Military History, 1959.

——. *Guadalcanal: The First Offensive*. Washington, DC: Department of the Army, Office of Chief of Military History, 1949.

O'Brien, Cyril J. *Liberation: Marines in the Recapture of Guam: Marines in World War II Commemorative Series*. Washington, DC: History & Museums Division, Headquarters, US Marine Corps, 1994.

Reichner, Henry H., Jr. *But One Life to Give*. Bloomington, IN: Xlibris Corp., 2009.

Rentz, John N. *Marines in the Central Solomons*. Washington, DC: Headquarters, US Marine Corps/Govt. Printing Office, 1952.

Shaw, Henry I., Jr. *First Offensive: The Marine Campaign for Guadalcanal: Marines in World War II Commemorative Series*. Washington, DC: History & Museums Division, Headquarters, US Marine Corps, 1992.

——. *The United States Marines in the Guadalcanal Campaign*. Washington, DC: Headquarters, US Marine Corps/Govt. Printing Office, 1962.

Shaw, Henry I., Jr., and Douglas T. Kane, *The Isolation of Rabaul: History of U.S. Marine Corps Operations in World War II*. Vol. 2. Washington, DC: Historical Branch, G-3 Division, Headquarters, US Marine Corps/Govt. Printing Office, 1963.

Stavisky, Samuel E. *Marine Combat Correspondent: World War II in the Pacific*. New York: Ivy Books, 1999.

Updegraph, Charles L., Jr. *Special Marine Corps Units of World War II*. Washington, DC: History & Museums Division, Headquarters, US Marine Corps, 1972.

Zimmerman, Maj. John L. *The Guadalcanal Campaign*. Washington, DC: Headquarters, US Marine Corps/Govt. Printing Office, 1949.

IV. GENERAL SOURCES AND READINGS ON WORLD WAR II, THE MARINES, AND THE PACIFIC THEATER

Adams, Captain Henry H. *1942: The Year that Doomed the Axis*. New York: Warner Paperback Library, 1973.

Alexander, Colonel Joseph H. *A Fellowship of Valor: The Battle History of the United States Marines*. New York: HarperCollins, 1996.

Ambrose, Stephen E. *Americans at War*. New York: Berkley Books, 1998.

——. *Citizen Soldiers*. New York: Simon & Schuster, 1997.

Angelucci, Enzo, and Paolo Matricardi. *World War II Airplanes*. Vol. 2. Chicago: Rand McNally & Company, 1977.

Ballard, Robert D., with Rick Archbold. *The Lost Ships of Guadalcanal*. New York: Warner/Madison Press Books, 1993.

Barker, Harold R. *History of the 43rd Division Artillery, World War II, 1941-1945*. Providence, RI: John F. Greene Co., Inc., 1960.

Berger, Carl. *B-29: The Superfortress*. New York: Ballantine Books, 1970.

Bergerud, Eric. *Fire in the Sky: The Air War in the South Pacific*. Boulder, CO: Westview Press, 1999.

Berry, Henry. *Semper Fi, Mac: Living Memories of the U.S. Marines in World War II*. New York: Quill/William Morrow, 1996.

Bradley, John H., Jack W. Dice, and Thomas E. Griess. *The West Point Military History Series—The Second World War: Asia and the Pacific*. Wayne, NJ: Avery Publishing Group, 1989.

Bradt, Hale. *Wilber's War: An American Family's Journey through World War II*. 3 vols. Salem, MA: Van Dorn Books, 2017.

Brokaw, Tom. *The Greatest Generation*. New York: Random House, 1998.

Caidin, Martin. *The Ragged, Rugged Warriors*. New York: Ballantine Books, 1973.

Calvocoressi, Peter, and Guy Wint. *Total War*. New York: Ballantine Books, 1973.

Dooly, William G., Jr. *Great Weapons of World War I*. New York: Bonanza Books, 1969.

Dower, John W. *War Without Mercy: Race and Power in the Pacific War*. New York: Pantheon Books, 1986.

Dull, Paul. *A Battle History of the Imperial Japanese Navy*. Annapolis, MD: Naval Institute Press, 1978.

Edgerton, Robert B. *Warriors of the Rising Sun: A History of the Japanese Military*. New York: W.W. Norton & Company, 1997.

Feifer, George. *Tennozan: The Battle of Okinawa and the Atomic Bomb*. New York: Ticknor & Fields, 1992.

Forty, George. *U.S. Army Handbook 1939-1945*. London, England: Ian Allan, 1979.

Fussell, Paul. *Wartime: Understanding and Behavior in the Second World War*. New York: Oxford Univ. Press, 1989.

Gamble, Bruce. *The Black Sheep: The Definitive Account of Marine Fighting Squadron 214 in World War II*. Novato, CA: Presidio Press, 1998.

Harries, Meirion and Susie. *Soldiers of the Sun: The Rise and Fall of the Imperial Japanese Army*. New York: Random House, 1991.

Harrington, Joseph D. *Yankee Samurai*. Detroit, MI: Pettigrew Enterprises, Inc., 1979.

Harrison, Simon. *Dark Trophies: Hunting and the Enemy Body in Modern War*. New York: Berghahn Books, 2012.

Hata, Ikuhiko, Yasuho Izawa, and Christopher Shores. *Japanese Naval Air Force Fighter Units and their Aces, 1932-1945*. London: Grub Street Publishing Ltd., 2011.

Hersey, John. *Into the Valley: A Skirmish of the Marines*. New York: Schocken Books, 1989.

Hogg, Ian V. *Barrage: The Guns in Action*. New York: Ballantine Books, 1970.

———. *The Encyclopedia of Infantry Weapons of World War II*. London: Bison Books, 1977.

Hynes, Samuel. *The Soldiers' Tale: Bearing Witness to Modern War*. New York: Penguin Books, 1997.

Hynes, Samuel, et al. *Reporting World War II*. 2 vols. New York: The Library of America, 1995.

Ienaga, Saburo. *The Pacific War, 1931-1945*. New York: Pantheon Books, 1978.

Jablonski, Edward. *Airwar*. Vol. 2, *Outraged Skies*. Garden City, NY: Doubleday & Company, Inc., 1971.

Jones, Captain (Ret'd) Wilbur D., Jr. *Gyrene: The World War II United States Marine*. Shippensburg, PA: White Mane Books, 1998.

Kirk, John, and Robert Young. *Great Weapons of World War II*. New York: Bonanza Books, 1961.

Leckie, Robert. *Strong Men Armed: The United States Marines vs. Japan*. New York: DaCapo Press, Inc., 1997.

Manchester, William. *Goodbye, Darkness: A Memoir of the Pacific War*. Boston: Little, Brown, 1979.

McManus, John C. *The Deadly Brotherhood: The American Combat Soldier in World War II*. Novato, CA: Presidio Press, 1998.

McPherson, James M. *For Cause and Comrades*. New York: Oxford Univ. Press, 1997.

Office of the Surgeon General, US Army. *Neuropsychiatry in World War II*. Vol. II, *Overseas Theaters*. Washington, DC: Gov't. Printing Office, 1973.

Orita, Zenji, with Joseph D. Harrington. *I-Boat Captain*. Canoga Park, CA: Major Books, 1976.

Rottman, Gordon, and Mike Chappell. *Fighting Elite—US Marine Corps 1941-45*. Edited by Lee Johnson. London: Osprey Military/Reed International, 1998.

Sakai, Saburo, with Martin Caidin. *Samurai!* New York: Nelson Doubleday, 1977.

Smith, S. E. *The United States Marine Corps in World War II*. New York: Random House, 1969.

Spector, Ronald H. *Eagle Against the Sun: The American War With Japan*. New York: Vintage Books, 1985.

US War Dep't. *Handbook on Japanese Military Forces*. London: Greenhill Books, 1991. Reprint of US War Department Technical Manual TM-E 30-480, Oct. 1, 1944.

Weinberg, Gerhard. *A World At Arms: A Global History of World War II*. New York: Cambridge Univ. Press, 1994.

Wyden, Peter. *Day One: Before Hiroshima and After*. New York: Warner Books, Inc., 1985.

V. PERIODICALS AND NEWSPAPERS

Allen, Thomas B., and Norman Polmar. "Gassing Japan." *Military History Quarterly* (Autumn 1997): 38-43.

Brooke, Jame. "Decades After Abuses by the Japanese, Guam Hopes the U.S. Will Make Amends." *New York Times*, Aug. 14, 2005. https://mobile.nytimes.com/2005/08/14/us/decades-after-abuses-by-the-japanese-guam-hopes-the-us-will-make-amends.html.

Crutchfield, James A. "World War Heroes Were Williamson Countians." *The Tennessean* (Nashville, TN), Nov. 7, 1996.

Drea, Edward J. "Previews of Hell." *Military History Quarterly* (Spring 1995): 74-81.

Falk, Stanley L. "A Nation Reduced to Ashes." *Military History Quarterly* (Spring 1995): 54-63.

Goldstein, Richard. "Col. Robert S. Scott Dies at 85; Won Medal of Honor in 1944." *New York Times*, Feb. 12, 1998.

LaPorta, James. "Honoring the Heroic Montford Pointers, The African American Marines the Corps Didn't Want." *Washington Post*, Aug. 1, 2016, online edition.

Maslowski, Peter. "Truman, The Bomb, and The Numbers Game." *Military History Quarterly* (Spring 1995): 103-7.

Meek, Lt. Col. H. B. "Marines Had Radar Too." *Marine Corps Gazette*, Oct. 1945, 16-19.

Miller, Sgt. Bill. "Ack Ack Etc." *The Leatherneck*, Pacific Edition, Sept. 15, 1944, 3-5.

Murphy, Charles J. V., and David E. Scherman. "The Sinking of the Zamzam."

Life Magazine, June 23, 1941. https://books.google.com/books?id=bU
oEAAAAMBAJ&pg=PA21&source=gbs_toc_r&cad=2#v=onepage&q&
f=false.

Murray, Williamson. "Armageddon Revisited." *Military History Quarterly*
(Spring 1995): 6-11.

Nashville Banner (Nashville, TN), Dec. 8, 1941, 1.

Oura, Toshihiro. "I Will Fight to the Last." Edited by Jack H. McCall. Translated by Dye Ogata and Frank Sanwo. *MHQ: The Quarterly Journal of
Military History* (Spring 2005): 70-79.

Paschall, Rod. "Tactical Exercises: Olympic Miscalculations." *Military History
Quarterly* (Spring 1995): 62, 63.

The Review-Appeal (Franklin, TN), various years and issues.

Seacoast Artillery Officers of a Marine Defense Battalion (various authors).
"We Had to Do It." *Coast Artillery Journal* (July-Aug. 1944): 4-13.

Suciu, Ron. "Christmas Tree Marines." *Leatherneck*, Jan. 1993, 48-50.

Thompson, Col. W. O. "News and Comment-Comment on Antiaircraft Firing."
Antiaircraft Journal (Jan.-Feb. 1949): 74-75.

VI. FILMS, UNPUBLISHED WORKS, AND MISCELLANEOUS SOURCES

Bowman, Virginia M. *Historic Williamson County.* Nashville, TN: Blue & Gray
Press, 1971.

Box, Colonel (Ret'd) William T., and Francis E. Chadwick. *Return to the Solomon Islands.* Videotape. Autumn 1988 (author's collection).

Bucheit, Jeffrey P., Assistant Director, Historical Electronics Museum. Letter
to Charles D. Melson, Feb. 16, 1993.

Caldwell, Ambrose W. "Red." *Secrets of a Diplomatic Courier—World War II.*
Nashville, TN: privately published, 1992.

Crutchfield, James A. *The Harpeth River: A Biography.* Nashville, TN: Blue &
Gray Press, 1972.

———. *Williamson County: A Pictorial History.* Virginia Beach, VA: The Donning
Company, 1980.

Heggen, Thomas. *Mister Roberts.* New York: Houghton Mifflin Co., 1946.

Lynch, Louise G. *Our Valiant Men.* Privately published, 1976.

Marshall, Joseph Frank. *The "Fighting Ninth"—9th Defense Battalion.* Edited by
Christopher S. Donner. Unpublished, undated manuscript, author's
collection.

McDonough, James Lee, and Thomas L. Connelly. *Five Tragic Hours: The Battle
of Franklin.* Knoxville: Univ. of Tennessee Press, 1983.

The Ninth Defense & AAA Battalion Association. *Poop! A Newsletter* and *Son of Poop!* Various years and issues, author's collection.

Sayen, Lt. Col. John. "Marine Heavy Artillery and the Defense Battalions." In *The Old Breed News.* Newsletter, 1st Marine Division Association, June 2000, 24.

Slater, David. *Jungle Vignettes.* Unpublished, undated manuscript, author's collection.

Sullivan, Lyn. *Back Home in Williamson County.* Nashville, TN: Williams Printing Co., 1986.

Sword, Wiley. *Embrace an Angry Wind: The Confederacy's Last Hurrah: Spring Hill, Franklin and Nashville.* HarperCollins Publishers, 1992.

U-Boat Net. Internet home page. Available at http://uboat.net/boats/u94.htm.

Uris, Leon. *Battle Cry.* New York: G. P. Putnam's Sons, 1953.

Watkins, Sam R. *Co. Aytch: A Side Show of the Big Show.* New York: Collier Books, 1962.

Index